Artificial Intelligence By Example

Develop machine intelligence from scratch using real artificial intelligence use cases

Denis Rothman

BIRMINGHAM - MUMBAI

Artificial Intelligence By Example

Commissioning Editor: Pravin Dhandre
Acquisition Editor: Tushar Gupta
Content Development Editor: Mayur Pawanikar
Technical Editor: Prasad Ramesh
Copy Editor: Vikrant Phadkay
Project Coordinator: Nidhi Joshi
Proofreader: Safis Editing
Indexer: Tejal Daruwale Soni
Graphics: Tania Dutta
Production Coordinator: Aparna Bhagat

First published: May 2018

Production reference: 2200618

Published by Packt Publishing Ltd.
Livery Place
35 Livery Street
Birmingham
B3 2PB, UK.

ISBN 978-1-78899-054-7

www.packtpub.com

*To my family and friends for bringing me joy on the good days
and comfort on the bad ones.*

-Denis Rothman

`mapt.io`

Mapt is an online digital library that gives you full access to over 5,000 books and videos, as well as industry leading tools to help you plan your personal development and advance your career. For more information, please visit our website.

Why subscribe?

- Spend less time learning and more time coding with practical eBooks and Videos from over 4,000 industry professionals

- Improve your learning with Skill Plans built especially for you

- Get a free eBook or video every month

- Mapt is fully searchable

- Copy and paste, print, and bookmark content

PacktPub.com

Did you know that Packt offers eBook versions of every book published, with PDF and ePub files available? You can upgrade to the eBook version at `www.PacktPub.com` and as a print book customer, you are entitled to a discount on the eBook copy. Get in touch with us at `service@packtpub.com` for more details.

At `www.PacktPub.com`, you can also read a collection of free technical articles, sign up for a range of free newsletters, and receive exclusive discounts and offers on Packt books and eBooks.

Contributors

About the author

Denis Rothman graduated from l'Université Paris-Sorbonne and l'Université Paris-Diderot, writing one of the very first word2matrix embedding solutions. He began his career authoring one of the first AI cognitive NLP chatbots applied as a language teacher for Moët et Chandon and other companies. He authored an AI resource optimizer for IBM and apparel producers. He then authored an Advanced Planning and Scheduling (APS) solution used worldwide.

> *I want to thank the corporations who trusted me from the start to deliver artificial intelligence solutions and share the risks of continuous innovation. I also thank my family, who believed I would make it big at all times.*

About the reviewers

Armando Fandango creates AI-powered products by leveraging his expertise in deep learning, machine learning, distributed computing, and computational methods. He advises Owen.ai Inc., Real Engagement, and Loyalty Inc. on AI product strategy. He founded NeuraSights to create insights using neural networks. He was the chief data scientist and CTO for Epic Engg., Consulting Group LLC, and director of data science for Sonobi. He has advised high-tech startups as an AI expert and advisory board member.

Nicolas Guet is a financial controller at GRDF. He was a project leader for ENGIE and a SAP BI consultant for Capgemini.

He graduated from Université Pierre et Marie Curie (Paris VI) and Université Paris Sud (Paris XI). He also designed a decision-making tool in Java that was part of an AI Advanced Planning System, managing hundreds of thousands of orders for 100+ suppliers worldwide. He is dedicated to promoting sustainable energy and smart grids.

Jérémie Rothman is an IT project manager at the French National Forest Office (ONF). He was an IT consultant for TCS France and worked on a Total SA route optimizing project. He graduated from Université Paris 1 Panthéon Sorbonne in economics and holds a degree in software mathematics (Université Paris 5 René Descartes).

He designed a Nash equilibrium theory of games algorithm to optimize warehouse locations for an AI Advanced Planning System (APS). The APS program is used to this day.

Packt is searching for authors like you

If you're interested in becoming an author for Packt, please visit authors.packtpub.com and apply today. We have worked with thousands of developers and tech professionals, just like you, to help them share their insight with the global tech community. You can make a general application, apply for a specific hot topic that we are recruiting an author for, or submit your own idea.

Table of Contents

Preface

This book will take you through all of the main aspects of artificial intelligence:

- The theory of machine learning and deep learning
- Mathematical representations of the main AI algorithms
- Real life case studies
- Tens of opensource Python programs using TensorFlow, TensorBoard, Keras and more
- Cloud AI Platforms: Google, Amazon Web Services, IBM Watson and IBM Q to introduce you to quantum computing
- An Ubuntu VM containing all the opensource programs that you can run in one-click
- Online videos

This book will take you to the cutting edge and beyond with innovations that show how to improve existing solutions to make you a key asset as a consultant, developer, professor or any person involved in artificial intelligence.

Who this book is for

This book contains the main artificial intelligence algorithms on the market today. Each machine learning and deep learning solution is illustrated by a case study and an open source program available on GitHub.

- Project managers and consultants: To understand how to manage AI input datasets, make a solution choice (cloud platform or development), and use the outputs of an AI system.
- Teachers, students, and developers: This book provides an overview of many key AI components, with tens of Python sample programs that run on Windows and Linux. A VM is available as well.
- Anybody who wants to understand how AI systems are built and what they are used for.

What this book covers

Chapter 1, *Become an Adaptive Thinker*, covers reinforcement learning through the Bellman equation based on the Markov Decision Process (MDP). A case study describes how to solve a delivery route problem with a human driver and a self-driving vehicle.

Chapter 2, *Think like a Machine*, demonstrates neural networks starting with the McCulloch-Pitts neuron. The case study describes how to use a neural network to build the reward matrix used by the Bellman equation in a warehouse environment.

Chapter 3, *Apply Machine Thinking to a Human Problem*, shows how machine evaluation capacities have exceeded human decision-making. The case study describes a chess position and how to apply the results of an AI program to decision-making priorities.

Chapter 4, *Become an Unconventional Innovator*, is about building a feedforward neural network (FNN) from scratch to solve the XOR linear separability problem. The business case describes how to group orders for a factory.

Chapter 5, *Manage the Power of Machine Learning and Deep Learning*, uses TensorFlow and TensorBoard to build an FNN and present it in meetings.

Chapter 6, *Don't Get Lost in Techniques – Focus on Optimizing Your Solutions*, covers a K-means clustering program with Lloyd's algorithm and how to apply to the optimization of automatic guided vehicles in a warehouse.

Chapter 7, *When and How to Use Artificial Intelligence*, shows cloud platform machine learning solutions. We use Amazon Web Services SageMaker to solve a K-means clustering problem. The business case describes how a corporation can analyze phone call durations worldwide.

Chapter 8, *Revolutions Designed for Some Corporations and Disruptive Innovations for Small to Large Companies*, explains the difference between a revolutionary innovation and a disruptive innovation. Google Translate will be described and enhanced with an innovative opensource add-on.

Chapter 9, *Getting Your Neurons to Work*, describes convolutional neural networks (CNN) in detail: kernels, shapes, activation functions, pooling, flattening, and dense layers. The case study illustrates the use of a CNN in a food processing company.

Chapter 10, *Applying Biomimicking to Artificial Intelligence,* describes the difference between neuroscience models and deep learning solutions when representing human thinking. A TensorFlow MNIST classifier is explained component by component and displayed in detail in TensorBoard. We cover images, accuracy, cross-entropy, weights, histograms, and graphs.

Chapter 11, *Conceptual Representation Learning,* explains Conceptual Representation Learning (CRL), an innovative way to solve production flows with a CNN transformed into a CRL Meta-model. The case study shows how to use a CRLMM for transfer and domain learning, extending the model to scheduling and self-driving cars.

Chapter 12, *Automated Planning and Scheduling,* combines CNNs with MDPs to build a DQN solution for automatic planning and scheduling with an optimizer. The case study is the optimization of the load of sewing stations in an apparel system, such as Amazon's production lines.

Chapter 13, *AI and the Internet of Things (IoT),* covers Support Vector Machines (SVMs) assembled with a CNN. The case study shows how self-driving cars can find an available parking space automatically.

Chapter 14, *Optimizing Blockchains with AI,* is about mining blockchains and describes how blockchains function. We use Naive Bayes to optimize the blocks of a Supply Chain Management (SCM) blockchain by predicting transactions to anticipate storage levels.

Chapter 15, *Cognitive NLP Chatbots,* shows how to implement IBM Watson's chatbot with intents, entities, and a dialog flow. We add scripts to customize the dialogs, add sentiment analysis to give a human touch to the system, and use conceptual representation learning meta-models (CRLMMs) to enhance the dialogs.

Chapter 16, *Improve the Emotional Intelligence Deficiencies of Chatbots,* shows how to turn a chatbot into a machine that has empathy by using a variety of algorithms at the same time to build a complex dialog. We cover Restricted Boltzmann Machines (RBMs), CRLMM, RNN, word to vector (word2Vec) embedding, and principal component analysis (PCA). A Python program illustrates an empathetic dialog between a machine and a user.

Chapter 17, *Quantum Computers That Think,* describes how a quantum computer works, with qubits, superposition, and entanglement. We learn how to create a quantum program (score). A case study applies quantum computing to the building of MindX, a thinking machine. The chapter comes with programs and a video.

Appendix, *Answers to the Questions,* contains answers to the questions listed at the end of the chapters.

To get the most out of this book

Artificial intelligence projects rely on three factors:

- Subject Matter Experts (SMEs). This implies having a practical view of how solutions can be used, not just developed. Find real-life examples around you to extend the case studies presented in the book.
- Applied mathematics and algorithms. Do not skip the mathematical equations if you have the energy to study them. AI relies heavily on mathematics. There are plenty of excellent websites that explain the mathematics used in the book.
- Development and production.

An artificial intelligence solution can be directly used on a cloud platform machine learning site (Google, Amazon, IBM, Microsoft, and others) online or with APIs. In the book, Amazon, IBM, and Google are described. Try to create an account of your own to explore cloud platforms.

Development still remains critical for artificial intelligence projects. Even with a cloud platform, scripts and services are necessary. Also, sometimes, writing an algorithm is mandatory because the ready-to-use online algorithms are insufficient for a given problem. Explore the programs delivered with the book. They are open source and free.

Download the example code files

You can download the example code files for this book from your account at `www.packtpub.com`. If you purchased this book elsewhere, you can visit `www.packtpub.com/support` and register to have the files emailed directly to you.

You can download the code files by following these steps:

1. Log in or register at `www.packtpub.com`.
2. Select the **SUPPORT** tab.
3. Click on **Code Downloads & Errata**.
4. Enter the name of the book in the **Search** box and follow the onscreen instructions.

Once the file is downloaded, please make sure that you unzip or extract the folder using the latest version of:

- WinRAR/7-Zip for Windows
- Zipeg/iZip/UnRarX for Mac
- 7-Zip/PeaZip for Linux

The code bundle for the book is also hosted on GitHub at `https://github.com/PacktPublishing/Artificial-Intelligence-By-Example`. We also have other code bundles from our rich catalog of books and videos available at `https://github.com/PacktPublishing/`. Check them out!

Download the color images

We also provide a PDF file that has color images of the screenshots/diagrams used in this book. You can download it here:
`http://www.packtpub.com/sites/default/files/downloads/ArtificialIntelligenceByExample_ColorImages.pdf`.

Code in Action

Visit the following link to check out videos of the code being run:
`https://goo.gl/M5ACiy`

Conventions used

There are a number of text conventions used throughout this book.

`CodeInText`: Indicates code words in text, database table names, folder names, filenames, file extensions, pathnames, dummy URLs, user input, and Twitter handles. Here is an example: "Mount the downloaded `WebStorm-10*.dmg` disk image file as another disk in your system."

A block of code is set as follows:

```
MS1='full'
MS2='space'
I=['1','2','3','4','5','6']
for im in range(2):
```

When we wish to draw your attention to a particular part of a code block, the relevant lines or items are set in bold:

```
Weights:
[[ 0.913269 -0.06843517 -1.13654324]
 [ 3.00969897 1.70999493 0.58441134]
 [ 2.98644016 1.73355337 0.59234319]
 [ 0.953465 0.08329804 -3.26016158]
 [-1.10051951 -1.2227973 2.21361701]
 [ 0.20618461 0.30940653 2.59980058]
 [ 0.98040128 -0.06023325 -3.00127746]]
```

Bold: Indicates a new term, an important word, or words that you see onscreen. For example, words in menus or dialog boxes appear in the text like this. Here is an example: "For this example, click on **Load data**."

Warnings or important notes appear like this.

Tips and tricks appear like this.

Get in touch

Feedback from our readers is always welcome.

General feedback: Email `feedback@packtpub.com` and mention the book title in the subject of your message. If you have questions about any aspect of this book, please email us at `questions@packtpub.com`.

Errata: Although we have taken every care to ensure the accuracy of our content, mistakes do happen. If you have found a mistake in this book, we would be grateful if you would report this to us. Please visit `www.packtpub.com/submit-errata`, selecting your book, clicking on the Errata Submission Form link, and entering the details.

Piracy: If you come across any illegal copies of our works in any form on the Internet, we would be grateful if you would provide us with the location address or website name. Please contact us at copyright@packtpub.com with a link to the material.

If you are interested in becoming an author: If there is a topic that you have expertise in and you are interested in either writing or contributing to a book, please visit authors.packtpub.com.

Reviews

Please leave a review. Once you have read and used this book, why not leave a review on the site that you purchased it from? Potential readers can then see and use your unbiased opinion to make purchase decisions, we at Packt can understand what you think about our products, and our authors can see your feedback on their book. Thank you!

For more information about Packt, please visit packtpub.com.

Become an Adaptive Thinker

In May 2017, Google revealed AutoML, an automated machine learning system that could create an artificial intelligence solution without the assistance of a human engineer. **IBM Cloud** and **Amazon Web Services** (**AWS**) offer machine learning solutions that do not require AI developers. GitHub and other cloud platforms already provide thousands of machine learning programs, reducing the need of having an AI expert at hand. These cloud platforms will slowly but surely reduce the need for artificial intelligence developers. Google Cloud's AI provides intuitive machine learning services. Microsoft Azure offers user-friendly machine learning interfaces.

At the same time, **Massive Open Online Courses** (**MOOC**) are flourishing everywhere. Anybody anywhere can pick up a machine learning solution on GitHub, follow a MOOC without even going to college, and beat any engineer to the job.

Today, artificial intelligence is mostly mathematics translated into source code which makes it difficult to learn for traditional developers. That is the main reason why Google, IBM, Amazon, Microsoft, and others have ready-made cloud solutions that will require fewer engineers in the future.

As you will see, starting with this chapter, you can occupy a central role in this new world as an adaptive thinker. There is no time to waste. In this chapter, we are going to dive quickly and directly into reinforcement learning, one of the pillars of Google Alphabet's DeepMind asset (the other being neural networks). Reinforcement learning often uses the **Markov Decision Process** (**MDP**). MDP contains a memoryless and unlabeled action-reward equation with a learning parameter. This equation, the Bellman equation (often coined as the Q function), was used to beat world-class Atari gamers.

The goal here is not to simply take the easy route. We're striving to break complexity into understandable parts and confront them with reality. You are going to find out right from the start how to apply an adaptive thinker's process that will lead you from an idea to a solution in reinforcement learning, and right into the center of gravity of Google's DeepMind projects.

The following topics will be covered in this chapter:

- A three-dimensional method to implement AI, ML, and DL
- Reinforcement learning
- MDP
- Unsupervised learning
- Stochastic learning
- Memoryless learning
- The Bellman equation
- Convergence
- A Python example of reinforcement learning with the Q action-value function
- Applying reinforcement learning to a delivery example

Technical requirements

- Python 3.6x 64-bit from `https://www.python.org/`
- NumPy for Python 3.6x
- Program on Github, `Chapter01 MDP.py`

Check out the following video to see the code in action:

`https://goo.gl/72tSxQ`

How to be an adaptive thinker

Reinforcement learning, one of the foundations of machine learning, supposes learning through trial and error by interacting with an environment. This sounds familiar, right? That is what we humans do all our lives—in pain! Try things, evaluate, and then continue; or try something else.

In real life, you are the **agent** of your thought process. In a machine learning model, the agent is the function calculating through this trial-and-error process. This thought process in machine learning is the **MDP**. This form of action-value learning is sometimes called **Q**.

To master the outcomes of MDP in theory and practice, a three-dimensional method is a prerequisite.

The three-dimensional approach that will make you an artificial expert, in general terms, means:

- Starting by describing a problem to solve with real-life cases
- Then, building a mathematical model
- Then, write source code and/or using a cloud platform solution

It is a way for you to enter any project with an adaptive attitude from the outset.

Addressing real-life issues before coding a solution

In this chapter, we are going to tackle Markov's Decision Process (Q function) and apply it to reinforcement learning with the Bellman equation. You can find tons of source code and examples on the web. However, most of them are toy experiments that have nothing to do with real life. For example, reinforcement learning can be applied to an e-commerce business delivery person, self-driving vehicle, or a drone. You will find a program that calculates a drone delivery. However, it has many limits that need to be overcome. You as an adaptive thinker are going to ask some questions:

- What if there are 5,000 drones over a major city at the same time?
- Is a drone-jam legal? What about the noise over the city? What about tourism?
- What about the weather? Weather forecasts are difficult to make, so how is this scheduled?

In just a few minutes, you will be at the center of attention, among theoreticians who know more than you on one side and angry managers who want solutions they cannot get on the other side. Your real-life approach will solve these problems.

A foolproof method is the practical three-dimensional approach:

- **Be a subject matter expert (SME)**: First, you have to be an SME. If a theoretician geek comes up with a hundred Google DeepMind TensorFlow functions to solve a drone trajectory problem, you now know it is going to be a tough ride if real-life parameters are taken into account.
  An SME knows the subject and thus can quickly identify the critical factors of a given field. Artificial intelligence often requires finding a solution to a hard problem that even an expert in a given field cannot express mathematically. Machine learning sometimes means finding a solution to a problem that humans do not know how to explain. Deep learning, involving complex networks, solves even more difficult problems.

- **Have enough mathematical knowledge to understand AI concepts**: Once you have the proper natural language analysis, you need to build your abstract representation quickly. The best way is to look around at your everyday life and make a mathematical model of it. Mathematics is not an option in AI, but a prerequisite. The effort is worthwhile. Then, you can start writing solid source code or start implementing a cloud platform ML solution.

- **Know what source code is about as well as its potential and limits**: MDP is an excellent way to go and start working in the three dimensions that will make you adaptive: describing what is around you in detail in words, translating that into mathematical representations, and then implementing the result in your source code.

Step 1 – MDP in natural language

Step 1 of any artificial intelligence problem is to transpose it into something you know in your everyday life (work or personal). Something you are an SME in. If you have a driver's license, then you are an SME of driving. You are certified. If you do not have a driver's license or never drive, you can easily replace moving around in a car by moving around on foot.

Let's say you are an e-commerce business driver delivering a package in an area you do not know. You are the operator of a self-driving vehicle. You have a GPS system with a beautiful color map on it. The areas around you are represented by the letters **A** to **F**, as shown in the simplified map in the following diagram. You are presently at **F**. Your goal is to reach area **C**. You are happy, listening to the radio. Everything is going smoothly, and it looks like you are going to be there on time. The following graph represents the locations and routes that you can possibly cover.

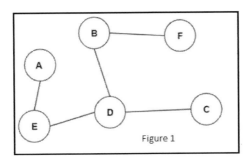

Figure 1

The guiding system's **state** indicates the complete path to reach **C**. It is telling you that you are going to go from **F** to **B** to **D** and then to **C**. It looks good!

To break things down further, let's say:

- The present **state** is the letter *s*.
- Your next **action** is the letter *a (action)*. This action *a* is not location A.
- The next action *a (not location A)* is to go to location **B**. You look at your guiding system; it tells you there is no traffic, and that to go from your present state **F** to your next state **B** will take you only a few minutes. Let's say that the next state **B** is the letter **B**.

At this point, you are still quite happy, and we can sum up your situation with the following sequence of events:

$$s, a, s'$$

The letter *s* is your present state, your present situation. The letter *a* is the action you're deciding, which is to go to the next area; there you will be in another state, *s'*. We can say that thanks to the action *a*, you will go from *s* to *s'*.

Now, imagine that the driver is not you anymore. You are tired for some reason. That is when a self-driving vehicle comes in handy. You set your car to autopilot. Now you are not driving anymore; the system is. Let's call that system the **agent**. At point **F**, you set your car to autopilot and let the self-driving **agent** take over.

The agent now sees what you have asked it to do and checks its mapping **environment**, which represents all the areas in the previous diagram from **A** to **F**.

In the meantime, you are rightly worried. Is the **agent** going to make it or not? You are wondering if its strategy meets yours. You have your **policy** *P*—your way of thinking—which is to take the shortest paths possible. Will the agent agree? What's going on in its mind? You observe and begin to realize things you never noticed before. Since this is the first time you are using this car and guiding system, the agent is **memoryless**, which is an MDP feature. This means the agent just doesn't know anything about what went on before. It seems to be happy with just calculating from this **state** *s* at area F. It will use machine power to run as many calculations as necessary to reach its goal.

Another thing you are watching is the total distance from **F** to **C** to check whether things are OK. That means that the agent is calculating all the states from **F** to **C**.

In this case, state **F** is state 1, which we can simplify by writing s_1. **B** is state 2, which we can simplify by write s_2. **D** is s_3 and **C** is s_4. The agent is calculating all of these possible states to make a decision.

The agent knows that when it reaches **D**, **C** will be better because the reward will be higher to go to **C** than anywhere else. Since it cannot eat a piece of cake to reward itself, the agent uses numbers. Our agent is a real number cruncher. When it is wrong, it gets a poor reward or nothing in this model. When it's right, it gets a reward represented by the letter **R**. This action-value (reward) transition, often named the Q function, is the core of many reinforcement learning algorithms.

When our agent goes from one state to another, it performs a *transition* and gets a reward. For example, the *transition* can be from **F** to **B**, state 1 to state 2, or s_1 to s_2.

You are feeling great and are going to be on time. You are beginning to understand how the machine learning agent in your self-driving car is thinking. Suddenly your guiding system breaks down. All you can see on the screen is that static image of the areas of the last calculation. You look up and see that a traffic jam is building up. Area **D** is still far away, and now you do not know whether it would be good to go from **D** to **C** or **D** to **E** to get a taxi that can take special lanes. You are going to need your agent!

The agent takes the traffic jam into account, is stubborn, and increases its reward to get to **C** by the shortest way. Its **policy** is to stick to the initial plan. You do not agree. You have another **policy**.

You stop the car. You both have to agree before continuing. You have your opinion and policy; the agent does not agree. Before continuing, your views need to **converge**. **Convergence** is the key to making sure that your calculations are correct. This is the kind of problem that persons, or soon, self-driving vehicles (not to speak about drone air jams), delivering parcels encounter all day long to get the workload done. The number of parcels to delivery per hour is an example of the workload that needs to be taken into account when making a decision.

To represent the problem at this point, the best way is to express this whole process mathematically.

Step 2 – the mathematical representation of the Bellman equation and MDP

Mathematics involves a whole change in your perspective of a problem. You are going from words to functions, the pillars of source coding.

Expressing problems in mathematical notation does not mean getting lost in academic math to the point of never writing a single line of code. Mathematics is viewed in the perspective of getting a job done. Skipping mathematical representation will fast-track a few functions in the early stages of an AI project. However, when the real problems that occur in all AI projects surface, solving them with source code only will prove virtually impossible. The goal here is to pick up enough mathematics to implement a solution in real-life companies.

It is necessary to think of a problem through by finding something familiar around us, such as the delivery itinerary example covered before. It is a good thing to write it down with some abstract letters and symbols as described before, with **a** meaning an action and **s** meaning a state. Once you have understood the problem and expressed the parameters in a way you are used to, you can proceed further.

Now, mathematics well help clarify the situation by shorter descriptions. With the main ideas in mind, it is time to convert them into equations.

From MDP to the Bellman equation

In the previous step 1, the agent went from **F** or state 1 or *s* to **B**, which was state 2 or *s'*.

To do that, there was a strategy—a policy represented by **P**. All of this can be shown in one mathematical expression, the MDP state transition function:

$$Pa(s, s')$$

P is the policy, the strategy made by the agent to go from **F** to **B** through action *a*. When going from **F** to **B**, this state transition is called **state transition function:**

- *a* is the action
- *s* is state 1 (*F*) and *s'* is state 2 (*B*)

This is the basis of MDP. The reward (right or wrong) is represented in the same way:

$$Ra(s, s')$$

That means **R** is the reward for the action of going from state *s* to state *s'*. Going from one state to another will be a random process. This means that potentially, all states can go to another state.

The example we will be working on inputs a reward matrix so that the program can choose its best course of action. Then, the agent will go from state to state, learning the best trajectories for every possible starting location point. The goal of the MDP is to go to **C** (line 3, column 3 in the reward matrix), which has a starting value of 100 in the following Python code.

```
# Markov Decision Process (MDP) - The Bellman equations adapted to
# Reinforcement Learning
# R is The Reward Matrix for each state
R = ql.matrix([ [0,0,0,0,1,0],
                [0,0,0,1,0,1],
                [0,0,100,1,0,0],
                [0,1,1,0,1,0],
                [1,0,0,1,0,0],
                [0,1,0,0,0,0] ])
```

Each line in the matrix in the example represents a letter from **A** to **F**, and each column represents a letter from **A** to **F**. All possible states are represented. The 1 values represent the nodes (vertices) of the graph. Those are the possible locations. For example, line 1 represents the possible moves for letter **A**, line 2 for letter **B**, and line 6 for letter **F**. On the first line, **A** cannot go to **C** directly, so a 0 value is entered. But, it can go to **E**, so a 1 value is added.

Some models start with -1 for impossible choices, such as **B** going directly to **C** and 0 values to define the locations. This model starts with 0 and 1 values. It sometimes takes weeks to design functions that will create a reward matrix (see `Chapter 2`, *Think like a Machine*).

There are several properties of this decision process. A few of them are mentioned here:

- **The Markov property**: The process is applied when the past is not taken into account. It is the memoryless property of this decision process, just as you do in a car with a guiding system. You move forward to reach your goal. This is called the Markov property.
- **Unsupervised learning**: From this memoryless Markov property, it is safe to say that the MDP is not supervised learning. Supervised learning would mean that we would have all the labels of the trip. We would know exactly what A means and use that property to make a decision. We would be in the future looking at the past. MDP does not take these labels into account. This means that this is unsupervised learning. A decision has to be made in each state without knowing the past states or what they signify. It means that the car, for example, was on its own at each location, which is represented by each of its states.
- **Stochastic process**: In step 1, when state **B** was reached, the agent controlling the mapping system and the driver didn't agree on where to go. A random choice could be made in a trial-and-error way, just like a coin toss. It is going to be a heads-or-tails process. The agent will toss the coin thousands of times and measure the outcomes. That's precisely how MDP works and how the agent will learn.
- **Reinforcement learning**: Repeating a trial and error process with feedback from the agent's environment.
- **Markov chain**: The process of going from state to state with no history in a random, stochastic way is called a **Markov chain**.

To sum it up, we have three tools:

- $P_a(s,s')$: A **policy**, **P**, or strategy to move from one state to another
- $T_a(s,s')$: A **T**, or stochastic (random) **transition**, function to carry out that action
- $R_a(s,s')$: An **R**, or **reward**, for that action, which can be negative, null, or positive

T is the transition function, which makes the **agent** decide to go from one point to another with a policy. In this case, it will be random. That's what machine power is for, and that's how reinforcement learning is often implemented.

Randomness is a property of MDP.

The following code describes the choice the *agent* is going to make.

```
next_action = int(ql.random.choice(PossibleAction,1))
return next_action
```

Once the code has been run, a new random action (state) has been chosen.

 The Bellman equation is the road to programming reinforcement learning.

Bellman's equation completes the MDP. To calculate the value of a state, let's use Q, for the Q action-reward (or value) function. The pre-source code of Bellman's equation can be expressed as follows for one individual state:

$$Q(s) = R(s) + \Upsilon * max(s')$$

The source code then translates the equation into a machine representation as in the following code:

```
# The Bellman equation
    Q[current_state, action] = R[current_state, action] + gamma * MaxValue
```

The source code variables of the Bellman equation are as follows:

- $Q(s)$: This is the value calculated for this state—the total reward. In step 1 when the agent went from **F** to **B**, the driver had to be happy. Maybe she/he had a crunch in a candy bar to feel good, which is the human counterpart of the reward matrix. The automatic driver maybe ate (reward matrix) some electricity, renewable energy of course! The reward is a number such as 50 or 100 to show the agent that it's on the right track. It's like when a student gets a good grade in an exam.
- $R(s)$: This is the sum of the values up to there. It's the total reward at that point.

- Υ = **gamma**: This is here to remind us that trial and error has a price. We're wasting time, money, and energy. Furthermore, we don't even know whether the next step is right or wrong since we're in a trial-and-error mode. **Gamma** is often set to 0.8. What does that mean? Suppose you're taking an exam. You study and study, but you don't really know the outcome. You might have 80 out of 100 (0.8) chances of clearing it. That's painful, but that's life. This is what makes Bellman's equation and MDP realistic and efficient.
- max(s'): s' is one of the possible states that can be reached with P_a (s,s'); max is the highest value on the line of that state (location line in the reward matrix).

Step 3 – implementing the solution in Python

In step 1, a problem was described in natural language to be able to talk to experts and understand what was expected. In step 2, an essential mathematical bridge was built between natural language and source coding. Step 3 is the software implementation phase.

When a problem comes up—and rest assured that one always does—it will be possible to go back over the mathematical bridge with the customer or company team, and even further back to the natural language process if necessary.

This method guarantees success for any project. The code in this chapter is in Python 3.6. It is a reinforcement learning program using the Q function with the following reward matrix:

```
import numpy as ql
R = ql.matrix([ [0,0,0,0,1,0],
                [0,0,0,1,0,1],
                [0,0,100,1,0,0],
                [0,1,1,0,1,0],
                [1,0,0,1,0,0],
                [0,1,0,0,0,0] ])

Q = ql.matrix(ql.zeros([6,6]))

gamma = 0.8
```

R is the reward matrix described in the mathematical analysis.

Q inherits the same structure as R, but all values are set to 0 since this is a learning matrix. It will progressively contain the results of the decision process. The gamma variable is a double reminder that the system is learning and that its decisions have only an 80% chance of being correct each time. As the following code shows, the system explores the possible actions during the process.

```
agent_s_state = 1

# The possible "a" actions when the agent is in a given state
def possible_actions(state):
    current_state_row = R[state,]
    possible_act = ql.where(current_state_row >0)[1]
    return possible_act

# Get available actions in the current state
PossibleAction = possible_actions(agent_s_state)
```

The agent starts in state 1, for example. You can start wherever you want because it's a random process. Note that only values > 0 are taken into account. They represent the possible moves (decisions).

The current state goes through an analysis process to find possible actions (next possible states). You will note that there is no algorithm in the traditional sense with many rules. It's a pure random calculation, as the following random.choice function shows.

```
def ActionChoice(available_actions_range):
    next_action = int(ql.random.choice(PossibleAction,1))
    return next_action

# Sample next action to be performed
action = ActionChoice(PossibleAction)
```

Now comes the core of the system containing Bellman's equation, translated into the following source code:

```
def reward(current_state, action, gamma):
    Max_State = ql.where(Q[action,] == ql.max(Q[action,]))[1]

    if Max_State.shape[0] > 1:
        Max_State = int(ql.random.choice(Max_State, size = 1))
    else:
        Max_State = int(Max_State)
    MaxValue = Q[action, Max_State]
```

```
# Q function
Q[current_state, action] = R[current_state, action] + gamma * MaxValue
```

```
# Rewarding Q matrix
reward(agent_s_state,action,gamma)
```

You can see that the agent looks for the maximum value of the next possible state chosen at random.

The best way to understand this is to run the program in your Python environment and `print()` the intermediate values. I suggest that you open a spreadsheet and note the values. It will give you a clear view of the process.

The last part is simply about running the learning process 50,000 times, just to be sure that the system learns everything there is to find. During each iteration, the agent will detect its present state, choose a course of action, and update the Q function matrix:

```
for i in range(50000):
    current_state = ql.random.randint(0, int(Q.shape[0]))
    PossibleAction = possible_actions(current_state)
    action = ActionChoice(PossibleAction)
    reward(current_state,action,gamma)
# Displaying Q before the norm of Q phase
print("Q :")
print(Q)

# Norm of Q
print("Normed Q :")
print(Q/ql.max(Q)*100)
```

After the process is repeated and until the learning process is over, the program will print the result in Q and the normed result. The normed result is the process of dividing all values by the sum of the values found. The result comes out as a normed percentage.

View the Python program at `https://github.com/PacktPublishing/Artificial-Intelligence-By-Example/blob/master/Chapter01/MDP.py`.

The lessons of reinforcement learning

Unsupervised reinforcement machine learning, such as MDP and Bellman's equation, will topple traditional decision-making software in the next few years. Memoryless reinforcement learning requires few to no business rules and thus doesn't require human knowledge to run.

Being an adaptive AI thinker involves three requisites—the effort to be an SME, working on mathematical models, and understanding source code's potential and limits:

- **Lesson 1**: Machine learning through reinforcement learning can beat human intelligence in many cases. No use fighting! The technology and solutions are already here.
- **Lesson 2**: Machine learning has no emotions, but you do. And so do the people around you. Human emotions and teamwork are an essential asset. Become an SME for your team. Learn how to understand what they're trying to say intuitively and make a mathematical representation of it for them. This job will never go away, even if you're setting up solutions such as Google's AutoML that don't require much development.

Reinforcement learning shows that no human can solve a problem the way a machine does; 50,000 iterations with random searching is not an option. The days of neuroscience imitating humans are over. Cheap, powerful computers have all the leisure it takes to compute millions of possibilities and choose the best trajectories.

Humans need to be more intuitive, make a few decisions, and see what happens because humans cannot try 50,000 ways of doing something. Reinforcement learning marks a new era for human thinking by surpassing human reasoning power.

On the other hand, reinforcement learning requires mathematical models to function. Humans excel in mathematical abstraction, providing powerful intellectual fuel to those powerful machines.

The boundaries between humans and machines have changed. Humans' ability to build mathematical models and every-growing cloud platforms will serve online machine learning services.

Finding out how to use the outputs of the reinforcement learning program we just studied shows how a human will always remain at the center of artificial intelligence.

How to use the outputs

The reinforcement program we studied contains no trace of a specific field, as in traditional software. The program contains Bellman's equation with stochastic (random) choices based on the reward matrix. The goal is to find a route to **C** (line 3, column 3), which has an attractive reward (`100`):

```
# Markov Decision Process (MDP) - Bellman's equations adapted to
# Reinforcement Learning with the Q action-value(reward) matrix
```

```
# R is The Reward Matrix for each state
R = ql.matrix([ [0,0,0,0,1,0],
                [0,0,0,1,0,1],
                [0,0,100,1,0,0],
                [0,1,1,0,1,0],
                [1,0,0,1,0,0],
                [0,1,0,0,0,0] ])
```

That reward matrix goes through Bellman's equation and produces a result in Python:

```
Q :
[[ 0.  0.  0.  0.  258.44 0.  ]
 [ 0.  0.  0.  321.8 0.  207.752]
 [ 0.  0.  500.  321.8 0.  0.  ]
 [ 0.  258.44 401.  0.  258.44 0.  ]
 [ 207.752 0.  0.  321.8 0.  0.  ]
 [ 0.  258.44 0.  0.  0.  0.  ]]
Normed Q :
[[ 0.  0.  0.  0.  51.688 0.  ]
 [ 0.  0.  0.  64.36 0.  41.5504]
 [ 0.  0.  100.  64.36 0.  0.  ]
 [ 0.  51.688 80.2 0.  51.688 0.  ]
 [ 41.5504 0.  0.  64.36 0.  0.  ]
 [ 0.  51.688 0.  0.  0.  0.  ]]
```

The result contains the values of each state produced by the reinforced learning process, and also a normed Q (highest value divided by other values).

As Python geeks, we are overjoyed. We made something rather difficult to work, namely reinforcement learning. As mathematical amateurs, we are elated. We know what MDP and Bellman's equation mean.

However, as natural language thinkers, we have made little progress. No customer or user can read that data and make sense of it. Furthermore, we cannot explain how we implemented an intelligent version of his/her job in the machine. We didn't.

We hardly dare say that reinforcement learning can beat anybody in the company making random choices 50,000 times until the right answer came up.

Furthermore, we got the program to work but hardly know what to do with the result ourselves. The consultant on the project cannot help because of the matrix format of the solution.

Being an adaptive thinker means knowing how to be good in all the dimensions of a subject. To solve this new problem, let's go back to step 1 with the result.

By formatting the result in Python, a graphics tool, or a spreadsheet, the result that is displayed as follows:

	A	B	C	D	E	F
A	-	-	-	-	258.44	-
B	-	-	-	321.8	-	207.752
C	-	-	500	321.8	-	-
D	-	258.44	401.	-	258.44	-
E	207.752	-	-	321.8	-	-
F	-	258.44	-	-	-	-

Now, we can start reading the solution:

- Choose a starting state. Take **F** for example.
- The **F** line represents the state. Since the maximum value is 258.44 in the **B** column, we go to state **B**, the second line.
- The maximum value in state **B** in the second line leads us to the **D** state in the fourth column.
- The highest maximum of the **D** state (fourth line) leads us to the **C** state.

Note that if you start at the **C** state and decide not to stay at **C**, the **D** state becomes the maximum value, which will lead you to back to **C**. However, the MDP will never do this naturally. You will have to force the system to do it.

You have now obtained a sequence: **F->B->D->C**. By choosing other points of departure, you can obtain other sequences by simply sorting the table.

The most useful way of putting it remains the normalized version in percentages. This reflects the stochastic (random) property of the solution, which produces probabilities and not certainties, as shown in the following matrix:

	A	B	C	D	E	F
A	-	-	-	-	51.68%	-
B	-	-	-	64.36%	-	41.55%
C	-	-	100%	64.36%	-	-
D	-	51.68%	80.2%	-	51.68%	-
E	41.55%	-	-	64.36%	-	-
F	-	51.68%	-	-	-	-

Now comes the very tricky part. We started the chapter with a trip on a road. But I made no mention of it in the result analysis.

An important property of reinforcement learning comes from the fact that we are working with a mathematical model that can be applied to anything. No human rules are needed. This means we can use this program for many other subjects without writing thousands of lines of code.

Case 1: Optimizing a delivery for a driver, human or not

This model was described in this chapter.

Case 2: Optimizing warehouse flows

The same reward matrix can apply to going from point **F** to **C** in a warehouse, as shown in the following diagram:

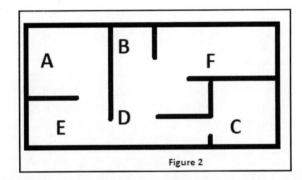

Figure 2

In this warehouse, the F->B->D->C sequence makes visual sense. If somebody goes from point **F** to **C**, then this physical path makes sense without going through walls.

It can be used for a video game, a factory, or any form of layout.

Case 3: Automated planning and scheduling (APS)

By converting the system into a scheduling vector, the whole scenery changes. We have left the more comfortable world of physical processing of letters, faces, and trips. Though fantastic, those applications are social media's tip of the iceberg. The real challenge of artificial intelligence begins in the abstract universe of human thinking.

Every single company, person, or system requires automatic planning and scheduling (see `Chapter 12`, *Automated Planning and Scheduling*). The six **A** to **F** steps in the example of this chapter could well be six tasks to perform in a given unknown order represented by the following vector *x:*

$$x = \begin{bmatrix} x1 \\ x2 \\ x3 \\ x4 \\ x5 \\ x6 \end{bmatrix}$$

The reward matrix then reflects the weights of constraints of the tasks of vector *x* to perform. For example, in a factory, you cannot assemble the parts of a product before manufacturing them.

In this case, the sequence obtained represents the schedule of the manufacturing process.

Case 4 and more: Your imagination

By using physical layouts or abstract decision-making vectors, matrices, and tensors, you can build a world of solutions in a mathematical reinforcement learning model. Naturally, the following chapters will enhance your toolbox with many other concepts.

Machine learning versus traditional applications

Reinforcement learning based on stochastic (random) processes will evolve beyond traditional approaches. In the past, we would sit down and listen to future users to understand their way of thinking.

We would then go back to our keyboard and try to imitate the human way of thinking. Those days are over. We need proper datasets and ML/DL equations to move forward. Applied mathematics has taken reinforcement learning to the next level. Traditional software will soon be in the museum of computer science.

An artificial adaptive thinker sees the world through applied mathematics translated into machine representations.

Use the Python source code example provided in this chapter in different ways. Run it; try to change some parameters to see what happens. Play around with the number of iterations as well. Lower the number from 50,000 down to where you find its best. Change the reward matrix a little to see what happens. Design your own reward matrix trajectory. It can be an itinerary or a decision-making process.

Summary

Presently, artificial intelligence is predominantly a branch of applied mathematics, not of neurosciences. You must master the basics of linear algebra and probabilities. That's a difficult task for a developer used to intuitive creativity. With that knowledge, you will see that humans cannot rival with machines that have CPU and mathematical functions. You will also understand that machines, contrary to the hype around you, don't have emotions although we can represent them to a scary point (See Chapter 16, *Improve the Emotional Intelligence Deficiencies of Chatbots*, and Chapter 17, *Quantum Computers That Think*) in chatbots.

That being said, a multi-dimensional approach is a requisite in an AI/ML/DL project—first talk and write about the project, then make a mathematical representation, and finally go for software production (setting up an existing platform and/or writing code). In real-life, AI solutions do not just grow spontaneously in companies like trees. You need to talk to the teams and work with them. That part is the real fulfilling aspect of a project—imagining it first and then implementing it with a group of real-life people.

MDP, a stochastic random action-reward (value) system enhanced by Bellman's equation, will provide effective solutions to many AI problems. These mathematical tools fit perfectly in corporate environments.

Reinforcement learning using the Q action-value function is memoryless (no past) and unsupervised (the data is not labeled or classified). This provides endless avenues to solve real-life problems without spending hours trying to invent rules to make a system work.

Now that you are at the heart of Google's DeepMind approach, it is time to go to Chapter 2, *Think Like a Machine*, and discover how to create the reward matrix in the first place through explanations and source code.

Questions

The answers to the questions are in *Appendix B,* with more explanations.

1. Is reinforcement learning memoryless? (Yes | No)
2. Does reinforcement learning use stochastic (random) functions? (Yes | No)
3. Is MDP based on a rule base? (Yes | No)
4. Is the Q function based on the MDP? (Yes | No)
5. Is mathematics essential to artificial intelligence? (Yes | No)
6. Can the Bellman-MDP process in this chapter apply to many problems? (Yes | No)
7. Is it impossible for a machine learning program to create another program by itself? (Yes | No)
8. Is a consultant required to enter business rules in a reinforcement learning program? (Yes | No)
9. Is reinforcement learning supervised or unsupervised? (Supervised | Unsupervised)
10. Can Q Learning run without a reward matrix? (Yes | No)

Further reading

Andrey Markov: https://www.britannica.com/biography/Andrey-Andreyevich-Markov

The Markov Process: https://www.britannica.com/science/Markov-process

2
Think like a Machine

The first chapter described a reinforcement learning algorithm through the Q action-value function used by DQN. The agent was a driver. You are at the heart of DeepMind's approach to AI.

DeepMind is no doubt one of the world leaders in applied artificial intelligence. Scientific, mathematical, and applications research drives its strategy.

DeepMind was founded in 2010, was acquired by Google in 2014, and is now part of Alphabet, a collection of companies that includes Google.

One of the focuses of DeepMind is on reinforcement learning. They came up with an innovate version of reinforcement learning called **DQN** and referring to deep neural networks using the Q function (Bellman's equation). A seminal article published in February 2015 in *Nature* (see the link at the end of the chapter) shows how DQN outperformed other artificial intelligence research by becoming a human game tester itself. DQN then went on to beat human game testers.

In this chapter, the agent will be an **automated guided vehicle (AGV)**. An AGV takes over the transport tasks in a warehouse. This case study opens promising perspectives for jobs and businesses using DQN. Thousands upon thousands of warehouses require complex reinforcement learning and customized transport optimization.

This chapter focuses on creating the **reward matrix**, which was the entry point of the Python example in the first chapter. To do so, it describes how to add a primitive McCulloch-Pitts neuron in TensorFlow to create an intelligent adaptive network and add an N (network) to a Q model. It's a small N that will become a feedforward neural network in Chapter 4, *Become an Unconventional Innovator*, and more in Chapter 12, *Automated Planning and Scheduling*. The goal is not to copy DQN but to use the conceptual power of the model to build a variety of solutions.

The challenge in this chapter will be to think literally like a machine. The effort is not to imitate human thinking but to beat humans with machines. This chapter will take you very far from human reasoning into the depth of machine thinking.

The following topics will be covered in this chapter:

- AGV
- The McCulloch-Pitts neuron
- Creating a reward matrix
- Logistic classifiers
- The logistic sigmoid
- The softmax function
- The one-hot function
- How to apply machine learning tools to real-life problems such as warehouse management

Technical requirements

- Python 3.6x 64-bit from `https://www.python.org/`
- NumPy for Python 3.6x
- TensorFlow from `https://deepmind.com/` with TensorBoard

The following files:

- `https://github.com/PacktPublishing/Artificial-Intelligence-By-Example/blob/master/Chapter02/MCP.py`
- `https://github.com/PacktPublishing/Artificial-Intelligence-By-Example/blob/master/Chapter02/SOFTMAX.py`

Check out the following video to see the code in action:

`https://goo.gl/jMWLg8`

Designing datasets – where the dream stops and the hard work begins

As in the previous chapter, bear in mind that a real-life project goes through a three-dimensional method in some form or the other. First, it's important to just think and talk about the problem to solve without jumping onto a laptop. Once that is done, bear in mind that the foundation of machine learning and deep learning relies on mathematics. Finally, once the problem has been discussed and mathematically represented, it is time to develop the solution.

 First, think of a problem in natural language. Then, make a mathematical description of a problem. Only then, start the software implementation.

Designing datasets in natural language meetings

The reinforcement learning program described in the first chapter can solve a variety of problems involving unlabeled classification in an unsupervised decision-making process. The Q function can be applied indifferently to drone, truck, or car deliveries. It can also be applied to decision-making in games or real life.

However, in a real-life case study problem (such as defining the reward matrix in a warehouse for the AGV, for example), the difficulty will be to design a matrix that everybody agrees with.

This means many meetings with the IT department to obtain data, the SME and reinforcement learning experts. An AGV requires information coming from different sources: daily forecasts and real-time warehouse flows.

At one point, the project will be at a standstill. It is simply too complicated to get the right data for the reinforcement program. This is a real-life case study that I modified a little for confidentiality reasons.

The warehouse manages thousands of locations and hundreds of thousands of inputs and outputs. The Q function does not satisfy the requirement in itself. A small neural network is required.

In the end, through tough negotiations with both the IT department and the users, a dataset format is designed that fits the needs of the reinforcement learning program and has enough properties to satisfy the AGV.

Using the McCulloch-Pitts neuron

The mathematical aspect relies on finding a model for inputs for huge volumes in a corporate warehouse.

In one mode, the inputs can be described as follows:

- Thousands of forecast product arrivals with a low priority weight: $w1 = 10$
- Thousands of confirmed arrivals with a high priority weight: $w2 = 70$
- Thousands of unplanned arrivals decided by the sales department: $w3 = 75$
- Thousands of forecasts with a high priority weight: $w4 = 60$
- Thousands of confirmed arrivals that have a low turnover and so have a low weight: $w5 = 20$

These weights represent vector w:

$$x = \begin{bmatrix} w1 \\ w2 \\ w3 \\ w4 \\ w5 \end{bmatrix} = \begin{bmatrix} 10 \\ 70 \\ 75 \\ 60 \\ 20 \end{bmatrix}$$

All of these products have to be stored in optimal locations, and the distance between nearly 100 docks and thousands of locations in the warehouse for the AGV has to be minimized.

Let's focus on our neuron. Only these weights will be used, though a system such as this one will add up to more than 50 weights and parameters per neuron.

In the first chapter, the reward matrix was size 6x6. Six locations were described (**A** to **F**), and now six locations (l1 to l6) will be represented in a warehouse.

A 6x6 reward matrix represents the target of the McCulloch-Pitts layer implemented for the six locations.

Also, this matrix was the input in the first chapter. In real life, and in real companies, you will have to find a way to build datasets from scratch. The reward matrix becomes the output of this part of the process. The following source code shows the input of the reinforcement learning program used in the first chapter. The goal of this chapter describes how to produce the following reward matrix.

```
# R is The Reward Matrix for each location in a warehouse (or any other
problem)

R = ql.matrix([ [0,0,0,0,1,0],
                [0,0,0,1,0,1],
                [0,0,100,1,0,0],
                [0,1,1,0,1,0],
                [1,0,0,1,0,0],
                [0,1,0,0,0,0] ])
```

For this warehouse problem, the McCulloch-Pitts neuron sums up the weights of the priority vector described previously to fill in the reward matrix.

Each location will require its neuron, with its weights.

$$INPUTS-> WEIGHTS - BIAS-> VALUES$$

- Inputs are the flows in a warehouse or any form of data
- Weights will be defined in this model
- Bias is for stabilizing the weights
- Values will be the output

 There are as many ways as you can imagine to create reward matrices. This chapter describes one way of doing it that works.

The McCulloch-Pitts neuron

The McCulloch-Pitts neuron dates back to 1943. It contains inputs, weights, and an activation function. This is precisely where you need to think like a machine and forget about human neuroscience brain approaches for this type of problem. Starting from Chapter 8, *Revolutions Designed for Some Corporations and Disruptive Innovations Small to Large Companies*, human cognition will be built on top of these models, but the foundations need to remain mathematical.

The following diagram shows the McCulloch-Pitts, neuron model.

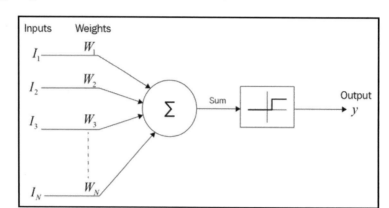

This model contains a number of input x weights that are summed to either reach a threshold which will lead, once transformed, to $y = 0$, or 1 output. In this model, y will be calculated in a more complex way.

A Python-TensorFlow program, MCP.py will be used to illustrate the neuron.

When designing neurons, the computing performance needs to be taken into account. The following source code configures the threads. You can fine-tune your model according to your needs.

```
config = tf.ConfigProto(
    inter_op_parallelism_threads=4,
    intra_op_parallelism_threads=4
)
```

In the following source code, the placeholders that will contain the input values (x), the weights (w), and the bias (b) are initialized. A placeholder is not just a variable that you can declare and use later when necessary. It represents the structure of your graph:

```
x = tf.placeholder(tf.float32, shape=(1, 6), name='x')
w = tf.placeholder(tf.float32, shape=(6, 1), name='w')
b = tf.placeholder(tf.float32, shape=(1), name='b')
```

In the original McCulloch-Pitts artificial neuron, the inputs (x) were multiplied by the following weights:

$$w_1 x_1 + \ldots + w_n x_n = \sum_{j=1}^{n} w_j x_j$$

The mathematical function becomes a one-line code with a logistic activation function (sigmoid), which will be explained in the second part of the chapter. Bias (b) has been added, which makes this neuron format useful even today shown as follows.

```
y = tf.matmul(x, w) + b
s = tf.nn.sigmoid(y)
```

Before starting a session, the McCulloch-Pitts neuron (1943) needs an operator to directly set its weights. That is the main difference between the McCulloch-Pitts neuron and the perceptron (1957), which is the model of modern deep learning neurons. The perceptron optimizes its weights through optimizing processes. Chapter 4, *Become an Unconventional Innovator*, describes the modern perceptron.

The weights are now provided, and so are the quantities for each x stored at l_1, one of the locations of the warehouse:

$$x = \begin{bmatrix} w1 \\ w2 \\ w3 \\ w4 \\ w5 \end{bmatrix} = \begin{bmatrix} 10 \\ 70 \\ 75 \\ 60 \\ 20 \end{bmatrix}$$

The weight values will be divided by 100, to represent percentages in terms of 0 to 1 values of warehouse flows in a given location. The following code deals with the choice of *one* location, l_1 **only**, its values, and parameters.

```
with tf.Session(config=config) as tfs:
    tfs.run(tf.global_variables_initializer())
    w_t = [[.1, .7, .75, .60, .20]]
    x_1 = [[10, 2, 1., 6., 2.]]
    b_1 = [1]
    w_1 = np.transpose(w_t)
    value = tfs.run(s,
        feed_dict={
            x: x_1,
            w: w_1,
            b: b_1
        }
    )
print ('value for threshold calculation',value)
```

The session starts; the weights (w_t) and the quantities (x_1) of the warehouse flow are entered. Bias is set to 1 in this model. w_1 is transposed to fit x_1. The placeholders are solicited with `feed_dict`, and the value of the neuron is calculated using the sigmoid function.

The program returns the following value.

```
print ('value for threshold calculation',value)
value for threshold calculation [[ 0.99971133]]
```

This value represents the activity of location l_1 at a given date and a given time. The higher the value, the higher the probable saturation rate of this area. That means there is little space left for an AGV that would like to store products. That is why the reinforcement learning program for a warehouse is looking for the **least loaded** area for a given product in this model.

Each location has a probable **availability**:

$$A = \text{Availability} = 1 - \text{load}$$

The probability of a load of a given storage point lies between 0 and 1.

High values of availability will be close to 1, and low probabilities will be close to 0 as shown in the following example:

```
>>>print ('Availability of 1x',1-value)
Availability of 1x [[ 0.00028867]]
```

For example, the load of l_1 has a probable load of 0.99 and its probable *availability* is 0.002. The goal of the AGV is to search and find the closest and most available location to optimize its trajectories. l_1 is obviously not a good candidate at that day and time. **Load** is a keyword in production activities as in the Amazon example in Chapter 12, *Automated Planning and Scheduling*.

When all of the six locations' availabilities has been calculated by the McCulloch-Pitts neuron—each with its respective *x* quantity inputs, weights, and bias—a location vector of the results of this system will be produced. This means that the program needs to be implemented to run all six locations and not just one location:

$$A(L) = \{a(l_1), a(l_2), a(l_3), a(l_4), a(l_5), a(l_6)\}$$

The availability (*1 - output value of the neuron*) constitutes a six-line vector. The following vector will be obtained by running the previous sample code on **all** six locations.

$$lv = \begin{bmatrix} 0.0002 \\ 0.2 \\ 0.9 \\ 0.0001 \\ 0.4 \\ 0.6 \end{bmatrix}$$

lv is the vector containing the value of each location for a given AGV to choose from. The values in the vector represent availability. *0.0002* means little availability. *0.9* means high availability. Once the choice is made, the reinforcement learning program presented in the first chapter will optimize the AGV's trajectory to get to this specific warehouse location.

The *lv* is the result of the weighing function of six potential locations for the AGV. It is also a vector of transformed inputs.

The architecture of Python TensorFlow

Implementation of the McCulloch-Pitts neuron can best be viewed with TensorBoard, as shown in the following graph:

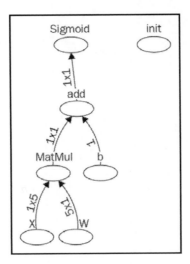

This is obtained by adding the following TensorBoard code at the end of your session. This data flow graph will help optimize a program when things go wrong.

```
#_____Tensorboard_____

#with tf.Session() as sess:

Writer = tf.summary.FileWriter("directory on your machine", tfs.graph)
Writer.close()


def launchTensorBoard():
    import os
    #os.system('tensorboard --logdir=' + 'your directory')
    os.system('tensorboard --logdir=' + 'your directory')
    return

import threading
t = threading.Thread(target=launchTensorBoard, args=([]))
t.start()

tfs.close()
#Open your browser and go to http://localhost:6006
#Try the various options. It is a very useful tool.
#close the system window when your finished.
```

When you open the URL indicated in the code on your machine, you will see the following TensorBoard data flow graph:

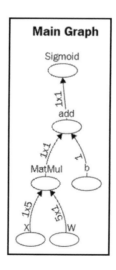

Logistic activation functions and classifiers

Now that the value of each location of $L=\{l1,l2,l3,l4,l5,l6\}$ contains its availability in a vector, the locations can be sorted from the most available to least available location. From there, the reward matrix for the MDP process described in the first chapter can be built.

Overall architecture

At this point, the overall architecture contains two main components:

- **Chapter 1**: *Become an Adaptive Thinker*: A reinforcement learning program based on the value-action Q function using a reward matrix that is yet to be calculated. The reward matrix was given in the first chapter, but in real life, you'll often have to build it from scratch. This could take weeks to obtain.
- **Chapter 2**: A set of six neurons that represent the flow of products at a given time at six locations. The output is the availability probability from 0 to 1. The highest value is the highest availability. The lowest value is the lowest availability.

At this point, there is some real-life information we can draw from these two main functions:

- An AGV is moving in a warehouse and is waiting to receive its next location to use an MDP, in order to calculate an optimal trajectory of its mission, as shown in the first chapter.
- An AGV is using a reward matrix that was given in the first chapter, but it needs to be designed in a real-life project through meetings, reports, and acceptance of the process.
- A system of six neurons, one per location, weighing the real quantities and probable quantities to give an availability vector lv has been calculated. It is almost ready to provide the necessary reward matrix for the AGV.

To calculate the input values of the reward matrix in this reinforcement learning warehouse model, a bridge function between lv and the reward matrix R is missing.

That bridge function is a logistic classifier based on the outputs of the y neurons.

At this point, the system:

- Took corporate data
- Used y neurons calculated with weights
- Applied an activation function

The activation function in this model requires a logistic classifier, a commonly used one.

Logistic classifier

The logistic classifier will be applied to *lv* (the six location values) to find the best location for the AGV. It is based on the output of the six neurons (*input x weight + bias*).

What are logistic functions? The goal of a logistic classifier is to produce a probability distribution from 0 to 1 for each value of the output vector. As you have seen so far, AI applications use applied mathematics with probable values, not raw outputs. In the warehouse model, the AGV needs to choose the best, most probable location, l_i. Even in a well-organized corporate warehouse, many uncertainties (late arrivals, product defects, or a number of unplanned problems) reduce the probability of a choice. A probability represents a value between 0 (low probability) and 1 (high probability). Logistic functions provide the tools to convert all numbers into probabilities between 0 and 1 to *normalize* data.

Logistic function

The logistic sigmoid provides one of the best ways to normalize the weight of a given output. This will be used as the activation function of the neuron. The threshold is usually a value above which the neuron has a *y=1* value; or else it has *y=0*. In this case, the minimum value will be 0 because the activation function will be more complex.

The logistic function is represented as follows.

$$\frac{1}{1 + e^{-x}}$$

- *e* represents Euler's number, or 2.71828, the natural logarithm.
- *x* is the value to be calculated. In this case, x is the result of the logistic sigmoid function.

The code has been rearranged in the following example to show the reasoning process:

```
#For given variables:
x_1 = [[10, 2, 1., 6., 2.]]       # the x inputs
w_t = [[.1, .7, .75, .60, .20]]   # the corresponding weights
b_1 = [1]                          # the bias
# A given total weight y is calculated
y = tf.matmul(x, w) + b
```

```
# then the logistic sigmoid is applied to y which represents the "x" in the
formal definition of the Logistic Sigmoid
s = tf.nn.sigmoid(y)
```

Thanks to the logistic sigmoid function, the value for the first location in the model comes out as 0.99 (level of saturation of the location).

To calculate the availability of the location once the 0.99 has been taken into account, we subtract the load from the total availability, which is 1, as follows:

As seen previously, once all locations are calculated in this manner, a final availability vector, *lv*, is obtained.

$$lv = \begin{bmatrix} 0.0002 \\ 0.2 \\ 0.9 \\ 0.0001 \\ 0.4 \\ 0.6 \end{bmatrix} \rightarrow [?]$$

When analyzing *lv*, a problem has stopped the process. Individually, each line appears to be fine. By applying the logistic sigmoid to each output weight and subtracting it from 1, each location displays a probable availability between 0 and 1. However, the sum of the lines in *lv* exceeds 1. That is not possible. Probability cannot exceed 1. The program needs to fix that. In the source code, *lv* will be named y.

Each line produces a [0,1] solution, which fits the prerequisite of being a valid probability.

In this case, the vector *lv* contains more than one value and becomes a multiple distribution. The sum of *lv* cannot exceed 1 and needs to be normalized.

The *softmax* function provides an excellent method to stabilize *lv*. *Softmax* is widely used in machine learning and deep learning.

Bear in mind that these *mathematical tools are not rules*. You can adapt them to your problem as much as you wish as long as your solution works.

Softmax

The softmax function appears in many artificial intelligence models to normalize data. This is a fundamental function to understand and master. In the case of the warehouse model, an AGV needs to make a probable choice between six locations in the *lv* vector. However, the total of the *lv* values exceeds 1. *lv* requires normalization of the softmax function *S*. In this sense, the softmax function can be considered as a generalization of the logistic sigmoid function. In the code, *lv* vector will be named y.

$$S(y_i) = \frac{e^{y_i}}{\sum_{j=1}^{n} e^{y_j}}$$

The following code used is SOFTMAX.py; y represents the *lv* vector in the following source code.

```
# y is the vector of the scores of the lv vector in the warehouse example:
y = [0.0002, 0.2, 0.9,0.0001,0.4,0.6]
```

e^{y_i} is the *exp*(i) result of each value in y *(lv* in the warehouse example), as follows:

```
y_exp = [math.exp(i) for i in y]
```

$\sum_{j=1}^{n} e^{y_j}$ is the sum of e^{y_i} iterations, as shown in the following code:

```
sum_exp_yi = sum(y_exp)
```

Now, each value of the vector can be normalized in this type of multinomial distribution stabilization by simply applying a division, as follows:

```
softmax = [round(i / sum_exp_yi, 3) for i in y_exp]

#Vector to be stabilized [2.0, 1.0, 0.1, 5.0, 6.0, 7.0]
#Stabilized vector [0.004, 0.002, 0.001, 0.089, 0.243, 0.661]
```

$$lv = \begin{bmatrix} 0.0002 \\ 0.2 \\ 0.9 \\ 0.0001 \\ 0.4 \\ 0.6 \end{bmatrix} \rightarrow softmax(lv) \rightarrow \begin{bmatrix} 0.111 \\ 0.135 \\ 0.273 \\ 0.111 \\ 0.165 \\ 0.202 \end{bmatrix}$$

softmax(lv) provides a normalized vector with a sum equal to 1 and is shown in this compressed version of the code. The vector obtained is often described as containing **logits.**

The following code details the process:

```
def softmax(x):
    return np.exp(x) / np.sum(np.exp(x), axis=0)

y1 = [0.0002, 0.2, 0.9,0.0001,0.4,0.6]
print("Stablized vector",softmax(y1))
print("sum of vector",sum(softmax(y1)))
# Stabilized vector [ 0.11119203 0.13578309 0.27343357 0.11118091
0.16584584 0.20256457]
# sum of vector 1.0
```

The softmax function can be used as the output of a classifier (pixels for example) or to make a decision. In this warehouse case, it transforms *lv* into a decision-making process.

The last part of the softmax function requires softmax(lv) to be rounded to 0 or 1. The higher the value in softmax(lv), the more probable it will be. In clear-cut transformations, the highest value will be close to 1 and the others will be closer to 0. In a decision-making process, the highest value needs to be found, as follows:

```
print("highest value in transformed y vector",max(softmax(y1)))
#highest value in normalized y vector 0.273433565194
```

Once line 3 (value 0.273) has been chosen as the most probable location, it is set to 1 and the other, lower values are set to 0. This is called a **one-hot** function. This **one-hot** function is extremely helpful to encode the data provided. The vector obtained can now be applied to the reward matrix. The value 1 probability will become 100 in the R reward matrix, as follows.

$$
lv = \begin{bmatrix} 0.0002 \\ 0.2 \\ 0.9 \\ 0.0001 \\ 0.4 \\ 0.6 \end{bmatrix} \rightarrow softmax(lv) \rightarrow \begin{bmatrix} 0.111 \\ 0.135 \\ 0.273 \\ 0.111 \\ 0.165 \\ 0.202 \end{bmatrix} \rightarrow one-hot \rightarrow \begin{bmatrix} 0 \\ 0 \\ 1 \\ 0 \\ 0 \\ 0 \end{bmatrix} \rightarrow R \rightarrow \begin{bmatrix} 0 \\ 0 \\ 100 \\ 0 \\ 0 \\ 0 \end{bmatrix}
$$

The softmax function is now complete. Location l_3 or **C** is the best solution for the AGV. The probability value is multiplied by 100 in the *R* function and the reward matrix described can now receive the input.

Before continuing, take some time to play around with the values in the source code and run it to become familiar with softmax.

We now have the data for the reward matrix. The best way to understand the mathematical aspect of the project is to go to a paperboard and draw the result using the actual warehouse layout from locations **A** to **F**.

Locations={l_1-A, l_2-B, l_3-C, l_4-D, l_5-E, l_6-F}

Value of locations in the reward matrix={0,0,100,0,0,0} where C (the third value) is now the target for the self-driving vehicle, in this case, an AGV in a warehouse.

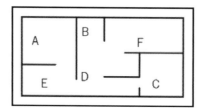

We obtain the following reward matrix R described in the first chapter.

State/values	A	B	C	D	E	F
A	-	-	-	-	1	-
B	-	-	-	1	-	1
C	-	-	100	1	-	-
D	-	1	1	-	1	-
E	1	-	-	1	-	-
F	-	1	-	-	-	-

This reward matrix is exactly the one used in the Python reinforcement learning program using the Q function in the first chapter. The output of this chapter is the input of the R matrix in the first chapter. The 0 values are there for the agent to avoid those values. This program is designed to stay close to probability standards with positive values, as shown in the following R matrix.

```
R = ql.matrix([ [0,0,0,0,1,0],
                [0,0,0,1,0,1],
                [0,0,100,1,0,0],
                [0,1,1,0,1,0],
```

```
                    [1,0,0,1,0,0],
                    [0,1,0,0,0,0] ])
```

At this point, the building blocks are in place to begin evaluating the results of the reinforcement learning program.

Summary

Using a McCulloch-Pitts neuron with a logistic activation function in a one-layer network to build a reward matrix for reinforcement learning shows how to build real-life applications with AI technology.

Processing real-life data often requires a generalization of a logistic sigmoid function through a softmax function, and a one-hot function applied to logits to encode the data.

This shows that machine learning functions are tools that must be understood to be able to use all or parts of them to solve a problem. With this practical approach to artificial intelligence, a whole world of projects awaits you.

You can already use these first two chapters to present powerful trajectory models such as Amazon warehouses and deliveries to your team or customers. Furthermore, Amazon, Google, Facebook, Netflix, and many others are growing their data centers as we speak. Each data center has locations with data flows that need to be calibrated. You can use the ideas given in this chapter to represent the problems and real-time calculations required to calibrate product and data flows.

This neuronal approach is the parent of the multi-layer perceptron that will be introduced in Chapter 5, *Manage The Power of Machine Learning and Deep Learning*. There, a shift from machine learning to deep learning will be made.

However, before that, machine learning or deep learning requires evaluation functions. No result can be validated without evaluation, as explained in Chapter 3, *Apply Machine Thinking to a Human Problem*. In the next chapter, the evaluation process will be illustrated with chess and a real-life situation.

Questions

1. Was the concept of using an artificial neuron discovered in 1990? (Yes | No)
2. Does a neuron require a threshold? (Yes | No)
3. A logistic sigmoid activation function makes the sum of the weights larger. (Yes | No)
4. A McCulloch-Pitts neuron sums the weights of its inputs. (Yes | No)
5. A logistic sigmoid function is a log10 operation. (Yes | No)
6. A logistic softmax is not necessary if a logistic sigmoid function is applied to a vector. (Yes | No)
7. A probability is a value between -1 and 1. (Yes | No)

Further reading

- Exploring DeepMind https://deepmind.com/
- The TensorFlow site, and support https://www.tensorflow.org/
- The original DQN article https://storage.googleapis.com/deepmind-media/dqn/DQNNaturePaper.pdf
- Automated solutions in logistics https://www.logistics-systems.ie/automated-solutions-apm

3
Apply Machine Thinking to a Human Problem

In the first chapter, the MDP reinforcement program produced a result as an output matrix. In Chapter 2, *Think Like a Machine*, the McCulloch-Pitts system of neurons produced an *input reward matrix*. However, the intermediate or final results of these two functions need to be constantly measured. Good measurement solves a substantial part of a given problem since decisions rely on them. Reliable decisions are made with reliable evaluations. The goal of this chapter is to introduce measurement methods.

The key function of human intelligence, decision-making, relies on the ability to evaluate a situation. No decision can be made without measuring the pros and cons and factoring the parameters.

Mankind takes great pride in its ability to evaluate. However, in many cases, a machine can do better. Chess represents the pride of mankind in thinking strategy. A chessboard is often present in many movies to symbolize human intelligence.

Today, not a single chess player can beat the best chess engines. One of the extraordinary core capacities of a chess engine is the evaluation function; it takes many parameters into account more precisely than humans.

This chapter focuses on the main concepts of evaluation and measurement; they set the path to deep learning gradient descent-driven models, which will be explained in the following chapter.

The following topics will be covered in this chapter:

- Evaluation of the episodes of a learning session
- Numerical convergence measurements
- An introduction to the idea of cross-entropy convergence
- Decision tree supervised learning as an evaluation method

- Decision tree supervised learning as a predictive model
- How to apply evaluation tools to a real-life problem you build on your own

Technical requirements

- Python version 3.6 is recommended
- NumPy compatible with Python 3.6
- TensorFlow with TensorBoard
- Graphviz 2.28 for use in Python

Programs are available on GitHub, Chapter03:

- Q_learning_convergence.py
- Decision_Tree_Priority_classifier.py

Check out the following video to see the code in action:

https://goo.gl/Yrgb3i

Determining what and how to measure

In Chapter 2, *Think Like a Machine*, the system of McCulloch-Pitts neurons generated a vector with a one-hot function in the following process.

$$lv = \begin{bmatrix} 0.0002 \\ 0.2 \\ 0.9 \\ 0.0001 \\ 0.4 \\ 0.6 \end{bmatrix} \rightarrow softmax(lv) \rightarrow \begin{bmatrix} 0.111 \\ 0.135 \\ 0.273 \\ 0.111 \\ 0.165 \\ 0.202 \end{bmatrix} \rightarrow one-hot \rightarrow \begin{bmatrix} 0 \\ 0 \\ 1 \\ 0 \\ 0 \\ 0 \end{bmatrix} \rightarrow R \rightarrow \begin{bmatrix} 0 \\ 0 \\ 100 \\ 0 \\ 0 \\ 0 \end{bmatrix}$$

R, the reward vector, represents the input of the reinforcement learning program and needs to be measured.

This chapter deals with an approach designed to build a reward matrix based on the company data. It relies on the data, weights, and biases provided. When deep learning forward feedback neural networks based on perception are introduced (`Chapter 4`, *Become an Unconventional Innovator*), a system cannot be content with a training set. Systems have a natural tendency to learn training sets through backpropagation. In this case, one set of company data is not enough.

In real-life company projects, a system will not be validated until tens of thousands of results have been produced. In some cases, a corporation will approve the system only after hundreds of datasets with millions of data samples have been tested to be sure that all scenarios are accurate. Each dataset represents a scenario consultants can work on with parameter scripts. The consultant introduces parameter scenarios that are tested by the system and measured. In systems with up to 200 parameters per neuron, a consultant will remain necessary for many years to come in an industrial environment. As of `Chapter 4`, *Become an Unconventional Innovator*, the system will be on its own without the help of a consultant. Even then, consultants often are needed to manage the hyperparameters. In real-life systems, with high financial stakes, quality control will always remain essential.

Measurement should thus apply to generalization more than simply applying to a single or few datasets. Otherwise, you will have a natural tendency to control the parameters and overfit your model in a too-good-to-be-true scenario.

Beyond the reward matrix, the reinforcement program in the first chapter had a learning parameter $\lambda = 0.8$, as shown in the following code source.

```
# Gamma : It's a form of penalty or uncertainty for learning
# If the value is 1 , the rewards would be too high.
# This way the system knows it is learning.
gamma = 0.8
```

The λ learning parameter in itself needs to be closely monitored because it introduces uncertainty into the system. This means that the learning process will always remain a probability, never a certainty. One might wonder why this parameter is not just taken out. Paradoxically, that will lead to even more global uncertainty. The more the λ learning parameter tends to 1, the more you risk overfitting your results. **Overfitting** means that you are pushing the system to think it's learning well when it isn't. It's exactly like a teacher who gives high grades to everyone in the class all the time. The teacher would be overfitting the grade-student evaluation process, and nobody would know whether the students have learned something.

The results of the reinforcement program need to be measured as they go through episodes. The range of the learning process itself must be measured. In the following code, the range is set to 50,000 to make sure the learning process reaches its goal.

```
for i in range(50000):
    current_state = ql.random.randint(0, int(Q.shape[0]))
    PossibleAction = possible_actions(current_state)
    action = ActionChoice(PossibleAction)
    reward(current_state,action,gamma)
```

All of these measurements will have a deep effect on the results obtained.

Convergence

Building the system was fun. Finding the factors that make the system go wrong is another story.

The model presented so far can be summed up as follows:

$$lv = \begin{bmatrix} 0.0002 \\ 0.2 \\ 0.9 \\ 0.0001 \\ 0.4 \\ 0.6 \end{bmatrix} \rightarrow softmax(lv) \rightarrow \begin{bmatrix} 0.111 \\ 0.135 \\ 0.273 \\ 0.111 \\ 0.165 \\ 0.202 \end{bmatrix} \rightarrow one - hot \rightarrow \begin{bmatrix} 0 \\ 0 \\ 1 \\ 0 \\ 0 \\ 0 \end{bmatrix} \rightarrow R \rightarrow \begin{bmatrix} 0 \\ 0 \\ 100 \\ 0 \\ 0 \\ 0 \end{bmatrix} \rightarrow gamma \rightarrow Q \rightarrow Results$$

From *lv* to *R*, the process creates the reward matrix (Chapter 2, *Think Like a Machine*) required for the reinforcement learning program (Chapter 1, *Become an Adaptive Thinker*), which runs from reading R (reward matrix) to the results. Gamma is the learning parameter, *Q* is the Q learning function, and the results are the states of Q described in the first chapter.

The parameters to be measured are as follows:

- The company's input data. The training sets found on the Web such as MNIST are designed to be efficient. These ready-made datasets often contain some noise (unreliable data) to make them realistic. The same process must be achieved with raw company data. *The only problem is that you cannot download a corporate dataset from somewhere. You have to build the datasets.*
- The weights and biases that will be applied.
- The activation function (a logistic function or other).

- The choices to make after the one-hot process.
- The learning parameter.
- Episode management through convergence.

The best way to start relies on measuring the quality of convergence of the system, the last step of the whole process.

If the system provides good convergence, it will avoid the headache of having to go back and check everything.

Implicit convergence

In the last part of `Reinforcement_Learning_Q_function.py` in the first chapter, a range of 50,000 is implemented.

The idea is to set the number of episodes at such a level that convergence is certain. In the following code, the range (`50000`) is a constant.

```
for i in range(50000):
    current_state = ql.random.randint(0, int(Q.shape[0]))
    PossibleAction = possible_actions(current_state)
    action = ActionChoice(PossibleAction)
    reward(current_state,action,gamma)
```

Convergence, in this case, will be defined as the point at which no matter how long you run the system, the Q result matrix will not change anymore.

By setting the range to `50000`, you can test and verify this. As long as the reward matrices remain homogeneous, this will work. If the reward matrices strongly vary from one scenario to another, this model will produce unstable results.

Try to run the program with different ranges. Lower the ranges until you see that the results are not optimal.

Numerical – controlled convergence

This approach can prove time-saving by using the target result, provided it exists beforehand. Training the reinforcement program in this manner validates the process.

In the following source code, an intuitive *cross-entropy* function is introduced (see `Chapter 9`, *Getting Your Neurons to Work*, for more on cross-entropy).

Cross-entropy refers to energy. The main concepts are as follows:

- Energy represents the difference between one distribution and another
- It is what makes the system continue to train
- When a lot of training needs to be done, there is a **high level of energy**
- When the training reaches the end of its cycles, **the level of energy is low**
- In the following code, **cross-entropy value (CEV)** measures the **difference between a target matrix and the episode matrix**
- Cross-entropy is often measured in more complex forms when necessary (see `Chapter 9`, *Getting Your Neurons to Work*, and `Chapter 10`, *Applying Biomimicking to Artificial Intelligence*)

In the following code, a basic function provides sufficient results.

```
for i in range(50000):
    current_state = ql.random.randint(0, int(Q.shape[0]))
    PossibleAction = possible_actions(current_state)
    action = ActionChoice(PossibleAction)
    reward(current_state,action,gamma)
    if Q.sum()>0:
    #print("convergent episode:",i,"Q.Sum",Q.sum(),"numerical convergent
value e-1:",Q.sum()-sum)
    #print("convergent episode:",i,"numerical convergent value:",ceg-
Q.sum())
        CEV=-(math.log(Q.sum())-math.log(ceg))
        print("convergent episode:",i,"numerical convergent value:",CEV)
        sum=Q.sum()
        if(Q.sum()-3992==0):
            print("Final convergent episode:",i,"numerical convergent
value:",ceg-Q.sum())
            break; #break on average (the process is random) before 50000
```

The previous program stops before 50,000 epochs. This is because, in the model described in this chapter (see the previous code excerpt), the system stops when it reaches an acceptable CEV convergence value.

```
convergent episode: 1573 numerical convergent value: -0.0
convergent episode: 1574 numerical convergent value: -0.0
convergent episode: 1575 numerical convergent value: -0.0
convergent episode: 1576 numerical convergent value: -0.0
convergent episode: 1577 numerical convergent value: -0.0
Final convergent episode: 1577 numerical convergent value: 0.0
```

The program stopped at episode `1577`. Since the decision process is random, the same number will not be obtained twice in a row. Furthermore, the constant `3992` was known in advance. This is possible in closed environments where a pre-set goal has been set. This is not the case often but was used to illustrate the concept of convergence. The following chapters will explore better ways to reach convergence, such as gradient descent.

The Python program is available at:

```
https://github.com/PacktPublishing/Artificial-Intelligence-By-Example/blob/
master/Chapter03/Q_learning_convergence.py
```

Applying machine thinking to a human problem

"An efficient manager has a high evaluation quotient. A machine has a better one, in chess and a number of increasing fields. The problem now is to keep up with what the machines are learning!"

-Denis Rothman

Evaluation is one of the major keys to efficient decision making in all fields: from chess, production management, rocket launching, and self-driving cars to data center calibration, software development, and airport schedules. Chess engines are not high-level deep-learning-based software. They rely heavily on evaluations and calculations. They evaluate much better than humans, and there is a lot to learn from them. The question now is to know whether any human can beat a chess engine or not. The answer is no.

To evaluate a position in chess, you need to examine all the pieces, their quantitative value, their qualitative value, cooperation between pieces, who owns each of the 64 squares, the king's safety, bishop pairs, knight positioning, and many other factors.

Evaluating a position in a chess game

Evaluating a position in a chess game shows why machines will surpass humans in quite some decision-making fields within the next few years.

The following position is after move 23 in the Kramnik-Bluebaum 2017 game. It cannot be correctly evaluated by humans. It contains too many parameters to analyze and too many possibilities.

It is white's turn to play, and a close analysis shows that both players are lost at this point. In a tournament like this, they must each continue to keep a poker face. They often look at the position with a confident face to hide their dismay. Some even shorten their thinking time to make their opponent think they know where they are going.

These unsolvable positions for humans are painless to solve with chess engines, even cheap, high-quality chess engines on a smartphone. This can be generalized to all human activity that has become increasingly complex, unpredictable and chaotic. Decision-makers will increasingly rely on artificial intelligence to help them make the right choices.

No human can play chess and evaluate the way a chess engine does by simply calculating the positions of the pieces, their squares of liberty, and many other parameters. A chess engine generates an evaluation matrix with millions of calculations. The following table is the result of an evaluation of only one position among many others (real and potential).

Position evaluated	0,3					
White	34					
	Initial position	position	Value		Quality Value	TotalValue
Pawn	a2	a2	1	a2-b2 small pawn island	0,05	1,05
Pawn	b2	b2	1	a2-b2 small pawn island	0,05	1,05

Pawn	c2	x	0	captured	0	0
Pawn	d2	d4	1	occupies center,defends Be5	0,25	1,25
Pawn	e2	e2	1	defends Qf3	0,25	1,25
Pawn	f2	x	0	captured	0	0
Pawn	g2	g5	1	unattacked, attacking 2 squares	0,3	1,3
Pawn	h2	h3	1	unattacked, defending g4	0,1	1,1
Rook	a1	c1	5	occupying c-file, attacking b7 with Nd5-Be5	1	6
Knight	b1	d5	3	attacking Nb6, 8 squares	0,5	3,5
BishopDS	c1	e5	3	central position, 10 squares, attacking c7	0,5	3,5
Queen	d1	f3	9	battery with Bg2, defending Ne5, X-Ray b7	2	11
King	e1	h1	0	X-rayed by Bb6 on a7-g1 diagonal	-0,5	-0,5
BishopWS	f1	g2	3	supporting Qf3 in defense and attack	0,5	3,5
Knight	g1	x	0	captured	0	0
Rook	h1	x	0	captured	0	0
			29		5	34
						White:34

The value of the position of white is 34.

White	34					
Black	33,7					
	Initial position	position	Value		Quality Value	TotalValue
Pawn	a7	a7	1	a7-b7 small pawn island	0,05	1,05
Pawn	b7	b7	1	a7-b7 small pawn island	0,05	1,05
Pawn	c7	x	0	captured	0	0
Pawn	d7	x	0	captured	0	0
Pawn	e7	f5	1	doubled, 2 squares	0	1
Pawn	f7	f7	1		0	1
Pawn	g7	g6	1	defending f5 but abandoning Kg8	0	1
Pawn	h7	h5	1	well advanced with f5,g6	0,1	1,1
Rook	a8	d8	5	semi-open d-file attacking Nd5	2	7
Knight	b8	x	0	captured	0	0
BishopDS	c8	b6	3	attacking d4, 3 squares	0,5	3,5
Queen	d8	e6	9	attacking d4,e5 , a bit cramped	1,5	10,5
King	e8	g8	0	f6,h6, g7,h8 attacked	-1	-1

BishopWS	f8	x	0	captured, White lost bishop pair	0,5	0,5
Knight	g8	e8	3	defending c7,f6,g7	1	4
Rook	h8	f8	5	out of play	-2	3
			31		2,7	Black:33,7

The value of black is 33.7.

So white is winning by *34-33.7 = 0.3.*

The evaluation system can easily be represented with two McCulloch-Pitts neurons, one for black and one for white. Each neuron would have 30 *weights = {w1,w2....w30}*, as shown in the previous table. The sum of both neurons requires an activation function that converts the evaluation into 1/100th of a pawn, which is the standard measurement unit in chess. Each weight will be the output of squares and piece calculations. Then the MDP can be applied to Bellman's equation with a random generator of possible positions.

 Present-day chess engines contain barely more intelligence than this type of pure calculation approach. They don't need more to beat humans.

No human, not even world champions, can calculate this position with this accuracy. The number of parameters to take into account overwhelms them each time they reach a position like this. They then play more or less randomly with some kind of idea in mind. It resembles a lottery sometimes. Chess expert annotators discover this when they run human-played games with powerful chess engines to check the game. The players themselves now tend to reveal their incapacity when questioned.

Now bear in mind that the position analyzed represents only one possibility. A chess engine will test millions of possibilities. Humans can test only a few.

Measuring a result like this has nothing to do with natural human thinking. Only machines can think like that. Not only do chess engines solve the problem, but also they are impossible to beat.

 At one point, there are problems humans face that only machines can solve.

Applying the evaluation and convergence process to a business problem

What was once considered in chess as the ultimate proof of human intelligence has been battered by brute-force calculations with great CPU/RAM capacity. Almost any human problem requiring logic and reasoning can most probably be solved by a machine using relatively elementary processes expressed in mathematical terms.

Let's take the result matrix of the reinforcement learning example of the first chapter. It can also be viewed as a scheduling tool. Automated planning and scheduling have become a crucial artificial intelligence field, as explained in Chapter 12, *Automated Planning and Scheduling*. In this case, evaluating and measuring the result goes beyond convergence aspects.

In a scheduling process, the input of the reward matrix can represent the priorities of the packaging operation of some products in a warehouse. It would determine in which order customer products must be picked to be packaged and delivered. These priorities extend to the use of a machine that will automatically package the products in a FIFO mode (first in, first out). The systems provide good solutions, but, in real life, many unforeseen events change the order of flows in a warehouse and practically all schedules.

In this case, the result matrix can be transformed into a vector of a scheduled packaging sequence. The packaging department will follow the priorities produced by the system.

The reward matrix (see Q_learning_convergence.py) in this chapter is R (see the following code).

```
R = ql.matrix([ [-1,-1,-1,-1,0,-1],
[-1,-1,-1,0,-1,0],
[-1,-1,100,0,-1,-1],
[-1,0,100,-1,0,-1],
[0,-1,-1,0,-1,-1],
[-1,0,-1,-1,-1,-1] ])
```

Its visual representation is the same as in Chapter 1, *Become an Adaptive Thinker*. But the values are a bit different for this application:

- **Negative values (-1)**: The agent cannot go there
- **0 values**: The agent can go there
- **100 values**: The agent should favor these locations

The result is produced in a Q function early in the first section of the chapter, in a matrix format, displayed as follows:

```
Q :
[[ 0. 0. 0. 0. 258.44 0. ]
 [ 0. 0. 0. 321.8 0. 207.752]
 [ 0. 0. 500. 321.8 0. 0. ]
 [ 0. 258.44 401. 0. 258.44 0. ]
 [ 207.752 0. 0. 321.8 0. 0. ]
 [ 0. 258.44 0. 0. 0. 0. ]]
Normed Q :
[[ 0. 0. 0. 0. 51.688 0. ]
 [ 0. 0. 0. 64.36 0. 41.5504]
 [ 0. 0. 100. 64.36 0. 0. ]
 [ 0. 51.688 80.2 0. 51.688 0. ]
 [ 41.5504 0. 0. 64.36 0. 0. ]
 [ 0. 51.688 0. 0. 0. 0. ]]
```

From that result, the following packaging priority order matrix can be deduced.

Priorities	O1	O2	O3	O4	O5	O6
O1	-	-	-	-	258.44	-
O2	-	-	-	321.8	-	207.75
O3	-	-	500	321.8	-	-
O4	-	258.44	401	-	258.44	-
O5	207.75	-	-	321.8	-	-
O6	-	258.44	-	-	-	-

The **non-prioritized vector (npv)** of packaging orders is *np.*

$$npv = \begin{bmatrix} O1 \\ O2 \\ O3 \\ O4 \\ O5 \\ O6 \end{bmatrix}$$

The *npv* contains the priority value of each cell in the matrix, which is not a location but an order priority. Combining this vector with the result matrix, the results become priorities of the packaging machine. They now need to be analyzed, and a final order must be decided to send to the packaging department.

Using supervised learning to evaluate result quality

Having now obtained the *npv*, a more business-like measurement must be implemented.

A warehouse manager, for example, will tell you the following:

- Your reinforcement learning program looks satisfactory (Chapter 1, *Become an Adaptive Thinker*)
- The reward matrix generated by the McCulloch-Pitts neurons works very well (Chapter 2, *Think Like a Machine*)
- The convergence values of the system look nice
- The results on this dataset look satisfactory

But then, the manager will always come up with a killer question, *How can you prove that this will work with other datasets in the future?*

The only way to be sure that this whole system works is to run thousands of datasets with hundreds of thousands of product flows.

The idea now is to use supervised learning to create relationships between the input and output data. It's not a random process like MDP. They are not trajectories anymore. They are priorities. One method is to used decision trees. In Chapter 4, *Become an Unconventional Innovator*, the problem will be solved with a feedforward backpropagation network.

In this model, the properties of the customer orders are analyzed so that we can classify them. This can be translated into decision trees depending on real-time data, to create a distribution representation to predict future outcomes.

1. The first step is to represent the properties of the orders O1 to O6.

    ```
    features = [ 'Priority/location', 'Volume', 'Flow_optimizer' ]
    ```

In this case, we will limit the model to three properties:

- Priority/location, which is the most important property in a warehouse flow in this model
- Volumes to transport
- Optimizing priority—the financial and customer satisfaction property

2. The second step is to provide some priority parameters to the learning dataset:

```
Y = ['Low', 'Low', 'High', 'High', 'Low', 'Low
```

3. Step 3 is providing the dataset input matrix, which is the output matrix of the reinforcement learning program. The values have been approximated but are enough to run the model. This simulates some of the intermediate decisions and transformations that occur during the decision process (ratios applied, uncertainty factors added, and other parameters). The input matrix is X:

```
X = [ [256, 1,0],
      [320, 1,0],
      [500, 1,1],
      [400, 1,1],
      [320, 1,0],
      [256, 1,0]]
```

The features in step 1 apply to each column.

The values in step 2 apply to every line.

4. Step 4 is running a standard decision tree classifier. This classifier will distribute the representations (distributed representations) into two categories:

- The properties of high-priority orders
- The properties of low-priority orders

There are many types of algorithms. In this case, a standard `sklearn` function is called to do the job, as shown in the following source code.

```
classify = tree.DecisionTreeClassifier()
classify = classify.fit(X,Y)
```

Applied to thousands of orders on a given day, it will help adapt to real-time unplanned events that destabilize all scheduling systems: late trucks, bad quality products, robot breakdowns, and absent personnel. This means that the system must be able to constantly adapt to new situations and provide priorities to replan in real time.

The program will produce the following graph, which separates the orders into priority groups.

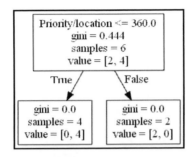

The goal now is to separate the best orders to replan among hundreds of thousands of simulating orders. In this case, the learning dataset has the six values you have been studying in the first two chapters from various angles.

- Priority/location<=360.0 is the division point between the most probable optimized orders (high) and less interesting ones (low).
- Gini impurity. This would be the measure of incorrect labeling if the choice were random. In this case, the dataset is stable.
- The false arrow points out the two values that are not <=360, meaning they are good choices, the optimal separation line of the representation. The ones that are not classified as False are considered as *don't eliminate* orders.
  The True elements mean: *eliminate orders as long as possible.*
- The value result reads as [*number of false elements, number of true elements*] of the dataset.

If you play around with the values in steps 1, 2, and 3, you'll obtain different separation points and values. This sandbox program will prepare you for the more complex scheduling problems of Chapter 12, Automated Planning and Scheduling.

You can use this part of the source code to generate images of this decision tree-supervised learning program:

```
# 5.Producing visualization if necessary
info =
tree.export_graphviz(classify,feature_names=features,out_file=None,filled=F
alse,rounded=False)
graph = pydotplus.graph_from_dot_data(info)

edges = collections.defaultdict(list)
for edge in graph.get_edge_list():
```

```
        edges[edge.get_source()].append(int(edge.get_destination()))

    for edge in edges:
        edges[edge].sort()
        for i in range(2):
            dest = graph.get_node(str(edges[edge][i]))[0]

    graph.write_png('warehouse_example_decision_tree.png')
    print("Open the image to verify that the priority level prediction of the
    results fits the reality of the reward matrix inputs")
```

The preceding information represents a small part of what it takes to manage a real-life artificial intelligence program on premise.

A warehouse manager will want to run this supervised learning decision tree program on top of the system described in Chapter 2, *Think Like a Machine*, and Chapter 3, *Apply Machine Thinking to a Human Problem*. This is done to generalize these distributed representations directly to the warehouse data to improve the initial corporate data inputs. With better-proven priorities, the system will constantly improve, week by week.

This way of scheduling shows that human thinking was not used nor necessary.

Contrary to the hype surrounding artificial intelligence, most problems can be solved with no human intelligence involved and relatively little machine learning technology.

 Human intelligence simply proves that intelligence can solve a problem.

Fortunately for the community of artificial intelligence experts, there are very difficult problems to solve that require more artificial intelligence thinking.

Such a problem will be presented and solved in Chapter 4, *Become an Unconventional Innovator*.

The Python program is available at https://github.com/PacktPublishing/Artificial-Intelligence-By-Example/blob/master/Chapter03/Decision_Tree_Priority_classifier.py.

Summary

This chapter led artificial intelligence exploration one more step away from neuroscience to reproduce human thinking. Solving a problem like a machine means using a chain of mathematical functions and properties.

The further you get in machine learning and deep learning, the more you will find mathematical functions that solve the core problems. Contrary to the astounding amount of hype, mathematics relying on CPUs is replacing humans, not some form of alien intelligence.

The power of machine learning with *beyond-human* mathematical reasoning is that generalization to other fields is easier. A mathematical model, contrary to the complexity of humans entangled in emotions, makes it easier to deploy the same model in many fields. The models of the first three chapters can be used for self-driving vehicles, drones, robots in a warehouse, scheduling priorities, and much more. Try to imagine as many fields you can apply these to as possible.

Evaluation and measurement are at the core of machine learning and deep learning. The key factor is constantly monitoring convergence between the results the system produces and the goal it must attain. This opens the door to the constant adaptation of the weights of the network to reach its objectives.

Machine evaluation for convergence through a chess example that has nothing to do with human thinking proves the limits of human intelligence. The decision tree example can beat most humans in classification situations where large amounts of data are involved.

Human intelligence is not being reproduced in many cases and has often been surpassed. In those cases, human intelligence just proves that intelligence can solve a problem, nothing more.

The next chapter goes a step further from human reasoning with self-weighting neural networks and introduces deep learning.

Questions

1. Can a human beat a chess engine? (Yes | No)
2. Humans can estimate decisions better than machines with intuition when it comes to large volumes of data. (Yes | No)
3. Building a reinforcement learning program with a Q function is a feat in itself. Using the results afterward is useless. (Yes | No)
4. Supervised learning decision tree functions can be used to verify that the result of the unsupervised learning process will produce reliable, predictable results. (Yes | No)
5. The results of a reinforcement learning program can be used as input to a scheduling system by providing priorities. (Yes | No)
6. Can artificial Intelligence software think like humans? (Yes | No)

Further reading

- For more on decision trees: `https://youtu.be/NsUqRe-9tb4`

- For more on chess analysis by experts such as Zoran Petronijevic: `https://chessbookreviews.wordpress.com/tag/zoran-petronijevic/`

Become an Unconventional Innovator

4

In corporate projects, there always comes the point when a problem that seems impossible to solve hits you. At that point, you try everything you learned, but it doesn't work for what's asked of you. Your team or customer begins to look elsewhere. It's time to react.

In this chapter, an impossible-to-solve business case regarding material optimization will be implemented successfully with an example of a **feedforward neural network (FNN)** with backpropagation.

Feedforward networks are the building blocks of deep learning. The battle around the XOR function perfectly illustrates how deep learning regained popularity in corporate environments. The XOR FNN illustrates one of the critical functions of neural networks: **classification**. Once information becomes classified into subsets, it opens the doors to **prediction** and many other functions of neural networks, such as representation learning.

An XOR FNN network will be built from scratch to demystify deep learning from the start. A vintage, start-from-scratch method will be applied, blowing the deep learning hype off the table.

The following topics will be covered in this chapter:

- How to hand build an FNN
- Solving XOR with an FNN
- Classification
- Backpropagation
- A cost function

- Cost function optimization
- Error loss
- Convergence

Technical requirements

- Python 3.6x 64-bit from `https://www.python.org/`
- NumPy for Python 3.6x

Programs from GitHub `Chapter04`:

- `FNN_XOR_vintage_tribute.py`
- `FFN_XOR_generalization.py`

Check out the following video to see the code in action:

`https://goo.gl/ASyLWz`

The XOR limit of the original perceptron

Once the feedforward network for solving the XOR problem is built, it will be applied to a material optimization business case. The material-optimizing solution will choose the best combinations of dimensions among billions to minimize the use of a material with the generalization of the XOR function. First, a solution to the XOR limitation of a perceptron must be fully clarified.

XOR and linearly separable models

In the academic world, like the private world, competition exists. Such a situation took place in 1969. Minsky and Papert published *Perceptrons.* They proved mathematically that a perceptron could *not* solve an XOR function. Fortunately, today the perceptron and its neocognitron version form the core model for neural networking.

One might be tempted to think, *So what*? However, the entire field of neural networks relies on solving problems such as this to classify patterns. Without pattern classification, images, sounds, and words mean nothing to a machine.

Linearly separable models

The McCulloch-Pitts 1943 neuron (see `Chapter 2`, *Think Like a Machine*) lead to Rosenblatt's 1957-1962 perceptron and the 1960 Widrow-Hoff adaptive linear element (Adaline).

These models are linear models based on *f(x,w)*, requiring a line to separate results. A perceptron cannot achieve this goal and thus cannot classify many objects it faces.

A standard linear function can separate values. **Linear separability** can be represented in the following graph:

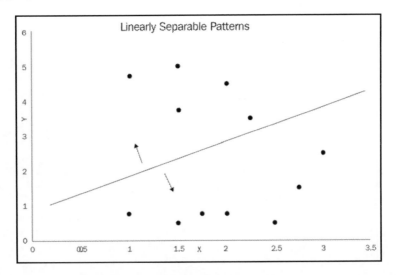

Imagine that the line separating the preceding dots and the part under it represent a picture that needs to be represented by a machine learning or deep learning application. The dots above the line represent *clouds* in the sky; the dots below the line represent *trees* on a hill. The line represents the slope of that hill.

To be linearly separable, a function must be able to separate the *clouds* from the *trees* to classify them. The prerequisite to classification is **separability** of some sort, linear or nonlinear.

The XOR limit of a linear model, such as the original perceptron

A linear model cannot solve the XOR problem expressed as follows in a table:

Value of x_1	Value of x_2	Output
1	1	0
0	0	0
1	0	1
0	1	1

The following graph shows the linear inseparability of the XOR function represented by one perceptron:

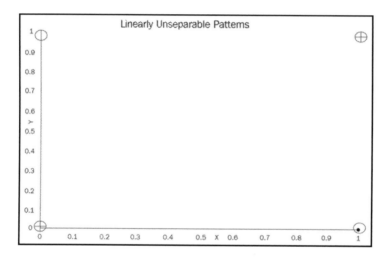

The values of the table represent the Cartesian coordinates in this graph. The circle with a cross at *(1,1)* and *(0,0)* cannot be separated from the circles at (1,0) and (0,11). That's a huge problem. It means that Frank Rosenblatt's *f(x,w)* perceptron cannot separate, and thus not classify, these dots into *clouds* and *trees*; an object used to identify that requires linear separability.

Having invented the most powerful concept of the 20th century—**a neuron that can learn**—Frank Rosenblatt had to bear with this limitation through the 1960s.

Let's vindicate this injustice with a vintage solution.

Building a feedforward neural network from scratch

Let's get into a time machine. In nanoseconds, it takes us back to 1969. We have today's knowledge but nothing to prove it. Minsky and Papert have just published their book, *Perceptrons*. They've proven that a perceptron cannot implement the exclusive OR function XOR.

We are puzzled. We know that deep learning will be a great success in the 21st century. We want to try to change the course of history. Thanks to our time machine, we land in a small apartment. It's comfortable, with a vinyl record playing the music we like! There is a mahogany desk with a pad, a pencil, sharpener, and eraser waiting for us. We sit. A warm cup of coffee appears in a big mug. We're ready to solve the XOR problem from scratch. We have to find a way to classify those dots with a neural network.

Step 1 – Defining a feedforward neural network

We look at our piece of paper. We don't have a computer. We're going to have to write code; then we'll hopefully find a computer in a university or a corporation that has a 1960 state-of-the-art language to program in.

We have to be unconventional to solve this problem. First, we must ignore Minsky and Papert's publication and also forget complicated words and theory of the 21st century. In fact, we don't remember much anyway. Time travel made our future fuzzy!

A perceptron is usually represented by a graph. But that doesn't mean much right now. After all, I can't compute circles and lines. In fact, beyond seeing circles and lines, we type characters in computer languages, not circles. So, I decide to simply to write a layer in high-school format. A hidden layer will simply be:

$$h_1 = x * w$$

Ok, now I have one layer. In fact, I just realized that a layer is merely a function. This function can be expressed as:

$$f(x, w)$$

In which *x* is the input value and *w* is some kind of value to multiply *x* by. I also realized that hidden just means that it's the computation, just as *x*=2 and *x*+2 is the hidden layer that leads to 4.

At this point, I've defined a neural network in three lines:

- Input *x*.
- Some kind of function that changes its value, like *2 x 2 = 4*, which transformed 2. That is a layer. And if the result is superior to 2, for example, then great! The output is 1, meaning yes or true. Since we don't see the computation, this is the *hidden* layer.
- An output.

Now that I know that basically any neural network is built with values transformed by an operation to become an output of something, I need the logic to solve the XOR problem.

Step 2 – how two children solve the XOR problem every day

Let's see how two children solve the XOR problem using a plain everyday example. I strongly recommend this method. I have taken very complex problems, broken them down into small parts to children's level, and often solved them in a few minutes. Then, you get the sarcastic answer from others such as *Is that all you did*? But, the sarcasm vanishes when the solution works over and over again in high-level corporate projects.

First, let's convert the XOR problem into a candy problem in a store. Two children go to the store and want to buy candy. However, they only have enough money to buy one pack of candy. They have to agree on a choice between two packs of different candy. Let's say pack one is chocolate and the other is chewing gum. Then, during the discussion between these two children, 1 means yes, 0 means no. Their budget limits the options of these two children:

- Going to the store and not buying any of chocolate **or** chewing gum = no, no (0,0). That's not an option for these children! So the answer is false.
- Going to the store and buying both chocolate **and** chewing gum = yes, yes (1,1). That would be fantastic, but that's not possible. It's too expensive. So, the answer is unfortunately false.
- Going to the store and either buying chocolate **or** chewing gum = (1,0 or 0,1) = yes or no/no or yes. That's possible. So, the answer is true.

Sipping my coffee in 1969, I imagine the two children. The eldest one is reasonable. The younger one doesn't know really how to count yet and wants to buy both packs of candy.

I decide to write that down on my piece of paper:

- x_1 (eldest child's decision yes or no, 1 or 0) * w_1 (what the elder child thinks). The elder child is thinking this, or:

$$x_1 * w_1 \quad or \quad h_1 = x_1 * w_1$$

The elder child weighs a decision like we all do every day, such as purchasing a car (x=0 or 1) multiplied by the cost (w1).

- x_2 (the younger child's decision yes or no, 1 or 0) * w_3 (what the younger child thinks). The younger child is also thinking this, or:

$$x_2 * w_3 \quad or \quad h_2 = x_2 * w_3$$

Theory: x_1 and x_2 are the inputs. h_1 and h_2 are neurons (the result of a calculation). Since h_1 and h_2 contain calculations that are not visible during the process, they are *hidden* neurons. h_1 and h_2 thus form a **hidden layer**.

Now I imagine the two children talking to each other.

Hold it a minute! This means that now each child is communicating with the other:

- x_1 (the elder child) says w_2 to the younger child. Thus *w2 = this is what I think and am telling you*:

$$x_1 * w_2$$

- x_2 (the younger child) says please add my views to your decision, which is represented by: w_4

$$x_2 * w_4$$

I now have the first two equations expressed in high-school-level code. It's *what one thinks + what one says to the other asking the other to take that into account*:

```
h1=(x1*w1)+(x2*w4)  #II.A.weight of hidden neuron h1
h2=(x2*w3)+(x1*w2)  #II.B.weight of hidden neuron h2
```

h1 sums up what is going on in one child's mind: personal opinion + other child's opinion.

h2 sums up what is going on in the other child's mind and conversation: personal opinion + other child's opinion.

Theory. The calculation now contains two input values and one hidden layer. Since in the next step we are going to apply calculations to h1 and h2, we are in a feedforward neural network. We are moving from the input to another layer, which will lead us to another layer, and so on. This process of going from one layer to another is the basis of deep learning. The more layers you have, the deeper the network is. The reason h1 and h2 form a hidden layer is that their output is just the input of another layer.

I don't have time to deal with complicated numbers in an activation function such as logistic sigmoid, so I decide to simply decide whether the output values are less than 1 or not:

if $h_1 + h_2 >= 1$ then $y_1 = 1$

if $h_1 + h_2 < 1$ then $y_2 = 0$

Theory: y_1 and y_2 form a second hidden layer. These variables can be scalars, vectors, or matrices. They are neurons.

Now, a problem comes up. Who is right? The elder child or the younger child?

The only way seems to be to play around, with the weights *W* representing all the weights.

I decided that at this point, I liked both children. Why would I have to hurt one of them? So from now on, $w_3 = w_2, w_4 = w_1$. After all, I don't have a computer and my time travel window is consuming a lot of energy. I'm going to be pulled back soon.

Now, somebody has to be an influencer. Let's leave this hard task to the elder child. The elder child, being more reasonable, will continuously deliver the bad news. You have to subtract something from your choice, represented by a minus (-) sign.

Each time they reach the point h_i, the eldest child applies a critical negative view on purchasing packs of candy. It's $-w$ of everything comes up to be sure not to go over the budget. The opinion of the elder child is biased, so let's call the variable a bias, b_1. Since the younger child's opinion is biased as well, let's call this view a bias too b_2. Since the eldest child's view is always negative, $-b_1$ will be applied to all of the eldest child's thoughts.

When we apply this decision process to their view, we obtain:

$$h_1 = y_1 * -b_1$$
$$h_2 = y_2 * b_2$$

Then, we just have to use the same result. If the result is $>=1$ then the threshold has been reached. The threshold is calculated as shown in the following function.

$$y = h_1 + h_2$$

Since I don't have a computer, I decide to start finding the weights in a practical manner, starting by setting the weights and biases to 0.5, as follows:

$$w_1 = 0.5; w_2 = 0.5; b_1 = 0.5$$
$$w_3 = w_2; w_4 = w_1; b_2 = b_1$$

It's not a full program yet, but its theory is done.

Only the communication going on between the two children is making the difference; I focus on only modifying w_2 and b_1 after a first try. An hour later, on paper, it works!

I can't believe that this is all there is to it. I copy the mathematical process on a clean sheet of paper:

```
Solution to the XOR implementation with
a feedforward neural network(FNN)

I.Setting the first weights to start the process
w1=0.5;w2=0.5;b1=0.5
w3=w2;w4=w1;b2=b1

#II hidden layer #1 and its output
h1=(x1*w1)+(x2*w4)  #II.A.weight of hidden neuron h1
h2=(x2*w3)+(x1*w2)  #II.B.weight of hidden neuron h2

#III.threshold I, hidden layer 2
if(h1>=1):h1=1;
```

```
if(h1<1):h1=0;
if(h2>=1):h2=1
if(h2<1):h2=0
h1= h1 * -b1
h2= h2 * b2

IV.Threshold II and Final OUTPUT y
y=h1+h2
if(y>=1):y=1
if(y<1):y=0

V. Change the critical weights and try again until a solution is found
w2=w2+0.5
b1=b1+0.5
```

I'm overexcited by the solution. I need to get this little sheet of paper to a newspaper to get it published and change the course of history. I rush to the door, open it but find myself back in the present! I jump and wake up in my bedroom sweating.

I rush to my laptop while this time-travel dream is fresh in my mind to get it into Python for this book.

 Why wasn't this deceiving simple solution found in 1969? Because *it seems simple today but wasn't so at that time like all inventions found by our genius predecessors.* Nothing is easy at all in artificial intelligence and mathematics.

Implementing a vintage XOR solution in Python with an FNN and backpropagation

I'm still thinking that implementing XOR with so little mathematics might not be that simple. However, since the basic rule of innovating is to be unconventional, I write the code.

To stay in the spirit of a 1969 vintage solution, I decide not to use NumPy, TensorFlow, Theano, or any other high-level library. Writing a vintage FNN with backpropagation written in high-school mathematics is fun.

This also shows that if you break a problem down into very elementary parts, you understand it better and provide a solution to that specific problem. You don't need to use a huge truck to transport a loaf of bread.

Furthermore, by thinking through the minds of children, I went against running 20,000 or more episodes in modern CPU-rich solutions to solve the XOR problem. The logic used proves that, basically, both inputs can have the same parameters as long as one bias is negative (the elder reasonable critical child) to make the system provide a reasonable answer.

The basic Python solution quickly reaches a result in 3 to 10 iterations (epochs or episodes) depending on how we think it through.

The top of the code simply contains a result matrix with four columns. Each represents the status (1=correct, 0=false) of the four predicates to solve:

```
#FEEDFORWARD NEURAL NETWORK(FNN) WITH BACK PROPAGATION SOLUTION FOR XOR
result=[0,0,0,0] #trained result
train=4 #dataset size to train
```

The train variable is the number of predicates to solve: (0,0), (1,1),(1,0),(0,1). The variable of the predicate to solve is `pred`.

The core of the program is practically the sheet of paper I wrote, as in the following code.

```
#II hidden layer 1 and its output
def hidden_layer_y(epoch,x1,x2,w1,w2,w3,w4,b1,b2,pred,result):
    h1=(x1*w1)+(x2*w4) #II.A.weight of hidden neuron h1
    h2=(x2*w3)+(x1*w2) #II.B.weight of hidden neuron h2

#III.threshold I,a hidden layer 2 with bias
    if(h1>=1):h1=1;
    if(h1<1):h1=0;
    if(h2>=1):h2=1
    if(h2<1):h2=0

    h1= h1 * -b1
    h2= h2 * b2
#IV. threshold II and OUTPUT y
    y=h1+h2
    if(y<1 and pred>=0 and pred<2):
        result[pred]=1

    if(y>=1 and pred>=2 and pred<4):
        result[pred]=1
```

`pred` is an argument of the function from 1 to 4. The four predicates can be represented in the following table:

Predicate (pred)	x_1	x_2	Expected result
0	1	1	0
1	0	0	0
2	1	0	1
3	0	1	1

That is why y must be <1 for predicates 0 and 1. Then, y must be >=1 for predicates 2 and 3.

Now, we have to call the following function limiting the training to 50 epochs, which are more than enough:

```
#I Forward and backpropagation
for epoch in range(50):
        if(epoch<1):
            w1=0.5;w2=0.5;b1=0.5
            w3=w2;w4=w1;b2=b1
```

At epoch 0, the weights and biases are all set to 0.5. No use thinking! Let the program do the job. As explained previously, the weight and bias of x_2 are equal.

Now the hidden layers and y calculation function are called four times, one for each predicate to train, as shown in the following code snippet:

```
#I.A forward propagation on epoch 1 and IV.backpropagation starting epoch 2
        for t in range (4):
            if(t==0):x1 = 1;x2 = 1;pred=0
            if(t==1):x1 = 0;x2 = 0;pred=1
            if(t==2):x1 = 1;x2 = 0;pred=2
            if(t==3):x1 = 1;x2 = 0;pred=3
            #forward propagation on epoch 1
            hidden_layer_y(epoch,x1,x2,w1,w2,w3,w4,b1,b2,pred,result)
```

A simplified version of a cost function and gradient descent

Now the system must train. To do that, we need to measure the number of predictions, 1 to 4, that are correct at each iteration and decide how to change the weights/biases until we obtain proper results.

A slightly more complex gradient descent will be described in the next chapter. In this chapter, only a one-line equation will do the job. The only thing to bear in mind as an unconventional thinker is: so what? The concept of gradient descent is minimizing loss or errors between the present result and a goal to attain.

First, a cost function is needed.

There are four predicates (0-0, 1-1, 1-0, 0-1) to train correctly. We simply need to find out how many are correctly trained at each epoch.

The cost function will measure the difference between the training goal (4) and the result of this epoch or training iteration (result).

When 0 convergence is reached, it means the training has succeeded.

`result[0,0,0,0]` contains a 0 for each value if none of the four predicates has been trained correctly. `result[1,0,1,0]` means two out of four predicates are correct. `result[1,1,1,1]` means that all four predicates have been trained and that the training can stop. 1, in this case, means that the correct training result was obtained. It can be 0 or 1. The `result` array is the result counter.

The cost function will express this training by having a value of 4, 3, 2, 1, or 0 as the training goes down the slope to 0.

Gradient descent measures the value of the descent to find the direction of the slope: up, down, or 0. Then, once you have that slope and the steepness of it, you can optimize the weights. A derivative is a way to know whether you are going up or down a slope.

In this case, I hijacked the concept and used it to set the learning rate with a one-line function. Why not? It helped to solve gradient descent optimization in one line:

```
if(convergence<0):w2+=0.05;b1=w2
```

By applying the vintage *children buying candy* logic to the whole XOR problem, I found that only w2 needed to be optimized. That's why b1=w2. That's because b1 is doing the tough job of saying something negative (-) all the time, which completely changes the course of the resulting outputs.

The rate is set at 0.05, and the program finishes training in 10 epochs:

```
epoch: 10 optimization 0 w1: 0.5 w2: 1.0 w3: 1.0 w4: 0.5 b1: -1.0 b2: 1.0
```

This is not a mathematical calculation problem but a logical one, a *yes or no* problem. The way the network is built is pure logic. Nothing can stop us from using whatever training rates we wish. In fact, that's what gradient descent is about. There are many gradient descent methods. If you invent your own and it works for your solution, that is fine.

This one-line code is enough, in this case, to see whether the slope is going down. As long as the slope is negative, the function is going downhill to *cost = 0*:

```
convergence=sum(result)-train #estimating the direction of the slope
if(convergence>=-0.00000001): break
```

The following graph sums up the whole process:

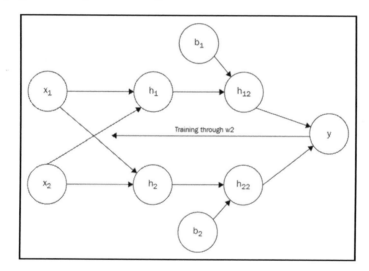

Too simple? Well, it works, and that's all that counts in real-life development. If your code is bug-free and does the job, then that's what counts.

Finding a simple development tool means nothing more than that. It's just another tool in the toolbox. We can get this XOR function to work on a neural network and generate income.

Companies are not interested in how smart you are but how efficient (profitable) you can be.

Linear separability was achieved

Bear in mind that the whole purpose of this feedforward network with backpropagation through a cost function was to transform a linear non-separable function into a linearly separable function to implement classification of features presented to the system. In this case, the features had 0 or 1 value.

One of the core goals of a layer in a neural network is to make the input make sense, meaning to be able to separate one kind of information from another.

h1 and h2 will produce the Cartesian coordinate linear separability training axis, as implemented in the following code:

```
h1= h1 * -b1
h2= h2 * b2
print(h1,h2)
```

Running the program provides a view of the nonlinear input values once they have been trained by the hidden layers. The nonlinear values then become linear values in a linearly separable function:

```
linearly separability through cartesian training -1.0000000000000004
1.0000000000000004
linearly separability through cartesian training -0.0 0.0
linearly separability through cartesian training -0.0 1.0000000000000004
linearly separability through cartesian training -0.0 1.0000000000000004
epoch: 10 optimization 0 w1: 0.5 w2: 1.0 w3: 1.0 w4: 0.5 b1: -1.0 b2: 1.0
```

The intermediate result and goal are not a bunch of numbers on a screen to show that the program works. The result is a set of Cartesian values that can be represented in the following linearly separated graph:

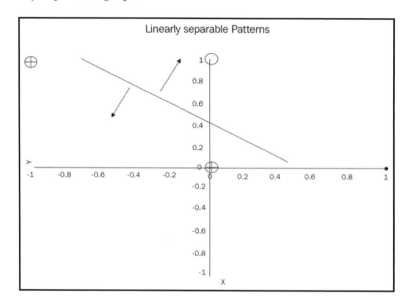

We have now obtained a separation between the top values (empty circle) representing the intermediate values of the 1,0 and 0,1 inputs, and the bottom values representing the 1,1 and 0,0 inputs. We now have *clouds* on top and *trees* below the line that separates them.

The layers of the neural network have transformed nonlinear values into linear separable values, making classification possible through standard separation equations, such as the one in the following code:

```
#IV. threshold II and OUTPUT y
y=h1+h2 # logical separation
if(y<1 and pred>=0 and pred<2):
result[pred]=1

if(y>=1 and pred>=2 and pred<4):
result[pred]=1
```

The ability of a neural network to make non-separable information separable and classifiable represents one of the core powers of deep learning. From this technique, many operations can be performed on data, such as subset optimization.

Applying the FNN XOR solution to a case study to optimize subsets of data

The case study described here is a real-life project. The environment and functions have been modified to respect confidentiality. But, the philosophy is the same one as that used and worked on.

We are 7.5 billion people breathing air on this planet. In 2050, there will be about 2.5 billion more. All of these people need to wear clothes and eat. Just those two activities involve classifying data into subsets for industrial purposes. **Grouping** is a core concept for any kind of production. Production relating to producing clothes and food requires grouping to optimize production costs. Imagine not grouping and delivering one t-shirt at a time from one continent to another instead of *grouping* t-shirts in a container and grouping many containers (not just two on a ship). Let's focus on clothing, for example.

A brand of stores needs to replenish the stock of clothing in each store as the customers purchase their products. In this case, the corporation has 10,000 stores. The brand produces jeans, for example. Their average product is a faded jean. This product sells a slow 50 units a month per store. That adds up to *10,000 stores x 50 units = 500,000 units* or **stock keeping unit (SKU)** per month. These units are sold in all sizes grouped into average, small, and large. The sizes sold per month are random.

The main factory for this product has about 2,500 employees producing those jeans at an output of about 25,000 jeans per day. The employees work in the following main fields: cutting, assembling, washing, laser, packaging, and warehouse. See Chapter 12, *Automated Planning and Scheduling*, for Amazon's patented approach to apparel production.

The first difficulty arises with the purchase and use of fabric. The fabric for this brand is not cheap. Large amounts are necessary. Each pattern (the form of pieces of the pants to be assembled) needs to be cut by wasting as little fabric as possible.

Imagine you have an empty box you want to fill up to optimize the volume. If you only put soccer balls in it, there will be a lot of space. If you slip tennis balls in the empty spaces, space will decrease. If on top of that, you fill the remaining empty spaces with ping pong balls, you will have optimized the box.

 Building optimized subsets can be applied to containers, warehouse flows and storage, truckload optimizing, and almost all human activities.

In the apparel business, if 1% to 10% of fabric is wasted while manufacturing jeans, the company will survive the competition. At over 10%, there is a real problem to solve. Losing 20% on all the fabric consumed to manufacture jeans can bring the company down and force it into bankruptcy.

 The main rule is to combine larger pieces and smaller pieces to make optimized cutting patterns.

Optimization of space through larger and smaller objects can be applied to cutting the forms which are patterns of the jeans, for example. Once they are cut, they will be assembled at the sewing stations.

The problem can be summed up as:

- Creating subsets of the 500,000 SKUs to optimize the cutting process for the month to come in a given factory
- Making sure that each subset contains smaller sizes and larger sizes to minimize loss of fabric by choosing six sizes per day to build 25,000 unit subsets per day
- Generating cut plans of an average of three to six sizes per subset per day for a production of 25,000 units per day

In mathematical terms, this means trying to find subsets of sizes among 500,000 units for a given day.

The task is to find six well-matched sizes among 500,000 units. This is calculated by the following combination formula:

$$C(n,r) = \frac{n!}{r!(n-r)!} = \frac{500000!}{6!(500000-6)!} = log_{10}10^{31.33}$$

At this point, most people abandon the idea and just find some easy way out of this even if it means wasting fabric. The problem was that in this project, I was paid on a percentage of the fabric I would manage to save. The contract stipulated that I must save 3% of all fabric consumption per month for the whole company to get paid a share of that. Or receive nothing at all. Believe me, once I solved that, I kept that contract as a trophy and a tribute to simplicity.

The first reaction we all have is that this is more than the number of stars in the universe and all that hype!

That's not the right way to look at it at all. The right way is to look exactly in the opposite direction. The key to this problem is to observe the particle at a microscopic level, at the **bits of information** level. This is a fundamental concept of machine learning and deep learning. Translated into our field, it means that to process an image, ML and DL process pixels. So, even if the pictures to analyze represent large quantities, it will come down to small units of information to analyze:

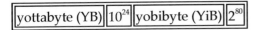

| yottabyte (YB) | 10^{24} | yobibyte (YiB) | 2^{80} |

Today, Google, Facebook, Amazon, and others have yottabytes of data to classify and make sense of. Using the word **big** data doesn't mean much. It's just a lot of data, and so what?

You do not need to analyze individual positions of each data point in a dataset, but use the probability distribution.

To understand that, let's go to a store to buy some jeans for a family. One of the parents wants a pair of jeans, and so does a teenager in that family. They both go and try to find their size in the pair of jeans they want. The parent finds 10 pairs of jeans in size *x*. All of the jeans are part of the production plan. The parent picks one at *random*, and the teenager does the same. Then they pay for them and take them home.

Some systems work fine with random choices: random transportation (taking jeans from the store to home) of particles (jeans, other product units, pixels, or whatever is to be processed) making up that fluid (a dataset).

Translated into our factory, this means that a stochastic (random) process can be introduced to solve the problem.

All that was required is that small and large sizes were picked at random among the 500,000 units to produce. If six sizes from 1 to 6 were to be picked per day, the sizes could be classified as follows in a table:

Smaller sizes= S={1,2,3}

Larger sizes=L=[4,5,6}

Converting this into numerical subset names, *S=1* and *L=6. By selecting large and small sizes to produce at the same time, the fabric will be optimized:*

Size of choice 1	Size of Choice 2	Output
6	6	0
1	1	0
1	6	1
6	1	1

Doesn't this sound familiar? It looks exactly like our vintage FNN, with 1 instead of 0 and 6 instead of 1. All that has to be done is to stipulate that subset *S=value 0,* and *subset L=value 1;* and the previous code can be generalized.

If this works, then smaller and larger sizes will be chosen to send to the cut planning department, and the fabric will be optimized. Applying the randomness concept of Bellman's equation, a stochastic process is applied, choosing customer unit orders at random (each order is one size and a unit quantity of 1):

```
w1=0.5;w2=1;b1=1
w3=w2;w4=w1;b2=b1
s1=random.randint(1,500000)#choice in one set s1
s2=random.randint(1,500000)#choice in one set s2
```

The weights and bias are now constants obtained by the result of the XOR training FNN. The training is done; the FNN is simply used to provide results. Bear in mind that the word *learning* in machine learning and deep learning doesn't mean you have to train systems forever. In stable environments, training is run only when the datasets change. At one point in a project, you are hopefully using deep *trained* systems and are not just stuck in the deep *learning* process. The goal is not to spend all corporate resources on learning but on using trained models.

 Deep learning architecture must rapidly become deep trained models to produce a profit or disappear from a corporate environment.

For this prototype validation, the size of a given order is random. 0 means the order fits in the S subset; 1 means the order fits in the L subset. The data generation function reflects the random nature of consumer behavior in the following six-size jean consumption model.

```
x1=random.randint(0, 1)#property of choice:size smaller=0
x2=random.randint(0, 1)#property of choice :size bigger=1
hidden_layer_y(x1,x2,w1,w2,w3,w4,b1,b2,result)
```

Once two customer orders have been chosen at random chosen at random in the right size category, the FNN is activated, the FNN is activated and runs like the previous example. Only the result array has been changed because no training is required. Only a yes (1) or no (0) is expected, as shown in the following code:

```
#II hidden layer 1 and its output
def hidden_layer_y(x1,x2,w1,w2,w3,w4,b1,b2,result):
  h1=(x1*w1)+(x2*w4) #II.A.weight of hidden neuron h1
  h2=(x2*w3)+(x1*w2) #II.B.weight of hidden neuron h2

#III.threshold I,a hidden layer 2 with bias
  if(h1>=1):h1=1;
  if(h1<1):h1=0;
  if(h2>=1):h2=1
  if(h2<1):h2=0
  h1= h1 * -b1
  h2= h2 * b2

#IV. threshold II and OUTPUT y
  y=h1+h2
  if(y<1):
  result[0]=0
  if(y>=1):
  result[0]=1
```

The number of subsets to produce needs to be calculated to determine the volume of positive results required.

The choice is made of six sizes among 500,000 units. But, the request is to produce a daily production plan for the factory. The daily production target is 25,000. Also, each subset can be used about 20 times. There is always, on average, 20 times the same size in a given pair of jeans available.

Each subset result contains two orders, hence two units:

$$R=2 \times 20 = 120$$

Each result produced by the system represents a quantity of 120 for 2 sizes.

Six sizes are required to obtain good fabric optimization. This means that after three choices, the result represents one subset of potential optimized choices:

$$R = 120 \times 3 \text{ subsets of 2 sizes} = 360$$

The magic number has been found. For every 3 choices, the goal of producing 6 sizes multiplied by a repetition of 20 will be reached.

The production per day request is 25,000:

The number of subsets requested = 25000/3=8333. 333

The system can run 8333 products as long as necessary to produce the volume of subsets requested. In this case, the range is set to 1000000 products because only the positive results are accepted. The system is filtering the correct subsets through the following function:

```
for element in range(1000000):
if(result[0]>0):
subsets+=1
print("Subset:",subsets,"size subset #",x1," and ","size subset #",x2,"
result:",result[0],"order #"," and ",s1,"order #",s2)
if(subsets>=8333):
break
```

When the 8333 subsets have been found respecting the smaller-larger size distribution, the system stops, as shown in the following output.

```
Subset: 8330 size subset # 1 and size subset # 0 result: 1 order # and
53154 order # 14310
Subset: 8331 size subset # 1 and size subset # 0 result: 1 order # and
473411 order # 196256
Subset: 8332 size subset # 1 and size subset # 0 result: 1 order # and
133112 order # 34827
Subset: 8333 size subset # 0 and size subset # 1 result: 1 order # and
470291 order # 327392
```

This prototype proves the point. Not only was this project a success with a similar algorithm, but also the software ran for years in various forms on key production sites, reducing material consumption and generating a profit each time it ran. The software later mutated in a powerfully advanced planning and scheduling application.

Two main functions, among some minor ones, must be added:

- After each choice, the orders chosen must be removed from the 500,000-order dataset. This will preclude choosing the same order twice and reduce the number of choices to be made.

- An optimization function to regroup the results by trained optimized patterns, by an automated planning program for production purposes, as described in `Chapter 12`, *Automated Planning and Scheduling*.

Application information:

- The core calculation part of the application is less than 50-lines long
- When a few control functions and dataset tensors are added, the program might reach 200 lines maximum
- This guarantees easy maintenance for a team

 It takes a lot of time to break a problem down into elementary parts and find a simple, powerful solution. It thus takes much longer than just typing hundreds to thousands of lines of code to make things work. The simple solution, however, will always be more profitable and software maintenance will prove more cost effective.

Summary

Building a small neural network from scratch provides a practical view of the elementary properties of a neuron. We saw that a neuron requires an input that can contain many variables. Then, weights are applied to the values with biases. An activation function then transforms the result and produces an output.

Neuronal networks, even one- or two-layer networks, can provide real-life solutions in a corporate environment. The real-life business case was implemented using complex theory broken down into small functions. Then, these components were assembled to be as minimal and profitable as possible.

Customers expect quick-win solutions. Artificial intelligence provides a large variety of tools that satisfy that goal. When solving a problem for a customer, do not look for the best theory, but the simplest and fastest way to implement a profitable solution no matter how unconventional it seems.

In this case, an enhanced perceptron solved a complex business problem. In the next chapter, an FNN will be introduced using TensorFlow.

Questions

1. Can the perceptron alone solve the XOR problem? (Yes | No)
2. Is the XOR function linearly non-separable? (Yes | No)
3. One of the main goals of layers in a neural network is classification. (Yes | No)
4. Is deep learning the only way to classify data? (Yes | No)
5. A cost function shows the increase in the cost of a neural network. (Yes | No)
6. Can simple arithmetic be enough to optimize a cost function? (Yes | No)
7. A feedforward network requires inputs, layers, and an output. (Yes | No)
8. A feedforward network always requires training with backpropagation. (Yes | No)
9. In real-life applications, solutions are only found by following existing theory. (Yes | No)

Further reading

Linear separability:

http://www.ece.utep.edu/research/webfuzzy/docs/kk-thesis/kk-thesis-html/node19.html

5
Manage the Power of Machine Learning and Deep Learning

Mastering machine learning and deep learning is proportional to your ability to design the architectures of these solutions. As developers, we tend to rush to some sample code, run it, and then try to implement it somehow. That's like going to a big city we don't know, with no map and no guiding system, and trying to find a street. Even worse, it's like trying to build a 50-storey building with no architect or plans.

An efficient, well-thought architecture will lead to a good solution. Deep learning networks are data flow graph calculations as shown in Chapter 4, *Become an Unconventional Innovator*. A node or edge is, in fact, a mathematical operation. The lines connecting these nodes are data flows and mathematical representations. Tools such as TensorFlow and TensorBoard have been designed for data flow graph representations and calculations. Without using TensorBoard, the graph representation of a network, there is little to no chance of understanding and designing deep networks.

The sponsors of a project need to understand the concepts of a given solution. This chapter explores how to use these tools and, at the same time, make a successful presentation to a CEO, top managers, or your team.

The following topics will be covered in this chapter:

- Building a **feedforward neural network (FNN)** with TensorFlow
- Using TensorBoard, a data flow graph, to design your program
- Using the data flow graph to write a program
- A cost function, a loss function
- Gradient descent
- Backpropagation in a feedforward network
- Presenting an FNN to a team or management

Technical requirements

- Python 3.6x 64-bit from `https://www.python.org/`
- NumPy for Python 3.6x
- TensorFlow from `https://deepmind.com/` with TensorBoard

Programs: GitHub `Chapter05`.

 The Python programs delivered with this chapter constitute a sandbox for you to play around with to become familiar with TensorFlow and TensorBoard. Feel free to run them, modify the TensorFlow data flow graphs, and see what happens in TensorBoard.

- `FNN_XOR_Tensorflow.py`: This program shows how to train an FNN to solve the XOR problem in a few lines.
- `FNN_XOR_Tensorflow_graph.py`: This program adds TensorBoard metadata to display the data flow graph of the program.
- `FNN_XOR_Tensorflow_graph_only.py`: This program contains a data flow graph of the program just to show that mastering the graph means mastering the program.
- `Tensorboard.reader.py`: This program runs with the preceding programs. It finds the `/log` file containing the data to display in TensorBoard and runs the TensorBoard local service.
- `FNN_XOR_Tensorflow_tensorboard_MODEL1.py`: This program shows how to tweak a `FNN_XOR_Tensorflow_graph_only.py` to add some labels to prepare a corporate presentation.

Check out the following video to see the code in action:

`https://goo.gl/QrKrSA`

Building the architecture of an FNN with TensorFlow

Before applying an FNN to a problem, an architecture of the network must be built. A TensorFlow architecture and solution to the XOR function is the place to start. The architecture of the example differs from the vintage, built-from-scratch solution but the concepts remain the same.

Writing code using the data flow graph as an architectural roadmap

TensorFlow is a graph-driven solution based on graph theory, a branch of mathematics. Designing deep learning without graphs would prove quite difficult. My XOR FNN built from scratch in Chapter 4, *Become an Unconventional Innovator*, fits the need of the case study described. However, if thousands of nodes are required, TensorFlow, Keras (with TensorFlow backend), or other similar solutions will be needed. In this chapter, a neural network will be developed in TensorFlow.

The building blocks of graphs are nodes (or vertices, or points) and edges (or lines) that connect the nodes to one another.

In TensorFlow parlance, nodes are cleverly named ops for operations. In Chapter 4, *Become an Unconventional Innovator*, the Python example shows exactly that: nodes as operations and calculations.

Mathematical models will be described through a data flow graph. The first step is to build the model, your architecture.

In a TensorFlow program, the first top source code lines are not just a new way to describe variables that you will use later. They are the program. They are critical to the computation of the graph. In fact, TensorFlow uses the graph to compute the operations. *The graph is the architecture, the roadmap that describes the whole computation process of a deep learning neural network.* The following graph has taken the code lines and transformed them into a graph. Imagine that the following graph is a network of water pipes in the city. First, the city builds the pipes. Only then does the water (data in our case) flow in those pipes. The pipes (TensorFlow variables, arrays, and other objects) are not a formality. They represent the core architecture of a system.

This graph is built with `FNN_XOR_Tensorflow_graph_only.py` to show how to use TensorBoard to analyze your network. It will prove easier to fix design errors with TensorBoard. Click on the nodes to explore the details of each part of the graph. Run the program; then run `TensorBoard_reader.py` to launch TensorBoard.

The following diagram illustrates this:

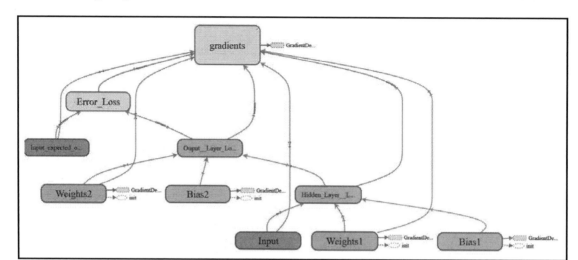

A dataflow graph

A data flow graph translated into source code

The data flow graph will be used to build the architecture of a project. It can be used as a project management tool and project optimization tool as shown in the last part of this chapter.

The input data layer

The input data on the graph represents each pair of two inputs computed at a time in this XOR model using `FNN_XOR_Tensorflow.py`.

This program shows how to build a TensorFlow network in a few lines. In other models, millions of pixels or other values can constitute the input. In this case, XOR is trained with this model:

```
XOR_X = [[0,0],[0,1],[1,0],[1,1]]
```

The first two inputs are (0,0), for example. The input will contain $x_1=0$ and $x_2=0$. Those inputs are sent to the hidden layer along with the weights and biases:

```
W1 = tf.Variable(tf.random_uniform([2,2], -1, 1), name = "Weights1")
B1 = tf.Variable(tf.zeros([2]), name = "Bias1")
```

The hidden layer

The hidden layer contains a multiplication function of weights and an addition of biases, as shown in the following diagram:

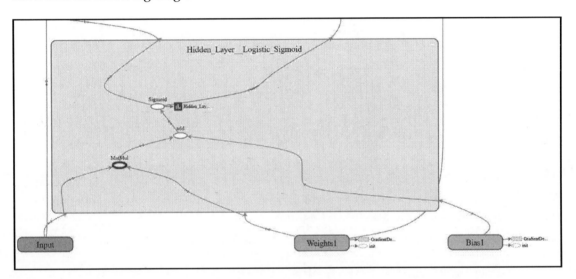

A dataflow graph with multiplication function

The input is sent to the multiplication function along with the weights. Thus x_1 and x_2 will be multiplied by the weights as explained in `Chapter 4`, *Become an Unconventional Innovator*. In this model, the bias variable is added to the result of the multiplications to each of the hidden neurons (one for each x). Go back to `Chapter 4`, *Become an Unconventional Innovator*, again to see the low-level mechanics of the system if necessary.

Bear in mind that there are several mathematical ways, and thus there are several architectures represented in graphs that can solve the FNN XOR problem. Once the multiplication and addition have been computed, a logistic sigmoid function (see `Chapter 2`, *Think like a Machine*) is applied to the result.

Why is a logistic sigmoid function needed here?

In Chapter 4, *Become an Unconventional Innovator*, in my vintage program, I did not use one. I just rounded the values to 0 or 1. That works in a limited environment. However, as explained in Chapter 2, *Think like a Machine*, the output of the neurons needs to be **normalized** to be useful when the input data starts increasing and diversifying. To sum it up, suppose we obtain 200 as an input of a neuron and 2 as an output of another neuron. That makes it very difficult to manage this in the next layer. It's as if you went to a shop and had to pay for one product in a given currency and another product in a different currency. Now the cashier has to add that up. It's not practical at all in a shop and even less in a network with thousands of neurons.

The following LS logistic sigmoid is thus a very handy tool for the outputs to level the values:

```
LS = tf.sigmoid(tf.matmul(x_, W1) + B1)
```

Basically, the values are squashed into small numbers that are compatible with the next step, which is the computation of the output layer.

The output layer

The output layer will now receive the result $y = (input * weights + bias)$ squashed by logistic sigmoid (y), as shown in the following diagram:

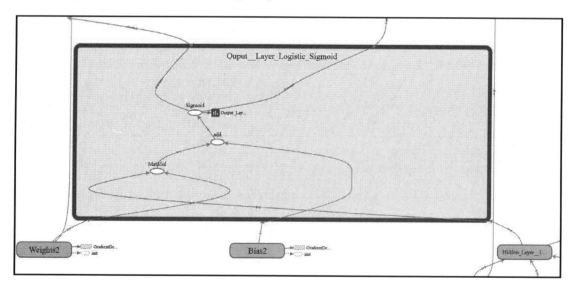

A dataflow graph with output layer

The output layer takes the *y* output of the hidden layer (on the right-hand side of the graph) and receives the weights and bias to apply to this layer in this model. Once the multiplication of weights and addition of bias are computed, the logistic sigmoid function squashes this output as well. This is a very nice way of keeping values homogeneous over the network. It's a tidy way of always sending small computable values to the next layer as implemented in the following code.

```
Output = tf.sigmoid(tf.matmul(LS, W2) + B2)
```

Now that the output has been obtained, what is it worth? How is it evaluated and how are the weights adjusted?

The cost or loss function

The following cost function compares the expected result `y_` with the present result produced by the network.

```
cost = tf.reduce_mean(( (y_ * tf.log(Output)) + ((1 - y_) * tf.log(1.0 -
Output)) ) * -1)
```

The `tf.log` is applied to the results to squash them for efficient comparisons.
The `tf.reduce_mean` supports a variety of cost functions; this is one way to calculate the error between the training dataset and the intermediate result.

Another way to calculate a cost function, as shown in the following code, is to compare the output of the current iteration with the target output and square both to obtain a visible difference.

```
cost = tf.reduce_mean(tf.square(y_-Output))
```

Choosing a cost function will depend on your model. This method in its minimized format is called **least squares**. It produces efficient results in this model.

Gradient descent and backpropagation

Gradient descent defines two concepts:

- Gradient or derivative measurement of the slope (up or down / how steep)
- Descent or reducing the error level between the present result, relying on the parameters (weights and biases), and the target training dataset

There are several ways to measure whether you are going up or down a slope. Derivatives are the most commonly used mathematical tool for this. Let us say you have 15 steps to go from one floor of a building down to the next floor. At each step, you feel you are going down.

The slope or derivative is the function describing you going down those stairs:

- S = slope of you going down the stairs
- dy = where you are once you have made a step (up, down, or staying on a step)
- dx = the size of your steps (one at a time, two at a time, and so on)
- f(x) = the fact of going downstairs, for example from step 4 to step 3, step by step.
- The derivative or slope is thus:

$$\frac{dy}{dx}$$

f(x) is the function of you going down (or up or stopping on a step). For example, when you move one step forward, you are going from step 4 to step 3 (down). Thus f(x)=x-b, in which b = 1 in this example. This is called a decreasing function. h = the number of steps you are going at each pace, for example, one step down if you are not in a hurry and two steps down if you are in a hurry. In this example, you are going down one step at a time from step 4 to 3; thus $h = 1$ (one step at a time).

We obtain the following formula:

$$\frac{dy}{dx} = \frac{f(x+h)-f(x)}{h} = -1$$

This means that we are at step 3 after taking one step. We started at step 4, so we went down -1 step. The minus sign means you are going downstairs from step 4 to step 3 or -1 step.

The gradient is the direction the function is taking. In this case, it is -1 step. If you go down two steps at a time, it would be -2. A straightforward way is just to take the derivative and use it. If it's 0, we're not moving. If it's negative we're going down (less computation or less remaining time to train).

If the slope is positive, we are in trouble, we're going up and increase the cost of the function (more training or more remaining time to train).

The goal of an FNN is to converge to 0. This means that as long as the parameters (weights and biases) are not optimized, the output is far from the target expected. In this case, for example, there are four predicates to train (1-1,0-0,1-0,0-1). If only two results are correct, the present situation is negative, which is *2 - 4 = -2*. When three results are correctly trained, the output gradient descent is *3 - 4 = -1*. This will be translated into derivative gradient descent form using the cost calculated. Descent means that 0 is the target when all four outputs out of four are correct. This arithmetic works for an example without complicated calculations. But TensorFlow provides functions for all situations to calculate the cost (cost function), see whether the training session is going well (down), and optimize the weights to be sure that the cost is diminishing (gradient *descent*). The following `GradientDescentOptimizer` will optimize the training of the weights.

```
cost = tf.reduce_mean(tf.square(y_-Output))
train_step = tf.train.GradientDescentOptimizer(0.10).minimize(cost)
```

A current learning rate for the gradient descent optimizer is 0.01. However, in this model, it can be sped up to `0.10`.

The `GradientDescentOptimizer` will make sure the slope is following a decreasing function's gradient descent by optimizing the weights of the network accordingly.

In this TensorFlow example, the means of the output values are calculated and then squashed with the logistic function. It will provide information for the inbuilt gradient descent optimizer to minimize the cost, with a small training step (0.01). This means that the weights will be slightly changed before each iteration. An iteration defines backpropagation. By going back running the FNN again, then measuring, and going back again, we are *propagating* many combinations of weights—hopefully in the right direction (down the slope)—to optimize the network.

Stochastic gradient descent (SGD) consists of calculating gradient descent on samples of random (stochastic) data instead of using the whole dataset every time.

Running the session

The last step is to run the architecture that has just been designed. The thinking was done in the previous steps.

To run the program, the minimum code is for opening a session and running iterations, as shown in the following code snippet:

```
#II.data

XOR_X = [[0,0],[0,1],[1,0],[1,1]]
XOR_Y = [[0],[1],[1],[0]]

#III.data flow graph computation

init = tf.global_variables_initializer()
sess = tf.Session()
sess.run(init)

for epoch in range(50000):
  sess.run(train_step, feed_dict={x_: XOR_X, y_: XOR_Y})
```

Feeding the data into the data flow graph is done with `feed_dict`. **Feed** is a keyword in FNN. This is an important feature. It is possible to feed parts of a dataset, not all of the data in stochastic (picking only parts of the dataset to train) gradient descent models as explained in Chapter 6, *Don't Get Lost in Techniques – Focus on Optimizing Your Solutions*.

Checking linear separability

The session has now taken the four XOR linearly non-separable (see Chapter 4, *Become an Unconventional Innovator*) predicates, that is, four possibilities, and computed a linearly separable solution:

The input of the output expected was the following:

```
XOR_Y = [[0],[1],[1],[0]]
```

One of the results obtained is the following:

```
Output [[ 0.01742549]
 [ 0.98353356]
 [ 0.98018438]
 [ 0.01550745]
```

The results are separable as described in Chapter 4, *Become an Unconventional Innovator*. If you plot the values, you can separate them with a line.

The results are displayed by printing the intermediate values as the session runs, as shown in the following code:

```
if epoch % 10000 == 0:
  print('Epoch ', epoch)
  print('Output ', sess.run(Output, feed_dict={x_: XOR_X, y_: XOR_Y}))
  print('Weights 1 ', sess.run(W1))
  print('Bias 1 ', sess.run(B1))
  print('Weights 2 ', sess.run(W2))
  print('Bias 2 ', sess.run(B2))
  print('cost ', sess.run(cost, feed_dict={x_: XOR_X, y_: XOR_Y}))
```

These source code lines are difficult to visualize. Using a graph to represent your architecture helps to see the strong and weak points of a solution.

Using TensorBoard to design the architecture of your machine learning and deep learning solutions

`FNN_XOR_Tensorflow_tensorbard_graph_only.py` contains no program in the traditional sense. It contains an essential aspect of developing machine learning and neural networks: the architecture. This program is overloaded with basic graph summaries to grasp the core concept of the data flow graph. In subsequent programs in this book, the summaries will be less literal.

Master the *architecture* of a machine learning and deep learning program and you'll master your solutions.

Designing the architecture of the data flow graph

First import TensorFlow with the following code:

```
import tensorflow as tf
```

Then use the following code to give a name of the `scope` of each object you want to display in one line. Write your variable or object on the second line and include it in the TensorBoard summary as an image (histograms, scalars, and other summaries are possible), as shown in the following code:

```
with tf.name_scope("Input"):
    x_ = tf.placeholder(tf.float32, shape=[4,2], name = 'x-input-predicates')
    tf.summary.image('input predicates x', x_, 10)
```

 name provides a label for the objects in the graph. `scope` is a way to group the names to simplify the visual representation of your architecture.

Repeat that with all the elements described in the previous section, as follows.

```
with tf.name_scope("Input_expected_output"):
    y_ = tf.placeholder(tf.float32, shape=[4,1], name = 'y-expected-output')
    tf.summary.image('input expected values of y', x_, 10)

...

with tf.name_scope("Error_Loss"):
    cost = tf.reduce_mean(( (y_ * tf.log(Output)) + ((1 - y_) * tf.log(1.0 -
Output)) ) * -1)
    tf.summary.image("Error_Loss", cost, 10)
```

Then, once the session is created, set up the log writer directory, as shown in the following code:

```
init = tf.global_variables_initializer()
sess = tf.Session()
writer = tf.summary.FileWriter("./logs/tensorboard_logs", sess.graph)
sess.run(init)
#THE PROGRAM DATE FEED CODE GOES HERE. See FNN_XOR_Tensorflow.py
writer.close()
```

Those are the basic steps to create the logs to display in TensorBoard.

 Note that this source code only contains the architecture of the data flow graph and no program running the data. The program is the architecture that defines computations. The rest is defining the datasets—how they will be fed (totally or partially) to the graph. I recommend that you use TensorBoard to design the architecture of your solutions with the TensorFlow graph code. Only then, introduce the dynamics of feeding data and running a program.

Displaying the data flow graph in TensorBoard

A practical way to obtain a visual display of your architecture and results is to have your own little `TensorBoard_reader.py`, as shown in the following lines of code:

```
def launchTensorBoard():
  import os
  os.system('tensorboard --logdir=' + './logs/tensorboard_logs')
  return

import threading
t = threading.Thread(target=launchTensorBoard, args=([]))
t.start()

#In your browser, enter http://localhost:6006 as the URL
#and then click on Graph tab. You will then see the full graph.
```

All you have to do is `git` the output directory to the log directory path in your program. It can be included in the main source code.

Once launched, you will see images of the previous section. You are now ready to enter corporate environments as a solid architect thinker and designer.

 Use a TensorBoard reader such as this for your meetings. You will be viewed as an architect. You can use Microsoft PowerPoint or other tools naturally. But at one point, even a single view of this data flow graph, from a few seconds up to as long as your audience is interested, shows that you master the architecture of the solution. That is, you master the subject.

The final source code with TensorFlow and TensorBoard

After running the programs, to make sure nothing is missing, the TensorFlow and TensorBoard models can be merged and simplified as shown in `FNN_XOR_Tensorflow_graph.py`.

The summaries have been simplified, the cost function uses the optimized least squares method, and XOR linear separability has been proven with this model.

Using TensorBoard in a corporate environment

Choosing the right architecture for your machine learning or deep learning solution is key to the technical success of your project.

Then, being able to explain it fewer than 2 minutes to a CEO, a top manager, or even a member of your team is key to the commercial success of your project. If they are interested, they will ask more questions and you can drill down. First, you have to captivate their attention. You spend time on your work. However, selling that idea or work to somebody else is extremely difficult.

A slight change in the inputs can do the job, as shown in `FNN_XOR_Tensorflow_tensorboard_MODELI.py` in the following code sample:

```
with tf.name_scope("input_store_products"):
x_ = tf.placeholder(tf.float32, shape=[4,2], name = 'x-input-
predicates')#placeholder is an operation supplied by the feed
tf.summary.image('input store products', x_, 10)

withtf.name_scope("input_expected_top_ranking"):
y_ = tf.placeholder(tf.float32, shape=[4,1], name = 'y-expected-output')
tf.summary.image('input expected classification', x_, 10)
```

Show the graph in full-screen mode and double-click on each node to highlight it while speaking about a particular aspect of your architecture. The graph can be grouped into large scopes by putting placeholders under the same `tr.name.scope`. For example, in the following code, `input_store_products` was added to make a presentation:

```
with tf.name_scope("input_store_products"):
x_ = tf.placeholder(tf.float32, shape=[4,2], name = 'x-input-
predicates')#placeholder is an operation supplied by the feed
y_ = tf.placeholder(tf.float32, shape=[4,1], name = 'y-expected-output')
```

Use your imagination to find the best and clearest way to make your architecture understood.

Display the graph in full-screen mode and double-click on each node to highlight it while speaking about it.

Using TensorBoard to explain the concept of classifying customer products to a CEO

Designing solutions seem fine, but if you can't sell them to your team or management, they won't go far. More often than not, we think that since we have a good technical background, we'll be recognized. Nothing is more deceiving. In a world where knowledge is everywhere, competition will be at your door everyday. Furthermore, managers will have less and less time to listen to what we have to say.

> The architecture of your solution depends on what your buyers (team managers, prospects, or customers) ask you. *Your freedom to implement your views depends on how well you present your architecture in a way that fits their needs.*

It's 8:30. The CEO has dropped into your office and is touring the company. The CEO is sharp, bright, and has no patience with people who can't express themselves clearly. You lower your head and look in the garbage can to find something that's not there. It doesn't work. The CEO comes straight to you, invites you to a meeting room and asks you to present what you are doing. A few other managers come in to see what's going on and whether you will survive the presentation.

Will your views on the project survive this meeting?

You can take your corporate PowerPoint out and bore your audience, or you can captivate it.

I have gone through these meetings hundreds of times with a 90% sales success rate and have refined a method that can be summed up in my 2-minute pitch, which always goes something like the following.

I will display a chart and the following graph and say:

"Let's go straight to the point. We're trying to analyze the details of products based on their images and find the most profitable ones. Here is a one-page chart showing the list of the most promising products. Here is TensorBoard; it comes with TensorFlow package. The computation power of TensorFlow's data flow guarantees disruptive innovative profits for this project.

At the bottom of the screen, you can see that we are going to input store products (point to the input_store_products *box). What we expect is the profitable classification of products: the best ones that represent our brand AND the ones that also generate the most profit. So basically, there are two main types of features to extract: forms, shapes, and colors of the most trendy products; and profit.*

To achieve that, we feed (that's literally the language we use in code) the system with the results we expect, a dataset of good choices (point to the input_expect_classification *box). Then we run the system; it optimizes until it has been trained through gradient descent (point your arm and finger downwards), which is simply a cost function to lower (CEO's understand lowering costs in 1/1,000,000th of a second) the errors. Once the weights (just as we weigh decisions) are optimized (I point to the weights), that's it. We will provide you each day with reports to drive the marketing department."*

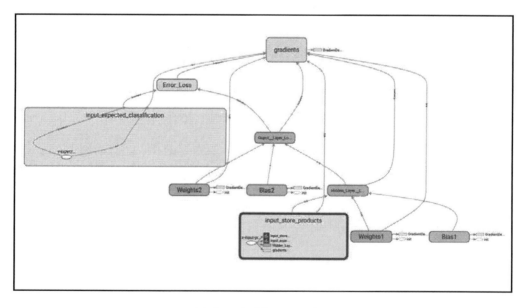

A dataflow graph with input_store_products

Then I stop immediately, slowly look at everybody, and say:

> *"To sum it up, we select the most profitable products in real time with this system and provide the marketing department with real-time AI reports to boost their marketing campaigns. By analyzing the features of the products, they will have more precise marketing data to drive their sales."*

If you read this aloud slowly, it should take you be under 2 minutes, which is your first-level survival time.

The rules I've applied successfully are as follows:

- Explain from off the top (global concepts).
- Use as few words as possible, but choose the right ones. Don't avoid technical concepts, but break them down into small key parts. This means that, once again, TensorBoard architecture will develop this ability.
- Speak slowly. Speaking slowly, stopping at each sentence, emphasizing each keyword, and pointing to the graph at the same time is the only way to make sure you are not losing anybody.
- After 2 minutes, sum your introduction up and ask: *"Am I clear? Do you want me to continue. Questions?"* If they want you to continue, then you can drill down, stopping at every key point to make sure that everybody is still with you.

 Bear in mind that many CEOs are *business visionaries*. They see things we don't. So, if they come up with an idea, be very constructive and innovative.

Was the sales pitch convincing?

At this point, if you have a good project, the CEO will most probably say one of the following:

- *"Gee, that was clear and I understand what you are doing. Thanks. Bye."* That's not too bad.

- *"That looks too simple to be true. Can you give some more details?"* This could be an opportunity. The CEO wants me to explain more. So I drill down another 2 minutes around the way the weights are optimized in a clear way just like the first 2 minutes. At that point, in 20% of my meetings, I ended up having lunch or dinner with the CEO, who always has 100 other ideas for uses of such a program. Bear in mind that many CEOs are *business visionaries*. They see things we don't. So, if a new idea comes up, I generally say, *"Great. I'll look into this and get back to you tomorrow."* Then I spend the night coming up with something that works and is explained clearly.
- *"Good. I'd like you to talk to X and see where this is going."* Not bad either. Hopefully, *X* will listen to the CEO.

Statistically, being short and concise with real technical tangible objects to show worked 90% of the time for me. The 10% failures are lessons to learn from to keep the statistic up the next time around.

 The percentage of failure of our presentations is our *cost function*. We have to bring that number down by learning from these failures by backpropagation as well. We need to go back and change our parameters to adapt to the next run.

Summary

Mastering the architecture of a machine learning and deep learning solution means first, and above all, becoming an expert in designing the architecture of a solution and being able to explain it.

The early lines of a source code program are not just variable declaration lines; they represent the data flow graph that drives the computation of a neural network. These lines define the architecture of your solutions. They are critical to the future of an artificial intelligence solution.

The architecture of the solution, represented by TensorBoard, for example, serves two purposes. The first purpose defines the way the computation of the graph will behave. The second purpose is to use the architecture as a communication tool to sell your project to your team, management, prospects, and customers. Our environment defines our project and not simply our technical abilities, no matter how much we know.

The next chapter focuses on analyzing the core problems of machine learning and deep learning programs.

Questions

1. TensorBoard is simply a nice displaying program. (Yes | No).
2. Defining functions at the beginning of the source code, is just like in standard programs. (Yes | No).
3. TensorFlow is a library add-on to Python to get some cool functions. (Yes | No).
4. TensorBoard is not necessary to deploy Machine Learning and Deep Learning programs. (Yes | No).
5. As long as we're technical experts, we don't have to worry about our environment. They will adapt. (Yes | No).
6. Presenting ML/DL projects doesn't change the architecture of a solution. (Yes | No).
7. Managers don't need to understand the technical aspect of a solution as long as it works. (Yes | No).

Further reading

- https://pythonprogramming.net/tensorflow-deep-neural-network-machine-learning-tutorial/?completed=/tensorflow-introduction-machine-learning-tutorial/https://www.tensorflow.org/programmers_guide/graphs
- https://www.tensorflow.org/versions/r0.12/get_started/basic_usage

References

https://aimatters.wordpress.com/2016/01/16/solving-xor-with-a-neural-network-in-tensorflow/

6
Don't Get Lost in Techniques – Focus on Optimizing Your Solutions

No matter how much we know, the key point remains being able to deliver an artificial intelligence solution or not. Implementing a **machine learning (ML)** or **deep learning (DL)** program remains difficult and will become more complex as technology progresses at exponential rates. This will be shown in Chapter 15, *Cognitive NLP Chatbots*, on quantum computing, which may revolutionize computing with its mind-blowing concepts. There is no such thing as a simple or easy way to design AI systems. A system is either efficient or not, beyond being either easy or not. Either the designed AI solution provides real-life practical uses or it builds up into a program that fails to work in various environments beyond the scope of training sets.

This chapter doesn't deal with how to build the most difficult system possible to show our knowledge and experience. It faces the hard truth of real-life delivery and ways to overcome obstacles. Without data, your project will never take off. Even an unsupervised ML program requires unlabeled data in some form or other.

Beyond understanding **convolutional neural networks (CNN)** that can recognize **Modified National Institute of Standards and Technology (MNIST)** training sets of handwritten images as described in Chapter 10, *Applying Biomimicking to Artificial Intelligence*, efficiency comes first. In a corporate environment, you will often have to deal with designing datasets and obtaining data. Doubts follow quickly. Are the datasets for a given project reliable? How can this be measured? How many features need to be implemented? What about optimizing the cost function and training functions?

This chapter provides the methodology and tools needed to overcome everyday artificial intelligence project obstacles. k-means clustering, a key ML algorithm, will be applied to the increasing need for warehouse intelligence (Amazon and all online product-selling sites). Quickly showing the solution to a problem will keep a project alive. Focusing on the solution, and not the techniques, will get you there.

The following topics will be covered in this chapter:

- Designing datasets
- The design matrix
- Dimensionality reduction
- Determining the volume of a training set
- k-means clustering
- Unsupervised learning
- Data conditioning management for the training dataset
- Lloyd's algorithm
- Building a Python k-means clustering program from scratch
- Hyperparameters
- Test dataset and prediction
- Presenting the solution to a team

Technical requirements

- Python 3.6x 64-bit from `https://www.python.org/`
- `sklearn`
- `pandas`
- `matplotlib`

Programs, `Chapter06`:

- `k-means_clustering_ch6.py` with `data.csv`

Check out the following video to see the code in action:

`https://goo.gl/kBzrp6`

Dataset optimization and control

On day one of a project, a manager or customer will inevitably ask the AI expert what kind of data is being dealt with, and in which format. Providing an answer to that will take some hard work. The AI expert never really thought of that, having acquired expertise using the available, optimized, and downloadable training datasets to test the programs. The expert's name is Pert Ex (an anagram of expert) in this chapter. The expert likes to be called **Pert**.

The CEO of the corporation (or boss or customer) wants Pert to lead an **Amazonization** project. Pert doesn't quite understand what that means. The CEO has the patience to explain that wholesale e-commerce has overtaken traditional ways of doing business. Wholesale means increasing use of warehouses. How those warehouses are managed will make a difference to the cost of each project and the sales price.

Although the business is now huge and the warehouse is expanding, the costs of retrieving products from the warehouse locations have been increasing. The corporation, which we will name AGV-AI in this chapter, represents the sum of several real-life projects I have managed on various warehouse and aerospace sites. Bear in mind that moving large components in an aerospace project requires precise scheduling. Moving large volumes of small products in an Amazonization process or small volumes of oversized products (25 meters or 82 feet for example) such as aerospace components can be costly if badly planned. In AGV-AI, **automatic guided vehicles** (**AGVs**) are surprisingly taking longer routes from a warehouse location to a pier. AGV-AI manufactures, stores, and delivers large volumes of consumer goods.

The CEO wants Pert's team to find out what is going on and Pert must lead the technical aspects of the project.

Designing a dataset and choosing an ML/DL model

Pert goes back to his desk in an open space occupied by a team of 50 people and tries to represent what is wrong in the Amazonization process at the warehouse level.

On paper, it comes down to moving from warehouse locations to piers represented by a distance. The sum of the distances **D** could be a way to measure the process:

$$D = \sum_{p1}^{pn} f(p)$$

f(p) represents the action of going from a warehouse location to a pier and the distance it represents. Exactly like the distance, it takes you from a location in a shop where you picked (*p*) something up and the door of the shop on your way out. You can imagine that if you go straight from that location, pay, and go out, then that is a shorter way. But if you pick the product up, wander around the shop first, and then go out, the distance (and time) is longer. The sum of all of the distances of all the people wandering in this shop is *D*.

Pert now has a clear representation of the concept of the problem to solve: **find the wanderers**. How can an AGV wander? It's automatic. After spending a few days watching the AGVs in the warehouse, Pert understands why the AGVs are taking longer routes sometimes.

 When an AGV encounters an obstacle either it stops or, in this case, it takes another route. Just like us in a shop when we have to walk around an obstacle to get where we want.

Pert smiles. Pert has a plan.

Approval of the design matrix

Pert's plan is to first obtain as much data as possible and then choose an ML/DL model. His plan is to represent all locations the AGVs come from on their way to the piers on a given day. It's a location-to-pier analysis. Since the AGVs were at that location at one point and their distances are recorded in their system, Pert goes over to the IT manager with a **design matrix.** A design matrix contains a different example on each row, and each column is a feature. Pert wants to play safe and comes up with the following format:

	AGV number	Start from location: Timestamp:yyyy,mm,dd,hh,mm	End at pier: Timestamp:yyyy,mm,dd,hh,mm	Location	Pier number	Distance
Ex1	1	year-month-day-hour-minute	year-month-day-hour-minute	80		
Ex2	2					
Ex3	3					
Ex4	4					
Ex5	5					

Agreeing on the format of the design matrix

The IT manager has been around AGV-AI for over 10 years and knows where all the existing data is stored. Pert explains that the design matrix is one of the best ways to start training a ML program. In this case:

- AGV number identifies the vehicle.
- Start indicates when the AGV left a location (*Location* column).

- End indicates when the AGV reached a pier (*Pier* column).
- Distance is expressed in the metric system. Pert explains that most space agencies around the world use the metric system.

The IT manager starts off by saying the following:

- The AGV number is not stored in the mainframe but the local system that manages the AGVs
- In the mainframe, there is a start time when an AGV picks up its load at the location and an end time when it reaches the pier
- The location can be obtained in the mainframe as well as the pier
- No distance is recorded

Pert would like to have access to the data in the AGV's local system to retrieve the AGV number and correlate it with the data in the mainframe.

The IT manager looks at Pert and decides to tell the artificial intelligence expert the simple truth:

1. Retrieving data from the AGV guiding system is not possible this fiscal year. Those vehicles are expensive and no additional budget can be allocated.
2. Nobody knows the distance it takes from a location to a pier. As long as the AGVs deliver the proper products on time at the right piers, nobody so far has been interested in distances.
3. The AGV mission codes in the mainframe are not the same as in the local AGV guiding system, so they cannot be merged into a dataset without development.

The project is slipping away. AGV-AI doesn't have the leisure or budget to invest man days in extracting data that may or may not be used to optimize warehouse distances in its Amazonization process. Pert has to find a solution very quickly before the very busy IT manager drops the whole idea. Pert decides to think of this overnight and come back quickly the next day.

     Keeping an AI project alive means moving quickly.

Dimensionality reduction

Pert is in trouble, and he knows it. Not all the data Pert would have liked can be obtained for the moment. Some features must be left aside for the moment. He thinks back to his walk from the IT manager's office to his office and looks at his cup of coffee.

Dimensionality reduction comes up!

DL uses dimensionality reduction to reduce the number of features in, for example, an image. Each pixel of a 3D image, for example, is linked to a neuron, which in turn brings the representation down to a 2D view with some form of function. For example, converting a color image into shades of a now-gray image can do the trick. Once that is done, simply reducing the values to, for example, 1 (light) or 0 (dark) makes it even easier for the network. Using an image converted to 0 and 1 pixels makes some classification processes more efficient, just like when we avoid a car on the road. We just see the object and avoid it. We are not contemplating the nice color or the car to avoid or other **dimensions**.

We perform dimensionality reduction all day long. When you walk from one office to another on the same floor of a building requiring no stairs or an elevator, you are not thinking that the earth is round and that you're walking over a slight curve. You have performed a **dimensionality reduction**. You are also performing a **manifold** operation. Basically, it means that locally, on that floor, you do not need to worry about the global roundness of the earth. Your manifold view of earth in your dimensionality reduction representation is enough to get you from your office to another one on that floor.

When you pick up your cup of coffee, you just focus on not missing it and aiming for the edges of it. You don't think about every single **feature** of that cup, such as its size, color, decoration, diameter, and the exact volume of coffee in it. You just identify the edge of the cup and pick it up. That is dimensionality reduction. Without **dimensionality reduction**, nothing can be accomplished. It would take you 10 minutes to analyze the cup of coffee and pick it up in that case!

When you pick that cup of coffee up, you test to see whether it is too hot, too cold, too warm, or just fine. You don't put a thermometer in the cup to obtain the precise temperature. You have again performed a **dimensionality reduction of the features** of that cup of coffee. Furthermore, when you picked it up, you computed a **manifold** representation by just observing the little distance around the cup, reducing the dimension of information around you. You are not worrying about the shape of the table, whether it was dirty on the other side, and other features.

Pert begins to imagine a (CNN) with dimensionality reduction. But the data will be insufficient for a CNN (see Chapter 9, *Getting Your Neurons to Work*).

There is no time to build a complicated DL program to compute dimensionality reduction and satisfy this need. Automatic dimensionality reduction will be dealt with later when the project has been accepted.

ML and DL techniques such as dimensionality reduction can be viewed as tools and be used in any field in which you find them useful. Reducing the number of features or modifying them can be done on a spreadsheet by selecting the useful columns and/or modifying the data. By focusing on the solution, you can use any tool in any way you want as long as it works in a reliable way.

Pert then turns to a k-means clustering ML algorithm and decides to perform dimensionality reduction by analysis of the data and defining it for a computation. Each location will form a cluster as explained in the next section. With this intuition, Pert goes back and presents the following format:

	Location	Start from location: Timestamp:yyyy,mm,dd,hh,mm	End at location: Timestamp:yyyy,mm,dd,hh,mm
Ex1			

The IT manager is puzzled. Pert explains that as long as each location represents a separate AGV task from start time to the end time and the pier, the rest will be calculated.

The IT manager says that it can be extracted in .csv format within a couple of days for a test but asks how that makes the project possible. Pert says, *"Provide the data, and I'll be back with a prototype within a couple of days as well."*

The volume of a training dataset

Pert decides to keep the dataset down to six locations over two days. Six locations are chosen in the main warehouse with a group of truck loading points. Taking around 5,000 examples into account, that should represent the work of all the 25 AGVs purchased by AGI-AI running 24 hours a day. The IT manager delivers the data.csv file the next day.

Implementing a k-means clustering solution

Pert now has a real data.csv dataset. The dataset needs to be converted into a prototype to prove the financial value of the project he has in mind. The amount of the money saved must capture the imagination of the CEO. *Making a machine learning program work in a corporate environment means nothing without profit to justify its existence.*

Do not speak about a project in a corporate environment without knowing how much **profit** it represents and the **cost** of getting the job done.

The vision

Pert's primary goal can be summed up in one sentence: finding profit by optimizing AGVs. Achieving that goal will lead to obtaining a budget for a full-scale project.

The data provided does not contain distances. However, an estimation can be made per location as follows:

distance=(end time- start time)/average speed of an AGV

The start location is usually a loading point near a pier in this particular warehouse configuration.

The data

The data provided contains start times (*st*), end times (*endt*), and delivery locations. To calculate distances, Pert needs to convert those times into a distance (*d$_i$*) with the following estimation for each location (*l$_l$*):

$$d_i(l_l)=(endt-st)/v$$

- v = velocity of the AGV per minute
- *endt-st* is expressed in minutes
- d_i = estimated distance an AGV has gone in a given time

A Python program reads the initial file format and data and outputs a new file and format as follows:

Distance	Location
55	53
18	17

Conditioning management

The data file is available at `https://github.com/PacktPublishing/Artificial-Intelligence-By-Example/blob/master/Chapter06/data.csv`.

Data conditioning means preparing the data that will become the input of the system. **Poor conditioning** can have two outcomes:

- Bad data making no difference (large volumes and minor errors)
- Bad data making a difference (regardless of volumes, the data influences the outcome)

In this particular case, out of the 5,000 records provided for the dataset, 25 distances are missing.

Pert has analyzed the warehouse and is lucky!

The location numbers start at #1. #1 is near the loading point of the products. The AGV has to bring the products to this point. To be more precise, in this warehouse configuration, the AGV goes and gets a box (or crate) of products and brings them back to location 1. At location 1, humans check the products and package them. After that, humans carefully load the products in the delivery trucks.

Having spent hours measuring distances in the warehouse, Pert knows that the distance from one location to the next is about 1 meter. For example, from location 1 to location 5, the distance is about 5 meters, or 5 m. Also since all locations lead to location 1 for the AGVs in this model, the theoretical distances will be calculated from location 1. Pert decides to generalize the rule and defines a distance d_i for a location l_j as follows:

$$d_i(l_j)=l_j$$

d_i is expressed in meters. Since the locations start at number 1 through n, the location number is equal to the approximate distance from the first location from which the AGVs depart. Looking at the data, it quickly appears that many distances are superior to their location numbers. That is strange because the distance should be about equal to the location.

The time has come to build a strategy and program.

The strategy

Pert's strategy can be summed up as follows:

- Quickly write a program to represent the AGV's trajectories in a visual way
- Go to the warehouse to check the results
- Calculate the potential optimized profit with a solution that is yet to be found
- Go back to present this to the top management to get a project budget approval

The k-means clustering program

k-means clustering is a powerful unsupervised learning algorithm. We often perform k-means clustering in our lives. Take, for example, a lunch you want to organize for a team of about 50 people in an open space that can just fit those people. It will be a bit cramped but a project must be finished that day and it is a good way to bind the team for the final sprint.

A friend and a friend first decide to set up a table in the middle. Your friend points out that the people in that room will form a big cluster k, and with only one table in the geometric center (or centroid) c, it will not be practical. The people near the wall will not have access to the main table.

You have an idea. You call Pert, who runs a computation to confirm your friend's intuition. Pert shows them the problem with the following one-table plan:

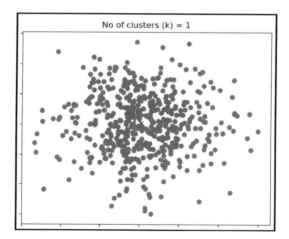

The people not close to the table (rectangle in the middle) will not have easy access to the table.

You go to the room with your friend and Pert and try moving two tables c_1 and c_2 in various places for two clusters of people k_1 and k_2.

The people x_1 to x_n form a dataset X. Your friend still has doubts and says, "*Look at table c_1. It is badly positioned. Some people x near the wall will be right next to it and the others too far away. We need the table c_1 to be in the center of that cluster k_1. The same goes for table c_2.*"

You and your friend move a table c, and then estimate that the mean distance of the people x around it will be about the same in their group or cluster k. They do the same for the other table. They draw a line with chalk on the floor to make sure that each group or cluster is at about the mean distance from its table.

Pert speaks up and says, "*Gee, we can simulate that with this Python program I am writing for my project!*":

- **Step 1**: You have been drawing lines with chalk to decide which group (cluster k) each person x will be in, by looking at the mean distance from the table c
- **Step 2**: You have been moving the tables around accordingly to optimize step 1

Pert shows them the two-table model computed by the k-means clustering program; it looks exactly like what you just did. Then they finally add a third table and it looks good. Pert says, "*Look at what you did on the following screenshot.*":

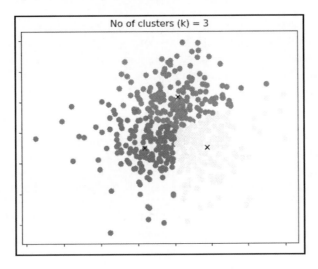

You and your friend look at Pert and say, "*So what?*"

Pert smiles and says, *"Well, you just re-invented Lloyd's algorithm to solve a k-means clustering problem!"*

You and your friend are curious. You want to know more. So you each get a paperboard, and ask Pert to explain to you the warehouse project or any project with this model in mathematical terms.

The mathematical definition of k-means clustering

The dataset X provides N points. These points or data points are formed by using distance as the x axis in a Cartesian representation and the location as the y axis in a Cartesian representation. If you have 1 person in on location 1 as the first record of your file, it will be represented as $x\ axis = 1$ and $y\ axis = 1$ by the black dot, which is the data point, as shown in the following diagram:

Cartesian representation

In this example, 5,000 records are loaded from `data.csv`, which is in the same directory as the program. The data is unlabeled with no linear separation. The goal is to allocate the X data points to K clusters. The number of clusters is an input value. Each cluster will have its geometric center or centroid. If you decide to have three clusters K, then the result will be as follows:

- Three clusters K in three colors in a visual representation
- Three geometric centers or centroids representing the center of the mean of the sum of distances of x data points of that cluster

If you decide on six clusters, then you will obtain six centroids, and so on.

Described in mathematical terms, the formula in respect of K_k, μ_k is as follows:

$$Min \sum_{k=1}^{K} \sum_{x_n \in K_k} \| x - \mu_k \|^2$$

This means that the sum of each k (cluster) from 1 to the number of clusters K of the sum of all distances of members x_i to x_n of each cluster K from their position to the geometric center (centroid) μ must be minimized.

The smaller the distance from each member x to centroid μ, the more the system is optimized. Note that the distance is squared each time because this is a Euclidean distance in this version of the equation.

Lloyd's algorithm

There are several variations of Lloyd's algorithm. But all of them follow a common philosophy.

For a given x_n (data point), the distance from the centroid μ in its cluster must be less than going to another center. Exactly like how a person in the lunch example wants to be closer to one table rather than having to go far to get a sandwich because of the crowd!

The best centroid μ for a given x_n is as follows:

$$x_n : \| x_n - \mu_k \|$$

This calculation is done for all μ (centroids) in all the clusters from k_1 to K.

Once each x_i has been allocated to a K_k, the algorithm recomputes μ by calculating the means of all the points that belong to each cluster and readjusts the centroid μ_k.

The goal of k-means clustering in this case study

The goal must be clear, not simple, not easy, for Pert's managers to understand. Pert decides to write a Python program first. Then if things go well, a full-scale project will be designed. The goal must be to find the *gain zone*. The gain zone will be the data points that could have been optimized in terms of distances.

In projects you build, distances can be replaced by costs, hours, or any optimization measurement feature. Location can be replaced by a feature such as the number of people, phone calls, or any other measurement.

k-means clustering can be applied to a range of applications as explained in Chapter 7, *When to Use Artificial Intelligence*.

The Python program

The Python program uses the `sklearn` library (which contains efficient algorithms), `pandas` for data analysis (only used to import the data in this program), and `Matplotlib` to plot the results as data points (the coordinates of the data) and clusters (data points classified in each cluster with a color). First the following models are imported:

```
from sklearn.cluster import KMeans
import pandas as pd
from matplotlib import pyplot as plt
```

NumPy is not a prerequisite since `sklearn` runs the computation.

1 – The training dataset

The training dataset consists of 5,000 lines. The first line contains a header for maintenance purposes (data checking), which is *not* used. k-means clustering is an **unsupervised learning** algorithm, meaning that it classifies unlabeled data into cluster-labeled data to make future predictions. The following code displays the dataset:

```
#I.The training Dataset
dataset = pd.read_csv('data.csv')
print (dataset.head())
print(dataset)
```

The `print(dataset)` line can be useful though not necessary to check the training data during a prototype phase or for maintenance purposes. The following output confirms that the data was correctly imported:

```
'''Output of print(dataset)
 Distance location
0 80 53
1 18 8
2 55 38
...
'''
```

2 – Hyperparameters

Hyperparameters determine the behavior of computation method. In this case, two hyperparameters are necessary:

- The k number of clusters that will be computed. This number can and will be changed during the case study meetings to find out the best organization process, as explained in the next section. After a few runs, Pert intuitively set k to 6.

- The *f* number of features that will be taken into account. In this case, there are two features: distance and location.

The program implements a k-means function as shown in the following code:

```
#II.Hyperparameters
# Features = 2
k = 6
kmeans = KMeans(n_clusters=k)
```

Note that the Features hyperparameter is commented. In this case, the number of features is implicit and determined by the format of the training dataset, which contains two columns.

3 – The k-means clustering algorithm

sklearn now does the job using the training dataset and hyperparameters in the following lines of code:

```
#III.k-means clustering algorithm
kmeans = kmeans.fit(dataset) #Computing k-means clustering
```

The gcenter array contains the geometric centers or centroids and can be printed for verification purposes, as shown in this snippet:

```
gcenters = kmeans.cluster_centers_
print("The geometric centers or centroids:"
print(gcenters)
'''Ouput of centroid coordinates
[[ 48.7986755  85.76688742]
 [ 32.12590799 54.84866828]
 [ 96.06151645 84.57939914]
 [ 68.84578885 55.63226572]
 [ 48.44532803 24.4333996 ]
 [ 21.38965517 15.04597701]]
'''
```

These geometric centers need to be visualized with labels for decision-making purposes.

4 – Defining the result labels

The initial unlabeled data can now be classified into cluster labels as shown in the following code:

```
#IV.Defining the Result labels
labels = kmeans.labels_
colors = ['blue','red','green','black','yellow','brown','orange']
```

Colors can be used for semantic purposes beyond nice display labels. A color for each top customer or leading product can be assigned, for example.

5 – Displaying the results – data points and clusters

To make sense to a team or management, the program now prepares to display the results as **data points** and **clusters**. The data will be represented as coordinates and the clusters as colors with a **geometric center** or **centroid**, as implemented in this code:

```
#V.Displaying the results : datapoints and clusters
y = 0
for x in labels:
plt.scatter(dataset.iloc[y,0], dataset.iloc[y,1],color=colors[x])
y+=1
for x in range(k):
lines = plt.plot(gcenters[x,0],gcenters[x,1],'kx')

title = ('No of clusters (k) = {}').format(k)
plt.title(title)
plt.xlabel('Distance')
plt.ylabel('Location')
plt.show()
```

The dataset is now ready to be analyzed. The data has been transformed into data points (Cartesian points) and clusters (the colors). The x points represent the geometric centers or centroids, as shown in the following screenshot:

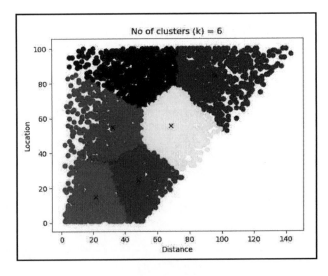

Output (data point and clusters)

Test dataset and prediction

In this case, the test dataset has two main functions. First, some test data confirms the **prediction** level of the trained and now-labeled dataset. The input contains random distances and locations. The following code implements the output that predicts which cluster the data points will be in:

```
#VI.Test dataset and prediction
x_test = [[40.0,67],[20.0,61],[90.0,90],
[50.0,54],[20.0,80],[90.0,60]]
prediction = kmeans.predict(x_test)
print("The predictions:")
print (prediction)
'''
Output of the cluster number of each example
[3 3 2 3 3 4]
'''
```

The second purpose, in future, will be to enter new warehouse data for **decision-making** purposes, as explained in the next section.

Analyzing and presenting the results

Pert knows the two-minute presentation rule.

If you have not captivated your manager or any audience within the two minutes of a presentation, it's over.

People will begin to look at their mail on their phones or laptops; pain replaces the pleasure of sharing a solution.

Pert decides to start the presentation with the following screenshot and a strong introduction:

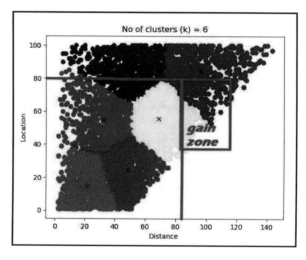

Gain zone area

Pert points to the gain zone area and says:

From the computations made, that gain zone is only part of the losses of the present way AGVs are used in our company. It takes only a few locations into account. I would say that we could save 10% of the distances of our 25 AGVs on this site only. If we add nine other major sites in the world that adds up to:

10% of (25 AGVs * 10 sites) = a gain of 25 AGVs

That's because the AGVs are not going directly to the right locations but are *wandering* around unplanned obstacles.

Pert has everybody's attention!

In real life, I started my career with major corporations by making the following statement in similar cases (factories, warehouses, purchasing department, scheduling departments, and many other fields):

> *Pay me a percentage of that gain, and I will do the project for free until that is proven.*

If the solution is mathematically solid and the data available, there is a risk to calculate to enter a corporation. When that is achieved once, it is easier the times after.

In this case, Pert's audience asks how this was estimated. The explanation is not simple but clear. The average distance from one location to another is 1 meter. The AGVs all start out from location 0 or 1. So the distance is strictly proportional to the locations in this particular example (which is not always the case).

To find the gain zone of a location, you draw a red horizontal line from location 80, for example, and a vertical line from distance 80 (add a couple of meters to take small variances into account).

None of the data points on the 80 location line should be beyond the maximum limit. The limit is 80 meters + a small variance of a few meters. Beyond that line, on the right-hand side of the figure, is where the company is losing money and something must be done to optimize the distances. This loss zone is the gain zone for a project. The gain zone on the k-means cluster results shows that some of the locations of 40 to 60 exceed 80 meters distance.

Something is wrong, and a project can fix it.

AGV virtual clusters as a solution

The planners anticipate AGVs tasks. They send them to probable locations from which they will have to pick up products and bring them back to the truck-loading points.

One of the solutions is to provide AGV virtual clusters as a business rule, as shown in the following screenshot:

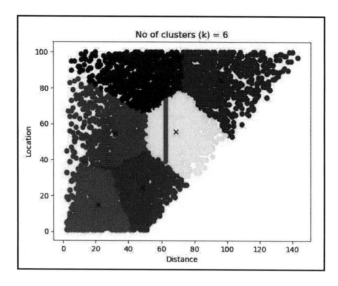

AGV virtual clusters

- **Rule 1**: The line in the middle represents a new business rule. In phase 1 of the project, an AGV used for locations 40 to 60 cannot go beyond that 60 meter + small variance line.
- **Rule 2**: A cluster will represent the pick-up zone for an AGV. The centroid will now be its parking zone. Distances will be optimized until all the clusters respect rule 1.

The financial manager and CEO approve Pert's prototype. But there now two conditions for this to become a project:

- Present an architecture for large volumes for 10 sites, not just this site.
- Present the *same* model but with different features to optimize the e-commerce of the corporation's websites that now represent 90% of all sales. Using the solution for another project will generate more profit with this approach.

Summary

Up to this point, we have explored Python with `NumPy`, `TensorFlow`, `sklearn`, `pandas`, and `matplotlib` libraries. More platforms and libraries will be implemented in this book. In the months and years to come, even more languages, libraries, frameworks, and platforms will appear on the market. *However, artificial intelligence is not only about development techniques.* It is a branch of applied mathematics that requires a real-life interest in the field to deliver. Building a k-means clustering program from scratch requires careful planning. The program relies on data that is rarely available as we expect it. That's where our imagination comes in handy to find the right features for our datasets.

Once the dataset has been defined, poor conditioning can compromise the project. Some small changes in the data will lead to incorrect results.

Preparing the training dataset from scratch takes much more time that we would initially expect. Artificial intelligence was designed to make life easier but that's after a project has been successfully implemented. The problem is that building a solution requires major dataset work and constant surveillance.

Then comes the hard work of programming a k-means clustering solution that must be explained to a team. Lloyd's algorithm comes in very handy to that effect by reducing development time.

k-means clustering can be applied to many fields and architectures as will be explained in `Chapter 7`, *When to Use Artificial Intelligence*.

Questions

1. Can a prototype be built with random data in corporate environments? (Yes | No)
2. Do design matrices contain one example per matrix? (Yes | No)
3. AGVs can never be widespread. (Yes | No)
4. Can k-means clustering be applied to drone traffic? (Yes | No)
5. Can k-means clustering be applied to forecasting? (Yes | No)
6. Llyod's algorithm is a two-step approach. (Yes | No)
7. Do hyperparameters control the behavior of the algorithm? (Yes | No)
8. Once a program works, the way it is presented does not really matter. (Yes | No)
9. k-means is only a classification algorithm. It's not a prediction algorithm. (Yes | No)

Further reading

The scikit-learn website contains additional information on k-means clustering:

`http://scikitlearn.org/stable/modules/generated/sklearn.cluster.KMeans.html`

You can find Python's Data Analysis Library here:

`https://pandas.pydata.org/`

7
When and How to Use Artificial Intelligence

Using **artificial intelligence (AI)** in a corporate environment follows a normal process of risk assessment. Managers evaluate the feasibility of a project and return on investment before giving a green signal to an AI implementation.

This chapter builds on the k-means clustering presentation that Pert Ex, our AI expert, made in `Chapter 6`, *Don't Get Lost in Techniques – Focus on Optimizing Your Solutions*. The time has come to carefully deploy a large number of datasets by first showing that a classical approach will not work. Then we use the proper architecture to get the project on track.

Amazon Web Services(AWS) SageMaker and Amazon S3 provide an innovative way to train machine learning datasets. The goal here is not to suggest that AWS could be the best solution but to show the best of AWS. AWS will constantly evolve, just like Google, IBM, Microsoft, and other platforms.

However, even though machine learning platforms might differ, the implementation method will necessarily remain the same.

The following topics will be covered in this chapter:

- Proving that AI must or not be used
- Data volume issues
- Proving the NP-hard characteristic of k-means clustering
- The central limit theorem (CLT)
- Random sampling
- Monte Carlo sampling
- Stochastic sampling

- Shuffling a training dataset
- How to use AWS SageMaker for a machine learning training model

Technical requirements

You will need Python 3.6x 64-bit from `https://www.python.org/`:

```
from sklearn.cluster import KMeans
import pandas as pd
from matplotlib import pyplot as plt
from random import randint
import numpy as np
```

You will need programs from GitHub `Chapter07`:

- `k-means_clustering_minibatch.py`
- `k-means_clustering_minibatch_shuffling.py`

Check out the following video to see the code in action:

`https://goo.gl/1nRPH6`

Checking whether AI can be avoided

Trying to avoid AI in a book on AI may seem paradoxical. However, AI tools can be compared to having a real toolkit in real life. If you are at home and you just need to change a light bulb, you do not have to get your brand new toolkit to show off to everybody around you. You just change the light bulb and that's it.

In AI, as in real life, use the right tools at the right time. If AI is not necessary to solve a problem, do not use it.

Use a **proof of concept (POC)** approach to prove your point for an AI project. A POC should cost much less than the project itself and helps to build a team that believes in the outcome. The first step is exploring the data volume and the method that will be used.

Data volume and applying k-means clustering

Anybody who has run MNIST with 60,000 handwritten image examples on a laptop knows that it takes some time for a machine learning program to train and test these examples. Whether a machine learning program or a deep learning convolutional network is applied, it uses a lot of the local machine's resources. Even if you run it on training on **GPUs** (short for **graphics processing unit**) hoping to get better performance than with CPUs, it still takes a lot of time for the training process to run through all the learning epochs.

If you go on and you want to train your program on images, CIFAR-10, a-60,000 image subset of the tiny image dataset, will consume even more resources on your local machine.

Suppose now, in this case, Pert Ex has to start using k-means clustering in a corporation with hundreds of millions of records of data to analyze in a SQL Server or Oracle database. Pert calls you in to manage the POC phase of the project. For example, you find that you have to work for the phone operating activity of the corporation and apply a k-means clustering program to the duration of phone calls to locations around the world every morning for several weeks. That represents about several million records per day, adding up to 3 billion records in a month. Once that has been implemented, the top marketing manager wants to use the visual result of the clusters and centroids for an investment meeting at the end of the month.

You go to the IT department and ask for a server to do the k-means clustering training and simulation process. You get a flat number. Everybody knows that a machine learning k-means clustering training program running over 3 billion records will consume too much CPU/GPU. A shrewd colleague points out that 3 billion records represent only one feature. If you talk about location and duration, that represents two features, bringing the data volume to 6 billion cells in a matrix.

You clearly understand the point and agree that there is a resource problem here. You go back to the marketing manager with your "No" for the project to run on local servers. You want to obtain permission to use AWS (Amazon Web Services). Your marketing manager immediately lets you use it. Obtaining those centroids per location cluster is critical to the business plan of the company.

Proving your point

While you are gone, the IT department try to run a query on the SQL server database on one continent and the Oracle database on another. They come up with the duration per location but simply cannot provide the centroids and clusters. They are puzzled because they would like to avoid using AWS. Now that they've tried and failed, they are ready to move forward and get the project rolling. They need an explanation first.

Never force a team to do what you think is necessary without proving why it is necessary. The explanation must be clear and each part of the project must be broken down into elementary parts that everybody can understand, including yourself!

You start by explaining that solving a k-means clustering problem is **NP-hard**. The **P** stands for **polynomial** and the **N** for **non-deterministic**.

NP-hard – the meaning of P

The *P* here means that the time to solve or verify the solution of a problem is polynomial (*poly*=many, *nomial*=terms). For example, x^3 is a polynomial.

Once x is known, then x^3 will be computed. Applied to 3,000,000,000 records, an estimation can be applied:

$x^3 = 3,000,000\verb|^|3$

It seems a lot but it isn't that much for two reasons:

- In a world of big data, the number can be subject to large-scale randomized sampling
- K-means clustering can be trained by mini-batches (subsets of the dataset) to speed up computations

The big difference between a polynomial function and an exponential function relies, in this case, on x being the variable, and 3 the exponent.

In an exponential function, x would be the variable and 3 the constant. With x as an exponent, the time to solve this problem would be exponential. It's certainly not a polynomial time you can predict.

$3^{3,000,000,000}$ is something you don't even want to think about!

Polynomial time means that this time will be more or less proportional to the size of the input. Even if the time it takes to train the k-means clustering remains a bit fuzzy, as long as the time it will take to verify the solution remains proportional to the size of the input, the problem remains a polynomial.

The IT department feels better about the problem. The volume of the training process will overload their servers. They do not have the time to purchase a server and set it up.

NP-hard – The meaning of non-deterministic

The IT department tried to find a solution with a query but did not succeed.

Non-deterministic problems require a heuristic approach, which implies some form of practical approach. The most widespread heuristic is trial and error. K-means goes beyond trial and error. It is more like a progressive-iterative approximation of the goals to attain.

In any case, k-means clustering requires a well-tuned algorithm to solve the volume of data involved in this project.

The meaning of hard

NP-hard, as opposed to NP, can solve a problem in a straightforward deterministic way, without a non-deterministic method.

The IT department is not only satisfied with the answer but also very pleased that you took the time to explain why AWS was necessary and did not just say, "*The boss said so.*"

 AI requires clear explanations and scientific proof of its necessity.

The last question comes up: *what are mini-batches and how are they used?*

Random sampling

A large portion of machine learning and deep learning contains random sampling in various forms. In this case, a training set of 3,000,000,000 elements will prove difficult to implement without random sampling.

Random sampling applies to many methods as described in this book: Monte Carlo, stochastic gradient descent, and many others. No matter what name the sampling takes, they share common concepts to various degrees depending on the size of the dataset. The following description fits the Monte Carlo philosophy.

The law of large numbers – LLN

In probability, the law of large numbers states that when dealing with very large volumes of data, significant samples can be effective enough to represent the whole set of data. We are all familiar with polling, for example, a population on all sorts of subjects.

This principle, like all principles, has its merits and limits. But whatever its limitations, this law applies to everyday machine learning algorithms.

In machine learning, sampling resembles polling. The right, smaller number of individuals makes up efficient datasets.

In machine learning, the word "mini-batch" replaces a group of people in the polling system.

Sampling mini-batches and averaging them can prove as efficient as calculating the whole dataset as long as a scientific method is applied:

- Training with mini-batches or subsets of data
- Using an estimator in one form or another to measure the progression of the training session until a goal has been reached

You may be surprised to see "until a goal has been reached" and not "the optimal solution."

The optimal solution may not represent the best solution. All the features and all the parameters are often not expressed. This makes being too precise useless.

In this case, the marketing manager wants to know where the centroids (geometric center) of each cluster (region of locations) have been computed for his marketing campaign. The corporation may decide to open a new company at the location of each centroid and provide additional services through local spin-offs to increase their market penetration.

Taking that into account, a centroid does not need to be extremely precise. Finding the nearest large city within a reasonable distance will prove good enough.

The LLN explains why random functions are widely used in machine learning and deep learning.

The central limit theorem

As shown in by the LLN applied to this business case, the k-means clustering project must provide a reasonable set of centroids and clusters (regions of locations for long-duration phone calls).

This approach can now be extended to the CLT, which states, in machine learning parlance, that when training a large dataset, a subset of mini-batch samples is sufficient. The following two conditions define the main properties of the central limit theorem:

- The variance between the data points of the subset (mini-batch) remains reasonable. In this case, filtering only long-duration calls solves the problem.
- The normal distribution pattern with mini-batch variances close to the variance of the whole dataset.

Using a Monte Carlo estimator

The name Monte Carlo comes from the casinos in Monte Carlo and gambling. Gambling represents an excellent memoryless random example. No matter what happens before a gambler plays, prior knowledge provides no insight.

Applied to machine learning, the sum of the distribution of $f(x)$ is computed. Then random samples are extracted from the following dataset: $x_1, x_2, x_3, ..., x_n$.

No matter what form $f(x)$ takes, such as in a k-means clustering process, to estimate the average result, it can be represented by the following equation:

$$\hat{e} = \frac{1}{n} \sum_{i=1}^{n} f(x_i)$$

The estimator $\hat{e}$ represents an average of the result of the k-means clustering algorithm or any model implemented.

Random sampling applications

Random sampling can be applied to many functions and methods as we will see in subsequent chapters in this book: Monte Carlo sampling, as described previously, and stochastic gradient descent by extracting samples from the dataset to evaluate the cost function and many other functions.

Randomness represents a key asset when dealing with large datasets.

Cloud solutions – AWS

Implementing large number data volumes involves using server resources in one form or the other. We have to use on-premise servers or cloud platforms. In this case, it has been decided to outsource server resources and algorithm development to face a large amount of data billion to train.

Several online cloud services offer the solution to machine learning projects. In this chapter, the project was carried out with AWS SageMaker on an AWS S3 data management platform.

Preparing your baseline model

3,000,000 records containing two features, adding up to a 6,000,000 cell matrix dataset, require mini-batches as defined in the next section through hyperparameters.

In the AWS interface, the size of a mini-batch will be a number. To see what it does, let's apply a mini-batch to the Python program example of Chapter 6, *Don't Get Lost in Techniques – Focus on Optimizing Your Solutions*.

Training the full sample training dataset

In Chapter 6, *Don't Get Lost in Techniques – Focus on Optimizing Your Solutions*, 5,000 records and a six-cluster configuration produced six centroids (geometric centers), as shown here:

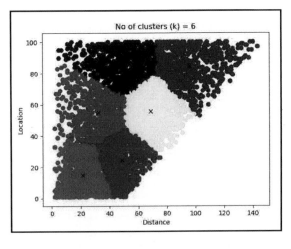

Six centroids

The problem now is how to avoid costly machine resources to train this k-means clustering dataset.

Training a random sample of the training dataset

Before spending resources on AWS, we must prepare a model locally and make sure it works. AWS possesses efficient mini-batch algorithms. But to master them, a local baseline will guarantee good AWS job management.

The `k-means_clustering_ch7_minibatch.py` file provides a way to verify the mini-batch solution.

The program begins by loading the data in the following lines of code:

```
dataset = pd.read_csv('data.csv')
print (dataset.head())
print (dataset)
```

Now a mini-batch dataset name `dataset1` will be randomly created using Monte Carlo's large data volume principle with a mini-batch size of 1,000. Many variations of the method's Monte Carlo approaches apply to machine learning. The estimator within the k-means function will be used as the Monte Carlo type averaging function, as shown in the following source code.

```
n=1000
dataset1=np.zeros(shape=(n,2))li=0
```

```
for i in range (n):
j=randint(0,4999)
dataset1[li][0]=dataset.iloc[j,0]
dataset1[li][1]=dataset.iloc[j,1]
li+=1
```

Finally, the k-means clustering algorithm runs on a standard basis, as shown in the following snippet.

```
#II.Hyperparameters
# Features = 2 :implict through the shape of the dataset (2 columns)
k = 6
kmeans = KMeans(n_clusters=k)

#III.K-means clustering algorithm
kmeans = kmeans.fit(dataset1) #Computing k-means clustering
gcenters = kmeans.cluster_centers_ # the geometric centers or centroids
print("The geometric centers or centroids:")
print(gcenters)
```

The following screenshot, displaying the result produced, resembles the full dataset trained by k-means clustering in Chapter 6, *Don't Get Lost in Techniques – Focus on Optimizing Your Solutions*.

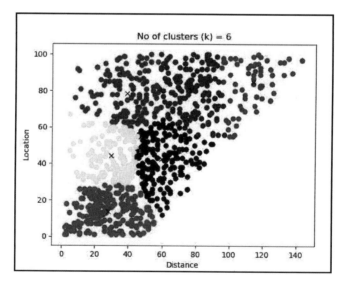

Output (k-means clustering)

The centroids obtained can solve the marketing problem as shown in this output.

```
The geometric centers or centroids:
[[ 19.6626506  14.37349398]
 [ 49.86619718 86.54225352]
 [ 65.39306358 54.34104046]
 [ 29.69798658 54.7852349 ]
 [ 48.77202073 23.74611399]
 [ 96.14124294 82.44067797]]
```

Shuffling as an alternative to random sampling

K-means clustering is an unsupervised training algorithm. As such, it trains *unlabeled* data. One random computation does not consume a high level of machine resources, but several random selections in a row can.

Shuffling can reduce machine consumption costs.

Proper shuffling of the data before starting training, just like shuffling cards before a *Poker* game, will avoid repetitive and random mini-batch computations. In this model, the loading data phase and training phase do not change. However, instead of one or several random choices for dataset1, the mini-batch dataset, we shuffle the complete dataset once before starting the training. The following code shows how to shuffle datasets.

```
sn=4999
shuffled_dataset=np.zeros(shape=(sn,2))
for i in range (sn):
  shuffled_dataset[i][0]=dataset.iloc[i,0]
  shuffled_dataset[i][1]=dataset.iloc[i,1]
```

Then we select the first 1,000 shuffled records for training, as shown in the following code snippet.

```
n=1000
dataset1=np.zeros(shape=(n,2))
for i in range (n):
dataset1[i][0]=shuffled_dataset[i,0]
dataset1[i][1]=shuffled_dataset[i,1]
```

The result in the following screenshot corresponds to the one with the full dataset and the random mini-batch dataset sample.

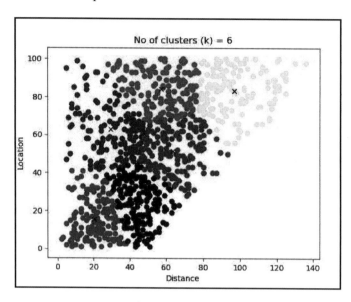

Full and random mini-batch dataset sample

The centroids produced can provide first-level results to confirm the model, as shown in the following output.

```
The geometric centers or centroids:
[[ 29.51298701  62.77922078]
 [ 57.07894737  84.21052632]
 [ 20.34337349  15.48795181]
 [ 45.19900498  23.95024876]
 [ 96.72262774  83.27737226]
 [ 63.54210526  51.53157895]]
```

Now that the model exists locally, the implementation on AWS can proceed.

 Using shuffling instead of random mini-batches has two advantages: limiting the number of mini-batch calculations and avoiding training the same samples twice.

AWS – data management

No matter which cloud solution you choose, data management will involve the following:

- Security and permissions—this will depend on your security policy and the cloud platform's policies
- Managing input data and output data related to your machine learning model

Buckets

AWS has a data repository named buckets. You can create a bucket on Amazon S3. On other platforms, different names are used but the concept remains the same. Your data has to reach the platform one way or the other with an API, a data connection, or loading of the data. In the present example, the best choice remains a bucket, as shown in the following screenshot:

Amazon S3 bucket creation

Uploading files

Once the bucket has been created, files can be loaded in various formats. In this example, data.csv was loaded without the headers. The data.csv used in the previous chapter has been loaded without headers. AWS requires format verification (number of columns, possible indexes) on an ever-evolving platform. The following screenshot shows how you can organize your data.

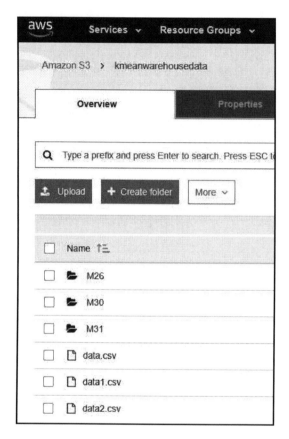

Amazon S3 bucket data

Access to output results

SageMaker automatically writes the results of the k-means clustering training session in an output directory in the following Amazon S3 bucket as shown in the following screenshot.

Output directory

SageMaker notebook

To create your machine jobs on any platform, you will have to configure an interface, use command lines, or write commands through APIs.

In this example, Amazon SageMaker notebooks will be managing the k-means clustering job. First, access AWS services with your account, as shown in this screenshot.

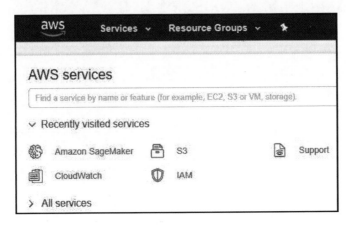

AWS services

Then go to SageMaker, as shown in the following screenshot.

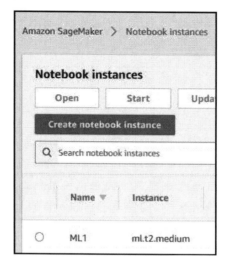

SageMaker notebook instances

ML1 is the notebook instance for the k-means clustering baseline model that will be run.

Creating a job

To create a job, we click on Create training job, as seen in the following screenshot.

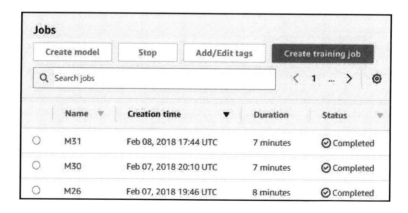

Job creation

Once the input data path and output path have been created, the most important part consists of setting up the right hyperparameters (see the following screenshot) that will control the behavior of the machine learning job.

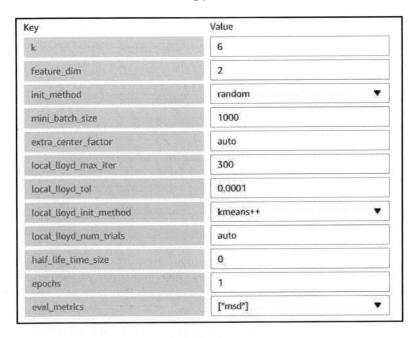

Key	Value
k	6
feature_dim	2
init_method	random ▼
mini_batch_size	1000
extra_center_factor	auto
local_lloyd_max_iter	300
local_lloyd_tol	0.0001
local_lloyd_init_method	kmeans++ ▼
local_lloyd_num_trials	auto
half_life_time_size	0
epochs	1
eval_metrics	["msd"] ▼

Setting hyperparameters

The main parameters are these:

- k: This determines the number of clusters and centroids that will be computed. For this example, setting it to 6 was used. If you are running handwritten letter recognition, you might want to have a centroid per letter.
- Feature_dim: The number of features in this example was set to 2. Many more features can be integrated into your model as long as they prove necessary.
- mini-batch_size: Mini-batch, as described in the previous section. The whole dataset batch cannot be trained with large data volumes. A batch size of 5,000 for large datasets can produce interesting results. However, finding the right parameter might take several tries.
- init_method: K-means generally starts with random *k*s centroids. The best way remains to get the system to work and then explore other avenues with AWS documentation.

- `extra_center_factor`: Keeping this value to auto to start with remains a good option. AWS put a lot of work into optimizing the algorithm by managing (adding centers when necessary) the number of *k*s. In the end, the algorithm will always return the right number of centroids.
- `local_lloyd_max_iter`: Lloyd's algorithm was described in the previous chapter. In brief, each data points goes to the closest centroid and becomes part of that cluster. The centroids are recalculated and the process continues until the data points stabilize. This parameter limits the number of iterations.
- `local_lloyd_tol`: Early stopping occurs when a local minimum is reached. The algorithm can reach stability although the optimizing process remains incomplete. The tolerance factor decides whether the variance is acceptable or not.
- `local_lloyd_num_trials`: The number of trials in a local computation measure with loss function.
- `half_life_time_size`: The k-means clustering algorithm has a loss function and evaluation metrics. As such, weights are updated as in other machine learning algorithms. Weight decay is just like when you are on a highway and have to get off at an exit. You must slow down or overshoot your exit goal. Weight decay reduces the values of weights exponentially has the loss function optimizes the clusters. At half-time, the weight will reach half of their value. You can choose not to trigger weight decay off by setting this parameter to 0.
- `epochs`: The number of episodes the algorithm will optimize the data points.
- `eval_metrics`: **["msd"]** or **["ssd"]** methods can be used as evaluation metrics. In any case, distance measurement remains a key factor in k-means optimizing algorithms.

Running a job

Running starts by clicking on **Create training job**:

Creating training job

After a few minutes or hours, depending on the volume of data provided or the complexity of the machine learning algorithm chosen, AWS SageMaker provides the status of the training session, as shown in the following screenshot.

Name	▼	Creation time	▼	Duration	Status
M31		Feb 08, 2018 17:44 UTC		7 minutes	⊘ Completed

Status of the training session—Completed

If the status column displays **Completed**, then the results will be analyzed. If not, we must solve the errors in the configuration process.

Reading the results

As explained previously, the results appear in the Amazon S3 bucket. In this case, a TAR file was created as shown in the following screenshot.

	Name ↑≡
☑	📄 model.tar.gz

TAR file

The TAR file contains `model_algo-1`, a data-serialized file.

To read the file, `mxnet` can be imported, the file opened, and the result displayed in a short `read.py` program, as shown in this code.

```
import mxnet as mxr=mx.ndarray.load('model_algo-1')
print(r)
```

The following result comes close to the local model.

```
[[ 23.70976257 16.17502213]
 [ 97.42507935 81.57003784]
 [ 58.39919281 45.75806427]
 [ 29.69905663 65.11740875]
 [ 61.08079529 81.22251892]
 [ 56.15731812 12.13902283]]
<NDArray 6x2 @cpu(0)>]
```

Recommended strategy

Taking the data volume issue into account, data shuffling could prove effective. Then, depending on corporate practices, the data could be streamed to AWS in batches or loaded in batches.

Training will take many hours of working on the hyperparameters and result analyzing.

Summary

In any machine learning project, we should start by proving that classical programs using SQL queries will not suffice. Then, a baseline or prototype using a sample should prove that the model will work.

Using a cloud platform such as AWS SageMaker with S3 will save corporate investment resources in order to focus on the training job. This proves once again that the future of artificial intelligence experts relies upon their ability to imagine solutions and not to get lost in programming.

No matter what happens, the basic steps will always remain the same, which include proving that artificial intelligence is necessary, building a prototype model, dataset management, and hyperparameter and job optimization.

Amazon, Google, IBM, Microsoft, and others will be offering more platforms, frameworks, and resources for machine learning. These platforms will constantly evolve and change. As these giants innovate, programming will become less and less necessary so that all companies, small or large, can access the AI cloud platforms. Programming AI will remain fascinating as well as standard non-AI development. However, nothing will stop cloud ready-to-use platforms from expanding.

These platforms are the cutting edge of artificial intelligence and will lead you to the fascinating frontier of present knowledge. You can cross the border into the wild and discover new ways of solving hard problems. A cloud platform has limits that you can push much further, as we will discover in the next chapter.

Questions

The questions will focus on the hyperparameters.

1. The number of k clusters is not that important. (Yes | No)
2. Mini-batches and batches contain the same amount of data. (Yes | No)
3. K-means can run without mini-batches. (Yes | No)
4. Must centroids be totally optimized for result acceptance? (Yes | No)
5. It does not take long to optimize hyperparameters. (Yes | No)
6. It sometimes takes weeks to train a large dataset. (Yes | No)
7. AWS SageMaker has a k-means algorithm only. (Yes | No)

Further reading

- Further information on Amazon Web Services, Sagemaker, and k-means clustering can be found here:
    - https://docs.aws.amazon.com/sagemaker/latest/dg/k-means.html
    - https://github.com/aws/sagemaker-python-sdk/blob/master/src/sagemaker/amazon/kmeans.py
- Further information on k-means clustering can be found here:
    - https://www.eecs.tufts.edu/~dsculley/papers/fastkmeans.pdf
    - https://docs.aws.amazon.com/sagemaker/latest/dg/algo-kmeans-tech-notes.html
    - https://pdfs.semanticscholar.org/0074/4cb7cc9ccbbcdadbd5ff2f2fee6358427271.pdf
- Further information on MXNET can be found here:
    - https://mxnet.incubator.apache.org/architecture/overview.html

8
Revolutions Designed for Some Corporations and Disruptive Innovations for Small to Large Companies

Contrary to media hype, artificial intelligence has just begun innovating human processes. A huge amount of work remains to be done. To achieve progress, everybody must get involved, as shown in this chapter. Even if Google, Amazon, Microsoft, IBM, and others offer a solution, it does not mean it cannot be improved by third parties as add-ons to existing solutions or new standalone products. After all, once Ford invented the Model T over a hundred years ago, it did not mean it was no use inventing other better cars. On the contrary, look around you!

This chapter first explains the differences between inventions, innovations, disruption, high-priced products, revolutions, and how to innovate in AI no matter what.

Then Google Translate will be explored to illustrate innovation concepts using natural language processing. This is a prerequisite to building not only translation solutions but also chatbots (see Chapter 15, *Cognitive NLP Chatbots*, and Chapter 16, *Improve the Emotional Intelligence Deficiencies of Chatbots*).

Google Translate entered the market in 2006 and was enhanced by neural networks in 2016, but still it often produces bad answers. Is that good news or bad news? Let's find out by exploring Google's API in a Python program, adding a k-nearest neighbor algorithm and measuring the results statistically.

The following topics will be covered in this chapter:

- The difference between inventions and innovations
- The difference between standard sales and disruptive marketing
- Google Translate API implementation in Python
- Introducing linguistics (prerequisites to building chatbots)
- Natural language processing prerequisites (for translations and chatbots)
- k-nearest neighbor (KNN) algorithm

Technical requirements

You will need Python 3.6x 64-bit from `https://www.python.org/`.

You will also need these libraries:

```
from googleapiclient.discovery import build
import html.parser as htmlparser
import pandas as pd
from matplotlib import pyplot as plt
from sklearn.neighbors import KNeighborsClassifier
```

And you will need programs from GitHub `Chapter08`:

- `google_translate.py`
- `Google_translate_a_few_test_expressions.py`
- `knn_polysemy.py` (download `V1.csv` in the same directory)
- `Google_Translate_customized.py` (download `V1.csv` in the same directory)

Check out the following video to see the code in action:

`https://goo.gl/aMcfcf`

Is AI disruptive?

The word "disruptive" is more often than not associated with artificial intelligence. Media hype tells us that AI robots will soon have replaced humans around the world. Although media hype made it much easier to obtain AI budgets, we need to know where we stand if we want to implement an AI solution. If we want to innovate, we need to find the cutting edge and build new ideas from there.

Why not just plunge into the tools and see what happens? Is that a good idea or a risky one? Unlike corporations with huge budgets, a single human has limited resources. If you spend time learning in the wrong direction, it will take months to gather enough experience in another better direction to reach your goal. For example, suppose you have trouble classifying large amounts of data (see the example in Chapter 7, *When and How to Use Artificial Intelligence*); you spend months on a project on a server in your company and fail. It could cost you your job. If you find the right cloud platform as shown in Chapter 7, *When and How to Use Artificial Intelligence* and learn the key concepts, your project can take off in a few days.

Before diving into a project, find out the best way to start it.

What is new and what isn't in AI

Most AI theory and tools have been around for decades, if not centuries. *We often tend to think that since something appears new to us, it has just been invented or discovered.* This mistake can prove fatal in many projects. If you know that a theory or function has been around for decades or centuries, you can do some deep research and use solutions found 100+ years ago to solve your present problems.

Finding out what is new and what is not will make a major difference in your personal or professional AI projects.

AI is based on mathematical theories that are not new

Artificial intelligence theory presently relies heavily on applied mathematics. In Chapter 1, *Become an Adaptive Thinker*, the **Markov Decision Process (MDP)** was described. Google Brain has proudly and rightly so won some competitions using the MDP combined with neural networks.

However, Andrey Andreyevich Markov was a Russian mathematician born in 1856 who invented the MDP among other functions. Richard Bellman published an enhanced version of the Markov Decision Process in 1957.

Bellman also coined the expression "curse of dimensionality" and published books on mathematical tools widely used today in AI. It is now well known that dimensionality reduction can be performed to avoid facing thousands of dimensions (features, for example) in an algorithm.

The logistic function (see `Chapter 2`, *Think like a Machine*) can be traced back to Pierre François Verhulst (1844-1845), a Belgian mathematician. The logistic function uses *e*, the natural logarithm base, which is also named after Euler's number. Leonhard Euler (1707-1783), a Swiss mathematician who worked on this natural logarithm.

Thomas Bayes (1701-1761) invented the theorem that bears his name: Bayes' Theorem. It is widely used in artificial intelligence.

In fact, almost all of the applied mathematics in artificial intelligence, machine learning, and deep learning can be traced from 17th-century to 20th-century mathematicians.

We must look elsewhere for 21st century AI innovations.

Neural networks are not new

Neural networks as explained in `Chapter 4`, *Become an Unconventional Innovator*, date back to the 1940s and 1950s. Even **convolutional neural networks** (**CNN**) date back to the 20th century. Yann LeCun, a French computer scientist, laid down the basics of a CNN (see `Chapter 9`, *Getting Your Neurons to Work*) in the 1980s; he successfully applied them as we know them today in the 1990s.

We must again look elsewhere for 21st AI innovations.

Cloud server power, data volumes, and web sharing of the early 21st century started to make AI disruptive

The first sign of AI's innovative disruption appeared between 2000 and 2010. Before then, the internet existed, and servers existed. But starting from around 2005, cloud servers were made widely available. With that kind of computer power, developers around the world could try using the highly greedy resources required by machine learning and deep learning.

 At the same moment, as powerful servers became available, the internet provided the largest library of knowledge in the history of mankind.

On top of that, social networking became widely used. Sharing discoveries and source code became commonplace. The **World Wide Web** (**WWW**) encouraged open source software, boosting local research and development.

The era of artificial intelligence became possible for local experts starting from the middle of the first decade of the 21st century.

 What makes artificial appear as an innovation today is the conjunction of more powerful machines and the availability of intellectual resources.

Public awareness contributed to making AI disruptive

Public awareness of artificial intelligence remained dim for several years after the cloud architectural revolution occurred from around 1995 to 2005.

Artificial intelligence hit us hard by around 2015 when we all woke up realizing that AI could massively replace humans and create job displacement at levels never seen in human history.

Worse, we realized that machines could beat us in fields we took pride in, such as chess (Chapter 3, *Apply Machine Thinking to a Human Problem*), the game of Go, other video games, manufacturing jobs with robots, office jobs with bots, and more fields that appear every day.

For the first time in human history, the human species can be surpassed by a new species: bots. As developers, we thought we were safe until Google presented AutoML, a solution that could create machine learning solutions better than humans. At the same time, ready-to-use machine learning platforms have spread that can reduce and even replace AI software development.

Artificial intelligence forces awe and fear upon us. How far will machines go? Will we simply experience job displacement or will it go as far as species replacement?

Could this be an opportunity for many? Who knows? In any case, this chapter provides solutions to constantly innovating and being useful as humans.

Inventions versus innovations

Some artificial intelligence programs, especially deep learning algorithms, remained inventions and not innovations until they were widely used by Google and other major players.

If you have invented a better algorithm than Google for some applications, it remains an invention until it actually *changes* something in your corporation or on the Web.

Suppose you find a quicker way to recognize an image through an optimized number of neurons and a new activation function. If nobody uses it, then that invention remains a personal theoretical fining no matter how good it appears. When others begin to use this new algorithm, then it becomes an innovation.

 An invention becomes an innovation only when it changes a process within a company or by a sufficient number of private users.

Revolutionary versus disruptive solutions

Suppose the new image recognition algorithm described just now becomes an innovation in a significant corporation. *This new algorithm has gone from being an **invention** (not really used) to an **innovation** (a solution making a difference).*

The corporation now widely uses the algorithm. Every subsidiary has access to it. For this corporation, the new image recognition algorithm has attained revolutionary status. Corporate sales have gone up, and profit margins have as well.

But maybe this corporation does not dominate the market and nobody has followed its example. The innovation remains revolutionary but has not become disruptive.

Then the person who created the algorithm decides to leave the company and start a business with the algorithm. It appears on GitHub as an open source program. Everybody wants it and the number of downloads increases daily until 1,000,000+ users have begun to implement it. Some very low priced add-ons are provided on the company website. Within a year, it becomes the new way of recognizing images. All companies must follow suit or stay behind. *The solution has become **disruptive** because it has globally changed its market.*

Where to start?

We have finished reading about such fantastic innovations and have tested mind-blowing AI solutions, knowing that all of this can be discouraging. Where to start? First of all, even if a solution exists, it has limits and can be improved, customized, packaged, and sold. *This means that if there is a limit, there is a market.*

Never criticize the flaws you find in an AI solution. They are gold mines!

 Where there is a limit, there lies an opportunity.

Let's go to the cutting edge and then over the border into unchartered territory using Google Translate to illustrate this.

Discover a world of opportunities with Google Translate

Starting out with Google Translate to explore **natural language processing (NLP)** is a good way to prepare for chatbots. Any disruptive web-based solution must be able to run in at least a few languages.

Google provides many resources to use, explore, or improve Google Translate. Getting a Python code to run and then assess the quality of the results will prove vital before implementing it for crucial translations in a company.

Getting started

Go the Google's developers API Client Libary page: `https://developers.google.com/api-client-library/`. On that page, you will see libraries for many languages: Java, PHP, .NET, JavaScript, Objective-C, Dart, Ruby,Node.js, Go, and probably more to come.

This does not change a thing about reaching the limits of Google Translate and entering the adventurous frontier of innovating the linguistic dimension of AI described in this chapter.

Then click on the **GET STARTED** option under **Python**. Follow the instructions to sign up, create a project in the Google API Console, and install the library.

To install the library, use `pip` (preferred):

```
$ pip install--upgrade google-api-python-client
```

If you encounter problems doing this part or do not wish to install anything yet, this chapter is self-contained. The source code is described in the chapter.

You are now ready to go ahead, whether you installed the tools or not.

The program

The goal of this section is to implement Google Translate functionality. You can follow the steps and get it working or simply read the chapter to get the idea.

The header

The standard Google header provided by Google was enough for the program I wrote, as shown in the following code.

```
from googleapiclient.discovery import build
```

Considering the many languages Google manages, special characters are a major problem to handle. Many forums and example programs on the Web struggle with the UTF-8 header when using Google Translate. Many solutions are suggested, such as the following source code header.

```
# -*- coding: utf-8 -*-
```

Then, when Google translate returns the result, more problems occur and many develop their own functions. They work fine but I was looking for a straightforward one-line solution. The goal here was not to have many lines of code but focus on the limit of Google Translate to discover the cutting-edge interpreting languages in AI.

So, I did not use the UTF-8 header but implemented this HTML parser.

```
import html.parser as htmlparser
parser = htmlparser.HTMLParser()
```

When confronted with a result, the following one-line HTML parser code did the job.

```
print("result:",parser.unescape(result))
```

It works well because, in fact, Google will return an HTML string or a text string depending on what option you implement. This means that the HTML parser can do the job.

Implementing Google's translation service

Google's translation service needs at least three values to return a result:

- `developerKey`: This is the API key obtained at the end of the "getting started" process described previously
- `q="text to translate"`: In my code, I used `source`
- `target="abbreviation of the translated text"`: `en` for English, `fr` for French, and so on

More options are available as described in the following sections.

With this in mind, the translation function will work as follows:

```
def g_translate(source,target1):
  service = build('translate', 'v2',developerKey='your Key')
  request = service.translations().list(q=source, target=target1)
  response = request.execute()
  return response['translations'][0]['translatedText']
```

In the `Google_translate.py` program, `q` and `target` will be sent to the function to obtain a parsed result:

```
source="your text"
 target1="abbreviation of the target language"
 result = g_translate(source,target1)
print(result)
```

To sum up the program, let's translate Google Translate into French, which contains accents parsed by the HTML parser:

```
from googleapiclient.discovery import build
import html.parser as htmlparser
parser = htmlparser.HTMLParser()

def g_translate(source,target1):
  service = build('translate', 'v2',developerKey='your key')
  request = service.translations().list(q=source, target=target1)
  response = request.execute()
  return response['translations'][0]['translatedText']

source='Google Translate is great!'

target1="fr"
result = g_translate(source,target1)
print(result)
```

`Google_Translate.py` works fine. The result will come out with the correct answer and the parsed accent:

```
Google Translate est génial!
```

At this point, everyone is happy in our corporation, named Example-Corporation:

- The developer has the starting point for whatever solution is requested
- The project manager has reached the goal set by the company
- The manager has a ready-to-use AI solution to translate commercial offers and contracts into many languages in many countries

Google Translate has satisfied everyone. It is disruptive, has changed the world, and can replace translators in many corporations for all corporate needs.

Fantastic!

In fact, we could end the chapter here, go to our favorite social network, and build some hype on our translation project!

Happy ending?

Well, not yet! The CEO, who happens to be the main shareholder of Example-Corporation, wants to make sure that everything really works before firing the 20 freelance translators working in the corporation.

The CEO phones a linguist from Example_University and asks for some expert advice. The next day, professor Ustiling comes in, gray-haired and smiling, *"You can call me Usty. So let's get to work!"*

Google Translate from a linguist's perspective

Usty is fascinated by Google Translate as presented previously. The possibilities seem endless.

Usty applies a linguist's approach to the program.

 By the time this book is published, maybe Google will have improved the examples in this chapter. But don't worry; in this case, you will quickly find hundreds of other examples that are incorrect. The journey has just begun!

Playing with the tool

They open the source code and Usty adds some paragraphs. This source code is saved as `Google_translate_a_few_test_expressions.py`. Usty has spent quite some time on automatic translating as a professor.

Usty, like many linguists, wants to play with the program first to get a feel of the program. The first two examples go well from English to French. Then Usty complicates the third example, as shown in the following code.

```
source='Hello. My name is Usty!'
 >>>result:Bonjour. Je m'appelle Usty!

source='The weather is nice today'
 >>>result: Le temps est beau aujourd'hui

source='Ce professor me cherche des poux.'
 >>>result: This professor is looking for lice!
```

The first two examples look fine in French although the second translation is a bit strange. But in the third test, the expression `chercher des poux` means *looking for trouble* in English not *looking for lice* as translated into French.

Usty has a worried look on his face. The corporate project teams ask him what is wrong.

Usty starts an assessment of Google Translate.

Linguistic assessment of Google Translate

Professor Usty both wants to assess Google Translate correctly and likes limits.

 Limits are the boundaries researchers crave for! We are frontiersmen!

Usty starts an expert assessment that will lead the project team to the frontier and beyond.

Lexical field theory

Lexical fields describe word fields. A word only acquires its full meanings in a context. This context often goes beyond a few other words or even a sentence.

Chercher des poux translated as such means *look for lice*. But in French, it can mean *looking for trouble* or literally *looking for lice*. The result Google Translate comes up with contains three basic problems.

```
source='chercher des poux'
>>result: look for lice
```

Problem 1, the lexical field: There is no way of knowing whether this means really looking for lice or looking for trouble without a context.

Problem 2, metaphors or idiomatic expressions: Suppose you have to translate *this is giving you a headache*. There is no way of knowing whether it is a physical problem or a metaphor meaning this is *driving you crazy*. These two idiomatic expressions happen to have the same metaphors when translated into French. But the *lice* metaphor in French means nothing in English.

Problem 3: *chercher* is an infinitive in French and the result should have been *looking* for lice in English. But *chercher des limites est intéressant* provides the right answer, which is *looking for*:

```
source='Chercher des limites est intéressant.'
>>>result:Looking for boundaries is interesting.
```

The answer is correct because *is* splits the sentence into two, making it easier for Google Translate to identify *chercher* as the first part of a sentence, thus using *looking* in English.

Professor Usty looks excited by these limits but this worries the project team. Will this project be shelved by the CEO or not?

Jargon

Jargon arises when fields specialize. In AI, hidden neurons are jargon. This expression means nothing for a lawyer for example. A lawyer may think you have hidden intelligence on the subject somewhere or are hiding money in a cryptocurrency called **hidden neuron**.

In the same way, if somebody asks an artificial intelligence expert to explain how to file a motion, that would prove difficult.

In a legal corporate environment, beyond using Google Translate as a dictionary, translating sentences might be risky if only a random number of results prove to be correct.

Translating is not just translating but interpreting

Usty likes challenges. He goes online and takes a sentence from a standard description of French commercial law:

```
source='Une SAS ne dispense pas de suivre les recommandations en vigueur
autour des pratiques commerciales.'

>>>result:An SAS does not exempt from following the recommendations in
force around commercial practices.
```

The French sentence means that a company such as a SAS (a type of company like inc., ltd., and so on). In English, **SAS** means **Special Air Forces**. Then comes the grammar that does not sound right.

A translator would write better English and also specify what a SAS is:

"A SAS (a type of company in France) must follow the recommendations that cover commercial practices."

Translating often means interpreting, not simply translating words.

In this case, a legal translator may interpret the text in a contract and go as far as writing:

The COMPANY must respect the legal obligation to treat all customers fairly.

The legal translator will suggest that *COMPANY* be defined in the contract so as to avoid confusions such as the one Google Translate just made.

At this point, the project team is ready to give up. They are totally discouraged!

When reading about natural language processing, chatbots, and translation, everything seems easy. However, really working on Google Translate can easily turn into a nightmare!

How can they go back to their CEO with Usty and explain that Google Translate provides a random quality of results?

In fact, Google Translate is:

- Sometimes correct
- Sometimes wrong
- Sometimes partly correct and partly wrong

Usty has much more to say but the team has had enough!

However, Usty will not give up and will want to explain a global fundamental problem. Then Usty offers to provide solutions. Google Translate is worth exploring and improving because of the available online datasets provided through the API.

He tries to translate the following:

```
The project team is all ears
```

Google Translate provides the output in French:

```
source:"The project team is all ears".
>>>result: L'équipe de projet est tout ouïe.
```

In French, as in English, it is better just to say *project team* and not use *of* to say *the team of the project*. In French *équipe projet* (équipe = team used before project).

How to check a translation

How can you check a translation if you do not know the language?

Be careful. If Google Translate provides randomly correct answers in another language, then you have no way of knowing whether the translation is reliable or not.

You may even send the opposite of what you mean to somebody important for you. You may misunderstand a sentence you are trying to understand.

In a travel company, you write an email stating that the coach stopped and people were complaining:

```
source='The coach stopped and everybody was complaining.'
```

Google Translate, for lexical field reasons, got it wrong and translated coach as a trainer (sports) in French, which would mean nothing in this context:

```
result: L'entraîneur s'est arrêté et tout le monde se plaignait.
```

Even in this situation, if you do not speak French, you have to trust professor Usty on this issue.

Now the situation gets worse. To help Google Translate, let's add some context.

```
source='The coach broke down and stopped and everybody was complaining.'
```

The answer is worse. Google Translate translates *broke down* correctly with the French expression *en panne* but still translates *coach* as *entraineur* (trainer) in French, meaning the *trainer* broke down, not the *coach* (bus).

```
result: L'entraîneur est tombé en panne et s'est arrêté et tout le monde se
plaignait.
```

Google will no doubt improve the program as it has done since 2006. Maybe this will be achieved even by the time you read this book or with some workarounds as shown in the next section. But a human translator will find hundreds of expressions Google Translate cannot deal with yet.

Understanding a sentence in your native language can prove difficult when a word or an expression has several meanings. Adding a translation function to the issue makes it even more difficult to provide a reliable answer.

And that is where we reach the frontier, just beyond the cutting edge.

As a researcher, Usty seems overexcited in contrast to the look of despair on the project team's faces. But soon the project team will share the excitement of discovering new AI lands.

AI as a new frontier

Google has a great but very limited translation program. Use the flaws to innovate! AI research and development has just scratched the surface of the innovations to come.

First, implement an AI solution. Then use it for what it is. But don't accept its limits. Don't be negative about it. Innovate! Imagine ideas or listen to other ideas you like, and build solutions in a team! Google might even publish your solutions!

Usty's excitement is contagious. The project team would like to build a prototype program. Usty suggests forgetting about generalizing the solution for the moment and just focusing on customizing Google Translation for their corporation. Usty decides to dive directly with the team into a prototype Python program: `Google_Translate_Customized.py`.

Lexical field and polysemy

A **lexical field** contains words that form sets and subsets. They differ from one language to another. A language itself forms a set and contain subsets of lexical fields.

Colder countries have more words describing water in its frozen form than tropical countries where snow hardly ever falls. A lexical field of cold could be a subset of C:

C = {ice, hail, snowflakes, snowman, slushy, powder, flake, snowball, blizzard, melting, crunch....n}

The curse of dimensionality, well known in artificial intelligence, applies here. Words contain an incredible number of dimensions and definitions. To translate certain expressions, Google Translate suppresses their dimension and reduces them.

 Google Translate often uses n-grams to translate. An n-gram is a fixed-length sequence of tokens. Tokens can be a word, a character or even numerical representations of words and characters.

The probability that token n means something is calculated given the preceding/following $n - x$ or $n + x$ tokens. x is a variable depending on the algorithm applied.

For example, slushy has a special meaning in the expression slushy snow. The snow is partly melting, it's watery and making slush sound when we walk through it. Melting is only a component of the meaning of slush.

Google Translate, at this point, will only translate slushy snow in French by:

neige (snow) fondante (melting)

Google Translate will also translate melting snow by:

neige (snow) *fondante* (melting)

To translate slushy into French, you have to use a phrase. To find that phrase, you need some imagination or have some parsed (searched) novels or other higher levels of speech representations. That takes time and resources. It will most probably take years before Google Translate reaches an acceptable native level in all the languages publicized.

Another dimension to take into account is polysemy.

 Polysemy means a word can have several very different meanings in a language. The equivalent word in another language may simply have one meaning or other, very different meanings.

"Go + over" in English can mean *go over a bridge* or *go over some notes*. At this point (hopefully, it will improve by the time you read this book), it is translated in both cases in French by *aller sur*. This means *to go on* (not over), which is incorrect in both cases. Prepositions in English constitute a field in themselves, generating many meanings with the same word. The verb go can have a wide list of meanings: go up (upstairs), go up (stock market), go down (downstairs), go down (fall apart), and many more possibilities.

Linguistics involves many more concepts and techniques than just statistics. More will be described in Chapter 15, *Cognitive NLP Chatbots*, and Chapter 16, *Improve the Emotional Intelligence Deficiencies of Chatbots*.

The prototype customized program starts with defining X, a small dataset to translate that will be more than enough to get things going:

```
X=['Eating fatty food can be unhealthy.',
   'This was a catch-22 situation.',
   'She would not lend me her tote bag',
   'He had a chip on her shoulder',
   'The market was bearish yesterday',
   'That was definitely wrong',
   'The project was compromised but he pulled a rabit out of his hat',
   'So just let the chips fall where they may',
   'She went the extra mile to satisfy the customer',
   'She bailed out when it became unbearable',
   'The term person includes one or more individuals, labor unions,
partnerships, associations, corporations, legal representatives, mutual
companies, joint-stock companies, trusts, unincorporated organizations,
trustees, trustees in bankruptcy, or receivers.',
   'The coach broke down, stopped and everybody was complaining']
```

These sentences will be automatically translated by Google Translate.

X1 , as implemented in the following code, defines some keywords statistically related to the sentences; it applies the n-gram probability theory described previously.

```
X1=['grasse',
  'insoluble',
  'sac',
  'agressif',
  'marché',
  'certainement',
  'chapeau',
  'advienne',
  'supplémentaire',
  'parti',
  'personne',
  'panne']
```

Each X1 line fits the corresponding X line. As explained, this only remains a probability and may not be correct.

We are not seeking perfection at this point but an improvement.

Exploring the frontier – the program

Now it's time to add some customized novelties. The use of the vectors in this section will be explained in the next section, again through the source code that uses them.

A trigger vector will force the program to try an alternate method to translate a mistranslated sentence. When the sentence has been identified and if its value in X2 **is** equal to 1, it triggers a deeper translation function as implemented here:

```
X2=[0,0,0,1,0,0,0,0,0,0,0,1]
```

0 and 1 are flags. Each value represents a line in X.

Note for developers: To use this method correctly, all the values of this vector should be set to 1. That will automatically use several alternate methods to translate Google Translate errors. A lot of work remains to be done here.

The case study is a transportation business. A transport phrase dictionary should be built. In this case, a general `phrase_translate` dictionary has been implemented with one expression, as shown in the following array.

```
phrase_translation=['','','','Il est agressif','','','','','','','','']
```

What remains to be done to fill up this dictionary ?

- Scan all the documents of the company—emails, letters, contracts, and every form of written documents.
- Store the words and sentences.
- Run an embedding Word2Vector program (see `Chapter 16`, *Improve the Emotional Intelligence Deficiencies of Chatbots*); it will find correlations between words. Add an expression correlation program to this search.
- Train the team to use the program to improve it by providing feedback (the right answer) in a learning interface when the system returns incorrect answers.

What Google Translate cannot do on a global scale, you can implement at a local scale to greatly improve the system.

k-nearest neighbor algorithm

No matter how you address a linguistic problem, it will always boil down to the word "context". When somebody does not understand somebody else, they say, *you took my words out of their context* or *that is not what I meant; let me explain...*

In `Chapter 16`, *Improve the Emotional Intelligence Deficiencies of Chatbots*, the embedding Word2Vector method will be explored. In any case, "proximity" and "nearness" remain the key concepts.

As explained before, in many cases, you cannot translate a word or expression without a lexical field. The difficulty remains proportional to the polysemy property as the program will show.

Using the **k-nearest neighbor (KNN)** algorithm as a classification method can prove extremely useful. In fact, any language interpretation (translation or chatbot) will have to use a context-orientated algorithm.

By finding the words closest (neighbors) to each other, KNN will create the lexical fields required to interpret a language. Even better, when provided with the proper datasets, it will solve the polysemy problem as shown in the upcoming sections.

The KNN algorithm

Generally, a word requires a context to mean something. Looking for "neighbors" close by provides an efficient way to determine where the word belongs.

KNN is supervised because it uses the labels of the data provided to train its algorithm. KNN, in this case, is used for classification purposes. For a given point p, KNN will calculate the distances to all other points. Then k represents the k-nearest neighbors to take into account.

Let's clear this up through an example. In English, the word "coach" can mean a trainer on a football field, a bus, or a railroad passenger car. Since the prototype is for a transportation company, "coach" will mostly be a bus that should not be confused with a trainer:

- **Step 1**: Parsing (examining in a detailed manner) texts with "coach" as a bus and "coach" as a trainer. Thus the program is searching for three target words: trainer, bus, and coach.
- **Step 2**: Finding some words that appear close to the target words we are searching. As recommended do the following:
  - Parse all the company documents you can use with a standard program
  - Use a Python function such as `if(ngram in the source) then store the data`

In this case, the `V1.csv` shown in the following output excerpt provided with the source code contains the result of such a parsing function:

```
broke,road,stopped,shouted,class
1,3.5,6.4,9,trainer
1,3.0,5.4,9,trainer
1,3.2,6.3,9,trainer
. . .
6.4,6.2,9.5,1.5,bus
2,3.2,9,1,bus
6.4,6.2,9.5,1.5,bus
. . .
3.3,7.3,3.0,2.5,coach
4.7,5.7,3.1,3.7,coach
2.0,6.0,2.7,3.1,coach
```

The program parsed emails, documents, and contracts. Each line represents the result of parsing of one document. The numbers represent the occurrences (number of times the word was present). The numbers have been "squashed" (divided again and again) to remain small and manageable.

Progressively, the words that came out with "trainer" were "shouted" more than "stopped." For a bus, "broke" (broken down as in breaking down), "road" and "stopped" appeared more than "shout."

"Coach" appeared on an average of "shouted", "stopped", "road" and broke because it could be either a trainer or a bus, hence the problem we face when translating this word. The polysemy (several meanings) of "coach" can lead to poor translations.

The KNN algorithm loaded the `V1.csv` file that contains the data to be trained and finds the following result:

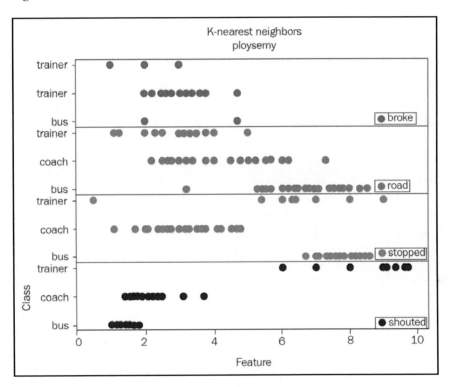

The `knn_polysemy.py` program determined the following:

- The verb "broke" in blue has a better chance of applying to a bus (*x* axis value >6) than to a trainer (*x* axis value <4). However, "coach" remains above trainer and below "bus" because it can be both.
- The word "road" follows the same logic as the blue chart.
- The verb "stopped" can apply to a trainer and more to a bus. "Coach" remains undecided again.

- The verb "shouted" applies clearly to a trainer more than a bus. "Coach" remains undecided again.

Note that the coordinates of each point in these charts are as follows:

- **y axis**: bus = 1, coach=2, trainer=3
- **x axis**: The value represents the "squashed" occurrence (the number of times the word appeared) values.

This is the result of the search of those words in many sources.

When a new point, a data point named P_n, is introduced in the system, it will find its nearest neighbor(s) depending on the value of k.

The KNN algorithm will calculate the Euclidean distance between P_n and all the other points from P_1 to P_{n-1} using the Euclidean distance formula. The k in KNN represents the number of "nearest neighbors" the calculation will take into account for classification purposes. The Euclidean distance (d_1) between two given points, for example, between $P_n(x1,y1)$ and $P_1(x2,y2)$, is:

$$d1(Pn, P1) = \sqrt[2]{(x1 - x2)^2 + (y1 - y2)^2}$$

Considering the number of distances to calculate, a function such as the one provided by sklearn.neighbors proves necessary.

The knn_polysemy.py program

The program imports the V1.csv file described before, prints a few lines, and prepares the labels in the right arrays in their respective x axis and y axis, as shown in this source code example.

```
import pandas as pd
from matplotlib import pyplot as plt
from sklearn.neighbors import KNeighborsClassifier
# Import data
df = pd.read_csv('V1.csv')
print (df.head())
# Classification labels
X = df.loc[:, 'broke':'shouted']
Y = df.loc[:, 'class']
```

Then the model is trained as shown in the following code:

```
# Trains the model
knn = KNeighborsClassifier()
knn.fit(X,Y)
```

Once the model is trained, a prediction is requested and is provided by the following code.

```
# Requesting a prediction
#broke and stopped are
#activated to see the best choice of words to fit these features.
# brock and stopped were found in the sentence to be interpreted.
# In X_DL as in X, the labels are : broke, road, stopped, shouted.
X_DL = [[9,0,9,0]]
prediction = knn.predict(X_DL)
print ("The prediction is:",str(prediction).strip('[]'))
```

This is the result displayed:

```
The prediction is: 'bus'
```

The initial data is plotted for visualization purposes, as implemented in the following code.

```
#Uses the same V1.csv because the parsing has
# been checked and is reliable as "dataset lexical rule base".
df = pd.read_csv('V1.csv')
# Plotting the relation of each feature with each class
figure, (sub1,sub2,sub3,sub4)=plt.subplots(4,sharex=True,sharey=True)
plt.suptitle('k-nearest neighbors')
plt.xlabel('Feature')
plt.ylabel('Class')
X = df.loc[:,'broke']
Y = df.loc[:,'class']
sub1.scatter(X, Y,color='blue',label='broke')
sub1.legend(loc=4, prop={'size': 5})
sub1.set_title('Polysemy')
X = df.loc[:,'road']
Y = df.loc[:,'class']
sub2.scatter(X, Y,color='green',label='road')
sub2.legend(loc=4, prop={'size': 5})
X = df.loc[:,'stopped']
Y = df.loc[:,'class']
sub3.scatter(X, Y,color='red',label='stopped')
sub3.legend(loc=4, prop={'size': 5})
X = df.loc[:,'shouted']
```

```
Y = df.loc[:,'class']
sub4.scatter(X, Y,color='black',label='shouted')
sub4.legend(loc=4, prop={'size': 5})
figure.subplots_adjust(hspace=0)
plt.show()
```

A compressed version of this program has been introduced in `Google_Translate_Customized.py` as shown here:

```
def knn(polysemy,vpolysemy,begin,end):
 df = pd.read_csv(polysemy+'.csv')
 X = df.loc[:,'broke':'shouted']
 Y = df.loc[:,'class']
 knn = KNeighborsClassifier()
 knn.fit(X,Y)
 prediction = knn.predict(vpolysemy)
 return prediction
```

The description is as follows:

- `polysemy` is the name of the file to read because it can be any file
- `vpolysemy` is the vector that needs to be predicted
- In future, in the to do list, `begin` should replace `broke` and `end` should replace `shouted` so that the function can predict the values of any vector
- The KNN classifier is called and the prediction returned

Implementing the KNN compressed function in Google_Translate_Customized.py

This program requires more time and focus because of the concepts of linguistics involved. The best way to grasp the algorithm is to run it in order.

Google Translate offers two translation methods, as shown in the following code:

```
#print('Phrase-Based Machine Translation(PBMT)model:base'): #m='base'
print('Neural Machine Translation model:nmt')
```

These are explained as follows:

- **Phrase-Based Machine Translation (PBMT)**: This translates the whole sequence of words. The phrase or rather phraseme (multi-word expression) is not always quite a sentence.

- **Neural Machine Translation (NMT)**: This uses neural networks such as **Recurrent Neural Network (RNN)**, which will be detailed later in this book. This method goes beyond the phraseme and takes the whole sentence into account. On the dataset presented in this chapter, this neural network method provides slightly better results.

Both methods, though interesting, still require the type of additional algorithms, among others, presented in this chapter. As you have seen so far, the subject is extremely complex if you take the lexical fields and structures of the many languages on our planet into account.

Step 1: Translating the X dataset line by line from English into French

The following code calls the translation function:

```
for xi in range(len(X)):
source=X[xi]
target1="fr";m='nmt'
result = g_translate(source,target1,m)
```

The code is explained here:

- `xi` is the line number in X.
- `source` is the `xi` line in X.
- `target1` is the target language, in this case, `fr` (French).
- `m` is the method (PBT or NMT) as described previously. In this case, `nmt` is applied.
- Then the Google Translate function is called as described earlier in this chapter. The result is stored in the `result` variable.

Step 2: Back translation

How can somebody know the correctness of a translation from language L1 to language L2 if L1 is the person's native language and L2 is a language the person does not understand at all?

This is one of the reasons, among others, that translators use back translation to check translations:

Translation = Initial translation from L1 to L2

Back translation = Translation back from L2 to L1

If the initial text is not obtained, then there is probably a problem. In this case, the length of the initial sentence L1 can be compared to the length of the same sentence translated back to L1. Back translation is called by the following code:

```
back_translate=result
back_translate = g_translate(back_translate,targetl,m)
print("source:",source,":",len(source))
print("result:",result)
print("target:",back_translate,":",len(back_translate))
```

Length comparison can be used to improve the algorithm :

Length of the initial n-gram = Length of back translation

If it's equal, then the translation may be correct. If not, it could be incorrect. More methods must be applied during each translation. In this case, the source (initial sentence) is compared to the back translation in the following code:

```
if(source == back_translate):
 print("true",)
 t+=1
else:
 f+=1;print("false")
```

- t is a true counter
- f is a false counter

The first line of X runs as follows:

```
source: Eating fatty food can be unhealthy. : 35
result: Manger de la nourriture grasse peut être malsain.
target: Eating fat food can be unhealthy. : 33
false
```

Eating fatty food is back translated as *eating fat food*, which is slightly wrong. Something may be wrong.

The French sentence sounds wrong too. Fatty food cannot be translated as such. Usually, the common sentence is *manger gras* meaning *eating (manger) fatty (gras)* which cannot be translated into English as such.

X[2] an X[3] come back as false as well.

At example X[4], I programmed a phrase-based translation using a trigger in the false condition in the following code.

```
else:
f+=1;print("false")
if(X2[xi]>0):
DT=deeper_translate(source,xi)
dt+=1
```

Since I did not write a complete application for this book but just some examples that can be extended in the future, I used `X2` as a trigger. If `X2[x1]>0`, then the `deeper_translation` function is activated.

Step 3: Deeper translation with phrase-based translations

`Deeper_translate` has two arguments:

- `source`: The initial sentence to translate
- `x1`: The target sentence

In this case, the problem to solve is an idiomatic expression that exists in English but does not exist in French:

```
source: He had a chip on his shoulder : 29
result: Il avait une puce sur son épaule
target: He had a chip on his shoulder : 29
false
```

To have *a chip on the shoulder* means to have an issue with something or somebody. It expresses some form of tension.

Google translated *chip* by assuming computer chip, or *puce* in French, which means both *computer chip* and *flea*. The translation is meaningless.

Chip enters three categories and should be labeled as such:

- Idiomatic expression
- Jargon
- Polysemy

At this point, the following function I created simulates the phrase-based solution to implement deeper translations.

```
def deeper_translate(source,index):
 dt=source
 deeper_response=phrase_translation[index]
 print("deeper translation program result:",deeper_response)
```

The deeper_translation looks for the translated sentence containing *chip* in the following phrase_translation array (list, vector, or whatever is necessary).

```
phrase_translation=['','','','Il est agressif','','','','','','','','']
```

The final result comes out with a translation, back translation, term search, and phrase translation. The following is the result produced, with comments added here before each line:

```
Initial sentence:
source: He had a chip on his shoulder : 29
Wrong answer:
result: Il avait une puce sur son épaule
The back-translation works:
target: He had a chip on his shoulder : 29
term: aggressif
false
ddeeper translation program result: Il est agressif
```

The question is, where did the term come from?

term comes from X1, a list of keywords that should be in the translation. X1 has been entered manually but it should be a list of possibilities resulting from a KNN search on the words in the sentence viewed as classes. This means that the sentence to be translated should have several levels of meaning, not just the literal one that is being calculated.

The actual true/false conditions contain the following deeper translation-level words to check:

```
if(source == back_translate):
 print("true")
 if((term not in words)and (xi!=4)):
 t+=1
 else:
 f+=1;print("false")
 if(X2[xi]>0):
 DT=deeper_translate(source,xi)
 dt+=1
```

In the present state of the prototype, only example four activates a phrase-based translation. Otherwise, true is accepted. If false is the case, the deeper translation is only activated for two cases in this sample code. The flag is in X2 (0 or 1).

`Deeper_translation` is called for either the phrase-based translation (described previously) or the KNN routine, which is activated if the phrase-based translation did not work.

If the translation did not work, an n-gram is prepared for the KNN algorithm, as shown in the following code:

```
if(len(deeper_response)<=0):
v1=0
for i in range(4):
ngram=V1[i]
if(ngram in source):
vpolysemy[0][i]=9
v1=1
```

`V1[i]` contains the keywords (n-grams) described in the preceding KNN algorithm for the transport lexical field, as shown in the following code:

```
V1=['broke','road','stopped','shouted','coach','bus','car','truck','break',
'broke','roads','stop']
```

The source (sentence to translate) is parsed for each n-gram. If the n-gram is found, the polysemy vector is activated with a nine value for that n-gram. The initial values are set to 0, as shown in the following code.

```
vpolysemy=[[0,0,0,0]]
```

The variable v1 is activated, which informs the program that V1.csv must be read for this case. An unlimited number of KNN references should be automatically created as described previously in the KNN section.

In this case, only v1 is activated. But after several months of working on the project for the company to customize their local needs, many other files should be created.

In this case, when `v1` is activated, it fills out the variables as follows.

```
if(v1>0):
polysemy='V1'
begin=str(V1[0]).strip('[]');end=str(V1[3]).strip('[]')
sememe=knn(polysemy,vpolysemy,begin,end)
```

- `polysemy` indicates the KNN file to open
- `begin` is the first label of the `V1` vector and `end` is the last label of the `V1` vector
- `sememe` is the prediction we expect

Now a condensed version of the KNN algorithm is called as described before for `knn.polysemy.py` is called in the following code:

```
def knn(polysemy,vpolysemy,begin,end):
 df = pd.read_csv(polysemy+'.csv')
 X = df.loc[:,begin:end]
 Y = df.loc[:,'class']
 knn = KNeighborsClassifier()
 knn.fit(X,Y)
 prediction = knn.predict(vpolysemy)
 return prediction
```

The example, in this case, is the polysemy feature of *a coach* as explained in the KNN section. The output will be produced as follows:

```
Source: The coach broke down, stopped and everybody was complaining : 59
result: L'entraîneur est tombé en panne, s'est arrêté et tout le monde se
plaignait
target: The coach broke down, stopped, and everyone was complaining : 59
term: bus
false
```

The translation is false because Google Translate returns *trainer* instead of *bus*.

The term *bus* is identical in English and French.

The KNN routine returned *bus* in English as the correct word to use when *broke down* and *stopped* were found as shown in the KNN section.

The goal of the rest of the source code in the `deeper_translate` function is to replace coach—the word increasing the polysemy feature to translate—by a better word (limited polysemy) to translate: `sememe`.

The `sememe` variable is initialized by the KNN function in the following code:

```
sememe=knn(polysemy,vpolysemy,beg in,end)
for i in range(2):
if(V1_class[i] in source):
replace=str(V1_class[i]).strip('[]')
sememe=str(sememe).strip('[]')
dtsource = source.replace(replace,sememe)
target1="fr";m='base'
result = g_translate(dtsource,target1,m)
print('polysemy narrowed result:',result,":Now true")
```

The function replaces *coach* by *bus* found by the KNN algorithm in the English sentence and then asks Google Translate to try again. The correct answer is returned.

 Instead of trying to translate a word with too many meanings (polysemy), the `deeper_translate` function first replaces the word with a better word (less polysemy). Better results will often be attained.

A frequentist error probability function is added to measure the performance, as shown in the following code:

```
def frequency_p(tnumber,cnumber):
ff=cnumber/tnumber #frequentist interpretation and probability
return ff
```

- `cnumber` is the number of false answers returned by Google Translate
- `tnumber` is the number of sentences translated
- `ff` gives a straightforward error (translation) probability, ETP

The function is called when a translation is false, or $f>0$, as implemented in the following code:

```
if(f>0):
B1=frequency_p(xi+1,f) #error detection probability before deep
translation
B2=frequency_p(xi+1,f-dt) #error detection probability after deep
translation
if(f>0):
print("ETP before DT",round(B1,2),"ETP with DT",round(B2,2))
else:
print('Insufficient data in probability distribution')
```

- B1 is the error (translation) probability (ETP) before the `deeper_translate` function is called
- B2 is the ETP after the `deeper_translate` function is called

At the end of the program, a summary is displayed, as shown in the following output:

```
print("------Summary------")
print('Neural Machine Translation model:nmt')
print('Google Translate:',"True:",t,"False:",f,'ETP',round(f/len(X),2))
print('Customized Google Translate:',"True:",t,"False:",f-
dt,'ETP',round((f-dt)/len(X),2))
a=2.5;at=t+a;af=f-a #subjective acceptance of an approximate result
print('Google Translate
acceptable:',"True:",at,"False:",af,'ETP',round(af/len(X),2))
#The error rate should decrease and be stabilized as the KNN knowledge base
increases
print('Customized Google Translate acceptable:',"True:",at,"False:",af-
dt,'ETP',round((af-dt)/len(X),2))
```

- A subjective acceptance of an approximate result has been added to increase the true probability.
- The error rate should decrease as the quality of the KNN knowledge base increases. In frequent probability theory, this means that a stabilized prediction rate should be reached.

Conclusions on the Google Translate customized experiment

The final error (translation) probability produced is interesting, as shown in the following output:

```
>>------Summary------
>>Neural Machine Translation model:nmt
>>Google Translate: True: 2 False: 8 ETP 0.67
>>Customized Google Translate: True: 2 False: 7 ETP 0.58
>>Google Translate acceptable: True: 4.5 False: 5.5 ETP 0.46
>>Customized Google Translate acceptable: True: 4.5 False: 4.5 ETP 0.38
```

Even with its NMT model, Google Translate is still struggling.

This provides great opportunities for AI linguists, as shown with some of the methods presented to improve Google Translate at a local level that could even go further.

This experiment with Google Translate shows that Google has just scratched the surface of real-life translations that sound right to the native speakers that receive these translations. It would take a real company project to get this on track with a financial analysis of its profitability before consuming resources.

The disruptive revolutionary loop

As you now see, Google Translate, like all artificial intelligence solutions, has limits. Once this limit has been reached, you are at the cutting edge.

 Cross the border into AI Frontierland; innovate on your own or with a team.

If you work for a corporation, you can create a revolutionary customized solution for hundreds of users. It does not have to go public. It can remain a strong asset to your company.

At some point or another, the revolutionary add-on will reach beyond the company and others will use it. It will become disruptive.

Finally, others will reach the limit of your now-disruptive solution. They will then innovate and customize it in their corporation as a revolutionary solution. This is what I call the disruptive revolutionary loop. It is challenging and exciting because it means that AI developers will not all be replaced soon by AutoAI bots!

Summary

Designing a solution does not mean it will be an invention, an innovation, revolutionary, or disruptive. But that does not really matter. What a company earns with a solution represents more than the novelty of what it sells as long as it is profitable. That is rule number #1. That said, without innovating in its market, that company will not survive through the years.

If a product requires quality for security reasons, it should remain in its invention state as long as necessary. If a product can produce sales at the low end of the market before its total completion, then the company should sell it. The company will acquire a reputation for innovation, get more money to invest, and take over the territory of its competitors.

Google Translate is a good example of disruptive marketing. As shown the theory, the model and even the cloud architecture are over 10 years old. But each time one of the hundreds of millions of users stumbles across it, it creates more disruption by hooking the user onto Google solutions. The user will come back again and again to view more advertisements, and everyone is happy!

Artificial intelligence has only begun. Google Translate has been around since 2006. However, the results still leave room for developers, linguists, and mathematicians to improve upon. Google has added a neural network, Google NMT, to improve translations by analyzing whole sentences. How long will it take to be really reliable? In the meantime, the next chapter will describe a CNN in more detail and provide ideas to help our community to move AI forward beyond the cutting edge into Frontierland. Before moving on to the next chapter, check your knowledge of some aspects of disruptive innovations.

Questions

1. It is better to wait until you have a top quality product before putting it on the market? (Yes | No)
2. Considering the investment made, a new product should always be priced high to reach the top segment of the market. (Yes | No)
3. Inventing a new solution will make it known in itself. (Yes | No)
4. Artificial Intelligence can solve most problems without using standard non-learning algorithms. (Yes | No)
5. Google Translate can translate all languages in a satisfactory way. (Yes | No)
6. If you are not creative, it is no use trying to innovate. (Yes | No)
7. If you are not a linguist, it is no use bothering with trying to improve Google Translate. (Yes | No)
8. Translation is too complicated to understand. (Yes | No)
9. Artificial intelligence has already reached its limits. (Yes | No)

Further reading

- The Harvard Business Review on disruptive innovations can be found here:
    - `https://hbr.org/2015/12/what-is-disruptive-innovation`
- Google Translate documentation can be found here:
    - `https://cloud.google.com/translate/docs/`
- Insights on English-French translations that can be extended to all languages with more difficulties:
    - `http://www.oneskyapp.com/blog/french-translation-challenges/`
    - `https://research.googleblog.com/2016/09/a-neural-network-for-machine.html`
    - `http://scikit-learn.org/stable/modules/neighbors.html#neighbors`

Getting Your Neurons to Work

9

The invention of convolutional neural networks (CNNs) applied to vision represents by far one of the most innovative achievements in the history of applied mathematics. With its multiple layers (visible and hidden), CNN has brought artificial intelligence from machine learning to deep learning.

A CNN relies on two basic tools of linear algebra: kernels and applying them to convolutions as described in this chapter. These tools have been used in applied mathematics for decades.

However, it took the incredible imagination of Yan LeCunn, Yoshua Bengio, and others—who built a mathematical model of several layers—to solve real-life problems with CNNs.

This chapter describes the marvels of CNNs, one of the pillars of Artificial Neural Networks (AANs). A CNN will be built from scratch, trained, and saved. The classification model described will detect production failures on a food-processing production line.

A Python Keras program running with TensorFlow on the backend will be built layer by layer and trained. Additional sample programs will illustrate key functions.

The following topics will be covered in this chapter:

- The differences between 1D, 2D, and 3D CNNs
- Adding layers to a convolutional neural network
- Kernels and filters
- Shaping images
- ReLU activation function
- Kernel initialization
- Pooling
- Flattening
- Dense layers

- Compiling the model
- Cross-entropy loss function
- Adam optimizer
- Training the model
- Saving the model
- Visualizing the PNG of a model

Technical requirements

You will need Python 3.6x 64-bit from `https://www.python.org/`:

You will also need the following libraries:

```
from keras.models import Sequential
from keras.layers import Conv2D
from keras.layers import MaxPooling2D
from keras.layers import Flatten
from keras.layers import Dense
from keras.preprocessing.image import ImageDataGenerator
from keras.models import model_from_json
from keras.models import save_model
from keras.models import load_model
from keras import backend as K
from pprint import pprint

import Numpy as np

import matplotlib.image as mpimg
import scipy.ndimage.filters as filter
import matplotlib.pyplot as plt
```

Programs, GitHub `Chapter09`:

- `CNN_STRATEGY_MODEL.py`
- `Edge_detection_Kernel.py`
- `ReLU.py`

Check out the following video to see the code in action:

`https://goo.gl/cGY1wK`

Defining a CNN

This section describes the basic components of a CNN. `01_CNN_SRATEGY_MODEL.py` will illustrate the basic CNN components the chapter used to build the case study model for a food-processing conveyor belt. CNNs constitute one of the pillars of deep learning (multiple layers and neurons).

In this chapter, a Keras neural network written in Python will be running on top of TensorFlow. If you do not have Python or do not wish to program, the chapter is self-contained with graphs and explanations.

Defining a CNN

A convolutional neural network takes an image, for example, and processes it until it can be interpreted.

For example, imagine you have to represent the sun with an ordinary pencil and a piece of paper. It is a sunny day, and the sun shines very brightly, too brightly. You put on a special pair of very dense sunglasses. Now you can look at the sun for a few seconds. You have just applied a color reduction filter, one of the first operations of a convolutional network. Then you try to draw the sun. You draw a circle and put some gray in the middle. You have just applied an edge filter. Finally, you go over the circle several times to make it easy to recognize, reducing the image you saw progressively into a representation of it. Now with the circle, some gray in the middle, and a few lines of the rays around it, anybody can see you drew a sun. You smile; you did it! You took a color image of the sun and made a mathematical representation of it as a circle, which would probably look something like this:

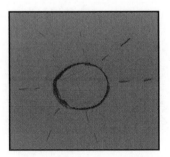

Mathematical representation of a circle

You just went through the basic processes of a convolutional network.

The word **convolutional** means that you transformed the image of the sun you were looking at into a drawing, area by area. But, you did not look at the whole sky at once. You made many eye movements to capture the sun, area by area, and you did the same when drawing. If you made a mathematical representation of the way you transformed each area from vision to your paper abstraction, it would be a kernel.

With that concept in mind, the following graph shows the successive mathematical steps to follow in this chapter's model for a machine to process an image just as you did. A convolutional network is a succession of steps that will transform what you see into a classification status. In your example, it would serve to find out whether your drawing represents the sun. This falls under the binary classification model (yes or no, 1 or 0).

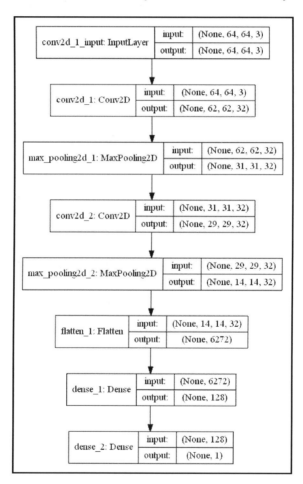

Notice that the size of the outputs diminishes progressively until the outputs reach 1, the binary classification status that will return (1 or 0). These successive steps, or layers, represent what you did when you went from observing the sun to drawing it. In the end, if we draw poorly and nobody recognizes the sun, it means that we have to go back to step 1 and change some parameters (weights in this case). That way, we train to represent the sun better until somebody says, "*Yes, it is a sun!*" That is probability = 1. Another person may say that it is not a sun (probability = 0; thus, more training would be required).

If you carry out this experiment of drawing the sun, you will notice that, as a human, you transform one area at a time with your eye and pencil. You repeat the way you do it in each area. That mathematical repetition you perform is your kernel. Using a kernel per area is the fastest way to draw. For us humans, in fact, it is the only way we can draw. A CNN is based on this process.

This section describes each component of this model. Hundreds of different models can be implemented. However, once you understand one model, you can implement the many others.

Initializing the CNN

The model used is a Keras `sequential()` model; it requires adding one layer at a time in a certain order with TensorFlow as the backend:

```
import matplotlib.pyplot as plt
import matplotlib.image as mpimg
import numpy as np
from keras.layers import Convolution2D, MaxPooling2D, Activation
from keras.models import Sequential
from keras.layers import Flatten
from keras.layers import Dense
from PIL import Image
from keras.preprocessing.image import ImageDataGenerator

model = Sequential()
```

The import libraries will be used for each layer of the model. The model can now be built.

Adding a 2D convolution

In the example of a drawing (image), we used our inbuilt human spacial module, working on a two-dimensional piece of paper with (x, y) coordinates. Two-dimensional relationships can be real-life images and also many other objects as described in this chapter. This chapter describes a two-dimensional network, although others exist:

- A one-dimensional CNN mostly describes a temporal mode, for example, a sequence of sounds (phonemes = parts of words), words, numbers and any other type of sequence
- A volumetric module is a 3D convolution, such as recognizing a cube or a video

In this chapter, a spatial 2D convolution module will be applied to images of different kinds. The main program, `CNN_STRATEGY_MODEL.py`, will describe how to build and save a model.

`classifier.add` will add a layer to the model. The name **classifier** does not represent a function but simply the arbitrary name that was given to this model in this particular program. The model will end up with *n* layers. Look at the following line of code:

```
classifier.add(Conv2D(32, (3, 3),input_shape = (64, 64, 3), activation = 'relu'))
```

This line of code contains a lot of information: the filters (applied with kernels), the input shape, and an activation function. The function contains many more options. Once you understand these in depth, you can implement other options one by one, as you deem necessary, for each project you have to work on.

Kernel

Just to get started, intuitively let's take another everyday model. This model is a bit more mathematical and closer to CNN's kernel representation. Imagine a floor of very small square tiles in an office building. You would like each tile of the floor to be converted from dirty to clean, for example. You can imagine a cleaning machine converting 3 x 3 small tiles (pixels) at a time from dirty to clean. You would laugh if you saw somebody come with 50 cleaning machines to clean all of the 32 x 32 tiles (pixels) at the same time. You know it would consume more resources, intuitively. Not only is a kernel an efficient way to filter but also a kernel convolution is a time-saving resource process. The single cleaning machine is the kernel (dirty-to-clean filter), which will save you that time to perform the convolution (going over all of the tiles to clean, 3 x 3 area by 3 x 3 area) of transforming the floor from dirty to clean.

In this case, 32 different filters have been added with 3 x 3 sized kernels:

```
classifier.add(Conv2D(32, (3, 3)...
```

The use of kernels as filters is the core of a convolutional network. (32, (3,3)) means (number of filters, (size of kernels)).

Intuitive approach

To understand a kernel intuitively, keep the sun and cleaning tiles examples in mind. In this section, a photograph of a cat will show how kernels work.

In a model analyzing cats, the initial photograph would look like this:

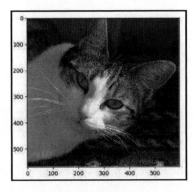

Cat photograph for model analyzing

On the first run of this layer, even with no training, an untrained kernel will transform the photograph.

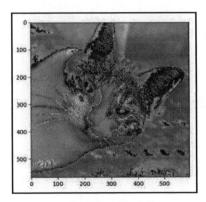

Cat photograph transformation

The first layer already has begun isolating the features of the cat. The edges have begun to appear: the cat's body, ears, nose, and eyes. In itself, this first filter (one of 32) with a size 3 x 3 kernel—in the first layer and with no training—already produces effective results.

Each subsequent layer will make the features stand out much better with smaller and smaller matrices and vectors until the program obtains a clear mathematical representation.

Developers' approach

Developers like to see the result first to decide how to approach a problem.

Let's take a quick, tangible shortcut to understand kernels through `Edge_detection_Kernel.py` with an edge detection kernel.

```
#I.An edge detection kernel
kernel_edge_detection = np.array([[0.,1.,0.],
[1.,-4.,1.],
[0.,1.,0.]])
```

The Kernel is a 3 x 3 matrix, like the cat example. But the values are preset, and not trained with weights. There is no learning here; only a matrix needs to be applied. The major difference with a CNN network is that it will learn how to optimize kernels itself through weights and biases.

`imp.bmp` is loaded, and the 3 x 3 matrix is applied to the pixels of the loaded image, area by area:

```
#II.Load image and convolution
image=mpimg.imread('img.bmp')[:,:,0]
shape = image.shape
```

The image before the convolution applying the kernel is the letter A (letter recognition):

Now the convolution transforms the image, as shown in the following code:

```
#III.Convolution
image_after_kernel =
filter.convolve(image,kernel_edge_detection,mode='constant', cval=0)
```

The edges of A now appear clearly in white, as shown in the following graph:

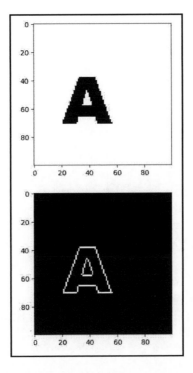

White edge of A is visible

The original image on top displayed a very thick A. In the preceding graph it displays a thin identifiable A feature through thin edges that a neural network can classify within a few mathematical operations. The first layers of a convolutional network train to find the right weights to generate the right kernel automatically.

Mathematical approach

The initial image has a set of values you can display, as follows:

```
#II.Load image
image=mpimg.imread('img.bmp')[:,:,0]
shape = image.shape
print("image shape",shape)
```

The code will print a numerical output of the image as follows:

```
image shape (100, 100)
image before convolution
[[255 255 255 ..., 255 255 255]
 [255 255 255 ..., 255 255 255]
 [255 255 255 ..., 255 255 255]
 ...,
```

The convolution filter is applied using `filter.convolve`, a mathematical function, to transform the image and filter it.

The convolution filter function uses several variables:

- The spatial index for the 3 x 3 kernel to apply; in this case, it must know how to access the data. This is performed through a spatial index, j, which manages data in grids. Databases also use spatial indexes to access data. The axes of those grids determine the density of a spatial index. Kernels and the image are convolved using j over W, the weights kernel.
- W is the weights kernel.
- I is the input image.
- k is the coordinate of the center of W. The default value is 0 in this case.

These variables then enter the `filter.convolve` function as represented by the following equation:

$$C_i = \sum_j I_{i+j-k} W_j$$

A CNN relies on kernels. Take all the time you need to explore convolutions through the three dimensions required to master AI: intuitive approach, development testing, and mathematical representation.

Shape

Shape defines the size of the image, which is 64 x 64 pixels (height x width), as shown here.

```
classifier.add(...input_shape = (64, 64, 3)...)
```

3 indicates the number of channels. In this case, 3 indicates the three parameters of an RGB color. Each number can have a given value of 0 to 255.

ReLu

Activation functions provide useful ways to influence the transformation of the input data weight bias calculations. Their output will change the course of a classification, a prediction, or whatever goal the network was built for. This model applies **rectified linear unit (ReLU)**, as shown in the following code:

```
classifier.add(..., activation = 'relu'))
```

ReLU activation functions apply variations of the following function to an input value:

$$f(x) = max\{0, x\}$$

The function returns 0 for negative values; it returns the positive values as x; it returns 0 for 0 values.

ReLU appears to be easier to optimize. Half of the domain of the function will return zeros. This means that when you provide positive values, the derivative will always be 1. This avoids the squashing effect of the logistic sigmoid function, for example. However, the decision to use one activation function rather than another will depend on the goal of each ANN model.

In mathematical terms, a rectified linear unit function will take all the negative values and apply 0 to them. And all the positive values remain unchanged.

The ReLu.py program provides some functions including a NumPy function to test how ReLu works.

You can enter test values or use the ones in the source code:

```
import numpy as np
nx=-3
px=1
```

nx expects a negative value and px expects a positive value for testing purposes for the relu(x) and lrelu(x) functions. Use the f(x) function if you wish to include zeros in your testing session.

The `relu(x)` function will calculate the ReLU value:

```
def relu(x):
if(x<0):ReLU=0
if(x>0):ReLU=1
return ReLU
```

In this case, the program will return the following result:

```
negative x= -3 positive x= 5
ReLU nx= 0
ReLU px= 5
```

The result of a negative value becomes 0, and the positive value remains unchanged. The derivative or slope is thus always one, which is practical in many cases and provides good visibility when debugging a CNN or any other ANN.

The NumPy function defined as follows will provide the same results.

```
def f(x):
 vfx=np.maximum(0,x)
 return vfx
```

Through trial and error, ANN research has come up with several variations of ReLU.

One important example occurs when many input values are negative. ReLu will constantly produce zeros, making gradient descent difficult if not impossible.

A clever solution was found using a leaky ReLU. A leaky ReLU does not return a zero for a negative value but a small value you can choose, 0.1 instead of 0, for example. See the following equation:

$$f(x) = max\{0.1, x\}$$

Now gradient descent will work fine. In the sample code, the function is implemented as follows:

```
def lrelu(x):
 if(x<0):lReLU=0.01
 if(x>0):lReLU=x
 return lReLU
```

Although many other variations of ReLUs exist, with this in mind, you have an idea of what it does.

Enter some values of your own, and the program will display the results as shown here:

```
print("negative x=",nx,"positive x=",px)
print("ReLU nx=",relu(nx))
print("ReLU px=",relu(px))
print("Leaky ReLU nx=",lrelu(nx))
print("f(nx) ReLu=",f(nx))
print("f(px) ReLu=",f(px))
print("f(0):",f(0))
```

The results will display the ReLU results as follows:

```
negative x= -3 positive x= 5
ReLU nx= 0
ReLU px= 5
Leaky ReLU nx= 0.01
```

Pooling

Pooling reduces the size of an input representation, in this case, an image. Max pooling consists of applying a max pooling window to a layer of the image:

```
classifier.add(MaxPooling2D(pool_size = (2, 2)))
```

This `pool_size` 2 x 2 window will first find the maximum value of the 2 x 2 matrix on the top left of the image matrix. This first maximum value is 4. It is thus the first value of the pooling window on the right.

Then the max pooling window hops over two squares and finds that 5 is the highest value. 5 is written in the max pooling window. The hop action is called a **stride**. A stride value of 2 will avoid overlapping although some CNN models have strides that overlap. It all depends on your goal. Look at the following diagram:

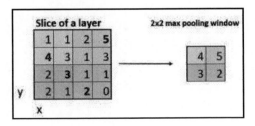

Pooling example

The output size has now gone from a 62 x 62 x 32 (number of filters) to a 31 x 31 x 32, as shown in the following diagram:

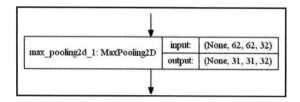

Output size changes (pooling)

Other pooling methods exist, such as average pooling, which will use the average of the pooling window and not the maximum value. This depends on the model and shows the hard work to put in to train a model.

Next convolution and pooling layer

The next two layers of the CNN repeat the same method as the first two described previously, and it is implemented as follows in the source code:

```
# Adding a second convolutional layer
print("Step 3a Convolution")
classifier.add(Conv2D(32, (3, 3), activation = 'relu'))
imp=classifier.input
outputs = [layer.output for layer in classifier.layers]

print("Step 3b Pooling")
classifier.add(MaxPooling2D(pool_size = (2, 2)))
```

These two layers have drastically downsized the input to 14 x 14 x 32, as shown in this diagram:

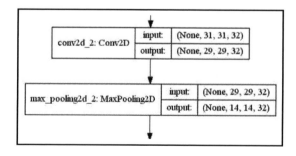

Convolution and pooling layer

The next layer can now flatten the output.

Flattening

The flattening layer takes the output of the max pooling layer and transforms into a vector of size $x * y * z$ in the following code:

```
# Step 4 - Flattening
print("Step 4 Flattening")
classifier.add(Flatten())
```

In this case, the layer vector will be *14 x 14 x 32 = 6,272*, as shown in the following diagram:

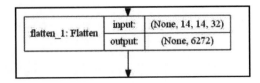

Flattening layer

This operation creates a standard layer with 6,272 very practical connections for the dense operations that follow. After flattening has been carried out, a fully connected, dense network can be implemented.

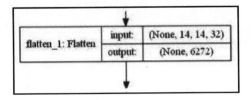

Flattening layer

Dense layers

Dense layers are fully connected. This has been made possible by the reductions in size calculated up to here, as shown before.

The successive layers in this sequential model have brought the size of the image down enough to use dense layers to finish the job. Dense 1 comes first, as shown here:

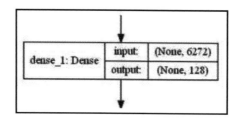

Dense layer

The flattening layer produced 14 x 14 x 32 size 6,272 layer with a weight for each input. If it had not gone through the previous layers, the flattening would have produced a much larger layer, and the features would not have been extracted by the filters. The result would produce nothing effective.

With the main features extracted by the filters through successive layers and size reduction, the dense operations will lead directly to a prediction using the ReLu on the dense 1 operation and the logistic sigmoid function on the dense operation.

Dense activation functions

This is how to apply the ReLU activation function.

The domain of the ReLU activation function is applied to the result of the first dense operation. The ReLU activation function will output the initial input for values >=0 and will output 0 for values <0:

$$f(input\ value) = max\{0,\ input\_value)$$

This is how to apply the logistic sigmoid activation function.

The logistic activation function applied to the second dense operation, as described in Chapter 2, *Think like a Machine*, will produce a value between 0 and 1:

$$LS(x)=\{0,1\}$$

We will now discuss the last dense layer after the LS activation function.

The last dense layer is size 1 and will classify the initial input, an image in this case:

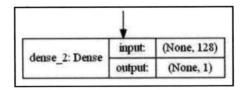

Dense layer 2

The layers of the model have now been added. Training can begin.

Training a CNN model

Training a CNN model involves four phases: compiling the model, loading the training data, loading the test data, and running the model through epochs of loss evaluation and parameter-updating cycles.

In this section, the choice of the theme of the training dataset will be a real-life case study from the food-processing industry.

The goal

The primary goal of this model consists of detecting production efficiency flaws on a food-processing conveyor belt. The use of CIFAR-10 (images) and MNIST (handwritten digit base) proves useful to understand and train some models (see Chapter 10, *Applying Biomimicking to Artificial Intelligence*). However, at one point, real-life datasets must be used to sell and implement deep learning and artificial intelligence in general.

The following photograph shows a section of the conveyor belt that contains an acceptable level of products, in this case, portions of chocolate cakes:

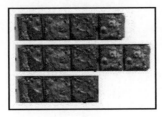

Portions of chocolate cake example

However, sometimes the production slows down, and the output goes down to an alert level, as shown in the following photograph:

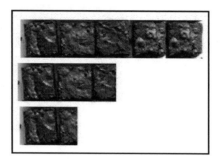

Portions of chocolate cake example

The alert-level image shows a gap that will slow down the packaging section of the factory dramatically.

Chapter 10, *Applying Biomimicking to Artificial Intelligence*, describes how this model can apply to the food-processing industry and be transferred to other applications.

Compiling the model

Compiling a Keras model requires a minimum of two options: a loss function and an optimizer. You evaluate how much you are losing and then optimize your parameters, just as in real life. A metric option has been added to measure the performance of the model. With a metric, you can analyze your losses and optimize your situation, as shown in the following code:

```
classifier.compile(optimizer = 'adam', loss = 'binary_crossentropy',
metrics = ['accuracy'])
```

Loss function

The loss function provides information on how far the state of the model *y1* (weights, biases) is from its target state *y*.

A description of the quadratic loss function precedes that of the binary cross-entropy functions applied to the case study model in this chapter.

Quadratic loss function

For gradient descent, see `Chapter 5`, *Manage the Power of Machine Learning and Deep Learning*. Let us refresh the concept. Imagine you are on a hill and want to walk down that hill. Your goal is to get to *y*, the bottom of the hill. Presently you are at *a*. Google Maps shows you that you still have to go a certain distance:

$$y - a$$

That formula is great for the moment. But now suppose you are almost at the bottom of the hill, and the person walking in front of you dropped a coin. You have to slow down now, and Google Maps is not helping much because it doesn't display such small distances that well. You open an imaginary application called **tiny maps** that zooms into small distances with a quadratic objective (or cost) function:

$$O = (y - a)2$$

To make it more comfortable to analyze, O is divided by 2, producing a standard quadratic cost function:

$$Cost = \frac{(y - a)^2}{2}$$

y is the goal. *a* is the result of the operation of applying the weights, biases, and finally the activation functions.

With the derivatives of the results, the weights and biases can be updated. In our hill example, if you move one meter (*y*) per step (*x*), that is much more than moving 0.5 meters (*y*) per step. Depending on your position on the hill, you can see that you cannot apply a constant learning rate (conceptually the length of your step); you adapt it just like Adam, the optimizer, does.

Binary cross-entropy

Cross-entropy comes in handy when the learning slows down. In the hill example, it slowed down at the bottom. But, remember, a path can lead you sideways, meaning you are momentarily stuck at a given height. Cross-entropy solves that by being able to function well with very small values (steps on the hill).

Suppose you have the following structure:

- Inputs is {x1, x2, ..., xn}
- Weights is {w1, w2, ..., wn}
- A bias (or sometimes more) is b
- An activation function(ReLU, logistic sigmoid, or other)

Before the activation, z represents the sum of the classical operations:.

$$z = \sum_{x_i} w_i x_i + b$$

Now the activation function is applied to z to obtain the present output of the model.

$$y1 = act(z)$$

With this in mind, the cross-entropy loss formula can be explained:

$$Loss = \frac{1}{n} \sum_{x} [y log y_1 + (1 - y) log(1 - y_1)]$$

In this function:

- n is the total number of items of the input training, with multiclass data. $M > 2$ means situations in which a separate loss of each class label is calculated. The choice of the logarithm base (2, e, 10) will produce different effects.
- y is the output goal.
- $y1$ is the present value, as described previously.

This loss function is always positive; the values have a minus sign in front of them, and the function starts with a minus. The output produces small numbers that tend to zero as the system progresses.

The loss function in Keras, which uses TensorFlow, uses this basic concept with more mathematical inputs to update the parameters.

A binary cross-entropy loss function is a binomial function that will produce a probability output of 0 or 1 and not a value between 0 and 1 as in standard cross-entropy. In the binomial classification model, the output will be 0 or 1.

In this case, the sum Σ is not necessary when *M (number of classes)* = 2. The binary cross-entropy loss function is then as follows:

$$Loss = -y log y_1 + (1 - y) log(1 - y_1)$$

The whole concept of this loss function method is for the CNN network to be used in specific real-life case studies described in the training dataset section and `Chapter 10`, *Applying Biomimicking to Artificial Intelligence*.

Adam optimizer

In the hill example, you first walked with big strides down the hill using momentum (larger strides because you are going in the right direction). Then you had to take smaller steps to find the object. You are adapting your estimation of your moment to your need; hence, the name **adaptive moment estimation (Adam)**.

Adam constantly compares the mean past gradients to present gradients. In the hill example, it compares how fast you were going.

The Adam optimizer represents an alternative to the classical gradient descent method or stochastic gradient descent method (see `Chapter 5`, *Manage the Power of Machine Learning and Deep Learning*). Adam goes further by applying its optimizer to random (stochastic) mini-batches of the dataset. This makes it a version of stochastic gradient descent.

Then, with even more inventiveness, Adam adds **root-mean-square deviation (RMSprop)** to the process by applying per-parameter learning weights. It analyzes how fast the means of the weights are changing (such as the gradients in our hill slope example) and adapts the learning weights.

Metrics

Metrics are there to measure the performance of your model. The metric function behaves like a loss function. However, it is not used to train the model.

In this case, the accuracy parameter was this:

```
...metrics = ['accuracy'])
```

Here, a value that descends towards 0 shows whether the training is on the right track and moves up to one when the training requires Adam function optimizing to set the training on track again.

Training dataset

The training dataset is available on GitHub, along with the installation instructions and explanations. The dataset contains the photo shown previously for the food-processing conveyor belt example.

The class A directory contains the acceptable level images of a production line that is producing acceptable levels of products. The class B directory contains the alert-level images of a production line that is producing unacceptable levels of products.

The number of images of the dataset is limited because of the following:

- For the purpose of training this limited industrial model, the images produced good results
- The training-testing phase runs faster to study the program

The goal of the model is to detect the alert levels as described in more detail in Chapter 10, *Applying Biomimicking to Artificial Intelligence,* when it will be applied to the trained images and generalized to similar ones.

Data augmentation

Data augmentation increases the size of the dataset by generating distorted versions of the images provided.

The ImageDataGenerator function generates batches of all images found in tensor formats. It will perform data augmentation by distorting the images (shear range, for example). Data augmentation is a fast way to use the images you have and create more virtual images through distortions:

```
train_datagen = ImageDataGenerator(re
scale = 1./255,
shear_range = 0.2,
zoom_range = 0.2,
horizontal_flip = True)
```

The code description is as follows:

- scale will rescale the input image if not 0 (or none). In this case, the data is multiplied by 1/255 before applying any other operation.
- shear_range will displace each value in the same direction determined, in this case by the 0.2. It will slightly distort the image at one point, giving some more virtual images to train.

- `zoom_range` is the value of zoom.
- `horizontal_flip` is set to true. This is a Boolean that randomly flips inputs horizontally.

`ImageDataGenerator` provides many more options for real-time data augmentation, such as rotation range, height shift, and more.

Loading the data

Loading the data goes through the `train_datagen` preprocessing `image` function (described previously) and is implemented in the following code:

```
print("Step 7b training set")
training_set = train_datagen.flow_from_directory(directory+'training_set',
target_size = (64, 64),
batch_size = batchs,
class_mode = 'binary')
```

The flow in this program uses the following options:

- `flow_from_directory` sets the directory + 'training_set' to the path where the two binary classes to train are stored.
- `target_size` will all be resized to that dimension. In this case, it is 64 x 64.
- `batch_size` is the size of batches of data. The default value is 32 and set to 10 in this case.
- `class_mode` determines the label arrays returned: none or categorical will be 2D one-hot encoded labels. In this case, binary returns 1D binary labels.

Testing dataset

The testing dataset flow follows the same structure as the training dataset flow described previously. However, for testing purposes, the task can be made easier or more difficult depending on the choice of the model. This can be done by adding images with defects or noise. This will force the system into more training and the project team into more hard work to fine-tune the model. Data augmentation provides an efficient way of producing distorted images without adding images to the dataset. Both methods, among many others, can be applied at the same time when necessary.

Data augmentation

In this model, the data only goes through rescaling. Many other options could be added to complicate the training task to avoid overfitting, for example, or simply because the dataset is small:

```
print("Step 8a test")
test_datagen = ImageDataGenerator(rescale = 1./255)
```

Loading the data

Loading the testing data remains limited to what is necessary for this model. Other options can fine-tune the task at hand:

```
print("Step 8b testing set")
test_set = test_datagen.flow_from_directory(directory+'test_set',
target_size = (64, 64),
batch_size = batchs,
class_mode = 'binary')
```

Never underestimate dataset fine-tuning. Sometimes, this phase can last weeks before finding the right dataset and arguments.

Training with the classifier

The classifier has been built and can be run:

```
print("Step 9 training")
print("Classifier",classifier.fit_generator(training_set,
steps_per_epoch = estep,
epochs = ep,
validation_data = test_set,
validation_steps = vs))
```

The `fit_generator` function, which fits the model generated batch by batch, contains the main hyperparameters to run the training session through the following arguments in this model. The hyperparameters settings determine the behavior of the training algorithm:

- `training_set` is the training set flow described previously.
- `steps_per_epoch` is the total number of steps (batches of samples) to yield from the generator. The variable used in the following code is estep.

- epochs is the variable of the total number of iterations made on the data input. The variable used is ep in the preceding code.
- validation_data=test_set is the testing data flow.
- validation_steps=vs is used with the generator and defines the number of batches of samples to test as defined by vs in the following code:

```
estep=100 #10000
vs=100 #5000
ep=2 #50
```

While the training runs, measurements are displayed: loss, accuracy, epochs, information on the structure of the layers, and the steps calculated by the algorithm.

Here is an example of the loss and accuracy data displayed:

```
Epoch 1/2
 - 23s - loss: 0.1437 - acc: 0.9400 - val_loss: 0.4083 - val_acc: 0.5000
Epoch 2/2
 - 21s - loss: 1.9443e-06 - acc: 1.0000 - val_loss: 0.3464 - val_acc:
0.5500
```

Saving the model

Saving the model, in this case, consists in saving three files.

First, we will discuss the model file.

model.json, saved in the following code, contains serialized data describing the model itself without weights. It contains the parameters and options of each layer. This information is very useful to fine-tune the model:

```
# serialize model to JSON
model_json = classifier.to_json()
with open("model.json", "w") as json_file:
json_file.write(model_json)
```

More details on this file are provided in the next section, in the *Loading the model* section.

- Now we will discuss the weights file.

  To understand a CNN model or any other type of model, having access to the weights can provide useful information when nothing works or to solve some of the problems that come up.

The weights are saved in the following code:

```
# serialize weights to HDF5
classifier.save_weights("model.h5")
from keras.utils import plot_model
plot_model(classifier, to_file='model.png',show_shapes=True )
print("Model saved to disk")
```

- A `model.png` file

This file will display the layers of the model, the input, and output sizes. The following code saves the model in `.png` format:

```
from keras.utils import plot_model
plot_model(classifier,
to_file=directory+'model/model.png',show_shapes=True )
print("Model saved to disk")
```

`model.png` can prove useful to understand how the model went down from the number of pixels of the original image to the binary classification layer containing the classification status. The diagram at the beginning of the chapter, displaying the layers and input/output values, was produced by this program.

Next steps

The model has been built and trained. In `Chapter 10`, *Applying Biomimicking to artificial intelligence*, it will be loaded and implemented in the food-processing company and other similar applications through transfer leaning.

Summary

Building and training a CNN will only succeed with hard work at choosing the model, the right dataset, and hyperparameters. Convolutions, pooling, flattening, dense layers, activations, and optimizing parameters (weights and biases) form solid building blocks to train and use a model.

Training a CNN to solve an everyday industrial problem helps sell AI to a manager or a sales prospect. In this case, using the model to help a food-processing factory solve a conveyor belt productivity problem takes artificial intelligence a step further into everyday corporate life.

Saving the model provides a practical way to use it by loading it and applying it to new images to classify them. This chapter concluded after we had trained and saved the model.

Chapter 10, *Applying Biomimicking to Artificial Intelligence,* will dive deeper into how neural networks were inspired by human neural networks and describe how to analyze a neural network with TensorBoard tools in more detail. Then the saved model CNN model will be applied to the food industry through transfer learning; and we'll expand far beyond those limits through domain learning in Chapter 11, *Conceptual Representation Learning.*

Questions

1. A CNN can only process images. (Yes | No)
2. A kernel is a preset matrix used for convolutions. (Yes | No)
3. Does pooling have a pooling matrix or is it random?
4. The size of the dataset always has to be large. (Yes | No)
5. Finding a dataset is not a problem with all the available image banks on the web. (Yes | No)
6. Once a CNN is built, training it does not take much time. (Yes | No)
7. A trained CNN model applies to only one type of images. (Yes | No)
8. A quadratic loss function is not very efficient compared to a cross-entropy function. (Yes | No)
9. The performance of a deep learning CNN does not a represent a real issue with modern CPUs and GPUs. (Yes | No)

Further reading and references

Keras provides good explanations and samples from its community that will lead the reader to interesting aspects of CNNs and practical issues:

- https://blog.keras.io/building-powerful-image-classification-models-using-very-little-data.html
- https://keras.io/activations/
- https://github.com/keras-team/keras/issues/

10
Applying Biomimicking to Artificial Intelligence

Heated debates have been raging over biomimicking humans in various forms of artificial intelligence for decades. In the 1940s, McCulloch and Pitts (see Chapter 2, *Think like a Machine*) came up with a *human* neuron. Then Rosenblatt came up with a *human* perceptron (Chapter 4, *Become an Unconventional Innovator*). Mimicking humans seemed to have conquered the world of artificial intelligence networks. Then, in 1969, Minsky slowed research down by proving that a perceptron could not solve the XOR problem (see Chapter 4, *Become an Unconventional Innovator*).

Today, deep learning networks reproduce our mental way of thinking. Neuroscientists now work on representing our physical brain functions. These two different fields, though different, still inspire each other.

Neural networks provide good mathematical models of how our mind works on the number side. Mental images on top of words and numbers to describe them constitute the larger part of human thinking. As shown in Chapter 8, *Revolutions Designed for Some Corporations and Disruptive Innovations Small to Large Companies*, the uncharted territory of AI must be continuously explored. Our community needs to make progress in this direction with tools that will represent our way of thinking at higher levels.

The following topics will be covered in this chapter:

- Showing how a neural network mimics the way a human mind represents images
- Showing how to use the graph structure representation of deep learning neural networks to build and debug them
- Exploring how the mathematical model neural networks are built today with TensorBoard

- Understanding the cutting edge of the mathematical data flow graph structures such as TensorFlow, which will lead us to the cutting edge of biomimicking humans with these methods
- The difference between neuroscience computing models and deep learning models
- A TensorFlow MNIST classifier
- TensorBoard dashboards
- TensorFlow scopes, placeholders, variables, and other components
- Analyzing accuracy, cross-entropy, and weights during the training process

This chapter prepares the reader for Chapter 11, *Conceptual Representation Learning*, which goes right over the cutting edge and into the uncharted territory of **conceptual representation learning** (CRL) and meta networks.

Technical requirements

You will need Python 3x with the following libraries:

```
from keras.preprocessing.image import load_img
from keras.preprocessing.image import img_to_array
import matplotlib.pyplot as plt
import keras
import numpy as np
from keras.preprocessing.image import ImageDataGenerator
from keras.models import model_from_json
from keras.models import load_model
import numpy as np
import cv2
from PIL import Image

import json
from pprint import pprint
```

For the TensorFlow classifier you will need this:

```
from __future__ import absolute_import
from __future__ import division
from __future__ import print_function

#argparse is a Python command-line parsing module
import argparse
import os
import sys
```

Programs from GitHub can be found here:

- `https://github.com/PacktPublishing/Artificial-Intelligence-By-Example/blob/master/Chapter10/Google_Tensor_Classifier.py`
- `https://github.com/PacktPublishing/Artificial-Intelligence-By-Example/blob/master/Chapter10/Tensorboard_reader.py`

Check out the following video to see the code in action:

`https://goo.gl/psrZzS`

Human biomimicking

In this section, the difference between neuroscience research on the brain and deep learning research on the mind has led to TensorFlow and TensorBoard. With TensorFlow, our representation of image recognition in a mathematical graph data flow structure has become an extremely efficient model. TensorBoard provides a visual representation of what we are building.

TensorFlow represents how our mind recognizes images (and other elements). TensorBoard enables our minds to visualize that representation and improve it.

TensorFlow, an open source machine learning framework

TensorFlow relies on graph representations of data flow. The graph computes dependencies between operations.

When using Keras, as in Chapter 9, *Getting Your Neurons to Work*, the details of graphs and sessions do not appear. However, to compare our brain with deep learning, some details need to be examined using `Google_Tensor_Classifier.py`, which classifies MNIST handwritten images and saves the summaries (information about the model).

The graph of the program is as shown in the following diagram:

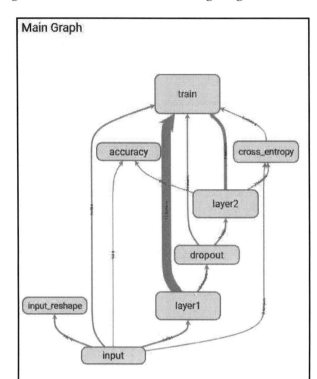

Main graph

The nodes (labels with lines around them) and edges (lines connecting the labels) constitute the graph structure. The graph structure, in turn, indicates how the operations are connected to one another.

Chapter 9, *Getting Your Neurons to Work,* described all the nodes except dropout. In that chapter, two **dense layer**s were added to the classifier model. Sometimes, when constructing a dense layer, some elements will not be trained. This is done to avoid overfitting (see the transfer learning section later), which means that the model will know the training set too well and will not adapt efficiently to new objects (images, sounds, or words). This method, among others, helps to fine-tune the model during the regularization process (methods to avoid overfitting, for example). The dropout regularization rate can be added to the graph structure. Dropouts can be used several times and at different places in a given model.

Does deep learning represent our brain or our mind?

After reading `Chapter 9`, *Getting Your Neurons to Work*, and the beginning of this chapter, it takes a major effort to see how a data flow graph structure representing a deep learning model has something to do with our brain.

We have gone a long way since the McCulloch-Pitts neuron proudly tried to represent a neuron in our brain (see `Chapter 2`, *Think like a Machine*).

Neuroscience research that tries to create computer models of our brain is now named **computational neuroscience**. Computer systems represent mathematical models of the brain. Understanding how the brain works remains a critical field of physiology, nervous system, cognitive ability, and related research. It sometimes provides some ideas for deep learning networks.

But a TensorFlow data flow graph structure represents a deep learning model (or other models) of a mathematical solution to a classification or prediction problem.

Deep learning networks have moved away from neuroscience, and their source of inspiration comes mostly from other areas such as applied mathematics (linear algebra), probability, information theory (for entropy, for example), and other related fields.

Naturally, the media hype surrounding artificial intelligence seems a bit confusing because marketing managers make some impressive demonstrations of robots that look like us, try to act like us, and speak like us. No matter what those systems do right now, their learning model relies on data flow graph structures based mostly on mathematical representations of our mind, not our brain.

Our mind thinks and reasons. When we think, we do not feel our brain following through neurons and synapses. Our mind acts like a high-level API between what we want to do and what our brain does for us.

To improve our API, we create abstract representations of almost everything around us. We try to make sense of the chaos of all the incoming perceptions and thoughts we have to manage. The better our representations, the more efficient our API to our brain will become.

The TensorFlow data flow graph structure represents our mind's API relaying information seamlessly to our brain, not our brain structure which we cannot see when we think.

In the end, a deep learning network is a way of mimicking humans.

Biomimicking in deep learning simply mimics **a deep learning network** and imitates our **mathematical mind**.

A TensorBoard representation of our mind

Nobody is sure how our brains can learn quickly with a few labeled objects and then apply the patterns to unsupervised, unlabeled learning. Research on the subject will eventually produce some helpful explanations.

In the meantime, we must rely on our mind's representations to train deep learning models.

If you want to follow the explanations of this chapter through programs, first run `Google_Tensor_Classifier.py` as it is. Then run `Tensorboard_reader.py` and follow the instructions in the code to open TensorBoard in your browser. Otherwise, the chapter is self-contained with source code excerpts and screenshots.

Many of the concepts in the `TensorFlow_Classifier.py` program were explained in `Chapter 9`, *Getting your Neurons to Work*.

The following sections focus on TensorFlow objects that are not always perceived with high-level interfaces, such as Keras.

Input data

This program is a **unit-testing** model. It uses unit-testing data in a unit-testing deep learning model:

```
mnist =
input_data.read_data_sets(FLAGS.data_dir,one_hot=True,fake_data=FLAGS.fake_
data)
```

`fake_data` refers to an MNIST (handwritten digits) unit testing dataset and `FLAGS` are command-line parameters (in this case, path information).

`one-hot=true` means that the labels of the data must be encoded into values. The presence of labels means that this is a supervised (with labels) training classifier and not an unsupervised (training with no labels) classifier.

The one-hot function (see `Chapter 2`, *Think like a Machine)* will encode labels into distinct one-hot values as in the following example:

```
# [[0, 1, 0, 0, 0, 0, 0, 0, 0, 0],
# [0, 0, 0, 0, 0, 0, 0, 0, 0, 1],
# ...]
```

The inputs are stored in placeholders as in the following code:

```
with tf.name_scope('input'):
x = tf.placeholder(tf.float32, [None, 784], name='x-input')
y_ = tf.placeholder(tf.float32, [None, 10], name='y-input')
```

Placeholders are **not** just variables that will be filled up later. They define one of the fundamental building blocks of a TensorFlow data flow graph. They contain the methods that will be used in the **node** they are in.

`tf.name.scope` is the title label that will appear on TensorBoard, and `name` identifies this element of the graph. The following graph displays the input scope with its two inputs.

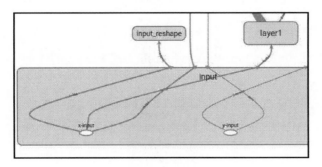

Input scope with two inputs

TensorBoard provides the visual representation our mind needs to think. The placeholders are in nodes that are linked to other operations through edges (lines) that represent the flow of data and operations.

`y-input`, as you can see, skips the `input_reshape` function in layer 1; it goes straight to the deeper operations of cross-entropy and accuracy as explained later.

`x-input` goes through the input-reshape node in the following code:

```
with tf.name_scope('input_reshape'):
image_shaped_input = tf.reshape(x, [-1, 28, 28, 1])
tf.summary.image('input', image_shaped_input, 10)
```

`tf.name_scope` defines the title, `input_reshape`. The interesting part is the details you will see if you click on the node and drill down, as shown in the following screenshot:

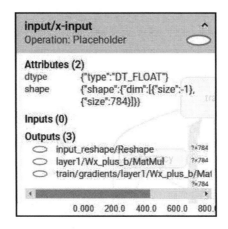

Input description

We usually represent the `reshape` function as one channel output when in fact there are three outputs to subsequent operations.

The **IMAGES** section provides a visual representation of the reshaped images as shown in the following screenshot:

Reshaped image

When building a model, TensorBoard visual representations of the reshaped images can prove helpful for validation purposes.

Layer 1 – managing the inputs to the network

As with the Keras, implementing a layer in TensorFlow is done in a few lines but with TensorBoard. Layer 1 takes `x-input`, calculates a weight, applies an activation function and sends its output directly to the training node and also to the dropout node. The following graph represents layer 1 and the result of the operations to **OUTPUTS** (dropout and train):

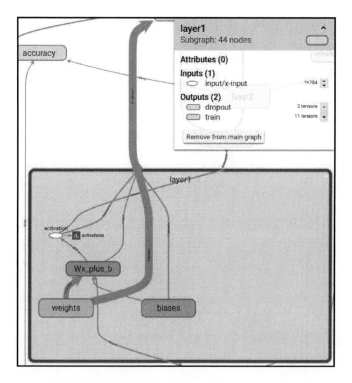

Layer 1 and result of operations

Weights, biases, and preactivation

The core lines have the visual representation TensorBoard `tf.name_scope` functions as described before as implemented in the following code.

```
with tf.name_scope(layer_name):
# This Variable will hold the state of the weights for the layer
with tf.name_scope('weights'):
weights = weight_variable([input_dim, output_dim])
variable_summaries(weights)
with tf.name_scope('biases'):
biases = bias_variable([output_dim])
variable_summaries(biases)
with tf.name_scope('Wx_plus_b'):
preactivate = tf.matmul(input_tensor, weights) + biases
tf.summary.histogram('pre_activations', preactivate)
activations = act(preactivate, name='activation')
tf.summary.histogram('activations', activations)
return activations
```

Notice the `tf.summary` module in the code. Not only does TensorFlow provide a data flow graph structure with the `tf.name.scope` that shows the operation, but also the values of the variables are stored with `tf.summary`. It stores the structure of the operations as well.

The values themselves can be viewed in following charts:

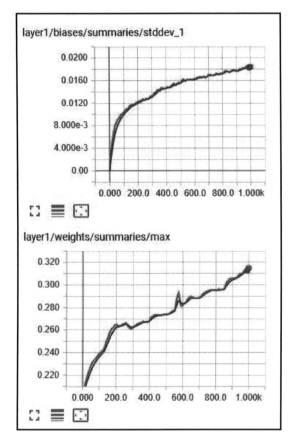

Data flow graph

Each chart has its statistics described in a `summary` function that defines the information needed to fine-tune and debug a model.

`def variables_summaries(var)` contains a list of very useful pieces of information. The following Python source code contains comments that provide information on the variables defined:

```
#Defining many summaries for TensorBoard Visualization of:
# a)weights that will send weights to this function
:variable_summaries(weights)
# b)biases that will send biasesto this function:
variable_summaries(biases)
# TensorBoard will then display charts of summaries described as follows on
the related
# TensorBoard dashboards
# These weight and bias summaries provide a clear view, in TensorBoard of
the direction
# the values are taking during training.It will help fine-tune the
hyperparameters when
# things go wrong or training does not go fast enough.
def variable_summaries(var):
with tf.name_scope('summaries'):
mean = tf.reduce_mean(var) #the mean of the elements of a tensor
tf.summary.scalar('mean', mean)
with tf.name_scope('stddev'):
stddev = tf.sqrt(tf.reduce_mean(tf.square(var - mean)))#var-mean will be
displayed
tf.summary.scalar('stddev', stddev) # calculates the standard deviation of
the input
tf.summary.scalar('max', tf.reduce_max(var)) #calculates the maximum of the
elements in the tensor
tf.summary.scalar('min', tf.reduce_min(var)) #calculates the minimum of the
elements in the tensor
tf.summary.histogram('histogram', var) # summarizes var for the histogram
tab on TensorBoard
```

With this number of quality controls, exploring TensorBoard will provide deep insights into the neural network.

Displaying the details of the activation function through the preactivation process

We often focus on the activation function in a layer. However, when a system fails and we have to debug it, having a peek at the preactivation function sometimes provides effective clues on what is going wrong. To visualize the preactivation output shown in the following graph, click on **Wx_plus_b** in layer 1, which shows that many events are influencing the training process:

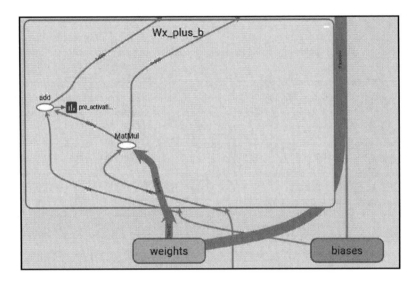

preactivation output

Several notable operations occur with `Wx_plus_b`:

- The weights and biases are connected to the training process, which is continuously modifying them; this happens even before the `MatMul` operation. Several tensors are sent to the training node and `Matmul`.
- The `Matmul` operation carries out the multiplications (Wx). But its output sends information to the training node and produces an output for the `add` node.
- The `add` node itself sends its output to the activation function and also to the preactivation data to the histogram summary so that we can analyze the behavior of this hidden layer.

Now when we click on the **HISTOGRAMS** section on TensorBoard, we can visualize the evolution of weight and bias training in the following diagrams:

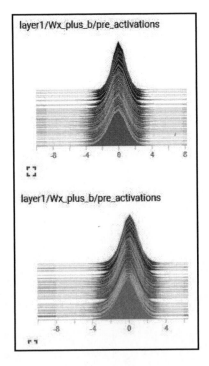

Evolution of weight and bias training

In this model, the preactivation diagrams show a smooth Gaussian-like bell (peak in the middle and similar slopes on each side). When building a model, everything seems fine. But if the curves become erratic and training the model fails, these histograms will provide critical information.

You can zoom in and check the values if necessary as shown in the following screenshot:

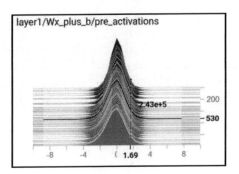

Evolution (Zoom in)

TensorBoard makes hidden layer intermediate values visible, which enhances our mental representation of a model.

In a real-life project, if the activation node goes wrong, checking the preactivation status of the layer eliminates a possible cause of design errors.

The activation function of Layer 1

The activation function of this model the is ReLU function (see `Chapter 9`, *Getting Your Neurons to Work*).

When we peek into its structure, once again we see that it is not just an activation function in a sequential process. Its output goes to the dropout and training nodes with complex intermediate calculations as shown in the following description of the activation function:

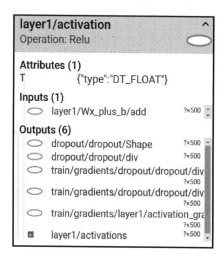

Activation function description

TensorBoard provides us with yet another visual representation to control the distribution of preactivation and, in this case, activations. The **DISTRIBUTIONS** section enables us to detect anomalies in the activation phase once we have verified that the preactivation functions produce acceptable results.

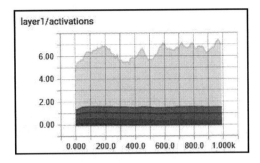

Visual representation complex node and edge structure

The visual representation of the complex node and edge structure of a TensorFlow data flow graph come in handy when design errors slow a project down.

Dropout and Layer 2

Dropouts and the designing of a layer were explained previously.

However, let us focus on some features of the dropout node: dropout keep probability and the outputs in the following diagram.

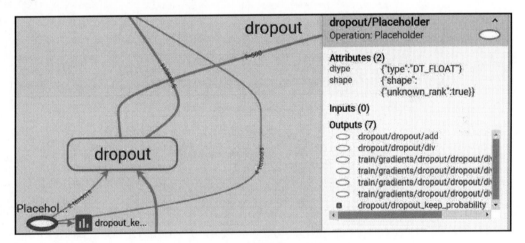

Dropout node

A dropout keep probability plays an overfitting reduction role. The probability leads to dropping neurons during the training process. The scaling is done automatically. Furthermore, this dropout feature is turned on and off during testing:

```
with tf.name_scope('dropout'):
keep_prob = tf.placeholder(tf.float32)
tf.summary.scalar('dropout_keep_probability', keep_prob)
dropped = tf.nn.dropout(hidden1, keep_prob)
```

TensorBoard receives the information through the `summary.scalar` and can be viewed in the following **SCALARS** section:

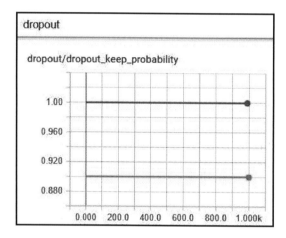

SCALARS view

Layer 2

The graph structure of layer 2 is the same as that of layer 1.

However, there are notable output differences in the connections (edges) to other nodes:

- Layer 1 sends an output to the drop node and the layer 2 node
- Layer 2 now sends its output to the training node, the accuracy node, and the cross-entropy node as shown in TensorBoard

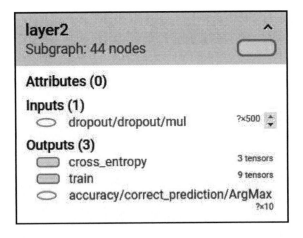

Layer 2 description

Measuring the precision of prediction of a network through accuracy values

The accuracy node contains two parts: correct prediction and accuracy. The output value is not sent to the training node but the correct predictions (see next section, *Correct prediction*) part of it is used by cross-entropy. Accuracy measures the performance of the system. You can stop training by limiting the number of epochs hyperparameter if you estimate that the accuracy is sufficient to achieve your goals. Or you can use accuracy to fine-tune the training model to increase its rate faster by modifying the hyperparameters or the design of your model.

Correct prediction

The following code implements `correct_prediction`, which uses an `argmax` function.

```
with tf.name_scope('accuracy'):
with tf.name_scope('correct_prediction'):
correct_prediction = tf.equal(tf.argmax(y, 1), tf.argmax(y_, 1))
```

`tf.argmax` will output the index of the largest value of the input tensors. This simplifies the task considerably by avoiding the need to manage scores of values. When things go wrong—and they often do in real-life projects—we can go back to the preceding nodes and debug the data flow or improve the design of the data flow graph structure.

When accuracy fails to meet expectations, TensorBoard provides us with a two-dimensional debugging approach: fine-tune the data flow graph structure itself and also explore the data flow values that the node operations produce and send to other nodes through the edges.

The following graph of the `correct_prediction` node has two inputs. The first one is the `y-input`, which comes straight from the input node. The second input is the output of layer 2, which has processed the `x-input` input that came from its preceding nodes and is communicating with the core training and cross-entropy nodes as well.

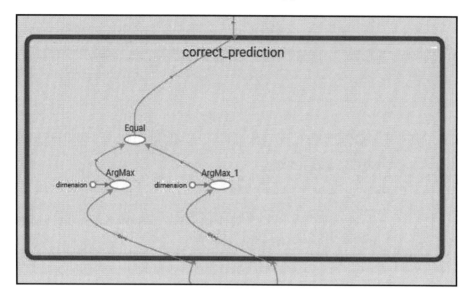

correct_prediction graph

`argmax` is applied separately to both inputs and sent to the accuracy node, and correct predictions are used by the cross-entropy node.

accuracy

The `accuracy` uses the output of the correct prediction to compute the mean of the elements of the tensor in the following code:

```
with tf.name_scope('accuracy'):
accuracy = tf.reduce_mean(tf.cast(correct_prediction, tf.float32))
tf.summary.scalar('accuracy', accuracy)
```

`tf.reduce.mean` calculates the mean in a standard way. For example, the mean of 2 and 4 is 3. Reducing the values of the input gives a good picture of how the model is doing during training without overloading the designer with too many values to analyze, as shown in the following diagram:

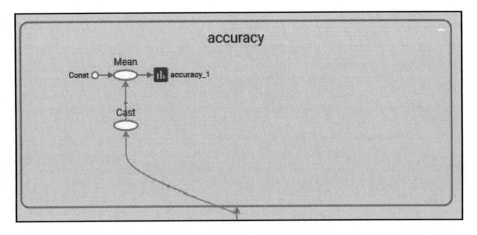

Accuracy scalar

The accuracy scalar is sent to `accuracy`, which can be viewed in the following screenshot of the **SCALARS** section.

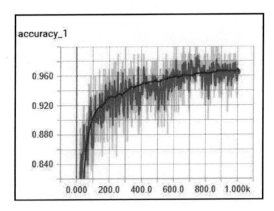

SCALARS section

You will notice that the accuracy values go up and up until we almost reach a **1** top score value.

Take another good look. This rarely happens in real-life projects.

 Accuracy fails to increase in many real-life projects without hard work and analysis.

Bad accuracy will tell you to go back and do the following:

- Check the data flow—initial datasets, initial hyperparameters, and any value that you can check and change in the data flow
- Check the data flow graph structure to find flaws and improve them

Then start the training process again.

Cross-entropy

Cross-entropy was described in Chapter 9, *Getting Your Neurons to Work*. The first input comes from layer 2, the result of the preceding nodes computing x-input. The second input, y-input, comes directly from the input node, as implemented in the following code:

```
with tf.name_scope('total'):
cross_entropy = tf.reduce_mean(diff)
tf.summary.scalar('cross_entropy', cross_entropy)
```

TensorFlow measures its progression as shown in the cross_entropy_1 and accuarcy_1 charts that follow:

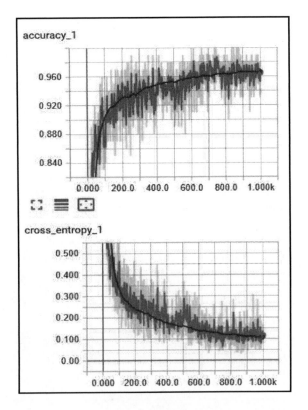

cross_entropy_1 and accuracy_1 charts

Note how nicely the value of cross-entropy goes down a nice gradient (slope) as the loss function as the training progresses. This curve shows that the errors are being reduced. Then note how nicely the accuracy curve goes up as the errors diminish.

Think about it. In real-life projects, the cross-entropy completely slows down at one point while accuracy becomes erratic. The effect of this will be limited because cross-entropy takes the correct predictions into account.

However, more often than not, hard work needs to be put in when facing our implementations.

Training

As in Chapter 9, *Getting Your Neurons to Work,* an algorithm with adaptive learning rates trains the model. The Adam algorithm using a cross-entropy loss function just like Chapter 9, *Getting Your Neurons to Work,* as shown here:

```
with tf.name_scope('train'):
train_step = tf.train.AdamOptimizer(FLAGS.learning_rate).minimize(
cross_entropy)
```

 The similarity between the Keras model in Chapter 9, *Getting Your Neurons to Work,* and this TensorFlow model does not come as a surprise since Keras uses TensorFlow as a backend.

The train node has several inputs from other nodes for its Adam optimizer—cross-entropy, layer2, dropout, layer1, and x-input, as shown in the following graph:

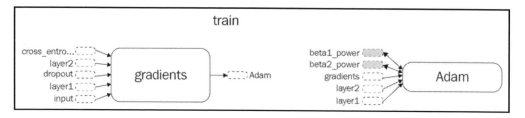

Train node

At this point, TensorFlow provides all the necessary information to build and debug the model.

 Drill down into all the nodes in this model on the **GRAPHS** dashboard. Explore all of the information about all the other sections: **SCALARS**, **IMAGES**, **DISTRIBUTIONS**, and **HISTOGRAMS** provided by this unit testing program. The more you know when things go wrong, the faster you will correct them.

Optimizing speed with Google's Tensor Processing Unit

Exploring a unit-testing model represents an effort on our part. Now, imagine having to build a model that is 10 times this size. Training the model to find out where and why things went wrong may prove time consuming.

Google has come up with an innovation: a **Tensor Processing Unit** (**TPU**). Google Search, Google Translate, and Google Photos use a TPU to speed up computations.

Making that available to us on its data centers will make a difference. TensorBoard already has a key function you might want to explore while building a complex and time-consuming model. This function is the TPU Compatibility option on TensorBoard (see the following screenshot).

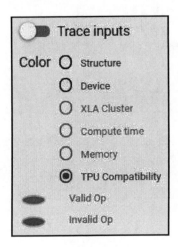

TPU Compatibility

Click on **TPU Compatibility** (this chapter used the **Structure** option until now).

The following graph will now display the levels of TPU compatibility of each node (green + red proportions):

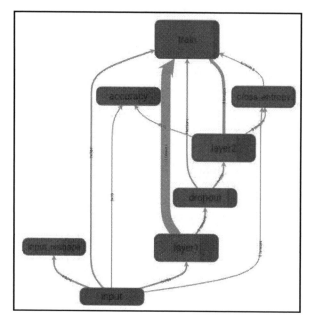

TPU compatibility of each node

This means that, in future when you are designing a complex model, you should keep an eye on TPU compatibility if you are going to consume a lot of CPU/GPU.

TensorBoard also provides the following list, for example, to display each level you are drilling down to:

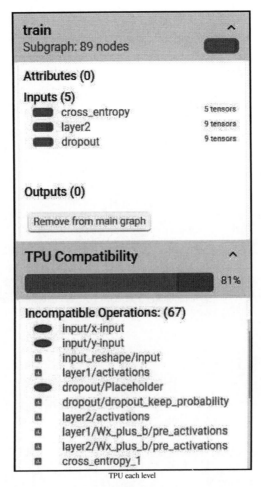

TPU each level

Even if you do not have access to a TPU, the read nodes will signal where you have to be careful. You may want to optimize the model before even starting to train it.

One of the main nodes to keep an eye on is the training node that contains the Adam optimizer, as shown in the following screenshot:

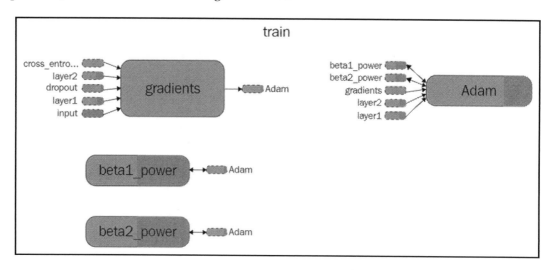

As models grow larger and larger, optimization will become a key field. Teams will have to optimize data graph structures, data flows, and machine configuration, including network speeds (and balancing).

Summary

The TensorFlow model represented in TensorBoard contains several basic building blocks of ANNs, whether they are CNNs, RNNs such as LTSM networks, or other forms. All of these models rely on numerical computation in one form or the other: weights, biases, `matmul` operations, activation functions (logistic sigmoid, ReLU, or others), layers, optimizers, loss functions, and more. All of these tools belong to the field of applied mathematics.

This approach has been around for decades. However, as time goes by, linguists, philosophers, historians, and many more people fascinated by AI will bring new ideas, new programming languages, interfaces, and APIs. Focus on the core concepts, not the tools, and you will always be able to keep up to date and innovate.

Biomimicking humans will inevitably be extended to conceptual representation learning, the fascinating world of our video-clipped minds.

Complex projects require conceptual representation.

Chapter 11, *Conceptual Representation Learning,* will lead you into the uncharted territory of conceptual representation learning.

Questions

1. Deep learning and machine learning mean the same thing. (Yes | No)
2. Deep learning networks mostly reproduce human brain functions (Yes | No)
3. Overfitting is unacceptable. (Yes | No)
4. Transfer learning can save the cost of building another model. (Yes | No)
5. Training a corporate model on MNIST is enough to implement it on a production line, for example. (Yes | No)
6. Exploring artificial intelligence beyond the cutting edge is not necessary. It is easier to wait for the next ideas that are published. (Yes | No)
7. Some researchers have reproduced all the physical and biological reasoning functions of the human brain in robots. In fact, some robots have human brain clones in them. (Yes | No)
8. Artificial general intelligence software, a program that can adapt to any human function (natural language processing, image processing, or sound streams) better than a human, already exists in some labs. (Yes | No)
9. Training deep learning networks has become a quick and easy task. (Yes | No)

Further reading

More on TensorFlow graphs and layers can be found here:

- https://www.tensorflow.org/programmers_guide/graphs
- https://www.tensorflow.org/tutorials/layers

11
Conceptual Representation Learning

Artificial intelligence has just begun its long tryst with human intellect. Chapter 9, *Getting Your Neurons to Work*, showed the possibilities of a CNN built with Keras. Chapter 10, *Applying Biomimicking to Artificial Intelligence*, reproduced what humans use the most to represent a problem: visualization.

Understanding cutting-edge machine learning, and deep learning theory only marks the beginning of your adventure. The knowledge you have acquired should help you become an AI visionary. Take everything you see as opportunities and see how it can fit in your projects. Reach the limits and skydive beyond them.

This chapter focuses on decision-making and visual representations and explains the motivation leading to **conceptual representation learning (CRL)** and **meta models (MM)**, which form **CRLMMs**. I developed this CRLMM method successfully for **automatic planning and scheduling (APS)** software (see Chapter 12, *Automated Planning and Scheduling*) for corporate projects. I also used this CRLMM method for cognitive NLP chatbots (see Chapter 15, *Cognitive NLP Chatbots*, and Chapter 16, *Improve the Emotional Intelligence Deficiencies of Chatbots*).

To plan, humans need to visualize necessary information (events, locations, and so on) and more critical *dimensions such as concepts*. A human being thinks in *mental images*. When we think, mental images flow through minds with numbers, sounds, odors, and sensations, transforming our environment into fantastic multidimensional representations similar to video clips.

The following topics will be covered in this chapter:

- An approach to CRLMM in three steps: transfer learning, domain learning, and the motivation for using CRLMM. Over the years, I've successfully implemented CRL in C++, Java, and logic programming (Prolog) in various forms on corporate sites. In this chapter, I used Python to illustrate the approach with the Keras **Convolutional Neural Network (CNN)** built in `Chapter 9`, *Getting Your Neurons to Work.*

- Transfer learning using the Keras model trained in `Chapter 9`, *Getting Your Neurons to Work,* to generalize image recognition.

- Domain learning to extend image recognition trained in one field to another field.

- Possible use of GANs (Generative Adversarial Networks) to produce CRL datasets.

- The use (or not) of Autoencoders.

Technical requirements

Python 3.6x 64-bit from `https://www.python.org/`:

Packages and modules:

```
from keras.models import model_from_json
from keras.models import load_model
from keras.models import Sequential
from keras.layers import Conv2D
from keras.layers import MaxPooling2D
from keras.layers import Flatten
from keras.layers import Dense
from keras.preprocessing.image import ImageDataGenerator
from keras.models import save_model
from keras import backend as K
from pprint import pprint

import Numpy as np
import matplotlib.image as mpimg
import scipy.ndimage.filters as filter
import matplotlib.pyplot as plt
```

Programs in GitHub `Chapter11`:

- `EAD_CNN_MODEL.py`
- `CNN_STRATEGY_MODEL.py`
- `CNN_TDC_TRAINING.py`
- `CNN_TDC_STRATEGY.py`

Check out the following video to see the code in action:

`https://goo.gl/e7p9Lg`

Generate profit with transfer learning

When it comes to reasoning and thinking in general, we use mental images with some words. Our thoughts contain concepts, on which we build solutions. The trained model of `Chapter 9`, *Getting Your Neurons to Work*, can now classify images of a certain type. In this section, the trained model will be loaded and then generalized through transfer learning to classify similar images.

The motivation of transfer learning

Transfer learning provides a cost-effective way of using trained models for other purposes within the same company, such as the food processing company described in `Chapter 9`, *Getting Your Neurons to Work*. This chapter describes how this food processing company used the model for other similar purposes.

The company that succeeds in doing this will progressively generalize the use of the solution. By doing so, inductive abstraction will take place and lead to other AI projects, which proves gratifying to the management of a corporation and the teams providing the solutions.

Inductive thinking

Induction uses inferences to reach a conclusion. For example, a food processing conveyor belt with missing products will lead to packaging productivity problems. If insufficient amounts of products reach the packaging section, this will slow down the whole production process.

By observing similar problems in other areas of the company, inferences from managers will come up, such as, *If insufficient amounts of products flow through the process, production will slow down.*

Inductive abstraction

The project team in charge of improving efficiency in the company needs to find an *abstract representation* of the problem to implement a solution through organization or software. This book deals with the AI side of solving the problem. Organizational processes need to define how AI will fit in with several on-site meetings.

The problem AI needs to solve

In this particular case, each section of the factory has an optimal production rate defined per hour or per day, for example. The equation of an **optimal production rate (OPR)** per hour can be summed up as follows:

$$OPR : min(p(s)){<}{=}opr{<}{=}max(p(s))$$

Where:

- p is the production rate of a given section (different production departments of a factory) s.
- $p(s)$ is the production rate of the section.
- $min(p(s))$ is the historical minimum (trial and error over months of analysis). Under that level, the whole production process will slow down.
- $max(p(s))$ is the historical maximum. Over that level, the whole production process will slow down as well.
- OPR is the optimal production rate.

The first time somebody sees this equation, it seems difficult to understand. The difficulty arises because one has to visualize the process, which is the goal of this chapter. Every warehouse, industry, and service uses production rates as a constraint to reach profitable levels.

Visualization requires representation at two levels:

- Ensuring that if a packaging department is not receiving enough products, it will have to slow down or even stop sometimes.
- Ensuring that if a packaging department receives too many products, it will not be able to package them. If the input is a conveyor belt with no intermediate storage (present-day trends), then it will have to be slowed down, slowing down or stopping the processes before that point.

In both cases, slowing down production leads to bad financial results and critical sales problems through late deliveries.

In both cases, an OPR gap is a problem. To solve it, another level of abstraction is required. First, let's separate the OPR equation into two parts:

$$OPR >= min(p(s))$$
$$OPR <= max(p(s))$$

Now let's find a higher control level through variance variable v:

$$vmin = |OPR - min(p(s))|$$
$$vmax = |OPR - max(p(s))|$$

v min and *v max* are the absolute values of the variance in both situations (not enough products to produce and too many to produce respectively).

The final representation is through a single control, detection, and learning rate (Greek gamma letter):

$$\Gamma = max(vmin, vmax)$$

This means that the variance between the optimal production rate of a given section of a company and its minimum speed (products per hour) will slow the following section down. If too few cakes (*vmin*), for example, are produced, then the cake packaging department will be waiting and stopping. If too many cakes are produced (*vmax*), then this section will have to slow down or stop. Both variances will create problems in a company that cannot manage intermediate storage easily, which is the case with the food processing industry.

With this single Γ parameter, Chapter 9, *Getting Your Neurons to Work*, Keras CNN, can start teaching a fundamental production concept: what a physical gap is.

The Γ gap concept

Teaching the CNN the gap concept will help it extend its thinking power to many fields:

- A gap in production, as explained before
- A gap in a traffic lane for a self-driving vehicle to move into
- Any incomplete, deficient area
- Any opening or window

Let's teach a CNN the Γ gap concept, **or simply Γ**. To achieve that goal, the CNN Keras model that was trained and saved in `Chapter 9`, *Getting Your Neurons to Work*, now needs to be loaded and used. To grasp the implications of the Γ concept, imagine the cost of not producing enough customer orders or having piles of unfinished products everywhere. The financial transposition of the physical gap is a profit **variance** on set goals. We all know the pain those variances lead to. Understanding and solving the Γ-gap problem will constitute a primary goal in `Chapter 12`, *Automated Planning and Scheduling.*

Loading the Keras model after training

The technical goal is to load and use the trained CNN Keras model and then use the same model for other similar areas. The practical goal is to teach the CNN how to use the Γ **concept** to enhance the thinking abilities of the scheduling, chatbot, and other applications.

Loading the model has two main functions:

- Loading the model to compile and classify new images without training the model
- Displaying the parameters used layer by layer and displaying the weights reached during the learning and training phase

Loading the model to optimize training

A limited number of headers suffice to read a saved model with `READ_CNN_MODEL.py,` as implemented in the following lines:

```
from keras.models import model_from_json
from keras.models import load_model
import json
from pprint import pprint
```

```
#Direction containing the model file
directory='dataset/'
print("directory",directory)
```

The .json model saved is now loaded from its file as shown here:

```
#_____LOAD MODEL_____
json_file = open(directory+'model/model.json', 'r')
loaded_jsonf = json_file.read()
loaded_json=json.loads(loaded_jsonf)
json_file.close()
print("MODEL:")
pprint(loaded_json)
```

I used the pprint function in the following code instead of print to obtain a *pretty print* formatted display of the model:

```
print("MODEL:")
pprint(loaded_json)
```

Reading the model is not a formality. The output of the program will help you train the model. Each layer starts with a marker. In this case, class name: indicates one of the layers added. For example, Conv2D in the following output provides vital information on the parameters and additional options of that layer:

```
MODEL:
{'backend': 'tensorflow',
 'class_name': 'Sequential',
 'config': [{'class_name': 'Conv2D',
 'config': {'activation': 'relu',
 'activity_regularizer': None,
 'batch_input_shape': [None, 64, 64, 3],
 'bias_constraint': None,
 'bias_initializer': {'class_name': 'Zeros',
 'config': {}},
 'bias_regularizer': None,
 'data_format': 'channels_last',
 'dilation_rate': [1, 1],
 'dtype': 'float32',
 'filters': 32,
 'kernel_constraint': None,
 'kernel_initializer': {'class_name': 'VarianceScaling',
 'config': {'distribution': 'uniform',
 'mode': 'fan_avg',
 'scale': 1.0,
 'seed': None}},
 'kernel_regularizer': None,
```

```
'kernel_size': [3, 3],
'name': 'conv2d_1',
'padding': 'valid',
'strides': [1, 1],
'trainable': True,
'use_bias': True}},
```

Each parameter contains very useful information. For example, `'padding':'valid'` means that padding has not been applied (no padding). In this model, the number and size of the kernels provide satisfactory results without padding and the shape decreases to the final status layer (classification) as shown here:

```
initial shape (570, 597, 4)
lay: 1 filters shape (568, 595, 3)
lay: 2 Pooling shape (113, 119, 3)
lay: 3 filters shape (111, 117, 3)
lay: 4 pooling shape (22, 23, 3)
lay: 5 flatten shape (1518,)
lay: 6 dense shape (128,)
lay: 7 dense shape (1,)
```

However, suppose you want to control the output shape of a layer so that the spatial dimensions do not decrease faster than necessary. One reason could be that the next layer will explore the edge of the image and that we need to explore them with kernels that fit in the shape.

In that case, a padding of size 1 can be added with 0 values as shown in the following matrix:

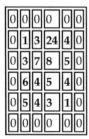

A padding of size 2 would add two rows and columns around the initial shape.

With that in mind, fine-tuning your training model by adding as many options as necessary will improve the quality of the results. The weights can be viewed by extracting them from the saved model file layer by layer, as shown in the following code snippet:

```
#_____ LOAD WEIGHTS_____

loaded_model=model_from_json(loaded_jsonf)
loaded_model.load_weights(directory+"model/model.h5")
print("WEIGHTS")
for layer in loaded_model.layers:
    weights = layer.get_weights() # list of numpy arrays
    print(weights)
```

Analyzing the weights used by the program will provide useful information about the way the optimizing process was carried out by the program. Sometimes, a program will get stuck, and the weights might seem off track. After all, a CNN can contain imperfections like any other program.

A look at the following output, for example, can help understand where the system went wrong:

```
WEIGHTS
[array([[[[-0.1005416 , -0.08582606, -0.058176 , 0.11453936, 0.04511052,
  0.05389464, 0.03316241, 0.10681037, 0.08743957, 0.0007824 ,
  0.09682989, 0.01926496, -0.00474238, -0.05053157, -0.07657856,
  -0.10017087, -0.08425587, 0.06652132, 0.04018607, 0.13323469,
  0.12131914, -0.11700463, -0.09595016, -0.08730403, -0.06408932,
  -0.0613227 , 0.13427697, -0.08226932, 0.09776273, 0.00540088,
  -0.02313543, -0.03464791],
```

 Much has been written about how to build CNNs and little about how to maintain them. This program provides one of the many tools to repair problems.

Loading the model to use it

Loading the model with `CNN_CONCEPT_STRATEGY.py` to use it requires more headers. I played it safe and loaded whatever would be needed to save the time otherwise spent in crashing and looking for imports as shown here:

```
from keras.preprocessing.image import load_img
from keras.preprocessing.image import img_to_array
import matplotlib.pyplot as plt
import keras
```

```
import numpy as np
from keras.preprocessing.image import ImageDataGenerator
from keras.models import model_from_json
from keras.models import load_model
import numpy as np
import cv2
from PIL import Image
```

Loading the `.json` file and weights is done by using the same code as in the `READ_CNN_MODEL.py` described previously. Once you load it, compile the model with the `model.compile` function, as follows:

```
# __compile loaded model
loaded_model.compile(loss='binary_crossentropy', optimizer='rmsprop',
metrics=['accuracy'])
```

The model used for this case study and the image identification function has been implemented in two parts. First, we're loading and resizing the image with the following function, for example:

```
def identify(target_image):
 filename = target_image
 original = load_img(filename, target_size=(64, 64))
 #print('PIL image size',original.size)
 plt.imshow(original)
 plt.show()
 numpy_image = img_to_array(original)
 arrayresized = cv2.resize(numpy_image, (64,64))
 #print('Resized',arrayresized)
 inputarray = arrayresized[np.newaxis,...] # extra dimension to fit model
```

Keras expects another dimension in the input array to predict, so one is added to fit the model. In this case study, one image at a time needs to be identified. These little details are time-savers in the development phase.

I added the following two prediction methods and returned one:

```
#___PREDICTION___
 prediction1 = loaded_model.predict_proba(inputarray)
 prediction2 = loaded_model.predict(inputarray)
print("image",target_image,"predict_proba:",prediction1,"predict:",predicti
on2)
 return prediction1
```

Two prediction methods are there because, basically, every component needs to be checked in a CNN during a project's implementation phase to choose the best and fastest ones. To test `prediction2`, just change the `return` instruction.

Once a CNN is running, it can prove difficult to find out what went wrong. Checking the output of each layer and component while building the network saves fine-tuning time once the full-blown model produces thousands of results.

The following example detects product **Γ gaps** on a conveyor belt in a food processing factory. The program loads the first image stored in the `classify` directory to predict its value. The program describes the prediction:

```
MS1='productive'
MS2='gap'

s=identify(directory+'classify/img1.jpg')
if (int(s)==0):
 print('Classified in class A')
 print(MS1)
```

The program displays (optional) the shaped image, such as the following frame, which shows that the conveyor belt has a sufficient number of products at that point:

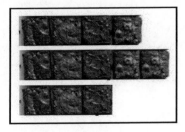

Output (shaped image)

The program then makes and displays its prediction 0, meaning no real gap has been found on the conveyor belt on this production line:

```
directory dataset/
Strategy model loaded from training repository.
image dataset/classify/img1.jpg predict_proba: [[ 0.]] predict: [[ 0.]]
Classified in class A
productive
Seeking...
```

`Seeking...` means it is going to analyze the second image in the classify direction. It loads, displays, and predicts its value as shown in the following frame:

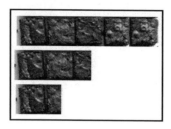

Output (shaped image)

The prediction (*value = 1*) correctly detected gaps on the conveyor belt, as shown in the following output:

```
image dataset/classify/img2.jpg predict_proba: [[ 1.]] predict: [[ 1.]]
Classified in class B
gap
```

Now that the predictions of the CNN have been verified, the implementation strategy needs approval. A convolutional neural network contains marvels of applied mathematics. CNNs epitomize deep learning in themselves. A researcher could easily spend hundreds of hours studying them.

However, applied mathematics in the business world requires profitability. As such, the components of CNNs appear as ever-evolving concepts. Added kernels, activation functions, pooling, flattening, dense layers, and compiling and training methods act as a starting point for architectures, not as a finality.

Using transfer learning to be profitable or see a project stopped

At one point, a company will demand results or shelve the project. If a spreadsheet represents a faster and a sufficient solution, a deep learning project will face potential competition and rejection. Many engineers learning artificial intelligence will have to assume the role of standard SQL reporting experts before accessing real AI projects.

Transfer learning appears as a solution to the present cost of building and training a CNN program. Your model might just pay off that way. The idea is to get a basic AI model rolling profits in fast for your customer and management. Then you will have everybody's attention. To do that, you must define strategies.

Defining the strategy

If a deep learning CNN expert, for example, our friend Pert Ex, comes to a top manager saying that this CNN model can classify CIFAR-10 images of dogs, cats, cars, plants, and more, the answer will be, *So what? My 3-year-old child can too. In fact, so can my dog!*

The IT manager in that meeting might even blurt out something like, *We have all the decision tools we need right now, and our profits are increasing. Why would we invest in a CNN?*

The core problem of marketing AI to real-world companies is that it relies upon the belief in the necessity of a CNN in the first place. Spreadsheets, SQL queries, standard automation, and software do 99% of the job. Most of the time, it does not take a CNN to replace many jobs; just an automated spreadsheet, a query, or standard and straightforward software is enough. Jobs have been sliced into simple-enough parts for decades to replace humans with basic software.

Before presenting a CNN, Pert Ex has to find out how much the company can earn using it. Pert has found an area with a quick win to show the power of the system in a cost-effective way.

Understanding, designing, building, and running a CNN does not mean much regarding business. All the hard work we put in to understanding and running these complex programs will add up to nothing if we cannot prove that a solution will generate profit. Without profit, the implementation costs cannot be recovered, and nobody will listen to a presentation about even a fantastic program.

Pert Ex describes the example in the previous section applied to this food processing company.

Applying the model

At the food processing company, one of the packaging lines has a performance problem. Sometimes, randomly, some of the cakes are missing on the conveyor belt, as shown in the following frame:

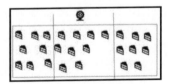

Food processing company example

Pert explains that to start a cost-effective project, a cheap webcam could be installed over the conveyor belt. It'll take a random sample picture every 10 seconds and process it to find the holes as shown in the interval between the two blue lines. If a hole is detected, it means some cakes have not made it to the conveyor belt (production errors).

 Pert estimates that a 2% to 5% productivity rate increase could be obtained by automatically sending a signal to the production robot when some cakes are missing.

The CEO decides to try this system out and approves a prototype test budget.

Making the model profitable by using it for another problem

The food processing experiment on the conveyor belt turns out to work well enough with dataset type d_1 and the CNN model M to encourage generalization to another dataset, d_2, in the same company.

Transfer learning consists of going from $M(d_1)$ to $M(d_2)$ using the same CNN model M, with some limited, cost-effective additional training. Variations will appear, but they will be solved by shifting a few parameters and working on the input data following some basic dataset preparation rules:

- **Overfitting**: When the model fits the training data quickly with 100% accuracy, this may or not be a problem. In the case of classifying holes on the conveyor, belt overfitting might not prove critical. The shapes are always the same and the environment remains stable. However, in an unstable situation with all sorts of different images or products, then overfitting will limit the effectiveness of a system.
- **Underfitting**: If the accuracy drops down to low levels such as 20%, then the CNN or any other model will not work. The datasets and parameters need optimizing. Maybe the number of samples needs to be increased for $M(d_2)$, or reduced, or split into different groups.
- **Regularization**: Regularization, in general, involves the process of finding how to fix the generalization problem of $M(d_2)$, not the training errors of $M(d_2)$. Maybe an activation function needs some improvements, or the way the weights have been implemented require attention.

There is no limit to the number of methods you can apply to find a solution, just like standard software program improvement.

Where transfer learning ends and domain learning begins

Transfer learning can be used for similar types of objects, or images in this case as explained. The more similar images you can train within a company with the same model, the more the **return on investment (ROI)** it will produce and the more this company will ask you for more AI innovations.

Domain learning takes a model such as the one described in Chapter 9, *Getting your Neurons to Work,* and that describe in this chapter to generalize it. The generalization process will lead us to domain learning.

Domain learning

This section on domain learning builds a bridge between classic transfer learning, as described previously, and another use of domain learning I found profitable in corporate projects: teaching a machine a concept (CRLMM). The chapter focuses on teaching a machine to learn to recognize a gap in situations other than at the food processing company.

How to use the programs

You can read the chapter first to grasp the concepts, or play with the programs first. In any case, CNN_TDC_STRATEGY.py loads trained models (you do not have to train them again for this chapter) and CNN_CONCEPT_STRATEGY.py trains the models.

The trained models used in this section

This section uses CNN_TDC_STRATEGY.py to apply the trained models to the target concept images. READ_CNN_MODEL.py (as shown previously) was converted into CNN_TDC_STRATEGY.py by adding variable directory paths (for the model.h5 files and images) and classification messages, as shown in the following code:

```
#loads,traffic,food processing
A=['dataset_O/','dataset_traffic/','dataset/']
MS1=['loaded','jammed','productive']
MS2=['unloaded','change','gap']
```

```
#_____LOAD MODEL_____
json_file = open(directory+'model/model.json', 'r')
....
s=identify(directory+'classify/img1.jpg')
```

Each subdirectory contains four subdirectories:

- `classify`: Contains the images to classify
- `model`: The trained `model.h5` used to classify the images
- `test_set`: The test set of conceptual images
- `training_set`: The training set of conceptual images

`Chapter 9`, *Getting Your Neurons to Work*, describes the whole process.

The training model program

For this chapter, you do not need to train the models; they were already trained using `CNN_TDC_TRAINING.py`. This program is an extension of the training program in `Chapter 9`, *Getting Your Neurons to Work*. The directory paths have become variables to access the subdirectories described previously. The paths can be called, as shown in the following code:

```
A=['dataset_O/','dataset_traffic/','dataset/']
scenario=3 #reference to A
directory=A[scenario] #transfer learning parameter (choice of images)
print("directory",directory)
```

You do not need to use this program for this chapter. The models were trained and automatically stored in their respective subdirectories on the virtual machine delivered with the book.

 For this chapter, focus on understanding the concepts. You can read the chapter without running the programs, open them without running them, or run them, whatever makes you comfortable. The main goal is to grasp the concepts to prepare for the subsequent chapters.

GAP – loaded or unloaded

In `Chapter 12`, *Automated Planning and Scheduling*, CRLMM will be applied to **automatic planning and scheduling (APS)**. When planning in general, in a factory for example, a key concept of a gap is unloaded, loaded.

Set the scenario to 0 in `CNN_TDC_STRATEGY.py` to run this conceptual model: `scenario=0 #reference to A,MS1,MS2`.

The gap concept has just become a polysemy word concept (polysemy means different meanings; see `Chapter 8`, *Revolutions Designed for Some Corporations and Disruptive Innovations Small to Large Companies*).

In the cake situation, the Γ gap was negative in its $g1$ subset of meaning and concepts applied to a CNN, relating it to negative images $n+g1$:

$$ng1=\{missing, not\ enough, slowing\ production\ down...bad\}$$

The full-of-products image was positive, $p+g2$:

$$pg2=\{good\ production\ flow, no\ gap\}$$

In this example, the CNN is learning how to distinguish an abstract representation, not an image like for the cakes. Another subset of Γ(gap conceptual dataset) is loaded/unloaded.

The following abstract image is loaded. The squares represent some kind of production machine and the arrows represent the load-in time. This means that the x axis represents time and the y axis represents machine production resources.

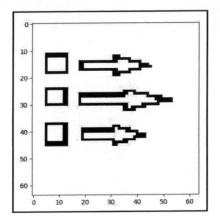

Abstract image

The CNN model runs and produces the following result:

```
directory dataset_O/
Strategy model loaded from training repository.
image dataset_O/classify/img1.jpg predict_proba: [[ 0.]] predict: [[ 0.]]
Classified in class A
loaded
Seeking...
```

The CNN recognizes this as loaded. The task goes beyond classifying. The system needs to recognize this to make a decision.

Another image produces a different result. In this case, an unloaded gap appears in the following screenshot:

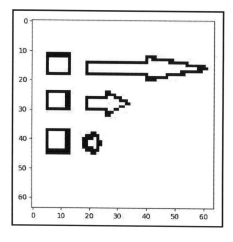

Abstract image

And the CNN has a different output, as shown here:

```
Seeking...
image dataset_O/classify/img2.jpg predict_proba: [[ 1.]] predict: [[ 1.]]
Classified in class
unloaded
```

The gap concept Γ has added two other subsets, $g3$ and $g4$, to its dataset. We now have:

$$\Gamma=\{ng1,g2,g3,g4...gn\}$$

The four *g1* to *g4* subsets of **Γ** are:

$$ng1 = \{missing,\ not\ enough,\ slowing\ production\ down...bad\}$$

$$pg2 = pg2 = \{good\ production\ flow,\ no\ gap\}$$

$$g3 = \{loaded\}$$

$$g4 = \{unloaded\}$$

The remaining problem will take some time to solve. *g4* (gap) can sometimes represent an opportunity for a machine that does not have a good workload to be open to more production. In some cases, *g4* becomes *pg4*(*p = positive*). In other cases, it will become *ng4* (*n=negative*) if production rates go down.

As in Chapter 8, *Revolutions Designed for Some Corporations and Disruptive Innovations for Small to Large Companies*, the context had become strategic when a bus (coach) broke down and the translation came out as a trainer (coach) and not as a vehicle. The problem in these situations relies on the fact that additional input information is required. More words will not help. CRLMM will bring additional concepts into the model.

GAP – jammed or open lanes

A self-driving car needs to recognize whether it is in a traffic jam or not. Also, the self-driving car has to know how to change lanes when it detects enough space (a gap) to do that.

This produces two new subsets:

$$g5 = \{traffic\ jam,\ heavy\ traffic...too\ much\ traffic\}$$

$$g6 = \{open\ lane,\ light\ traffic...normal\ traffic\}$$

The model now detects *g*5 (traffic jam), as shown in the following screenshot:

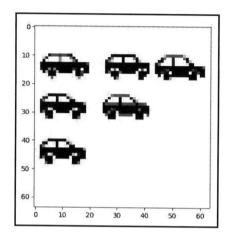

Traffic jam example

The following output appears correctly:

```
directory dataset_traffic/
Strategy model loaded from training repository.
image dataset_traffic/classify/img1.jpg predict_proba: [[ 0.]] predict: [[
0.]]
Classified in class A
jammed
```

*g*6 comes out right as well, as shown in this screenshot:

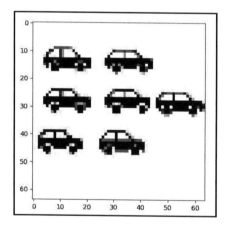

Traffic jam example

A potential lane change has become possible, as detected by the following code:

```
Seeking...
image dataset_traffic/classify/img2.jpg predict_proba: [[ 1.]] predict: [[
1.]]
Classified in class B
change
```

The gap dataset

At this point, the **Γ(gap conceptual dataset)** has begun to learn several subsets:

$$\Gamma=\{g1,g2,g3,g4,g5,g6\}$$

In which:

$$ng1=\{missing,\ not\ enough,\ slowing\ production\ down...bad\}$$

$$pg2=pg2=\{good\ production\ flow,\ no\ gap\}$$

$$g2=\{loaded\}$$

$$g3=\{unloaded\}$$

$$pg4=\{traffic\ jam,\ heavy\ traffic...too\ much\ traffic\}ng5=\{open\ lane,\ light\ traffic...normal\ traffic\}$$

Notice that $g2$ and $g3$ do not have labels yet. The food processing context provided the label. Concept detection requires a context, which CRLMMs will provide.

Generalizing the Γ(gap conceptual dataset)

The generalization of **Γ(gap conceptual dataset)** will provide a conceptual tool for meta-models.

Γ(gap conceptual dataset) refers to negative, positive, or undetermined space between two elements (objects, locations, or products on a production line).

Γ (gamma) also refers to a gap in time: too long, not long enough, too short, or not short enough.

Γ represents the distance between two locations: too far or too close.

Γ represents a misunderstanding or an understanding between two parties: a divergence of opinions or a convergence.

All of these examples refer to gaps in space and time viewed as space.

Generative adversarial networks

Using GANs to generate concept-word images can boost the production CRL datasets and produce millions of concept-word images. No single solution will suffice. CNNs can do the job; GANs can also.

Suppose the **Γ gap** concept needs to be generalized to thousands of situations. Millions of images with words could be analyzed and automatically stored in a **Γ dataset**, with tens of thousands of image-word concepts of gaps.

A GAN could be built in a few lines with the following components:

- Input data for the generator
- The generator
- Real data input
- A discriminator (detects fake data from real data)
- An optimizer (training)

The network starts by inputting real data and fake data (with the generator), as shown in the following diagram:

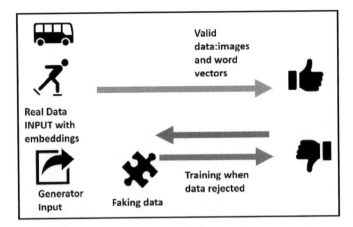

The discriminator function accepts or rejects the generated data. If the data is rejected, then we are back to known territory (see `Chapter 9`, *Getting Your Neurons to Work*) with cross-entropy to measure the loss and an Adam optimizer, for example.

The system will train until it distinguishes right images from fake images like other networks.

 What makes GANs interesting is the fact that the generator data has no direct connection with the real data.

It has to go through the discriminator and be trained if it's wrong. Furthermore, the generated data can be labeled with accurate or inaccurate labels although the real data is correctly labeled.

Generating conceptual representations

A GAN can be used to generate the large datasets required for CRLMMs. The real data could be a set of images with the correct word vectors. The generator could then produce millions of images and labels that the discriminator would work on. The accurately generated datasets could be stored in a CRL repository.

A GAN can be implemented in a few lines of code in TensorFlow, for example. The *Further reading* section at the end of the chapter provides links that detail this simple but effective type of network.

The use of autoencoders

The use of autoencoders must be explored although not recommended for the generation of a conceptual learning dataset.

Data compression has become a part of our daily life through MP3 algorithms, for example. Autoencoding in machine learning is a data compression algorithm.

It takes the original data, compresses it, and can then reconstruct it:

- Original input
- The **encoder** compresses the data (compressed representation)
- The **decoder** reconstructs the data
- The reconstructed output is produced

They were used for CNNs at a time for data representations. But as shown in Chapter 9, *Getting Your Neurons to Work,* random weight initialization scenarios are as effective if not more reliable and flexible.

Two main limitations of autoencoders have restrained their use:

- Autoencoders need to be trained on **specific** data. Being data-specific makes transfer learning tedious.
- The decompressed output is not 100% reliable. They are **lossy**, which means that information is lost during the encoding-decoding phase, unlike standard lossless compression algorithms.

Autoencoders can be used in some cases of dimensionality reduction for data visualization and data denoising.

Beyond that, present-day random weight initialization methods are favored for CNN applications.

The motivation of conceptual representation learning meta-models

A CRLMM converts images into concepts. These abstract concepts will then be embedded in vectors that become logits for a softmax function and in turn be converted into parameters for complex artificial intelligence programs such as :

- Automated planning and scheduling (see `Chapter 12`, *Automated Planning and Scheduling*)
- Cognitive NLP Chatbots (see `Chapter 15`, *Cognitive NLP Chatbots*, and `Chapter 16`, *Improve the Emotional Intelligence Deficiencies of Chatbots*)

At one point, in some artificial intelligence projects, dimension reduction does not produce good results. When scheduling maintenance on airplanes, rockets, and satellite launcher, for example, thousands of features enter the system without leaving any out. A single missing screw in the wrong place can create a disaster.

The curse of dimensionality

The features for a given project can reach large numbers. The following example contains 1,024 dimensions:

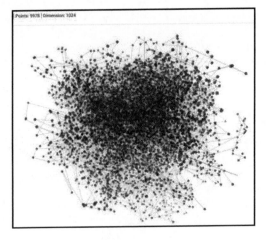

The curse of dimensionality

In Chapter 9, *Getting Your Neurons to Work,* and Chapter 10, *Applying Biomimicking to Artificial Intelligence,* kernels and pooling reduced the number of dimensions to extract key features. With those key features in tensors, arrays and/or vectors, classification and prediction processes are possible. This process produces effective results in many areas.

The limit of this approach occurs when the result does not reach expectations, such as in some of the cases we will discover in the following chapters. In those cases, CRLMMs will increase the productivity of the solution providing a useful abstract model.

When a solution requires a large number of unreduced dimensions, kernels, pooling, and other dimension reduction methods cannot be applied. CRLMMs will provide a *pair of glasses* to the system.

The blessing of dimensionality

In some projects, when the model reaches limits that comprise a project, dimensionality is a blessing. Let's focus on three examples described in the next chapters: scheduling, chatbots, and self-driving cars.

Scheduling and blockchains

An artificial neural network (ANN) system built on dimension reduction might sometimes be seriously underfitted. As long as it was trained with ready-to-use datasets (MNIST, CIFAR, and others), the system worked fine. It even ran perfectly on small datasets.

Then all of a sudden, on the first week in the food processing industry, for example, it mistakes a positive gap (an available resource) for a negative gap (not enough production).

For example, since a gap meant missing products for several days, the AI system wrongly predicted a negative gap when it was not supposed to. In this circumstance, this was a deliberate choice of the management to slow production down due to resource shortages (see Chapter 12, *Automated Planning and Scheduling*). Dimensionality enhancements will solve the problem.

Humans reduce the number of possibilities of a problem with logic and inbuilt decision trees. Machines can beat humans in some forms of computation with no logic at all using random memoryless algorithms (MDP; see Chapter 1, *Become an Adaptive Thinker*). However, present-day deep learning networks, however innovative they are, reduce the dimensions of representation, layer by layer. They flatten them out, drop out information and more to reach a result.

The future of AI will no doubt rely on increasing the number of dimensions way beyond human limits and performing powerful calculations without present-day levels of reduction. Today's state-of-the-art is tomorrow's past. Blow the number of dimensions up to indefinite numbers when it is necessary and possible!

Chatbots

Most NLP algorithms use probabilities to predict the next words. Or they use preset sentences to answer questions *without analyzing the real meaning.*

This means building systems that guess, sometimes effectively, sometimes with errors. In any case, they do not *think.* Many applications produce good results with statistical approaches. But for some projects, customizing a chatbot comes in handy.

For example, imagine that somebody is speaking to you in a language you do not know at all. You have the inbuilt ability of present NLP algorithms to predict representations through statistics on your smartphone.

Although you do not understand a single word, you produce words, statistically, that could fit the situation. For isolated words and simple sentences, you are doing well.

Then all of a sudden, the person frowns. You are totally off track, like many NLP systems today. The person is astonished by your ability to speak and has just said in French, for example, "tu *as la* patate!"

You understand what Google Translate tells you: "*You have the potato!*" You have a big question mark on your face. The other person frowns. Oops!

You just spoke in body language: your question mark, the person's frown. Body language constitutes a major part of real communication between humans. Body language needs to be compensated for with empathy as we will explore in the chatbot chapters.

In the meantime, in French colloquial or slang language *potate* means *pep* (lots of energy) in English.

Classifying documents, finding keywords, and doing first-level translations (see `Chapter 8`, *Revolutions Designed for Some Corporations and Disruptive Innovations for Small to Large Companies*) is one thing; building a smart chatbot beyond language statistics when necessary is another. A CRLMM solution will provide a deeper interaction between a system and humans such as described in the chatbot chapters.

Self-driving cars

Self-driving cars will progressively drive everywhere for everything. In the meantime, accidents caused by self-driving cars grab the headlines. Let's imagine some solutions to help them avoid accidents and improve maintenance problems with small but effective CRLMM enhancements.

 Humans increase dimensionality to solve problems, find new ideas, clear misunderstandings up, and adapt.

The CRLMMs built as add-ons on the awesome tools we all have access to, give us the opportunity to push the limits of AI further every day.

Summary

In this chapter, the **Convolution Neural Network (CNN)** architecture built in Chapter 9, *Getting Your Neurons to Work,* was loaded to classify physical gaps in a food processing company.

Then the trained models were applied to transfer learning by identifying similar types of images. Some of these images represented concepts that lead the trained CNN to identify Γ **concept gaps**.

Γ **concept gaps** were applied to different fields using the CNN as a training and classification tool in domain learning.

Γ **concept gaps** have two main properties: negative n-gaps and positive p-gaps. To distinguish one from the other, a CRLMM provides a useful add-on. In the food processing company, installing a webcam on the right food processing conveyor belt provided a context for the system to decide whether the gap was positive or negative.

With these concepts in mind, let's build a solution for **advanced planning and scheduling (APS)** in the next chapter.

Questions

1. The curse of dimensionality leads to reducing dimensions and features in machine learning algorithms. (Yes | No)
2. Transfer learning determines the profitability of a project. (Yes | No)
3. Reading model.h5 does not provide much information. (Yes | No)
4. Numbers without meaning are enough to replace humans. (Yes | No)
5. Chatbots prove that body language doesn't mean that much. (Yes | No)
6. Present-day ANNs provide enough theory to solve all AI requests. (Yes | No)
7. Chatbots can now replace humans in all situations. (Yes | No)
8. Self-driving cars have been approved and do not need conceptual training. (Yes | No)
9. Industries can implement AI algorithms for all of their needs. (Yes | No)

Further reading

- **More on convolutional networks:** `http://ufldl.stanford.edu/tutorial/supervised/ConvolutionalNeuralNetwork/`
- **A Keras introduction to autoencoders:** `https://blog.keras.io/building-autoencoders-in-keras.html`
- **More on GANs:** `https://medium.com/@devnag/generative-adversarial-networks-gans-in-50-lines-of-code-pytorch-e81b79659e3f`

12
Automated Planning and Scheduling

Amazon is one of the world's leading e-retailers, with sales exceeding US$ 170 billion US. Amazon's e-store sales exceed all of their other activities, such as AWS subscription services (premium, for example), retail third-party seller services, and physical stores.

This chapter focuses on *Amazon Fashion*, one of Amazon's web stores for which Amazon recently registered a patent. *Prime Wardrobe* even offers a try-and-easy-return service. This new activity requires planning and scheduling. Amazon took the matter seriously and registered a patent for an apparel manufacturing system to control the production process of its apparel products.

 Artificial intelligence already plays a role in automatic planning and scheduling in the apparel business, from customer order to delivery.

Recently, Google—through its **DeepMind** projects—is also working on improving the **Deep Q-Network (DQN)**, a system that can beat humans at video games.

This chapter unites both systems with an innovation for the apparel manufacturing industry and adds a **Conceptual Representation Learning Meta Model (CRLMM)** to DQN. Going from scratch to a prototype that could be implemented on site, the foundations are being set for more applications in the coming chapters.

The following topics will be covered in this chapter:

- Further generalization of the CRLMM described in Chapter 11, *Conceptual Representation Learning*, applied to an apparel production process
- Feeding the CRLMM **Convolutional Neural Network (CNN)** with a simulation of frames coming from a webcam on a production line

- Introducing an optimizer that will use weights applied to production stations to input a reward matrix to a **Markov Decision Process (MDP)**, which will then update the weights
- Building a program that will run continuously (no beginning, no end) on a production line using all the three components mentioned previously

Technical requirements

Python 3.6x 64-bit from `https://www.python.org/`.

Packages and modules:

```
import numpy as ql
from matplotlib.ticker import FuncFormatter
import matplotlib.pyplot as plt
from matplotlib.path import Path
import matplotlib.patches as patches
import random
import math
import time
from keras.preprocessing.image import load_img
from keras.preprocessing.image import img_to_array
import keras
from keras.preprocessing.image import ImageDataGenerator
from keras.models import model_from_json
from keras.models import load_model
import scipy.misc
from PIL import Image
```

GitHub `Chapter12`:

- `CNN_CONCEPT_STRATEGY.py`
- `MDP_Graph.py`

Check out the following video to see the code in action:

`https://goo.gl/vScnD3`

Planning and scheduling today and tomorrow

When Amazon decided to launch **Prime Wardrobe**, it brought a new service to its customers. The customer can establish a purchase plan, the list of tasks to carry out:

- Fill a box with clothing, for example
- Try the clothing at home
- Return the clothing if it does not fit
- Purchase the items that are kept

Once the customer agrees to follow this plan, the time sequence becomes crucial:

- First, a box must be chosen
- Then there is a delivery time
- Then there is a trying time (you cannot try the products forever)
- Finally, the customer has a purchase time

Whether Amazon Prime Wardrobe will remain a service in the years to come or not, the precedent is set; just as physical bookstores disappear every year, shopping for clothing online will continue its progression.

On top of that distribution, corporations will continue to expand their own production sites to become manufacturing-distributing giants. Warehouses will progressively replace many stores as per the warehouse examples provided in some of the chapters in this book.

Supply Chain Management (SCM) combined with APS has become a necessity. Blockchains ensure the transactions (see Chapter 14, *Optimizing Blockchains with AI*) and this technology will only expand with these trends.

SCM-APS constraints (depending on the manufacturer) have encouraged Amazon to produce its own clothing. Amazon has produced its own in-house fashion labels with apparel and accessories sold worldwide.

To prove that it means business, Amazon registered patents for a *blended reality mirror*, an apparel manufacturing system, and more. This way a person can actually visualize how the clothing will fit.

We will explore the planning and scheduling side of Amazon's apparel in-house manufacturing plans which will have the same effect on apparel factories as it did on physical bookstores and all types of shops. Many new jobs will emerge, such as hundreds of thousands of jobs in the artificial intelligence business, on websites, and in marketing and SCM. Many jobs will disappear as well. The improvement made will boost medical progress and also the defense industry. The social and economical implications are beyond the scope of this book and possibly beyond our comprehension as in all disruptive eras in the past.

We will focus in depth on the main aspects of Amazon's patented custom clothing process. As mentioned before, whether it turns into a success or not, the precedent is set.

A real-time manufacturing process

The key concept in Amazon's approach is real-time. Pushing the physical limits of centuries of commerce, Amazon's brand takes the manufacturing process right beyond the cutting edge.

Amazon must expand its services to face competition

Amazon could have continued to purchase products from its suppliers and not manufacture them. Instead of using artificial intelligence to solve the conveyor belt problem, several sensors could be installed with traditional software solutions.

Mankind could also have continued to use horses instead of cars and paper instead of computers. However, once a disruptive innovation has been successfully launched by a company, competition must either follow or disappear. Amazon needs to get involved in manufacturing somehow with this apparel manufacturing patent, 3-D printers, and other innovations in order to increase its productivity.

Artificial intelligence needs to be confronted with difficult industrial problems to improve its experience and progress to achieve higher machine learning levels and meet greater challenges.

A real-time manufacturing revolution

Artificial intelligence software, though spectacular, is not the only revolution changing our lives forever. Real-time is a strong force that will change every process in the world.

Apparel manufacturing and manufacturing, in general, follow an advanced planning and scheduling process today. Amazon's manufacturing department, just like Elon Musk's Tesla self-driving cars (see `Chapter 13`, *AI and The Internet of Things (IoT)*, and `Chapter 14`, *Optimizing Blockchains with AI*), require automated planning and scheduling, not advanced planning and scheduling.

The fundamental difference between the two systems relies on the time factor as shown in the following comparison table. The difference between an advanced and an automated system seems small but Amazon, like others, will change the course of history with those differences. Both systems, in theory, can do both types of tasks. In practice, these methods will specialize in the years to come:

- A **plan** consists of processes preparing production for the future: purchasing material components and adapting human resources and physical resources. Amazon, for example, has a yearly business plan: putting together the necessary resources in advance in order to be ready for production. This means purchasing or building warehouses, hiring employees, and purchasing basic material resources (boxes, labels, and other components).
- **Scheduling** confronts the plan with the time factor on a shorter horizon. Scheduling determines when each part of the plan will come first and be produced. For example, now that the warehouse is built or purchased (plan), at what time (schedule) should the packaging start working next Monday and for the weeks to come?

 A schedule can be seen as a zoomed version of a plan.

If somebody walks into Jeff Bezos' office with a plan to build a warehouse at a given location with the cost and general timing of the implementation, that is fine.

Then, that person might (I suggest not!) say: *The plan is great since it will be ready in 10 months. But I'm worried about the daily schedule in 1 year of shift #2. Should they start at 7:30 am or 7:45?* Jeff Bezos will not be listening anymore. That zoom level is not part of his job description. He has to focus on a higher level.

The trend of automated planning and scheduling is becoming a time-squashed version of advanced planning and scheduling. The figures in the following table do not reflect the exact numbers but the trends:

Function	Advanced planning and scheduling	Automated planning and scheduling
Long-term plan	1 month to 5 years	A few days to less than a month
Short-term plan	1 day	1 minute
Production or event measurement	Taken into account on a daily basis in general	Real-time
Scheduling	An hour to 1 week	Real-time
Re-planning when there is a problem	1 hour to 1 month	Real-time
Re-scheduling	1 hours to 1 week	Real-time
Resource adjustment	1 day to 1 month	Real-time
Load balancing	1 hour to 1 week	Real-time
Automatic functions of planning and scheduling	80%	99%

Although this table contains approximate information, the underlying trend is extremely strong.

An advanced planning and scheduling system mostly imports data from ERPs to make plans in the future. An automated planning and scheduling program mostly detects data with sensors to react and optimize in real time. The present chapter deals with automated planning programs, not advanced planning and scheduling systems.

Think of the evolution between an advanced APS and an automated APS as a logistic sigmoid function applied to planning-scheduling time squashing. Here are some examples:

- The advanced plan to manufacture a car spans a month to a year
- The Google Maps itinerary automated plan for a self-driving car at its starting point: a few seconds to a minute depending on the connection status of that location
- The schedule to manufacture a car: 1 day to 1 month
- The schedule to pilot a self-driving car following the Google Map *itineray=real time*

To sum it up, the present trend represents a revolution in the history of human processes.

 Amazon's manufacturing patent reflects the revolution of real-time applied to every field.

Planning in advance has moved up to planning in real time as shown in the following equation.

$$Z = \sum_{tx_n}^{tx_n} \frac{1}{1+e^{-tx}} \lambda$$

In which:

- x is a quantity to produce or any unit event
- t_x is the time (t) it takes for x to start and end
- A logistic function squashes t_x
- λ (lambda) is the learning factor; the more a task is carried out, the more it is optimized

X_t is the total weight of a group of n tasks at a given time t:

$$X_t = \{x_1, x_2, x_3 ... x_n\}$$

The difference between X_t and $Z(X_t)$ is:

- X_t is the actual time it takes to produce products
- $Z(X_t)$ is not the actual time it takes. $Z(X_t)$ is the result of an activation function that squashes times as an output of X_t in a DQN-CRLMM network. $Z(X_t)$ is a weighting factor.

The key to reducing the weighting factory further is a physical production process and other physical events (outputs, for example), that I call lambda: λ all the improvements in real-life production that can reduce the production cycle as well as the natural events such as production output.

In Chapter 11, *Conceptual Representation Learning*, Γ was introduced to reduce gaps. In this chapter, Γ will be generalized a step further to optimize λ (lambda)

This means a DQN-CRLMM system will optimize a manufacturing process.

CRLMM applied to an automated apparel manufacturing process

With an automated planning and scheduling system, not an advanced planning and scheduling system, Amazon has brought apparel manufacturing closer to the consumer.

Artificial intelligence will boost existing processes. In this section, a DQN-CRLMM will optimize an apparel manufacturing process.

An apparel manufacturing process

Amazon's apparel manufacturing patent can be summed up as follows:

- **P1**: Grouping apparel customer orders by products and sizes. This process is around since the origins of industrial apparel manufacturing centuries ago.
- **P2**: Automatically cutting lays (such as cutting a circle in several pieces of paper at the same time).
- **P3**: Moving the packs of the parts of clothing to the assembly lines on conveyor belts (see Chapter 11, *Conceptual Representation Learning*).
- **P4**: Other operations depending on the products (packaging or printing or other).
- **P5**: Storing and optimizing the distribution process through warehouses and deliveries and many more processes (tracking and data analysis, for example, finding late deliveries and optimizing their routes).

The following figure represents the production flow at an apparel manufacturing company. First, the fabric is cut; then it is stacked in piles and sent by a conveyor belt to sewing stations to assemble the clothing:

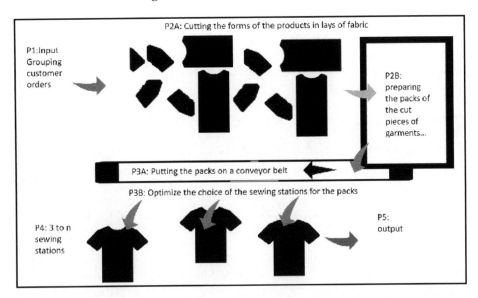

A webcam is set up right over P3, the conveyor belt. The following image represents the webcam above the conveyor belt:

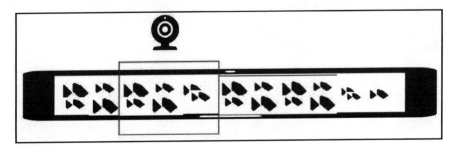

Webcam overview

The webcam freezes a frame (within the red rectangle) every n seconds. The frame is the input of the CRL-CNN described later.

This image is a representation of the concepts. In reality, the webcam might be located at the beginning of the conveyor belt or even over the output of the cutting process. For the purpose of the prototype in this chapter, just keep in mind that every n seconds a frozen frame is sent to the trained CNN.

This P1 to P5 flowchart provides a general idea of an apparel manufacturing process. In a real-life company, many more processes are required: market studies, designing products, testing prototypes, adding manufacturing processes for jeans (making holes with a laser, for example), and much more.

Every process described so far was individually invented 30+ years ago, including automatic cutting and conveyor belts applied to the apparel business. *What's new here?* comes up in the minds of many apparel experts reading about Amazon. And that is the mind trap! Thinking that Amazon's apparel patent does not contain new components.

Time squashing is the innovation. Bringing manufacturing closer to the consumer in near-real time is a revolution that will become disruptive. Add 3-D printers to the time squashing equation and you will easily picture the future of our consumer markets. However, artificial intelligence has the right to enter the optimizing competition as well.

To illustrate this, let's build an AI model that optimizes P3, the conveyor belt. Many solutions already exist as well, but DQN can most probably beat them just as it will in many fields.

The first step is to generalize the Γ model described in Chapter 11, *Conceptual Representation Learning*, a bit further. Then the DQN-CRLMM can be built.

Training the CRLMM

In Chapter 9, *Getting Your Neurons to Work*, and Chapter 11, *Conceptual Representation Learning*, the CRLMM program CNN_STRATEGY_MODEL.py was trained to identify gaps in outputs on the conveyor belt of a food processing factory. Chapter 11, Conceptual Representation Learning, introduced CRLMMs using Γ (gap concept) to illustrate one.

In the previous, chapters, conceptual subsets around Γ (gap concepts) were designed as follows:

- $\Gamma=\{g1,g2,g3,g4,g5,g6\}$ which contains pg_i (p=positive) and ng_i (n=negative subsets)
- $ng1$ is a subset of Γ; $ng1=\{$missing, not enough, slowing production down...bad$\}$,
- $pg2$ is a subset of Γ; $pg2=pg2=\{$good production flow, no gap$\}$
- $g2=\{$loaded$\}$
- $g3=\{$unloaded$\}$,
- $pg4=\{$traffic jam, heavy traffic...too much traffic$\}$
- $ng5=\{$open lane, light traffic...normal traffic$\}$

CNN_STRATEGY_MODEL.py needs to be trained to recognize Γ in an apparel production environment as well as remember how to recognize former Γ *concepts:*

- The cutting section P2(A and B) output of apparel packs flowing on a conveyor belt (P3)
- Remember know how to classify the cakes of the food processing company to teach the model to recognize more situations.
- Remember how to perform a traffic analysis (see Chapter 11, *Conceptual Representation Learning*)
- Learn how to be able to classify an abstract representation of a gap

Generalizing the unit-training dataset

To generalize the unit training dataset, six types of images were created. Each image represents a webcam frame taken over a conveyor build every *n* seconds. Four images are figurative in the sense of figurative painting. Two images bring the CRLMM program to a higher level of abstraction, which will be applied to cognitive chatbots (Chapter 15, *Cognitive NLP Chatbots, and* Chapter 16, *Improve the Emotional Intelligence Deficiencies of Chatbots*) with further training.

Food conveyor belt processing – positive pγ and negative nγ gaps

In the food processing industry example (see Chapter 9, *Getting Your Neurons to Work, and* Chapter 11, *Conceptual Representation Learning*), a gap on the conveyor built was most often negative, a *negative gamma= nγ*.

The following frame shows that the first line of production is complete but not lines two and three:

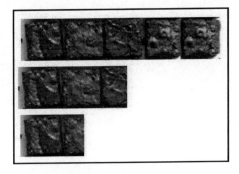

Food conveyor belt processing frame

On the contrary, with approximately no gaps, the load on the conveyor built was viewed as positive, a *positive gamma= $p\gamma$*.

The following frame shows that there is an acceptable number of products per line:

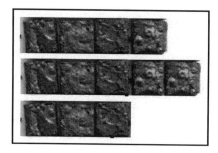

Food conveyor belt processing frame

Apparel conveyor belt processing – undetermined gaps

A gap in an apparel conveyor belt process is most often undetermined. This constitutes a major optimization problem in itself. Naturally, if the conveyor belt is empty or totally saturated, the variance will attract the attention of a human operator. However, most of the time, optimization solves the problem.

The following frame shows a relatively well-loaded production flow of apparel packs of pieces of clothing to be assembled (by sewing them together) further down the line:

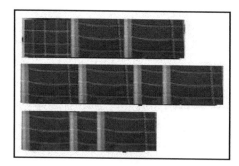

Well-loaded production flow

The following frame clearly shows a gap, meaning that the quantity that will be sent to a sewing station will not be high:

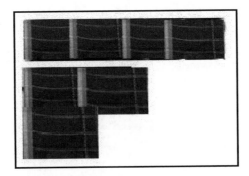

Production flow (gap)

Several observations are necessary to optimize this problem:

- The conveyor built real-time problem excludes running an advanced planning and scheduling
- This problem requires real-time automated planning and scheduling
- The automated planning and scheduling solution will have to both plan and schedule in real time
- It will take planning constraints into account (as explained in the following sections) to predict outputs
- It will take scheduling constraints into account to optimize the sewing sections

 Amazon and others have slowly but surely brought many planning horizon problems (longer) down to shorter scheduling horizons, pushing the limits of SCM further and further.

The beginning of an abstract notion of gaps

The gaps shown have negative or positive properties depending on the context. The CRLMM model now has to learn a metaconcept, an abstract representation of all the gaps mentioned up to now. These gaps are all flow gaps of one sort or the other. Something is moving from one point to another in small packs. The packs, so are often not the same size and gaps form.

These concepts can be applied to cattle herds, horse races, team sports attacks (football, soccer, rugby, basketball, handball, and other fields), Olympic races, marathons, conveyor belts, and much more, as will be detailed in the chatbot in `Chapter 15`, *Cognitive NLP Chatbots*, and `Chapter 16`, *Improve the Emotional Intelligence Deficiencies of Chatbots*.

When the packs in the flow are close to each other, an individual mental image comes up. Each person has a customized version. The following image is a generalized representation of a no gap concept:

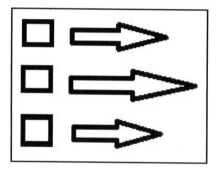

Generalized representation of a no gap concept

Then the packs have leaders and followers, then an abstract representation comes up as well. The following image shows a generalized representation of a gap concept:

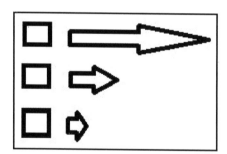

Generalized representation of a gap concept

Humans do not have a flow detection gap function for each thing they are observing. Humans have one brain that contains physical memories or other datasets, but more importantly, they have abstract datasets.

Every single of us billions of thinking bipeds have extremely efficient abstract datasets. The meta-concept shown before means that through inferences, a human has a central meta-concept with a dataset of memories that fit with it through experience.

A meta-model uses these datasets. The dataset in the directory "dataset" contains the beginning of a CRLMM system. The program will learn what a *flow gap* is and then apply to what it sees by analyzing the context.

This goal of this dataset leads to a CLR-MM, as explained in the following sections in which:

- The abstract learned meta-concept is applied to a situation, in this case, a frame.
- The CRLMM then determines whether it is a gap or no gap situation.
- The CRLMM then makes a decision using a thinking optimizer based on a decision weight orientated activation function. This means that it is more than a mathematical *squash*. It's literally *weighing* the pros and cons of a decision-making process.

> To apply this model in real life, the next step would be to spend the necessary time to build a dataset from experience with thousands upon thousands of frames. This would take months of painful work.

Modifying the hyperparameters

The training was done with the same CNN_STRATEGY_MODEL.py program described in Chapter 9, *Getting Your Neurons to Work*, which was designed to be generalized for subsequent chapters.

Once the dataset of the previous section has been installed, there are only two hyperparameters to change in the following code snippet:

```
estep=5000 #5000 steps per epoch
...
ep=3 #epochs
```

This forces the program to train longer:

- **Three epochs**: ep=3
- **5,000 steps per epoch**: estep=5000

As the code that follows shows, the hyperparameters have been modified; the program runs and the new model is saved with its graph flow structure and weights:

```
# serialize model to JSON
model_json = classifier.to_json()
with open(directory+"model/model.json", "w") as json_file:
  json_file.write(model_json)
# serialize weights to HDF5
classifier.save_weights(directory+"model/model.h5")
```

The model has been trained to deal with a meta-concept. It now needs to go through a prediction program to check the network.

Running a prediction program

The same CNN_CONCEPT_STRATEGY.py described in Chapter 11, *Conceptual Representation Learning*, was used. However, some new features were added to make this prediction testing phase comfortable to use and watch.

The model is loaded and compiled as described in Chapter 11, *Conceptual Representation Learning*. The identify(target_name) function contains the same philosophy. However, instead of showing the pre-processed image and having to click on it to close the window, a matplotlib plt.close function was added, as in the following code:

```
if(display==1):
   plt.imshow(original)
   plt.show(block=False)
   time.sleep(5)
   plt.close()
```

display is a variable that can be set to 0. In that case, no image will be displayed. However, when developing convolutional networks, displaying images remains a practical way of testing the program.

The image will be displayed for 5 seconds and automatically closed. To keep things automatic, the four frames and two meta-concepts run in a loop as in the code that follows:

```
I=['1','2','3','4','5','6']
for im in range(6):
imgc=directory+'classify/img'+ I[im] + '.jpg'
print(imgc)
s=identify(imgc)
if (int(s)==0):
print('Classified in class A')
print(MS1)
```

```
if (int(s)==1):
print('Classified in class B')
print(MS2)
```

The predictions come out as 0 with an MS1 message or 1 with an MS2 message. The messages can be changed or come from a message dataset depending on the goal of the program. The program will then display the classification, as follows:

```
#_SEARCH STRATEGY_
MS1='no gap'
MS2='gap'
```

The CRLMM has now learned to represent real-life memories and an inference of the associated memories in a meta-concept.

Building the DQN-CRLMM

The full code of the DQN-CRLMM program is `MDP_Graph.py`. It is built on the knowledge and programs of the previous chapters and previous sections of this chapter.

The DQN-CRLMM contains three components:

- A CRLMM convolutional network that will analyze each frame it receives from the webcam that is located right over the pieces of garment packs on the conveyor belt coming from the cutting section.
- An optimizer using a modified version of the Z(X) described before that plans how the assembly stations will be loaded in real-time.
- An MDP that will receive the input of the optimizer function and schedule the work of the assembly stations. It also produces the modified Z(X) updated value of the weights of each assembly station for the next frame.

In the physical world, the conveyor belt transports the garment packs, a picture (frame) is taken every *n* seconds, and the DQN-CRL-MN runs. The output of the DQN-CRL-MN sends instructions to the conveyor belt and directs the garment backs to the optimized load of the assembly stations as explained before.

Since `MPP_graph.py` describes a continuous DQN-CRLMM process, there is no beginning or end to the program. The components are independent and are triggered by the input sent to them and they trigger others with their output.

Thus, components will be described in the processing order but not in the code-in-line order. This is due to the fact that the functions defined by *def + function()* precede the function calls to them. Code line numbers will thus be inserted in the description of the code.

38: is the code line number. It is not in the actual code but only given in the book to find the functions. The code is complete and you can view the line numbers in an editor.

A circular process

Once the three main components of the system are explained later (CNN, MDP, optimizer); the circular property of this DQN-CRLMM is a *stream-like system that never starts nor ends*.

There is no beginning and no end to the flow of functions in this virtually memoryless system.

The conveyor belt's webcam provides a *stream* of frames, forcing the system into circular stream-like behavior.

Implementing a CNN-CRLMM to detect gaps and optimize

The CNN-CRLMM function was described in the *Running a prediction program* section and in Chapter 11, *Conceptual Representation Learning*. The prediction function is part of the MDP output analysis described later. The CRLMM function is called as shown in the following code:

```
180: def CRLMM(Q,lr,e):
```

The first part of this function squashes the W vector described in the following section. The second part of this function analyzes the input frame.

Since no webcam is connected to the system at this point (that must be done during project implementation), a random image (frame) choice is made. The following random code simulates the random occurrences of real-life production:

```
status=random.randint(0,1)
```

In a real-life situation, random quantities will be going through the conveyor belt. Status being determined, the CNN simulates adding a frozen frame from the video stream coming from the webcam located right on the conveyor belt. It runs the identify (image) function described before and returns a gap or no gap scenario for the optimizer (see the optimizer section). The following code describes a gap identification process:

```
if(status==0):
        #Add frame from video stream (connect to webcam)
        s=identify(directory+'classify/img1.jpg',e)
if(status==1):
        #Add frame from video stream (connect to webcam)
        s=identify(directory+'classify/img2.jpg',e)
s1=int(s[0])
if (int(s1)==0):
    print('Classified in class A')
    print(MS1[scenario])
    print('Seeking...')
if (int(s1)==1):
    print('Classified in class B')
    print(MS2[scenario])
return s1
```

Once status has been detected, whether the load output of the cutting system is high or low, a decision must be made. This will be done with the MDP.

Q-Learning – MDP

By adding an MDP Q-Learning decision function (see Chapter 1, *Become an Adaptive Thinker*) in this CNN-CRLMM program, we are now entering the family of DQNs, such as Google's DeepMind programs.

> In this real-time system, there is no beginning, no end, and no real memory beyond a few frames.

The `MDP.py` MDP program has been incorporated into `MDP_Graph.py`. Thus, only the changes made are described in this chapter.

MDP parameters come right after the import packages. Each vertex of the graph has its own letter and its own location, as shown in the following code snippet:

```
38:L=['A','B','C','D','E','F']
```

When the program runs, the following graph will be displayed with red (target vertices) for this frame. It is then up to the MDP to choose, as described as follows:

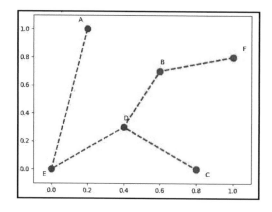

Output (target vertices)

Notice that this is an undirected graph with vertices (the colored dots) and no edge (lines) directions. The MDP will provide directions for each frame in this model.

Each vertex represents an assembly station in this model. Each assembly station has a high workload or a low workload. The workload is rarely stabilized because products keep flowing in and out as they are produced.

MDP inputs and outputs

The MDP process in this model uses a reward matrix as an input and produces a weight vector.

The input is a neutral reward matrix

The MDP reward matrix (see `Chapter 1, Become an Adaptive Thinker`) is set to zero except for the values representing the edges of the graph that can be physically accessed; these are set to one, a small neutral value.

As it is, the MDP cannot provide a satisfactory result beyond reproducing the structure of this undirected graph. The reward matrix is now initialized and duplicated as shown in the following code, starting from line 41; at line 43, R, the reward matrix is built, and at line 50, Ri, a duplicate of R is created:

```
41:# R is The Reward Matrix for each state built on the physical graph
# Ri is a memory of this initial state: no rewards and undirected

43:R = ql.matrix([ [0,0,0,0,1,0],
[0,0,0,1,0,1],
[0,0,0,1,0,0],
[0,1,1,0,1,0],
[1,0,0,1,0,0],
[0,1,0,0,0,0] ])

50:Ri = ql.matrix([ [0,0,0,0,1,0],
[0,0,0,1,0,1],
[0,0,0,1,0,0],
[0,1,1,0,1,0],
[1,0,0,1,0,0],
[0,1,0,0,0,0] ])
```

Ri, on line 50, is a copy of the initial-state zero-reward matrix. R is reset to Ri at every new frame. MDP trains the assembly location plan for each new frame in a memoryless, undirected graph and unsupervised approach.
Q is the learning matrix in which rewards will be learned/stored, as shown in the code on line 59:

```
59:Q = ql.matrix(ql.zeros([6,6]))
```

The standard output of the MDP function

The load of the assembly stations is not the exact quantities produced. They are weights that are updated continuously during this continuous process as explained further in the chapter.

At an initial state of the program, the initial weight of the vertices is set to 0 in the following line of code (line 40):

```
40:W=[0,0,0,0,0,0]
```

The weight vector (represented as an array) contains one value per assembly station location or vertex.

An initial state is not a real beginning. It is like a pause button on a video. The initial state can come from a holiday (no production), a maintenance day (no production), or a lack of input orders (no production). The initial state is just a case when the weights are equal to 0 because there is nothing on the conveyor or assembly stations.

The weight vector is part 1 of the optimizer (see the following section). The MDP produces an output matrix (see Chapter 1, *Become an Adaptive Thinker*) after having optimized the undirected graph. The optimizer will have provided a target.

The program contains the same source code as in Chapter 1, *Become an Adaptive Thinker,* with Bellman's equation from start line 117. The MDP produces its result (Chapter 1, *Become an Adaptive Thinker*) as shown in the following output:

```
[[ 0.  0.  0.  0.  105.352 0. ]
 [ 0.  0.  0.  130.44 0.  201. ]
 [ 0.  0.  0.  130.44 0.  0. ]
 [ 0.  161.8 105.352 0.  105.352 0. ]
 [ 85.2816 0.  0.  130.44 0.  0. ]
 [ 0.  0.  0.  0.  0.  250. ]]
Normed Q :
[[ 0.  0.  0.  0.  42.1408 0. ]
 [ 0.  0.  0.  52.176 0.  80.4 ]
 [ 0.  0.  0.  52.176 0.  0. ]
 [ 0.  64.72 42.1408 0.  42.1408 0. ]
 [ 34.11264 0.  0.  52.176 0.  0. ]
 [ 0.  0.  0.  0.  0.  100. ]]
```

 Bear in mind that this whole NDQ-CRLMM is not only based on the undirected memoryless MDP function but also has no real beginning nor end since it's a continuous and virtually memoryless process.

A graph interpretation of the MDP output matrix

After each run, the MDP matrix also produces a graph interpretation of the values of paths between the vertices from point to point (letter to letter), and displays it in the following output:

```
State of frame : 3 D
0 A E 161.8
1 B D 201.0
2 C D 201.0
```

```
3  D  D  250.0
4  E  A  130.44
4  E  D  201.0
5  F  B  161.8
```

This way, if the values are taken from the highest to the lowest edges (lines and thus values between two letters), it gives a visual idea of how the MDP function calculated its way through the graph.

RL is the letter vector. It is empty after each frame. It will be filled by finding the values of each edge. It will contain the letters of the vertices (nodes and dots) connected by the edges (lines represented by the values).

RN is the value of the edges. The following code shows how to implement RL and RN and update the weights of the locations in the weight vector (W):

```
187: #Graph structure
RL=['','','','','','']
RN=[0,0,0,0,0,0]
print("State of frame :",lr,L[lr])
for i in range(6):
maxw=0
for j in range(6):
W[j]+=logistic_sigmoid(Q[i,j])
if(Q[i,j]>maxw):
RL[i]=L[j]
RN[i]=Q[i,j]
maxw=Q[i,j]
print(i,L[i],RL[i],RN[i])
```

The logistic function in the preceding code is being updated while RL and RN are being updated.

The optimizer

I have written a number of optimizers for fabric optimization in the apparel industry. In this case, the optimizer will be used to regulate the flow of production.

The optimizer is not the CNN rmsprop optimizer used in the previous chapters:

```
88:loaded_model.compile(loss='binary_crossentropy', optimizer='rmsprop',
metrics=['accuracy'])
```

This `optimizer` is both an activation function and a regulator that was built from scratch. This shows that you must sometimes invent the `optimizer` you need to generate a profitable solution for your customer or company.

The optimizer as a regulator

The whole concept of this DQN-CRL-MNN of real-time production, applied to P3, is to optimize Z over the load distribution of the assembly stations, as explained before. This means reducing Z as much as possible through the following equation:

$$Z = \sum_{tx_n}^{tx_n} \frac{1}{1+e^{-tx}} \lambda$$

To achieve that optimization goal, Z needs to be taken apart and applied to strategic parts of the code.

Implementing Z – squashing the MDP result matrix

The output of the MDP functions provides the following Q matrix:

```
Q :
[[ 0. 0. 0. 0. 321.8 0. ]
 [ 0. 0. 0. 401. 0. 258.44]
 [ 0. 0. 0. 401. 0. 0. ]
 [ 0. 0. 0. 500. 0. 0. ]
 [ 258.44 0. 0. 401. 0. 0. ]
 [ 0. 321.8 0. 0. 0. 0. ]]
```

Each line represents a vertex in the graph: A, B, C, D, E, and F. Each value obtained needs to be squashed in the following z(x) function:

$$z(x) = \frac{1}{1+e^{-tx}}$$

The first step in the code that follows is to squash the weights provided by the MDP process for each line (vertex) x with a `logistic_sigmoid` function:

```
119:#Logistic Sigmoid function to squash the weights
def logistic_sigmoid(w):
return 1 / (1 + math.exp(-w))
```

The function is called by the transformation of the MDP Q output matrix into the weight vector for each column of each line, as shown in the following code:

```
191: for i in range(6):
 maxw=0
 for j in range(6):
 W[j]+=logistic_sigmoid(Q[i,j])
```

At this point, each value of the MDP has lost any real-life value. It is a weight, just as in any other network. The difference is that the whole system is controlled. In a real-life project, keeping an eye on the calculations through reports is necessary for maintenance purposes. Even an automatic system requires quality control.

The MDP matrix has now been flattened into a weight matrix, as shown in the following output:

```
Vertice Weights [3.5, 3.5, 3.0, 5.0, 3.5, 3.5]
```

Each vertex (letter in the graph) now has a weight.

Implementing Z – squashing the vertex weights vector

Squashed W (vertex weights) grow after each frame analysis and each MDP run since $W[j]+$ is applied continuously and W is never set to zero.

The main reasons:

- Once launched, the DQN-CRLMM is a continuous process, with no beginning and no end as long as the conveyor belt is running
- The conveyor belt is sending assembly (mostly sewing) work to the assembly stations that take some time (t) to get the job (x) represented by t_x in the Z equation and the W vector in the program
- So work is piling up on each vertex (A to F), which represents an assembly station

This is why the λ (lambda) variable in the Z equation is implemented as shown in the initial equation early in the chapter, as follows:

$$Z = \sum_{tx_n}^{tx_n} \frac{1}{1+e^{-tx}} \lambda$$

λ (lambda) is implemented for two reasons:

- The sewing or assembly stations send their finished work to the next operation on the production line, packaging for example. So every *m* minutes, their workload goes down and so does the load feature weight.
- Production managers are constantly working on learning curves on assembly lines. When a new product arrives, it takes some time for the teams to adapt. Their output is a bit slower than usual. However, well-trained teams bring the learning period down regularly.

λ (lambda) combines both concepts in one variable. This might be enough for some projects. If not, more work and variables need to be added.

In this model, λ (lambda) is activated by the following:

- `oif` represents the frequency of a `W` vector λ update. In this example, `oif` is set to 10. This means that every 10 frames, `oir` will be applied.
- `oir` represents the output rate for the two reasons described before. This variable will squash the `W` vector by the `%` given. In this example, `oir=0.2`. That means that only 20% of the weights will be retained. The rest has been finished.

The following code shows how to implement `oif` and `oir`:

```
314:input_output_frequency : output every n frames/ retained memory
oif=10
#input_output_rate p% (memory retained)
oir=0.2
fc=0 #frequencey counter : memory output
for e in range(episodes):
 print("episode:frame #",e)
 fc=fc+1
 #memory management : lambda output
 if(fc>=10):
 for fci in range(6):
 W[fci]=W[fci]*oir
 fc=0
 print("OUTPUT OPERATION - MEMORY UPDATED FOR ",L[fci]," ",oir,"%
retained")
```

The W vector has been squashed again, as shown in this output:

```
OUTPUT OPERATION - MEMORY UPDATED FOR A 0.2 % retained
OUTPUT OPERATION - MEMORY UPDATED FOR B 0.2 % retained
OUTPUT OPERATION - MEMORY UPDATED FOR C 0.2 % retained
OUTPUT OPERATION - MEMORY UPDATED FOR D 0.2 % retained
OUTPUT OPERATION - MEMORY UPDATED FOR E 0.2 % retained
OUTPUT OPERATION - MEMORY UPDATED FOR F 0.2 % retained
```

Finding the main target for the MDP function

W, the weight vector, is updated after each frame with a short-term memory of *n* frames. This means that in every n frames, it's memory is emptied of useless information.

The goal of the optimizer is to provide a target for the MDP function. On the first episode, since it does not have any information, the optimizer selects a random state, as shown in the following code excerpt:

```
#first episode is random
if(e==0):
lr=random.randint(0,5)
```

This means that a random assembly station will be chosen on the MPD graph, which represents the six assembly sewing stations. Once this episode has been completed, the system enters a circular real-time cycle (see next section).

The second episode has the W vector to rely upon.

It runs the crlmm (described before) CNN-CRLMM network to determine whether the frame has a gap or no gap feature as shown in the following code:

```
383:crlmm=CRLMM(Q,lr,e)
```

The optimizer will use W to:

- Choose the vertex (sewing station) with *somewhat* the smallest weight if the CNN on the frame produces a result with no gap (probability is zero). Since there is no gap that means that there are many pieces to sew. Thus, it is much better to give the work to an assembly station that has a lower load than others.

- Choose the vertex (sewing station) with *somewhat* the highest weight if the CNN on the frame produces a result with a `gap` (probability is one). Since there is a gap, it means there are not that many pieces to sew. Thus it is much better to give the work to an assembly station that already has a higher workload. It will balance the loads and optimize the load distribution over all the stations.
- Introduce a choice to find one target assembly station for the MDP function in each of these cases. It will look for stations (vertices, letters, dots in the graph) with the highest weight in one case and the lowest in another.
- Add the **somewhat** concept referred to before. The system must remain relatively free or it will keep choosing the same best sewing stations, depriving others of work. Thus each possibility (`gap` or `no gap`) is limited to a random choice of only three among the six locations for each weight class (higher or lower).

The optimizing function, shown in the following snippet, can prove extremely profitable on real-life industrial production lines:

```
if(e>0):
    lr=0
    minw=10000000
    maxw=-1
#no G => Finding the largest gap (most loaded resource or a distance)
if(crlmm==0):
for wi in range(3):
op=random.randint(0,5)
if(W[op]<minw):
lr=op;minw=W[op]
#G => Finding the smallest gap (a least loaded resource or a distance)
if(crlmm==1):
for wi in range(3):
op=random.randint(0,5)
if(W[op]>maxw):
lr=op;maxw=W[op]
```

`lr` is the main location chosen for the MDP reinforcement learning function, as shown in the following code:

```
print("LR TARGET STATE MDP number and letter:",lr,L[lr])
```

Reinforcement learning has to run every time since it faces new frames in the continuous process of the conveyor belt in the automated apparel system.

Now the MDP reward matrix is reset to its initial state, as implemented in these lines of the program:

```
#initial reward matrix set again
  for ei in range(6):
      for ej in range(6):
          Q[ei,ej]=0
          if(ei !=lr):
              R[ei,ej]=Ri[ei,ej]
          if(ei ==lr):
              R[ei,ej]=0 #to target, not from
```

The target location is initialized with a value that fits the gap or no gap philosophy of the program. If there is no gap, the value is higher and so will be the weight (represented load of the station) in the end. If there is a gap, the value is lower and so will be the weight for that station, as shown in the following lines of code:

```
#no G
rew=100
#G
if(crlmm==1):
    rew=50
R[lr,lr]=rew
print("Initial Reward matrix withe vertice locations:",R)
```

Circular DQN-CRLMM – a stream-like system that never starts nor ends

A linear stream of a conveyor line has been converted into a circular process. The DQN-CRLMM solution:

- Captures a frame of the output of the cutting section with a webcam and a CNN-CRLMM
- Analyses the load (histograms of each sewing section) with the CRLMM
- Optimizes the sewing stations with an MDP

The following graph represents the process:

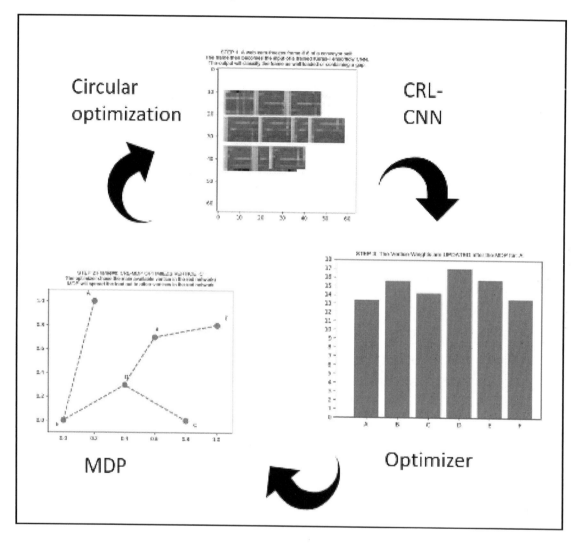

Circular DQN-CRLMM

Let's explore these steps in more detail.

Step X: When the following frame arrives, the CRL-CNN is activated:

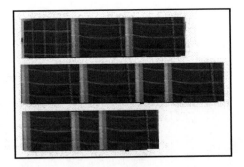

CRL-CNN gets activated

The solution calls the CRLMM function, as shown in the following code:

```
383:crlmm=CRLMM(Q,lr,e)
 print("GAP =0 or GAP =1 status: ",crlmm)
```

The following code displays the status of the image: gap, no gap:

```
image dataset/classify/img1.jpg predict_probability: [[ 0.]] prediction: [[
0.]]
Classified in class A
productive
Seeking...
GAP =0 or GAP =1 status: 0
```

The following weights of each sewing station (vertices A to F) are taken into account:

```
385:MDP_GRAPH(lr,e)
print("Vertice Weights",W)
```

The program displays them in text form:

```
Vertice Weights [9.4, 11.100000000000001, 10.2, 12.0, 11.7, 10.0]
```

The program also displays the following bar chart of the weights of each sewing station:

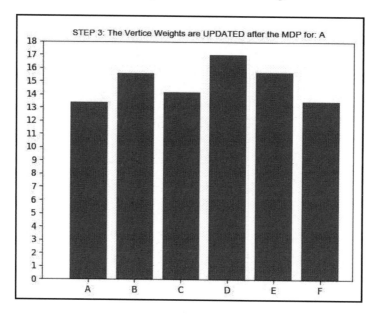

Bar chart of the weighs of each sewing station

STEP X+1 optimizer analyzes the weights to make a decision: *Send small quantities to the sewing stations that have a lot of work and large quantities to sewing stations that have less work to do.*

Γ **(gamma)** has now reached a point at which it understands that a gap is a comparison between two states and an inference of a conceptual distance:

- **Overloading**: Too much
- **Underloading**: Not enough

Γ **(gamma)** now contains two abstract concepts:

- Enough to too much
- Not enough to lacking

 The goal of the circular process is to keep the bars at an approximately similar height—not an exact height, but also not a situation in which A would have no work to do and E would be overloaded.

STEP X+2 the MDP, as described in this chapter, receives instructions to optimize a given sewing station and spreads work out to its neighbors. This is often a production constraint: one station sews the sleeves of a t-shirt. For example, the station nearby sews a pocket on the t-shirt. The MDP spreads out the work starting with the target location, as shown in the following graph:

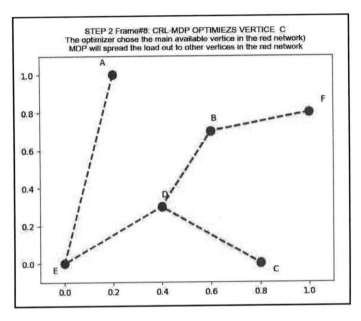

MDP spreads out

The MDP sends its results directly to the conveyor belt, which automatically follows the path instructions sent to it.

Then the MDP updates the weights, empties its reward matrix, and waits for a new one. The system goes back to Step X.

As you might have noticed, no human operator is involved in this whole process at all. This application is part of the IoT family of applications. Chapter 13, *AI and The Internet of Things (IoT)*, will take the application to the streets of our cities.

Summary

Applying artificial intelligence to Amazon's real-time sales, production, and delivery forces projects into reality.

Learning machine learning and deep learning with MNIST, CIFAR, and other ready-to-use datasets with ready-to-use programs is a prerequisite to mastering artificial intelligence. Learning mathematics is a must.

Building a few programs that can do various theoretical things cannot be avoided. But managing a real project under corporate pressure will bring an AI expert up to another level. The constraints of corporate specifications make machine learning projects exciting. During those projects, experts learn valuable information on how AI solutions work and can be improved.

This chapter described a DQN-CRLMM-CNN model with an optimizer and an MDP function. The next chapter explores an application of this solution with an SVM applied to a self-driving car situation in an IoT context.

Questions

1. A CNN can be trained to understand an abstract concept? (Yes | No)
2. Is it better to avoid concepts and only use real-life images? (Yes | No)
3. Planning and scheduling mean the same thing? (Yes | No)
4. Is Amazon's manufacturing patent a revolution? (Yes | No)
5. Learning how warehouses function is not useful. (Yes | No)
6. Online marketing does not require artificial intelligence. (Yes | No)

Further reading

More on Amazon's apparel manufacturing innovation:

- `https://www.nytimes.com/2017/04/30/technology/detailing-amazons-custom-clothing-patent.htm`
- `http://money.cnn.com/2018/01/03/technology/amazon-smart-mirror-patent/index.html`

13
AI and the Internet of Things (IoT)

Some say **Internet of Things (IoT)** will turn out to become the fourth Industrial Revolution. I think we should wait a few years until the smoke clears and let historians figure out what sort of revolution we went through.

In any case, **connected objects** have been changing our lives for 20+ years. In the past years, we can safely say that IoT has become disruptive.

Artificial intelligence has just begun its long journey through the human intellect. New, incredible innovations await us. Understand cutting-edge machine learning and deep learning theory is only the beginning of your adventure. The knowledge you have acquired should help you become an AI visionary. Take everything you see seriously and see how it can fit in your projects.

Your mind must remain open to what may seem the strangest things to come. For example, conceptual representation learning (see previous chapters) will bring new dimensions to a machine's thinking mind.

This chapter takes the technology of the previous chapter and applies it to a self-driving car working for the mayor's office in a city called **Iotham City**. The previous chapter used a webcam and a program and sent instructions to the conveyor belt. It was in the family of IoT. Let's add a **support vector machine** to the program and take it out on the streets of Iotham City to see what happens.

The chapter is divided into three main sections: Iotham City's project, the configuration of the model, and running the model.

The following topics will be covered in this chapter:

- A self-driving solution
- Introducing a safe route parameter in trip planners
- Applying CNNs to parking lots
- Applying SVMs to safety on a trip planning
- Teaching an MDP to find the safest route (not necessarily the shortest way)

Technical requirements

Python 3.6x 64-bit from `https://www.python.org/`.

Packages and modules:

```
import numpy as ql
 from matplotlib.ticker import FuncFormatter
 import matplotlib.pyplot as plt
 from matplotlib.path import Path
 import matplotlib.patches as patches
 import random
 import math
 import time
 from keras.preprocessing.image import load_img
 from keras.preprocessing.image import img_to_array
 import keras
 from keras.preprocessing.image import ImageDataGenerator
 from keras.models import model_from_json
 from keras.models import load_model
 import scipy.misc
 from PIL import Image
```

GitHub, `Chapter13`:

- `CNN_CONCEPT_STRATEGY.py`
- `CRL-MM-IoT_SVM.py`

Check out the following video to see the code in action:

`https://goo.gl/UQmAJb`

The Iotham City project

A few years from now, the mayor and the city council of Iotham have decided to implement a self-driving, home-to-homeless-shelter service:

- Families at homes have clothing and food they would like to give to others that need them.
- The self-driving car can be started at a distance and goes to homes and takes the goods to the shelters.
- The self-driving car does not need to have a base. It can park anywhere, go anywhere, and refuel at service stations with automatic electric recharging.

Some IoT projects plan to put sensors on every parking space and send the information to control centers. Iotham City finds that too expensive. Instead, the city council has decided to use a more cost-effective solution. A webcam will be installed on all the possible parking lots in the project's grid. This smart grid is for transporting products from homes to shelters.

The model in this chapter can start at any point. This is circular, as described in the previous chapter. Our scenario starts after the self-driving car has just delivered clothing to a shelter. Now the self-driving vehicle has to find a parking lot to park in until its next mission.

Setting up the DQN-CRLMM model

This section describes how to set up the previous chapter's model for this project and add a few functions.

A DQN-CRLMM model contains a **convolutional neural network (CNN)** and a **Markov Decision Process (MDP)** linked together by an optimizer.

A conceptual representation learning meta-model contains:

- A CNN
- An optimizer linking it to an MDP
- An MDP function

This system will now be referred to as a **CRLMM.**

Training the CRLMM

In previous chapters, the CRLMM program CNN_STRATEGY_MODEL.py was trained to identify Γ (gamma concept) in outputs on the conveyor belt of a food processing factory. The end of the previous chapter brought Γ up to a higher abstraction level.

As long as a member of γ (gamma) of the Γ dataset is in an undetermined state, its generalization encompasses ambivalent but similar concepts. Up to this chapter, these are the concepts Γ has learned (conceptual representation learning).

Γ = { a gap, no gap, a load, no load, not enough load, enough load, too much load, a space on a lane for a car, a distance between a high load of products and missing products on a conveyor belt, weights on sewing stations...n}

The next step in the chapter is to train the CRLMM built in the previous chapters to recognize a parking space in a parking lot and send a signal to the self-driving vehicle:

- Γ will now see gaps as space
- Γ will now perceive space as a distance (gap) between two objects
- Γ will need a **context** to find out whether this space between two objects is a positive or negative distance

The dataset

As in the previous chapters, the dataset directory of this chapter on GitHub contains:

- The training set
- The test set
- The model trained by 01_CNN_STRATEGY_MODEL.py
- The classify directory used by 01_CNN_STRATEGY_MODEL.py

As explained in the previous chapters, a full dataset would take weeks, if not months, to prepare. They are projects in themselves.

For this example, Γ has evolved into space (gap detection between (distance)) cars to find a parking space.

The following is a simulated frozen frame with no **Γ-space** taken by a webcam located on a building, pointing down to a parking lot:

Simulated frozen frame

The following frame represents a small but sufficient parking space on the left of the screen. I copied the pavement over it to free the **Γ-space**. It shows something like several available parking spaces:

Sufficient parking space frame

Training and testing the model

The model was trained by using the same `01_CNN_STRATEGY_MODEL.py` program as in `Chapter 9`, *Getting Your Neurons to Work*.

Just be sure the directory in the header of the following program is pointing to /dataset, which is scenario number 2:

```
A=['dataset_O/','dataset_traffic/','dataset/']
scenario=2 #reference to A
directory=A[scenario] #transfer learning parameter (choice of images)
print("directory",directory)
```

The model is stored in `/dataset/model`. To test the model, the `CNN_STRATEGY_MODEL.py` improved in the previous chapter was used. Just change the messages and limit the frame classification loop to 2 as shown in the following code snippet:

```
MS1='full'
MS2='space'
I=['1','2','3','4','5','6']
for im in range(2):
```

The following loaded image was already resized before applying the kernels of the CNN:

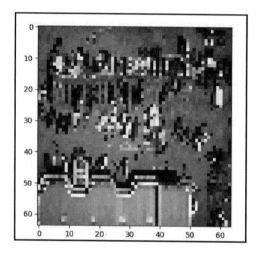

Resized image

Classifying the parking lots

Now that the CRLMM has been trained to distinguish a full parking lot from a parking lot with available space, once an available parking lot has been found, an SVM takes over as an intermediate step.

Adding an SVM function

The self-driving car has delivered its packages to the shelters. Now it has to find a parking lot and park there. Instead of having a base like many other systems, this saves Iotham City many useless trips.

Motivation – using an SVM to increase safety levels

The support vector system adds a new function to itinerary calculations—**safety**.

Most systems such as Google Maps focus on:

- Shortest trip
- Fastest trip
- Traffic

However, self-driving cars have to take extra precautions. In fact, many humans do not feel secure on some roads. Iotham City has a good management policy. Safety will come first, no matter what. Once a suitable parking lot has been found, the SVM has to **avoid traffic**.

The goal is to find a path through traffic even if the distance is longer. A **p** parameter allows for a p% variance of the distance. For example, 10% allows a 10% longer distance and will provide a safe passage, as shown in the following SVM result:

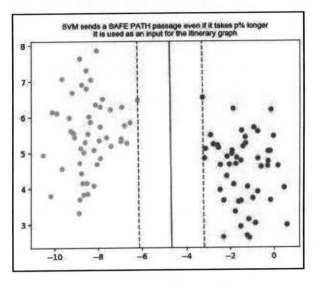

Traffic path

It is important to note that the data points are **not** the actual coordinates but a representation in a higher dimension, as explained in the following section.

Definition of a support vector machine

A **support vector machine (SVM)** classifies data by transforming it into higher dimensions. It will then classify data into two classes, for example.

In the following example, the SVM will be used to separate risky driving locations from safer driving locations:

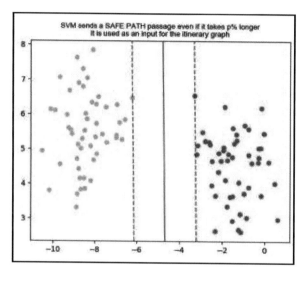

Traffic path

The example in the code is random (as in real-life traffic) but the model can be developed much further.

Safety is the key to this model, so each driving location (road, crossing) possesses features related to this goal:

- Number of accidents at that location
- Traffic at that location
- Experience of driving through that location (near misses and no problems)

All of this data can be fed into an SVM program. The program will transform the data to make it linearly separable (see Chapter 4, *Become an Unconventional Innovator*).

The blue dots on the left will be the good locations, and the brown ones on the left will be the risky ones. To convert it back into GPS format, a function will just read the latitude and longitude features of the data point.

For example, a blue dot on the left might be:

- Location A
- One accident in the past 10 years
- Zero problems driving through that point in 1 year

A brown dot might be:

- Location D (a few blocks from A)
- Seventy-four accidents in 10 years
- Fifteen problems driving through that point in 1 year

The blue dots and brown dots thus have nothing to do with the real location on the preceding graph. The locations are **labels**. Their features have been separated as expected.

> To send the data to a GPS guiding system, all that needs to be done is to find the GPS coordinates of the locations that are part of the initial dataset.

Location A will be chosen, for example, instead of location D; so the program looks into the dataset and finds its GPS location.

Let's put some words on the following SVM graph:

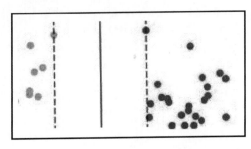

SVM graph

- The space between the dotted vertical lines is the **margin**. It's somewhat like the margin between two lines of a rugby or football team. When the players (data points) are lined up, an invisible space or margin separates them.

- The dots that touch those **margins** are critical because they are the ones that decide where the margin will be in the first place. As the rugby or football players line up in clusters, the SVM will calculate this (see the following Python function). These special data points are called **support points**. They can also be called **support vectors**.
- The vertical line running in the middle of the **margin** is the **decision line**.
- Since the dots are separated by a line, the dataset is linearly separable (see Chapter 4, *Become an Unconventional Innovator*). This means that a line can be drawn between the data points and can separate them into classes. In this case, the system wants to obtain safe locations (blue dots) and avoid unsafe locations (brown dots).

Python function

The `sklearn` packages provide the following `svm` function:

```
from sklearn import svm
from sklearn.datasets import make_blobs
```

The `make_blobs` function generates uniform data for this example in all directions. It is thus an **isotropic** distribution (*iso*=equal, *tropy*=way) of random data. A **blob** contains points of data.

`scikit-learn` contains a **Gaussian** factor for the generation function. A Gaussian kernel applies standard deviations from a mean. Imagine you are playing in a sandbox and you make a little hill. Then, with your hand, you cut the pile in two. The mean is where you cut the sand pile; the standard deviation is shown by the slopes going down on both sides.

It might take days, and sometimes weeks, to put a good dataset together. But with `scikit-learn`, you can do it in one line, as shown in the following code snippet:

```
323:#100 cars clusters(concentration of cars) represented
X, y = make_blobs(n_samples=100, centers=2, random_state=7)
```

This function offers many parameters. The ones used are as follows:

- `n_samples`, which represents the number of points spread out between the clusters. In this example, 100 already represents subclusters of car concentrations in an area.

- `centers` is the number of centers to generate data from. In this example, 2 represents areas close to the present location of the self-driving car and its future destination.
- `random_state` is the seed by the random number generator. It is where the sequence of random numbers will start. This is because what we think is random is pseudo-random, so it has some deterministic basis.

In this example, a `linear` kernel is used to fit the model, as shown in the following code:

```
325:# the model is directly fitted. The goal is a global estimate
clf = svm.SVC(kernel='linear', C=1000)
clf.fit(X, y)
```

scikit-learn's SVM contains a parameter penalty, which explains the `C` in `svm.SVC`. There are many more options, but the key option is the kernel. A linear kernel will produce a linear separation, as shown in the preceding screenshot.

An RBF kernel would produce a different result. The structure looks more regularized. As shown in the following screenshot, an RBF kernel acts as an efficient structural regularizer:

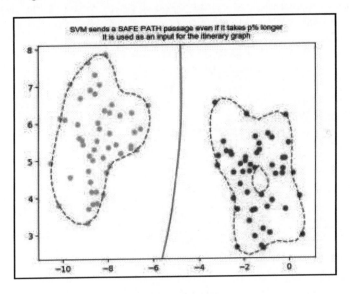

Regularized structure path

Bear in mind that the SVM can be used for image recognition on the MNIST and CIFAR datasets, for example. Artificial intelligence provides more than one way to solve a given problem. It is up to you to choose the right tools by having a flexible trial-and-error approach where necessary.

The plot lines start at line 300. The main line to take into account is the function that will find and use the **decision line** (see preceding definition) and scatter the data points on both sides of the margin. This is achieved by using the following decision_function:

```
Z = clf.decision_function(xy).reshape(XX.shape)
```

The result will be displayed as shown previously. The SVM is now a component of the CRLMM in this self-driving car model.

Running the CRLMM

The self-driving car's mission is a circular (no beginning, no end) one like the CRLMM described in the previous chapter:

- If it is in a parking lot, it can be activated by a home or a shelter
- If it is at a given home, it will go to a shelter
- If at a shelter, it can go to a home or a parking space
- If it needs recharging, this can be done at a recharging space (or more probably at a parking space), which is already the case in some cities

At one point, the self-driving car has to go from a home to a parking space. This part of its itinerary is the subject of the following sections.

Finding a parking space

CRL-MM-IoT_SVM.py uses a fine-tuned version of the MDP_Graph.py described in the previous chapter.

A no-Γ (no gamma, no gap, no space) is not acceptable.

If the crlmm function, which classifies parking lot images into full or available space, returns a 0, the program detects it and displays a message. The code samples contain the line number of the following code excerpt:

```
389: if(crlmm==0):
     full = load_img("FULL.JPG")
     plt.subplot(111)
```

```
    plt.imshow(full)
    plt.title('PARKING LOT STATUS : This          parking lot is full.'
+'\n'+'Another webcam        is        consulted',fontname='Arial',
fontsize=10)
    #plt.text(0.1,2, "The frame is the input of      a trained CNN")
    plt.show(block=False)
    time.sleep(5)
    plt.close()
    print("This parking lot is full,      searching...")
```

The program displays the following full sign and closes it after a few seconds:

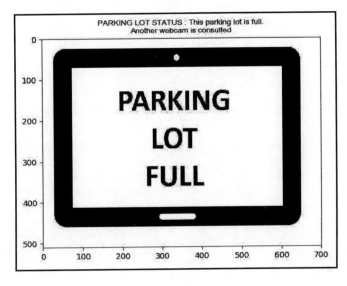

Parking lot status

The program must find a parking space. It will thus try searches of good parking lots as shown in line 388 of this code snippet:

```
388:for search in range(1000):
    if(crlmm==0):
```

A thousand searches looks like a lot, but it isn't. Some cities already have parking spaces near sidewalks with recharging stations.

Furthermore, looking for available parking spaces in a large city can be excruciating. More often than not, it will not be suitable: there will be not enough available parking spaces to be sure to find one in the time it will take to get there.

For this prototype, the number of optimal searches is limited to 2. Beyond that value, the following CRLMM function is activated:

```
399:if(search>2):
    a=1
    crlmm=CRLMM(Q,lr,e,a)
```

After two fruitless searches, the program activates a, a flag for the crlmm function.

The crlmm function now contains a random search function, which simulates the choice of a parking lot and provides a first-level status:

```
204:  status=random.randint(0,10)
   if(status>5):
        status=1
   if(status<=5):
        status=0
```

The status represents a probabilistic estimate of the availability of the parking lot. The a flag simulates a program yet to be added that will scan all the parking lots and run this function to find an available space.

 To present a prototype on a first meeting, you will always need enough to convince, but if you go too far, the cost of doing this becomes a risk if your idea is rejected.

So if a is activated, the system simulates a scan (to be developed) and forces the status to 1, as shown in the following code snippet:

```
209:if(a>0 and status==0):
#add an available search function here that scans all the
#webcams of then network until it finds one that suits the model (not too
far parameter and available)
status=1
```

The program then continues and runs the convolutional neural network (CNN) trained to identify an available parking lot (see the screenshot that follows), as explained in the preceding configuration section.

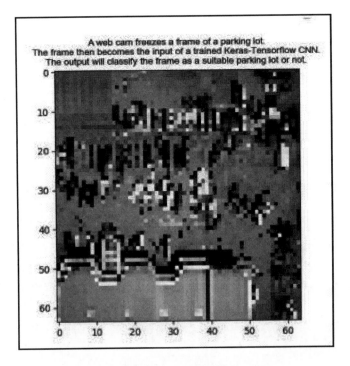

A web cam freezes a frame of a parking lot.
The frame then becomes the input of a trained Keras-Tensorflow CNN.
The output will classify the frame as a suitable parking lot or not.

Web came freezes a frame of parking lot

Now that a parking lot with available space has been found (the empty spaces on the top left of the frame), the search function stops and the following break instruction is activated:

```
402: if(crlmm==1):
a=0
break
```

Deciding how to get to the parking lot

The CRLMM program has found a suitable parking lot, as shown in the following code, when crlmm==1:

```
406:if(crlmm==1):
    available = load_img("AVAILABLE.JPG")
    plt.subplot(111)
    plt.imshow(available)
    plt.title('PARKING LOT STATUS : This parking lot has available space.'
+'\n'+'Now an SVM will suggest a safe route ',fontname='Arial',
```

```
    fontsize=10)
   #plt.text(0.1,2, "The frame is the input of a trained CNN"
      plt.show(block=False)
      time.sleep(5)
      plt.close()
      print("This parking lot has available space...")
```

It displays this message and a sign:

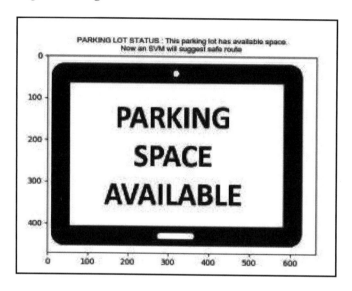

Parking lot status

Support vector machine

The CRLMM now **demands a safe route** even if it means taking longer (time or distance). For Iotham, safety comes first.

The program reaches the following SVM function:

```
415:print("This parking lot has available space...")
SAFE_SVM()
```

The SVM described in the configuration section provides a safe passage through traffic, as shown in this screenshot of the result:

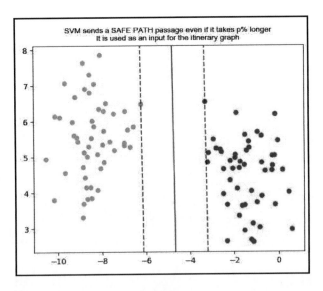

Traffic graph

For example, in this random case (traffic will be random most of the time), the blue dots on the left represent sparser traffic and the brown dots represent areas with denser traffic. Explained as follows, the weights of the statistics of past accidents and the car's experience can be added to create a deeper vision of this **safety** model trip planner.

Suppose the self-driving car has to go to a point in the brown area. The SVM will:

- Suggest an itinerary that goes through blue dot areas as much as possible and then only in brown areas
- Send the information to Google Maps

Many drivers feel unsafe on loaded freeways or in dense cities. Adding the safest route function to mapping software would help.

The SVM brought the data points to a higher level (see the explanation in the configuration section of the chapter).

 The points represented in an SVM function are **not** the actual locations but an abstract representation. The dividing line needs to go through a function that will transform that information into a real location data point.

Once the SVM boundaries have been converted into location data points, the itinerary or trip graph is activated.

The itinerary graph

The prototype shows a simulation of an itinerary graph based on the SVM recommendations and its weight vector through the following function call:

```
421:print("SAFE PASSAGE SUGGESTED")
MDP_GRAPH(lr,e)
```

The following graph displays the **safest** itinerary in red even if it takes longer (time or distance):

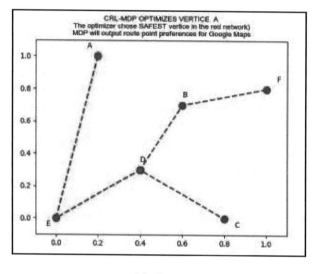

Safest itinerary

For the purpose of the prototype, the SVM was not directly connected to the graph, which would require costly hours. Instead, the following `random.randint` function was inserted, which simulates the random availability of parking space anyway:

```
417:for wi in range(6):
    op=random.randint(0,5)
    if(W[op]>maxw):
        lr=op;maxw=W[op]
```

Bear in mind that it would be useless to develop more for a prototype for the first presentation to a prospect or manager.

This type of prototype is more powerful than a slide show because it proves your legitimacy. Slideshows are static and don't prove your abilities on this particular subject. A prototype will show your expertise. But do not overdo it unless you have a budget!

The weight vector

The weight vector is displayed. In this model, the weights represent the locations just like in the previous chapter. However, in this chapter, the weights are a rating:

- Each weight has a high safety rank when few accidents have occurred around that area in the past n years. It is a **safety rank**. This ranking should be part of our itinerary software. We should be informed.
- Each weight will be customized by the self-driving car's experience. It is its own driving record. Near misses because of its faulty software will bring the weight down. Good track records will take the weights up. What seems easy for a human might be difficult for software and vice versa.

The system now displays the weights used with an internal update program to be developed if the prototype is accepted. The following code calls the function that manages the weights of the safest routes for the self-driving vehicle and displays a histogram:

```
423: print("Vertice Weights",W)
MDP_CRL_graph(W,lr)
```

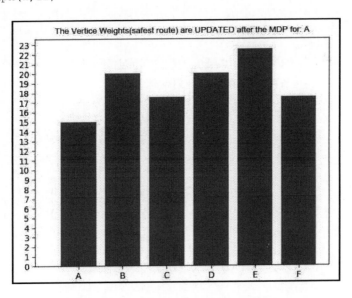

Histogram of weights used with an internal update program

Summary

This chapter, like the previous chapter, described a connected IoT process with no humans involved. This trend will expand into every field in the years to come.

This also shows that knowing how to use a tool requires hard work, especially when learning artificial intelligence. Imagining a solution for a given market requires more than hard work. Creativity does not come with work. It develops by freeing your mind from any form of constraint.

Once the solution has been imagined, then comes the fine line between developing too much for a presentation and not showing enough. A CRLMM provides the kind of framework that helps build a technical solution (CNN, MDP, SVM, and optimizers) while keeping everyday concepts that others understand in mind.

For the first meeting with Iotham or any other city council members, a good slide show with a working prototype, along with some past references, would be a good start. A realistic approach would be to ask how far the prototype should be developed to have a chance to be on the shortlist.

The next chapter will lead us deeper into the corporate world by applying artificial intelligence to blockchains.

Questions

1. Driving quickly to a location is better than safety in any situation. (Yes | No)
2. Self-driving cars will never really replace human drivers. (Yes | No)
3. Will a self-driving fire truck with robots be able to put out a fire one day? (Yes | No)
4. Do major cities need to invest in self-driving cars or avoid them? (Invest | Avoid)
5. Would you trust a self-driving bus to take children to school and back? (Yes | No)
6. Would you be able to sleep in a self-driving car on a highway? (Yes | No)
7. Would you like to develop a self-driving program for a project for a city? (Yes | No)

Further reading

For more information on self-driving cars:

https://www.mckinsey.com/industries/automotive-and-assembly/our-insights/self-driving-car-technology-when-will-the-robots-hit-the-road

References

How to implement an SVM:

http://scikit-learn.org/stable/modules/svm.html
http://scikit-learn.org/stable/auto_examples/svm/plot_separating_hyperplane.html#sphx-glr-auto-examples-svm-plot-separating-hyperplane-py

14
Optimizing Blockchains with AI

IBM was founded in 1911, making it the most experienced company today in its field. Google, Amazon, and Microsoft also offer history-making machine learning platforms. However, IBM offers machine learning platforms with its valuable 100+ years of experience.

Some of IBM's 100+ years in the computer and software market were bumpy. Some terrible decisions cost the company a lot of problems across the world. IBM learned from those mistakes and now offers robust solutions:

- IBM Hyperledger for blockchain solutions (this chapter)
- IBM Watson for artificial intelligence applications, including chatbots (see `Chapter 15`, *Cognitive NLP Chatbots*, and `Chapter 16`, *Improve the Emotional Intelligence Deficiencies of Chatbots*)
- IBM quantum computing (see `Chapter 17`, *Quantum Computers That Think*)

This chapter offers an overview of what blockchains mean for companies around the world, introduces naive Bayes, and explains where it could fit in a CRLMM.

Mining cryptocurrency represents one side of the use of blockchains. IBM advocates using blockchains for corporate transactions and brings 100+ years of experience into the field.

The following topics will be covered in this chapter:

- Using blockchains to mine bitcoins
- Using blockchains for business transactions
- How the blocks of a blockchain provide a unique dataset for artificial intelligence
- Applying artificial intelligence to the blocks of a blockchain to predict and suggest transactions
- Naive Bayes
- How to use naive Bayes on blocks of a blockchain to predict further transactions and blocks

Technical requirements

Python 3.6x 64-bit from `https://www.python.org/`.

Package and modules:

```
import numpy as np
import pandas as pd
from sklearn.naive_bayes import GaussianNB
```

Programs from GitHub `Chapter14`:

`naive_bayes_blockchains.py`

Check out the following video to see the code in action:

`https://goo.gl/kE3yNc`

Blockchain technology background

Blockchain technology will transform transactions in every field.

For 1,000+ years, transactions have been mostly local bookkeeping systems. For the past 100 years, even though the computer age changed the way information was managed, things did not change that much. Each company continued to keep its transactions to itself, only sharing some information through tedious systems.

Blockchain makes a transaction **block** visible to the global network it has been generated in.

The fundamental concepts to keep in mind are **sharing** and **privacy control**. The two ideas seem to create a cognitive dissonance, something impossible to solve. Yet it has been solved, and it will change the world.

When a block (a transaction of any kind) is generated, it is shared with the whole network. Permissions to read the information within that block remain manageable and thus private if the regulator of that block wants the information to stay private.

Whether the goal is to mine bitcoins through blocks or use blocks for transactions, artificial intelligence will enhance this innovation shortly.

Mining bitcoins

Mining a bitcoin means creating a mathematical block for a valid transaction and adding this block to the chain, the blockchain:

$$Blockchain = \{block_1, block_2, the\ block\ just\ added...block_n\}$$

The blockchain cannot go back in time. It is like a time-dating feature in life. On minute m, you do something, on minute $m+1$ something else, on minute $m+n$ something else, and so on. You cannot travel back in time. **What is done is done**.

When a block is added to the bitcoin chain, there is no way of undoing the transaction.

The global network of bitcoin mining consists of **nodes**. With the appropriate software, you leave a port open, allocate around 150+ GB of disk space, and generate new blocks. The nodes communicate with each other, and the information is relayed to the other nodes around the whole network.

For a node to be a miner, it must solve complex mathematical puzzles that are part of the bitcoin program.

To solve the puzzle, the software must find a number that fits in a specific range when combined with the data in the block being generated. The number is passed through a hash function.

You can call the number a **nonce** and it's used only once. For example, an integer between 0 and 4,294,967,296 for a bitcoin must be generated.

The process is random. The software generates a number, passes it through the hash function, and sends it out to the network. The first **miner** who produces a number in the expected range informs the whole network that that particular block has been generated. The rest of the network stops working on that block and moves on to another one.

The reward for the miner is naturally paid out in bitcoins. It represents a lot of money, but it's hard to get, considering the competition in the network and the cost required (CPU, electricity, disk space, and time) to produce correct results.

 Keep an eye on quantum computers (see `Chapter 17`, *Quantum Computers That Think*) because their exponential power could dramatically change the mining market.

Using cryptocurrency

Be very careful with cryptocurrency. The concept sounds fascinating, but the result remains currency. Currency can be volatile, and you can lose your life's savings in less than an hour if a crash occurs.

 Golden rule: If you cannot resist investing in cryptocurrencies, do not invest more than you can afford to lose.

That being said, to use cryptocurrency, first set up a wallet to store your bitcoins, for example. The wallet can be online, through a provider, or even offline.

Once that is done, you will be able to purchase bitcoins as you wish in hard cash, or using credit cards, debit cards, and transfers.

Remember, you are buying these currencies like any other currency with all the potential, but also all the risks, involved.

Using blockchains

IBM blockchain, based on Hyperledger Fabric, provides a way for companies around the world to share a blockchain transaction network without worrying about mining or using cryptocurrencies.

The system is based on the Linux Foundation project. Hyperledger is an open source collaborative project hosted by the Linux Foundation.

At this level, Hyperledger uses blockchains to guarantee secure transactions without trying to optimize the cryptocurrency aspect. The software generates blocks in a blockchain network shared by all the parties involved, but they do not have to purchase cryptocurrencies in the currency sense—only in the technological sense.

The following graph, used in previous chapters to illustrate the Markov Decision Process, is applied to a blockchain.

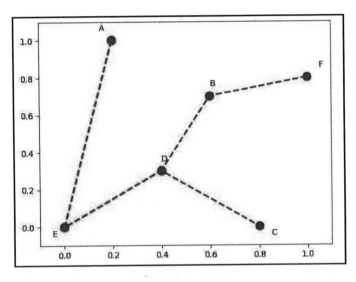

Markov Decision Process graph

Each vertex represents a company that takes part in an IBM Hyperledger network set up for those six companies, as described in the following table:

Company	Activity	Weight in a CRLMM
A buys and sells clothing and also other products in this network.	Provide goods to the network but keep the stock levels down	Stock levels
B buys and sells fabric and also other products in this network.	Provide goods to the network but keep the stock levels down	Stock levels
C buys and sells buttons and also other products in this network.	Provide goods to the network but keep the stock levels down	Stock levels
D buys and sells printed fabric and also other products in this network.	Provide goods to the network but keep the stock levels down	Stock levels
E buys and sells accessories (belts, bracelets) and also other products in this network.	Provide goods to the network but keep the stock levels down	Stock levels
F buys and sells packaging boxes and also other products in this network.	Provide goods to the network but keep the stock levels down	Stock levels

With millions of commercial transactions per year with a huge amount of transportation (truck, train, boat, air), it is impossible to manage this network effectively in the 21st century without a solution like IBM Hyperledger.

With IBM Hyperledger, the companies have **one** online transaction ledger with smart contracts (online) and real-time tracking.

The transactions are secure; they can be private or public among the members of the network and they provide real-time optimization information for an artificial intelligence solution.

Using blockchains in the A-F network

IBM Hyperledger provides artificial intelligence developers with a unique advantage over any other dataset—a 100% reliable dataset updated in real time.

Creating a block

A block is formed with the method described for mining a bitcoin, except that this time currency is not a goal. The goal is a secure transaction with a smart contract when necessary. The following screenshot is a standard IBM interface that can be customized:

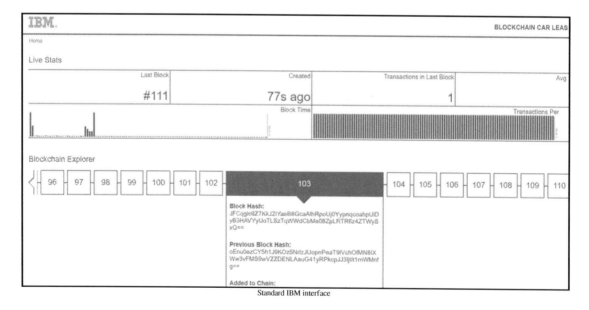

Standard IBM interface

You can see the individual and unique blocks that make up a blockchain. Each block in IBM Hyperledger has a unique number. In this example, it is **111** with a zoom on block **103**.

A block in the preceding A to F example can be the purchase of a product X with a contract. The next block can be the transportation of that product to another location and any transaction within the A-F blockchain network.

The information attached to that block is in the Hyperledger repository: company name, address, phone number, transaction description, and any other type of data required by the network of companies. Each block can be viewed by all or some depending on the permission properties attached to it.

Exploring the blocks

Exploring the blocks provides an artificial intelligence program with a gold mine: a limitless, real-life, and 100% reliable dataset.

The interesting part for AI optimization is the block information, as described in the following screenshot. The present block was added to the chain along with the previous block and the transaction code.

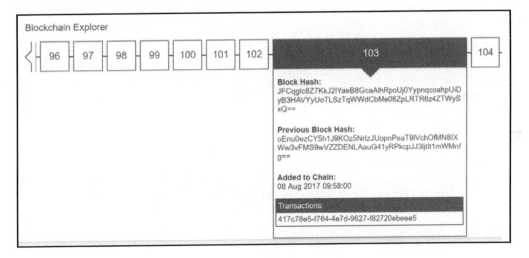

Notice that the block hash (see the preceding mining section) of a given block is linked to the previous block hash and possesses a unique transaction code.

The CRLMM will use some of the critical information as **features** to optimize warehouse storage and product availability in a real-time process.

To implement the CRLMM, an additional component is required: a naive Bayes learning function. The naive Bayes learning function will learn the previous block to predict and output the next blocks that should be inserted in the blockchain.

Using naive Bayes in a blockchain process

Naive Bayes is based on Bayes' theorem. Bayes' theorem applies conditional probability, defined as follows:

$$P(A|B) = \frac{P(B|A)P(A)}{P(B)}$$

- $P(A|B)$ is a **posterior probability**, the probability of A after having observed some events (B). It is also a **conditional probability**: the likelihood of A happening given B has already happened.
- $P(B|A)$ the probability of B given the prior observations A. It is also a conditional probability: the likelihood of B happening given A has already happened.
- $P(A)$ is the probability of A prior to the observations.
- $P(B)$ is the probability of the predictions.

Naive Bayes, although based on Bayes' theorem, assumes that the features in a class are **independent** of each other. In many cases, this makes predictions more practical to implement. The statistical presence of features, related or not, will produce a prediction. As long as the prediction remains sufficiently efficient, naive Bayes provides a good solution.

A naive Bayes example

Chapter 12, *Automated Planning and Scheduling*, described an apparel-manufacturing process. The CRLMM program used there optimized the load of the sewing stations.

The load of a sewing station in an apparel industry is expressed in quantities, in **stock keep units (SKUs)**. An SKU, for example, can be product P: a pair of jeans of a given size.

Once the garment has been produced, it goes into storage. At that point, a block in a blockchain can represent that transaction with two useful features for a machine learning algorithm:

- The day the garment was stored
- The total quantity of that SKU-garment now in storage

Since the blockchain contains the storage blocks of all A, B, C, D, E, and F locations that are part of the network, a machine learning program can access the data and make predictions.

The goal is to spread the stored quantities of the given product evenly over the six locations, as represented in the following histogram:

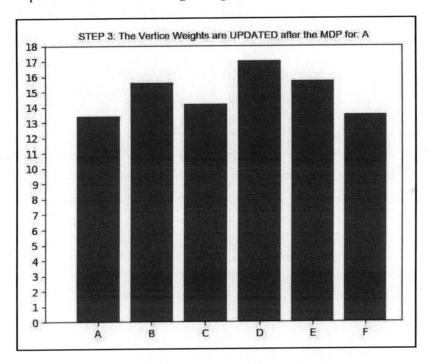

Storage level of product distributed over six locations Histogram

This screenshot shows the storage level of product P distributed over six locations. Each location in this blockchain network is a **hub**. A hub in **supply chain management (SCM)** is often an intermediate storage warehouse. For example, to cover the area of these six locations, the same product will be stored at each location. This way, local trucks can come and pick the goods for delivery.

The goal is to have an available product P at point A when needed. The delivery time from A to a location point a_1 (a store or home) will only take a few hours. If A did not store P, then the finer consumer would have to wait for the product to travel from C to A, for example.

If the blockchain network is well organized, one location can specialize in producing product P (best production costs) and evenly distribute the quantity stored in the six locations, including itself.

This load optimization approach is the same as the CRLMM Chapter 12, *Automated Planning and Scheduling*. Reusing a model in domain learning will generate profit and lower costs. The more an AI solution can be applied to transfer, domain, and conceptual learning, the more powerful it will become. It will learn more and solve an endless number of problems.

The blockchain anticipation novelty

In former days, all the warehouses at those six locations (A to F) had to ensure the minimum storage level for each location.

In a world of real-time producing and selling, distributors need to predict **demand**. The system needs to be **demand driven**. Naive Bayes can solve that problem.

It will take the first two features into account:

- **DAY**: The day the garment was stored
- **STOCK**: The total quantity of that SKU-garment now in storage

Then it will add a novelty—the number of blocks related to product P.

A high number of blocks at a given date means that this product was in demand in general (production, distribution). The more blocks there are, the more transactions there are. Also, if the storage levels (STOCK feature) are diminishing, this is an indicator; it means storage levels must be replenished. The DAY feature time-stamps the history of the product.

The block feature is named **BLOCK**. Since the blockchain is shared by all, a machine learning program can access reliable global data in seconds. The dataset reliability provided by blockchains constitutes a motivation in itself to optimize blocks.

The goal

This CRLMM is the same one as in Chapter 11, *Conceptual Representation Learning*. The difference is that instead of analyzing a conveyor belt to make a decision, the system will analyze the blocks of a blockchain.

The program will take the DAY, STOCK, and BLOCKS (number of) features for a given product P and produce a result. The result predicts whether this product P will be in demand or not. If the answer is yes or 1, the demand for this product requires anticipation.

Step 1 the dataset

The dataset contains raw data from prior events in a sequence, which makes it perfect for prediction algorithms. This constitutes a unique opportunity to see the data of all companies without having to build a database. The raw dataset will look like the following list:

BLOCKS	STATUS
Blocks	No
Some_blocks	Yes
No_Blocks	Yes
Blocks	Yes
Blocks	Yes
Some_blocks	Yes
Blocks	Yes
No_Blocks	No
Blocks	Yes
No_Blocks	Yes

Raw dataset

This dataset contains the following:

- **Blocks** of product P present in the blockchain on day *x* scanning the blockchain back by 30 days. **No** means no significant amounts of blocks has been found. **Yes** means a significant number of blocks have been found. If blocks have been found, this means that there is a demand for this product somewhere along the blockchain.

- **Some_blocks** means that blocks have been found, but they are too sparse to be taken into account without overfitting the prediction. However, yes will contribute to the prediction as well as no.
- **No_blocks** means there is no demand at all, sparse or not (**Some_blocks**), numerous (blocks) or not. This means trouble for this product P.

The goal is to avoid predicting demand on sparse (**Some_blocks**) or absent (**No_blocks**) products. This example is trying to predict a potential **Yes** for numerous blocks for this product P. Only if **Yes** is predicted can the system trigger the automatic demand process (see the *Implementation* section later in the chapter).

Step 2 frequency

Looking at the following frequency table provides additional information:

STATUS:	No	No	No	Yes	Yes	Yes
	Some_blocks	No_Blocks	Blocks	Some_blocks	No_Blocks	Blocks
			1			
				1		
					1	
						1
						1
				1		
						1
		1				
						1
					1	
FREQUENCY	0	1	1	2	2	4

Frequency table

The **Yes** and **No** statuses of each feature (**Blocks, Some_blocks**, or **No_blocks**) for a given product P for a given period (past 30 days) have been grouped by frequency.

The sum is on the bottom line for each no feature and yes feature. For example, **Yes** and **No_Blocks** add up to 2.

Some additional information will prove useful for the final calculation:

- The total number of samples = 10
- The total number of yes samples = 8
- The total number of no samples = 2

Step 3 likelihood

Now that the **frequency** table has been calculated, the following **likelihood** table is produced using that data:

Weather	No	Yes		
Some_block	0	2	2	0,2
No Blocks	1	2	3	0,3
Blocks	1	4	5	0,5
	2	8		
	0,2	0,8		

Likelihood table

The table contains the following statistics:

- *No = 2 = 20% = 0.2*
- *Yes = 8 = 80%=0.8*
- *Some blocks = 2 = 20%=0.2*
- *No blocks = 3 = 30%=0.3*
- *Blocks = 5 = 50%=0.5*

Blocks represent an important proportion of the samples, which means that along with some blocks, the demand looks good.

Step 4 naive Bayes equation

The goal now is to represent each variable of the Bayes' theorem in a naive Bayes equation to obtain the probability of having **demand** for product P and trigger a purchase scenario for the blockchain network. Bayes' theorem can be expressed as follows:

$$P(A|B) = \frac{P(B|A)P(A)}{P(B)}$$

- *P(Yes|Blocks)=P(Blocks|Yes) * P(Yes)/P(Blocks)*
- *P(Yes)=8/10 = 0.8*
- *P(Blocks)=5/10 = 0.5*
- *P(Blocks|Yes)=4/8 = 0.5*
- *P(Yes|Blocks)=(0.5*0.8)/0.5 = 0.8*

The demand looks acceptable. However, penalties must be added and other factors must be considered as well (transportation availability through other block exploration processes).

This example and method show the concept of the naive Bayes approach. However, scikit-learn has excellent scientific functions that make implementation easier.

Implementation

This section shows how to use an advanced version of naive Bayes and where to insert this component in the CRLMM described in `Chapter 11`, *Conceptual Representation Learning*.

Gaussian naive Bayes

In implementation mode, a dataset with raw data from the blockchain will be used without the feature interpretation function of naive Bayes in the following table:

DAY	STOCK	BLOCKS	DEMAND
10	1455	78	1
11	1666	67	1
12	1254	57	1
14	1563	45	1
15	1674	89	1
10	1465	89	1
12	1646	76	1
15	1746	87	2
12	1435	78	2

Each line represents a block:

- **DAY**: The day of the month scanned (dd/mm/yyyy can be used beyond a prototype)
- **STOCK**: The total inputs in a given location (A, B, or... F) found in the blocks and totaled on that day
- **BLOCKS**: The number of blocks containing product P for location A, for example

A high number of blocks in the BLOCK column and a low number of quantities in the STOCK column mean that the demand is high.

- **DEMAND = 1**. The proof of demand is a transaction block that contains a purchase in the past. These transaction blocks provide vital information.

  A low number of blocks in the BLOCK column and a high number of quantities in the STOCK column mean that the demand is low.

- **DEMAND = 2**. Proof that no transaction was found.

However, in some cases, *DEMAND = 1* when the stock is high and the blocks are low. That's why strict correlation is not so useful where naive Bayes just analyzes the statistics and learns how to predict, ignoring the actual conditional probabilities.

The Python program

The Python `naive_bayes_blockchains.py` program uses a `skearn` class. Consider the following snippet:

```
import numpy as np
import pandas as pd
from sklearn.naive_bayes import GaussianNB
```

It reads the dataset into the data structure. The following code reads `data_BC.csv` into `df`:

```
#Reading the data
df = pd.read_csv('data_BC.csv')
print("Blocks of the Blockchain")
print (df.head())
```

It prints the top of the file in the following output:

```
Blocks of the Blockchain
  DAY STOCK BLOCKS DEMAND
0 10 1455 78 1
1 11 1666 67 1
2 12 1254 57 1
3 14 1563 45 1
4 15 1674 89 1
```

It prepares the training set, using X to find and predict Y in the following code:

```
# Prepare the training set
X = df.loc[:,'DAY':'BLOCKS']
Y = df.loc[:,'DEMAND']
```

It chooses the class and trains the following `clfG` model:

```
#Choose the class
clfG = GaussianNB()
# Train the model
clfG.fit(X,Y)
```

The program then takes some blocks of the blockchain, makes predictions, and prints them using the following `clfG.predict` function:

```
# Predict with the model(return the class)
print("Blocks for the prediction of the A-F blockchain")
blocks=[[28,2345,12],
        [29,2034,50],
        [30,7789,4],
        [31,6789,4]]
print(blocks)
prediction = clfG.predict(blocks)I
for i in range(4):
    print("Block #",i+1," Gauss Naive Bayes
Prediction:",prediction[i])
```

The blocks are displayed and the following predictions are produced. 2 means no demand for the moment; 1 will trigger a purchase block:

```
Blocks for the prediction of the A-F blockchain
[[14, 1345, 12], [29, 2034, 50], [30, 7789, 4], [31, 6789, 4]]
Block # 1 Gauss Naive Bayes Prediction: 1
Block # 2 Gauss Naive Bayes Prediction: 2
Block # 3 Gauss Naive Bayes Prediction: 2
Block # 4 Gauss Naive Bayes Prediction: 2
```

This is a replenishment program. It will mimic the demand. When no demand is found, nothing happens; when a demand is found, it triggers a purchase block. Some chain stores know the number of garments purchased on a given day (or week or another unit) and automatically purchase that amount. Others have other purchasing rules. Finding business rules is part of the consulting aspect of a project.

Implementing your ideas

Blocks in a blockchain provide sequences of unlimited data. Exploring the scikit-learn classes for naive Bayes is an excellent way to start a gold mining adventure in the world of blockchains.

Another way is to go back to the CRLMM MDP_Graph.py program used in Chapter 12, *Automated Planning and Scheduling,* and replace the content of the following crlmm function on line 383 with a Naive_Bayes:

```
383:crlmm=CRLMM(Q,lr,e)
print("GAP =0 or GAP =1 status: ",crlmm)
MDP_GRAPH(lr,e)
print("Vertice Weights",W)
MDP_CRL_graph(W,lr)
```

When crlmm is called instead of using a CNN, naive Bayes will provide the same type of information. It will predict a **Γ-gap** in the storage level (literally a space to fill in the warehouse) of the products in demand. You will have to modify the program a bit to have a parameter for crlmm to make it run a CNN or the naive Bayes approach.

Once that is processed, the **Markov decision function** in the CRLMM will take over to spread the load (products in demand) over the various locations in the blockchain network, precisely like the production stations in Chapter 9, *Getting Your Neurons to Work.* This load function can be found at line 377 in the following code:

```
377:for i in range(50000):
current_state = ql.random.randint(0, int(Q.shape[0]))
PossibleAction = possible_actions(current_state)
action = ActionChoice(PossibleAction)
reward(current_state,action,gamma)
```

The machine learning algorithms available on cloud platforms make blockchains a major field to optimize.

Summary

The reliable sequence of blocks in a blockchain has opened the door to endless machine learning algorithms. Naive Bayes appears to be a practical way to start optimizing the blocks of a blockchain. It calculates correlations and makes predictions by learning the independent features of a dataset, whether the relationship is conditional or not.

This freestyle prediction approach fits the open-minded spirit of blockchains that propagate by the millions today with limitless resources.

IBM Hyperledger takes blockchain's "Frontierland" development to another level with the Linux Foundation project. IBM also offers a cloud platform and services.

IBM, Microsoft, Amazon, and Google provide cloud platforms with an arsenal of disruptive machine learning algorithms. This provides a smooth approach to your market or department, along with the ability to set up a blockchain prototype online in a short time. With this approach, you can enter some real prototype data in the model, export the data, or use an API to read the block sequences. Then you will be able to apply machine learning algorithms to these reliable datasets.

The limit is our imaginations.

The next chapter will first take us into another IBM innovation, IBM Watson, applied to chatbots, and then beyond... into cognitive **natural language processing (NLP)**.

Questions

1. Cryptocurrency is the only use of blockchains today. (Yes | No)
2. Mining blockchains can be lucrative. (Yes | No)
3. Blockchains for companies cannot be applied to sales. (Yes | No)
4. Smart contracts for blockchains are more accessible to write than standard offline contracts. (Yes | No)
5. Once a block is in a blockchain network, everyone in the network can read the content. (Yes | No)
6. A block in a blockchain guarantees that absolutely no fraud is possible. (Yes | No)
7. There is only one way of applying Bayes' theorem. (Yes | No)
8. Training a naive Bayes dataset requires a standard function. (Yes | No)
9. Machine learning algorithms will not change the intrinsic nature of the corporate business. (Yes | No)

Further reading

For more on scikit: `http://scikit-learn.org/stable/`

To explore IBM's Hyperledger solution: `https://www.ibm.com/blockchain/hyperledger.html`

15
Cognitive NLP Chatbots

IBM Watson on IBM Cloud provides a set of tools to build a cognitive NLP chatbot. IBM proposes a well-thought process to design a chatbot. Good architecture remains the key to a chatbot's success.

To make a chatbot meet user demands, IBM Watson has many services libraries (speech to text, text to speech, and much more).

The whole process can be customized with one's programs. This makes IBM Cloud an excellent place to start creating chatbots. The TextBlob project offers another set of NLP modules that provide some interesting ways of improving a chatbot.

This chapter starts by setting up an IBM Watson chatbot following IBM's standard procedure and shows how to use IBM Watson to add one's cognitive chatbot functions. A cognitive service in Python will be described to solve a case study. The problem to address is that of a tourist on a bus that just broke down. He needs to communicate with a police chatbot to get help. The solution uses a CNN, Google Translate, **conceptual representation learning (CRL)** cognitive techniques, and sentiment analysis.

The following topics will be covered in this chapter:

- IBM Watson's chatbot solution
- Defining intents and entities
- Defining a dialog flow
- Adding scripts to the dialog flow
- Customizing scripts for a chatbot
- Using sentiment analysis to improve some dialogs
- Using **conceptual representation learning meta models (CRLMM)** to enhance some dialogs

Technical requirements

Python 3.6x 64-bit from https://www.python.org/.

Package and modules:

```
from keras.preprocessing.image import load_img
from keras.preprocessing.image import img_to_array
import matplotlib.pyplot as plt
import keras
import numpy as np
from keras.preprocessing.image import ImageDataGenerator
from keras.models import model_from_json
from keras.models import load_model
import numpy as np
import scipy.misc
from PIL import Image
import time
from textblob import TextBlob
```

Program: GitHub Chapter15/CRL-MM-Chabot.py.

Check out the following video to see the code in action:

https://goo.gl/R7qHk6

IBM Watson

IBM's Watson conversation service has many development tools for creating a chatbot with compatible standard services (translations, digitized voice, voice recognition, and so on). You can set up your own basic account in a few clicks.

To create a chatbot, you need three major objects: **intents, entities**, and a **dialog** flow. To complete the dialog flow, there are additional features: conditions, context, and expressions for example. Then services can be added such as digitalized voice, speech recognition, and more.

This section describes how to build an interview chatbot named **HobChat**, a diet bot that can interview users.

Intents

An **intent** represents the initial subject of the conversation that the chatbot is initiating. The user input needs to be **classified** just as images need to be in a CNN, for example.

Let's say HobChat needs two types of information from the user:

#whatkindof and #food

You'll notice a fundamental concept here. We are getting information from a person and not the other way around. In many chatbots, the user asks a question to obtain an answer. HobChat works the other way around. It's extracting information through interrogation techniques.

Chatbots have different points of view:

- Providing information for a user: tourism, online shopping, and other services
- Obtaining information from a user: medical applications, dietitians, sports trainers, and marketing
- Providing and gathering information

In this case, Hobchat's **intent** is to learn about *#whatkindof #food* the user likes. HobChat is prepared for the user to either answer or ask a question. To do that, we set up a list of variations of *#whatkindof* in the system in the following intents interface:

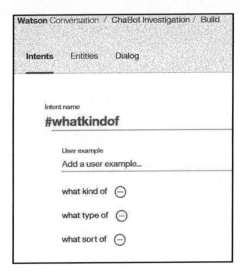

Intents interface

The intent name *#whatkindof* will be detected if a similar phrase comes up:

#whatkindof={what kindof, what type of, what sort ...n}

The number of sentences depends on the final use of the application. One similar phrase could suffice in some cases; in others, hundreds are required.

In this example, we can see that if HobChat asks *What kind of food do you like?* and if a user answers *What type of what?*, then the chatbot will apply a function *f* to the utterance.

f(utterance) will provide the intent. *f(What kind of what?)*, for example, would be parsed and classified in the *#whatkindof* intent.

The same has to be done with *#food*, for example, as shown in the following screenshot:

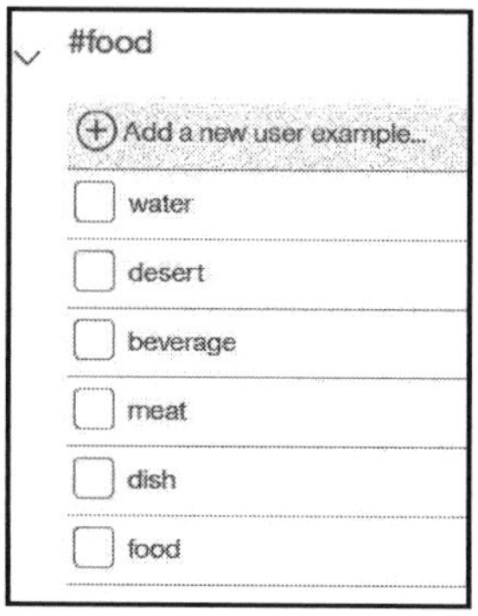

Food intent

The *#food* intent subset is now ready to use:

food = {water, dessert, beverage, meat, dish, food}

Now that some intents have been created, it's time to test these subsets.

Testing the subsets

IBM Watson provides a dialog tool to test the chatbot throughout the creation process. The dialog tool can be set up intuitively in a few steps, as described in the following dialog section.

The test dialog will run an initial dialog in the following dialog testing interface:

Dialog testing interface

We can see that HobChat was activated to start a conversation called **food interrogation**. HobChat classifies the chatbot subject in *#food* (blue in the screenshot) and starts the interview by asking a sort of generic text blob question **What kind of food do you like to eat?**.

This interview technology will also be beneficial for medical applications such as doctors asking patients questions to classify types of pathologies.

The user answers, *"What?"*

"What?" is processed as *f(utterance=f(what)= #whatkindof.*

To pursue this conversation, the chatbot needs **entities.**

Entities

Now, we need to clarify Hobchat's *#food* intent. What exactly are we talking about? What kind of food? To clarify our intent, we need entities that will describe our types of food in the following interface:

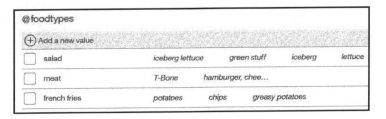

Food intent interface

Our food type entity is *#foodtypes={salad, meat, french fries}*. We also need as many synonyms for each member of the *#foodtype* group :

salad={iceberg lettuce, green stuff, iceberg, lettuce}

meat = {T-Bone, hamburger, cheeseburger}

french fries={potatoes, chips, greasy potatoes, greasy}

Now we can clarify our dialog with the food type entity in the following interface:

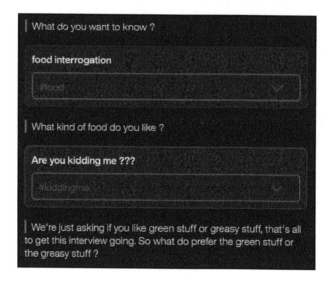

Food type entity interface

We've gone through the first part. Hobchat has asked the user, a person who visibly does not like such questions, *What kind of food do you like?*

A surprise entity was added so that *Hobchat* can detect surprise (emotion) in the answer:

The user answers: *Are you kidding me?*

Real-life conversations involve emotional answers a chatbot must deal with.

The chatbot offers a calm response: *We're just asking if you like green stuff or greasy stuff, that's all to get this interview going. So what do you prefer, the green stuff or the greasy stuff?*

To find out what's going to happen next, we have to set up the dialog flow.

Dialog flow

IBM Watson has an interface to configure the dialog flows shown previously.

To teach your chatbot how to conduct an interview using IBM Watson, or any other solution, requires a lot of cognitive science work to represent the expertise of a given field. Cognitive science involves linguistics, anthropology, psychology, philosophy, analyzing intelligence, and more.

The next section shows how to use services to implement a cognitive approach to solving a problem encountered by a chatbot.

First, a basic dialog flow must be configured. We are ready to create dialog scenarios for Hobchat. An IBM Watson conversation provides an efficient, ready-to-use platform, as shown in the following screenshot:

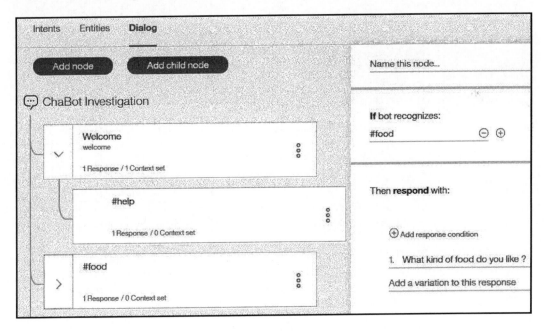

IBM Watson conversation flow chart

As you can see, it's a complex type of flowchart. You set up the dialog using your intents and entities, with all the possible linguistic variations you can provide. Then you can create an unlimited number of nodes in a combinatory tree.

You can add conditions, expressions, context, and also script as much as you want.

Scripting and building up the model

In the preceding dialog flow graph, you can enter scripts. For example, at *then respond with* nodes, you can write your script as shown in the following script-editing interface:

```
Then respond with:
1  {
2      "context": {
3          "foodtypes": [
4              "Salad",
5              "Meat",
6              "Dessert"
7          ]
8      },
9      "output": {
10         "text": {
11             "values": [
12                 "I can tell you about <? $foodtypes.join(', ') ?>",
13                 "What do you want to know ?"
14             ],
15             "selection_policy": "random"
16         }
17     }
18 }
```

Script-editing interface

In the preceding context script, on the top left, you can see *then respond with*. That means you can script your subdialogs within the dialog flow. You can add a random function such as `selection_policy:random` so that the system changes phrases every time.

Your intents and entities can also be enriched by importing data. I recommend using big data map and retrieving techniques to boost the power of the dialog. The dialog will come close to human dialogs.

IBM Watson entity features offer a vast number of entity feature add-ons, as the following screenshot shows:

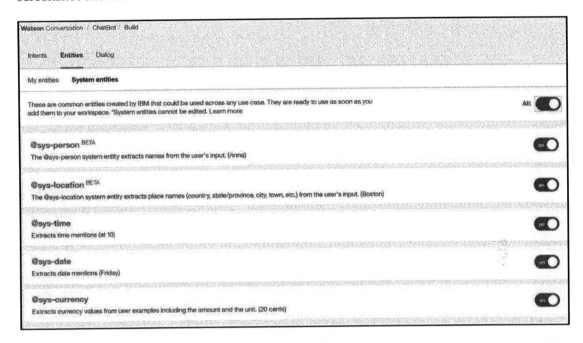

IBM Watson entity

The @Sys-person extracts names, the @sys-location system extracts place names (country, state/province, city, town, and so on), @sys-time extracts the time, @sys-date extracts the date, and @sys-currency extracts the currency and other features.

The quality of a chatbot will depend on:

- **Not** adding too many features, but just those required in some cases
- Adding **all** the necessary features when necessary, no matter how much time it takes

Adding services to a chatbot

IBM's Watson Conversation Service allows you to add all the services you want to your dialog flow, as shown in the following list:

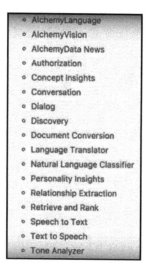

Watson Conversation Services

IBM Watson provides a robust framework and a cloud service to build a solid, reliable chatbot.

 With IBM Watson services, your imagination will be your only limit.

You can also implement a service of your own, such as a cognitive service.

A cognitive chatbot service

You now have a chatbot running on IBM Watson or another platform. The architecture of an efficient chatbot requires restricting the perimeter of the functions to a minimum and getting it to work as quickly as possible.

With a solid foundation, the chatbot can now expand its limitless potential in the areas required. Services such as these can be added to a personal assistant, for example.

The case study

A bus of English-speaking tourists is traveling through France. Somewhere in the countryside, on a small road, the bus breaks down. A tourist will use a personal assistant with inbuilt functions to communicate with a police chatbot.

Nobody speaks French. One of the tourists has a tablet and an internet connection. It also has a personal assistant on it. It could be Google Assistant, Siri, Bixby, Alexa, Cortana, or any other.

For our purpose, let's assume it's Google Assistant and say we built a backend with Google Translate, with the API described in `Chapter 8`, *Revolutions Designed for Some Corporations and Disruptive Innovations for Small to Large Companies.*

The tourist types or says as described in that chapter: `The coach broke down.` Google Translate produces a sentence in French, confusing "coach" with a sports coach and not translating it as "bus." As explained before, Google will no doubt correct this error, but there are still thousands more to correct.

This is not a problem but a limitation that we, as a worldwide community of artificial intelligence, must expand by sharing ideas.

A cognitive dataset

A cognitive NLP chatbot must provide cognition. Humans think in more than words. Mostly humans combine words and images.

Furthermore, for a human, a chat generates mental images, sounds, odors, feelings, sensations, and much more.

The scenario is expanded to images for this case study:

- The tourist will chat with the police chatbot using the inbuilt functions of a personal assistant.
- The police bot will answer that it does not understand the statement. The tourist's personal assistant will trigger off a deeper conversation level.
- They will find a way to understand each other using images to solve the problem.

In this section, `CRL-MM-Chabot.py` will be described in a chronological way, following the sequence of the dialog.

The program starts with an explanation of the scenario and shows where this new cognitive function could be inserted in `Google_Translate_Customized.py` (see `Chapter 8`, *Revolutions Designed for Some Corporations and Disruptive Innovations for Small to Large Companies*).

Cognitive natural language processing

Conceptual representation learning meta-model (CRLMM) means describing concepts in words plus images, beyond using mathematical numerical vectors.

If you run `CRL-MM-Chabot.py`, the output comes as a detailed explanation of what the program is doing while it is running, as shown in the following code block. You can also view the video that comes with this chapter to get a feel of the program before running and viewing the following output:

```
In chapter 8, the Google_Translate_Customized.py
program found an error in Google Translate.
Google Translate confused a sports coach with a vehicle-coach.
In the near future, Google will probably correct this example
but here are thousands of other confusions.
On line 48 of Google_Translate_Customized.py, a deeper_translate function
was added to correct such errors.
This was only possible because Google provides
the necessary tools for the AI community to help make progress.
The translation was corrected so that the word bus replaced coach
and Google translated the sentence correctly
This program extends polysemy deeper understanding to concepts:
words and images

This model can be added to
deep_translate in Google_Translate_Customized at line 114 or
deployed in a cognitive chabot as follows...
Press ENTER to continue
```

The tourist now enters a sentence in the personal assistant (text or voice) that Google Translate does not understand (but it will in the near future), as displayed in the following snippet:

```
PERSON IN A BUS THAT BROKE DOWN TEXTING THE POLICE
 A MESSAGE WITH A CHABOT TRANSLATOR:
 My sports coach broke down(the sentence is in French but came out that
way)
```

The police bot answers and a sentiment analysis function detects a negative feeling, as shown in the following code snippet:

```
POLICE RECEIVING THE SMARTPHONE MESSAGE:
I dont understand what you mean.
The sentiment analysis estimation is: -0.3125
```

The following sentiment analysis function comes from TextBlob:

```
ext = "I dont understand what you mean."
obj = TextBlob(text)
sentiment = obj.sentiment.polarity
print (text,"\n"," The sentiment analysis estimation is: ",sentiment)
```

The sentiment has been analyzed through the `polarity` function. Negative values mean negative feelings, positive feelings come out as positive values, and 0 is neutral. In this case study, 0 will be OK.

The sentiment estimation for the policeman's sentence is -0.3, which is not good at all.

Our dialog flow (see the explanation in the first section of the chapter) does not wish to add confusions to the present confusion. Since the sentiment is negative, instead of adding more words that might or might not be correctly translated, an image is displayed. In this example, a frown is displayed, as implemented in the following code:

```
if(sentiment<0):
print("IMAGE DISPLAYED: FROWN OR OTHER POLYSEMY")
imgc=directory+'cchat/notok.jpg'
imgcc = load_img(imgc, target_size=(64, 64))
plt.imshow(imgcc)
plt.show(block=False)
time.sleep(5)
plt.close()
```

The frown will appear and disappear automatically on the tablet or smartphone. The following image is displayed by the program:

Output image

A /cchat (conceptual chat) directory was added to this CRLMM model. The CRLMM is beginning to use words + images to form concepts to express itself.

Words are sometimes confusing, especially in foreign-language environments on global social networks or personal assistants. Images will help clarify the conversation.

 You can add a whole library of emoticons that will be activated by a sentiment analysis function such as TextBlob.

Activating an image + word cognitive chat

To resolve their misunderstanding the tourist and the police bot both have an inbuilt CRLMM function in their personal assistants and cloud chatbot platform.

On the policy side, a polysemy (several meanings to a word) function has automatically been triggered by the sentiment analysis value. The Polysemy function is activated and begins to clarify the situation, as shown in the following code:

```
This is sports coach.
Polysemy Activated
POLICE: Do you mean this coach?
Enter yes or no(show an icon also to avoid language):
```

The program has already loaded its trained image model and compiled it, and the following prediction function is ready:

```
#____LOAD MODEL_____
json_file = open(directory+'model/model.json', 'r')
loaded_model_json = json_file.read()
....
loaded_model=model_from_json(loaded_model_json)
#_____ load weights into new model
loaded_model.load_weights(directory+"model/model.h5")
loaded_model.compile(loss='binary_crossentropy', optimizer='rmsprop',
metrics=['accuracy'])
```

The images were trained by the same program described in the previous chapters. The training has been orientated towards defining images conceptually more than classifying them. The prediction function is also the same as described in earlier chapters.

Chapter 16, *Improve the Emotional Intelligence Deficiencies of Chatbots,* will detail this conceptual training approach for image-word concepts.

The police bot displays what was understood by its system. Using more words will add more confusion. This is why an image provides a clear message. The program will display the following image:

Output image providing clear message

The system displays the following message:

```
POLICE: Do you mean this coach?
Enter yes or no(show an icon also to avoid language):
```

I recommend adding a yes or no icon.

The user will answer: **no.**

The conceptual (images + words) polysemy has been triggered by the mistake the system made. Another image is displayed as follows, with a question:

Output image with question

The tourist may or may not understand the policeman's question. The question may or may not be correctly translated. But providing a yes or no answer to an image simplifies the communication problem.

The user answers yes (or clicks on a yes icon). The tourist + personal assistant bot and the police bot are now beginning to understand each other.

Solving the problem

The chatbot has escalated into image + word chat mode. Confusing words have been replaced by an image and a yes/no clarified communication function. The system now thinks it understands. However, the bot has to make sure that it understands as shown in the following screenshot of the program's dialog:

```
POLICE:I understand. Your bus broke down.
Bus+ brock down
Is this what you mean?
Enter yes or no:
```

It displays the following image of the situation (concept + words):

Output image (concept + words)

The tourist will recognize the bus and a sort of problem sign even if the words remain unclear.

The user answers yes. The following snippet runs a sentiment analysis and displays an image:

```
if(answer=="yes"):
 print("THE SYSTEM WRITES A SENTENCE:","\n")
 text = "Image to text: Yes that is correct"
 obj = TextBlob(text)
 sentiment = obj.sentiment.polarity
 print (text," : ",sentiment)
 if(sentiment>=0):
 imgc=directory+'cchat/ok.jpg'
```

The system produces a scenario sentence (see IBM Watson's dialog flow), the `sentiment.polarity` produces a value and displays the following image.

Output image

The police bot and the tourist now understand each other.

The police bot produces an image and a text in case the message is confusing. The following snippet shows the police reply with an image to clarify the message:

```
print("\n","POLICE : OK. We are already on our way.","\n","The bus
emergency sensor sent us a message 5 minutes ago.","\n","Thanks for
confirming","\n")
print("\n","POLICE : We will be there at 15:30")
imgc=directory+'cchat/ETA.jpg'
imgcc = load_img(imgc, target_size=(128, 200))
```

The image confirms or replaces the text. The police bot informs the tourist that the estimated time of arrival is 15:30.

The police bot had received a sensor message from the bus. The bus had an inbuilt alerting system. But the emphatic cognitive chatbot was glad to help, just like a real-life police officer.

Implementation

Implementing a cognitive chatbot using CRLMM, as for any chatbot, needs to follow some well-organized steps:

- Identify the intents and entities
- Create the dialog scenarios
- Dialog controls—all that the user clicks and answers
- Make an emoticon images repository
- Make a conceptual images repository
- Train and test the model with all sorts of scenarios; especially look out for the ones that fail to improve the system

Summary

IBM Watson provides a complete set of tools on IBM Cloud to build a chatbot, add services to it, and customize it with your own cognitive programs.

A good chatbot fits the need. Thinking the architecture through before starting development avoids underfitting (not enough functionality) or overfitting (functions that will not be used) of the model.

Determining the right intent (what is expected of the chatbot), determining the entities to describe the intent (the subsets of phrases and words), and creating a proper dialog will take quite some time.

If necessary, adding services and specially customized machine learning functions will enhance the quality of the system. The use of CRLMM introduces concepts (images + words) into chatbots, bringing them closer to how humans communicate.

NLP parses and learns words. CRL adds a higher dimension to those words with images. These images clarify interpretation and mistranslation problems. To close the gap between machines and humans, AI must bring emotional intelligence into chatbot dialogs.

The next chapter explores emotional intelligence through a Boltzmann machine (recently used by Netflix) and principal component analysis applied to a CRLMM's image + word (concept) approach.

Questions

1. Can a chatbot communicate like a human? (Yes | No)
2. Are chatbots necessarily artificial intelligence programs? (Yes | No)
3. Chatbots only need words to communicate. (Yes | No)
4. Do humans only chat with words? (Yes | No)
5. Humans only think in words and numbers. (Yes | No)
6. To build a cognitive chatbot, mental images are necessary. (Yes | No)
7. For a chatbot to function, a dialog flow needs to be planned. (Yes | No)
8. A chatbot possesses general artificial intelligence, so no prior development is required. (Yes | No)
9. A chatbot translates fine without any function other than a translation API. (Yes | No)
10. Chatbots can already chat like humans in most cases. (Yes | No)

Further reading

- For more on IBM Cloud Watson: https://www.ibm.com/cloud/ai
- For more on TextBlob: http://textblob.readthedocs.io/en/dev/

16
Improve the Emotional Intelligence Deficiencies of Chatbots

Recent disruptive AI technology provides all the tools to eliminate emotional deficiencies in artificial intelligence applications. **Conceptual representation learning meta-models (CRLMM)** can convert mathematical outputs into somewhat human mind models. Classical machine learning and deep learning programs mostly produce mathematical outputs. In previous chapters, CRLMM models produced enhanced conceptual representations, closing the gap between machine and human thinking.

The goal is clearly to build a mind, not an output, through several machine learning techniques: an RBM, sentiment analysis, CRLMM, RNN, LSTM, Word2Vec, and PCA. For each step, an application is available on a Windows or Linux platform, along with a video.

RBMs were presented in a Netflix competition for prediction purposes, namely to predict user choices. The ultimate goal of this model is not to predict what a person will say or do but to make an approximate mental clone of a human mind—to build thinking and feeling machines.

Building a mind requires teamwork between several AI models. This chapter describes a profiler solution that will build a profile of a person named **X**. A mental projection will be shown, representing part of the profile to prepare for a deeper profile by unleashing the power of quantum computing (see Chapter 17, *Quantum Computers That Think*).

Starting to build a mind is the beginning of what will be one of the major adventures of the 21st century.

The following topics will be covered in this chapter:

- **Restricted Boltzmann Machine (RBM)**
- CRLMM
- Sentiment analysis
- **Recurrent neural networks (RNN)** and **Long Short-Term Memory (LSTM)** RNNs
- Word2Vec (word to vector) embedding
- **Principal Component Analysis (PCA)**
- Jacobian matrix

Technical requirements

Python 3.6x 64-bit from `https://www.python.org/`.

Package and modules:

```
import numpy
from __future__ import print_function
import numpy as np
from textblob import TextBlob
from PIL import Image
from keras.preprocessing.image import load_img
from keras.preprocessing.image import img_to_array
import matplotlib.pyplot as plt
import time
import scipy.misc
from keras.preprocessing.image import load_img
from keras.preprocessing.image import img_to_array
import keras
from keras.preprocessing.image import ImageDataGenerator
from keras.models import model_from_json

import tensorflow as tf
from tensorflow.contrib import rnn
from __future__ import absolute_import
from __future__ import division
from __future__ import print_function
import collections
import math
import os
import random
from tempfile import gettempdir
```

```
import zipfile
import numpy as np
from six.moves import urllib
from six.moves import xrange # pylint: disable=redefined-builtin
from tensorflow.contrib.tensorboard.plugins import projector
import tensorflow as tf
```

Programs needed:

- `RBM.py`
- `CNN_CONCEPT_STRATEGY.py`
- `LSTM.py` **with its** `Tensorboard_reader.py`
- `RNN.py`
- `Embedding.py` **and its** `Tensorboard_reader.py`

Check out the following video to see the code in action:

`https://goo.gl/SKPUZA`

Building a mind

The following method represents a starting point to build a mind in a machine.

It is based on a cognitive NLP chatbot I successfully delivered many years ago. It was designed for language teaching and would teach a student, but more importantly, it would **learn** who that student was by **memorizing** the chats and storing words, images, and sounds. The bot would know more about the student after each session and ask questions about past conversations.

A random memory sentence was produced among many, such as:

```
Oh, I remember you. You like.....
```

Then the profile dataset of the person was used to add:

```
Oh, I remember you. You like + football
```

The voice was digitized (and a bit bumpy because of intonation problems), but it scared one of the first users enough to make the student stand up and go look to see if there was somebody behind the computer playing a prank.

I had to build everything from scratch, which was excruciating but incredibly exhilarating. This project was fun and very profitable for a while, but that was 25+ years ago! There was no internet and no need to replace people. So that was it. I got some media attention but had to move on.

I then used the CRLMM model I had been describing during the previous chapters to introduce deep human concepts in an advanced planning and scheduling system; this is not meant to be a real-time planning tool like the one described in Chapter 12, *Automated Planning and Scheduling*.

This proves that building a mind is possible and will now happen. Maybe you can take everything in this book and become the architect of a thinking machine, and sell it to a corporation for deep decision-making purposes or as an advanced cognitive NLP chatbot.

Outer space, way above the sky, is the limit and might lead you to build the technology for a smart rocket on its road to Mars. It's at the touch of your fingertips.

How to read this chapter

The goal is to show how to build a mind using several artificial intelligence techniques. Each technique will be briefly explained and then applied. At this point in the book, you know that all the network models encountered in machine learning contain inputs, activation functions, and outputs going through layers (visible and hidden). The flow is trained with an optimizer (loss function) and weights (with biases). There are many combinations of these models.

Each section contains a Python program you can run, explore, and view through a video. The video shows how a mind thinks in a 3D projection of thoughts and concepts. Image embedding was used to represent concepts (conceptual representation learning). Then PCA was applied.

The target scenario is for us to use machine learning tools and bots to gather data on a person named X. In Chapter 17, *Quantum Computers That Think*, we will explore the mind of X—the very beginning of its machine clone that can be used to make decisions, chat, or simply dream and have fun.

The profiling scenario

The goal is to learn who X is and build a mind for X through a CRLMM approach added to other techniques.

> Building a machine mind requires using all the machine learning techniques we can put together. It would take several months to produce a thinking machine for decision-making or chatbot purposes.

This *x* step scenario will provide enough data to start building a mind:

- An RBM that will not try to predict what a user will do but will profile person X based on their Netflix ratings in an advanced approach
- A sentiment analysis function to gather information through X's social networks
- A CRLMM function to gather images and begin to fit them with the words as X would do
- Using an RNN to generate sentences X could say in a data augmentation approach
- Applying word embedding (word2vec) to the text to gather information on how X perceives words, not their general statistical meaning
- Representing some of X's professional environment words with word2vec in TensorFlow projector with PCA, to obtain a personal mental representation of how X sees the world (not the statistical representation)

> The goal is not to classify X or predict what X would do, but to understand X by representing X's mind.

Restricted Boltzmann Machines

RBMs are random and undirected graph models generally built with a visible and a hidden layer. They were used in a Netflix competition to predict future user behaviors. The goal here is **not** to predict what X will do but **find out who X is** and store the data in X's profile-structured mind-dataset.

The input data represents the features to be trained to learn about person X. Each column represents a feature of X's potential personality and tastes. The following code (and this section) is in `RBM.py`:

```
F=["love","happiness","family","horizons","action","violence"]
```

Each of the following lines is a movie X watched containing those six features; for them, X gave a five-star rating:

```
r = RBM(num_visible = 6, num_hidden = 2)
training_data = np.array([[1,1,0,0,1,1],
                          [1,1,0,1,1,0],
                          [1,1,1,0,0,1],
                          [1,1,0,1,1,0],
                          [1,1,0,0,1,0],
                          [1,1,1,0,1,0]])
```

The goal of this RBM is to find out more about X's personality through the output of the RBM.

The connections between visible and hidden units

The RBM model used contains two layers:

- A visible layer
- A hidden layer

Many types of RBMs exist, but generally, they contain these properties:

- There is no connection between the visible units
- There is no connection between the hidden units

- The visible and hidden layers are connected by a weight matrix and a bias vector, as shown in the following diagram:

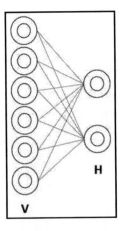

The connections between visible and hidden units

The network contains six visible and two hidden units, producing a weight matrix of 2 x 6 values. Note that there are no connections between the visible or hidden units. The following Python code initializes the model with the units:

```
self.num_hidden = num_hidden
self.num_visible = num_visible
```

The weight matrix is initialized with random weights between the following:

- *-sqrt(6./(num_hidden+visible)*
- *+sqrt(6./(num_hidden+visible)*

It is implemented with the following random states and values:

```
np_rng = np.random.RandomState(1234)
self.weights = np.asarray(np_rng.uniform(
low=-0.1 * np.sqrt(6. / (num_hidden + num_visible)),
high=0.1 * np.sqrt(6. / (num_hidden + num_visible)),
size=(num_visible, num_hidden)))
```

The bias will now be inserted in the first row and the first column in the following code:

```
self.weights = np.insert(self.weights, 0, 0, axis = 0)
self.weights = np.insert(self.weights, 0, 0, axis = 1)
```

The goal of this model will be to observe the behavior of the weights. Observing the weights will determine how to interpret the result in this model based on calculations between the visible and hidden units. The following output displays the weight values:

```
[[ 0.91393138 -0.06594172 -1.1465728 ]
 [ 3.01088157 1.71400554 0.57620638]
 [ 2.9878015 1.73764972 0.58420333]
 [ 0.96733669 0.09742497 -3.26198615]
 [-1.09339128 -1.21252634 2.19432393]
 [ 0.19740106 0.30175338 2.59991769]
 [ 0.99232358 -0.04781768 -3.00195143]]
```

The first row and column are the biases. Only the weights will be analyzed for the *profiling* functions. The weights and biases are now in place.

Energy-based models

An RBM is an **energy-based model (EBM)**. An EBM uses probabilistic distributions defined by an energy function.

For a given *x*, *E(x)* or *E(v,h)* is one way of expressing the energy function of an RBM in a simplified, conceptual line. It is:

$$E(v, h) = -bv - hWv$$

This **energy function drives** the model and will be used to direct weight and bias optimization:

- The *v* (visible) and *h* (hidden) units are connected by *W* (the weights)
- *b* is an offset of the units that acts as a bias

Then the energy will be measured with a probabilistic function *p*:

$$p(x) = \frac{e^{-E(x)}}{Z}$$

Z is a **partition function** for making sure that the sum of the probabilities of each x input does not exceed 1:

$$\sum_x p(x) = 1$$

The partition function is the sum of all the individual probabilities of each x:

$$Z = \sum_x e^{-E(x)}$$

With each $p(x)$ divided by Z (the sum of all the probabilities), we will reach 1. The whole system is based on the energy between the visible and hidden units until the loss is optimized, as shown in the following RBM.py code:

```
error = np.sum((data - neg_visible_probs) ** 2)
if self.debug_print:
print("Epoch %s: error is %s" % (epoch, error))
```

Gibbs random sampling

An RBM increases in efficiency when random variable sampling is applied during the training process. Gibbs sampling generates a Markov chain of samples that takes the nearby samples into account as well.

Random sampling makes the system more objective. Hidden units remain latent (this is a two-layer system), which confers its dream property.

Running the epochs and analyzing the results

Once the RBM has optimized the weight-bias matrix for n epochs, the matrix will provide the following information for the profiler system of person X:

```
[[ 0.91393138 -0.06594172 -1.1465728 ]
 [ 3.01088157 1.71400554 0.57620638]
 [ 2.9878015 1.73764972 0.58420333]
 [ 0.96733669 0.09742497 -3.26198615]
 [-1.09339128 -1.21252634 2.19432393]
 [ 0.19740106 0.30175338 2.59991769]
 [ 0.99232358 -0.04781768 -3.00195143]]
```

When RBM.py reaches this point, it asks you if you want to profile X, as shown in the following output:

```
Press ENTER if you agree to start learning about X
```

 I strongly recommend that only bots access this type of data and that the provider protects the data as much as possible. For users to accept these models, they must first trust them.

If you accept, it will train the input and display the features added to X's profile.

The weights of the features have been trained for person X. The first line is the bias and examines column 2 and 3. The following six lines are the weights of X's features:

```
Weights:
[[ 0.913269 -0.06843517 -1.13654324]
 [ 3.00969897  1.70999493  0.58441134]
 [ 2.98644016  1.73355337  0.59234319]
 [ 0.953465   0.08329804 -3.26016158]
 [-1.10051951 -1.2227973   2.21361701]
 [ 0.20618461  0.30940653  2.59980058]
 [ 0.98040128 -0.06023325 -3.00127746]]
```

The weights (in bold) are lines 2 to 6 and columns 2 to 3. The first line and first column are the biases.

The weight matrix will provide a profile of X by summing the weight lines of the feature, as shown in the following code:

```
for w in range(7):
 if(w>0):
  W=print(F[w-1],":",r.weights[w,1]+r.weights[w,2])
```

The features are now **labeled,** as displayed in this output:

```
love : 2.25265339223
happiness : 2.28398311347
family : -3.16621250031
horizons : 0.946830830963
action : 2.88757989766
violence : -3.05188501936
```

A value>0 is positive, close to 0 slightly positive.
A value<0 is negative, close to 0 slightly negative.

We can see that beyond standard movie classifications, X likes horizons somewhat, does not like violence, and likes action. X finds happiness and love important but not family at this point.

The RBM has provided a personal profile of X—not a prediction but getting ready for a suggestion through a chatbot or just building X's machine mind-dataset.

RBM.py will now begin sentiment analysis.

Sentiment analysis

RMB.py leaves the realm of RBMs and enters a tone analyzer phase using sentiment analysis to parse X's social networks.

The following code triggers the bot to ask you once again whether you agree (the mind-dataset-building bot) to parse X's social networks:

```
Press ENTER if you agree to learn more about X.
The AI program will now enter social networks
to scan X's social media profile.

First words(Tweets, posts, messages on Facebook and much more) will be
analyzed then images

Press ENTER if you agree to scan X's social networking...
```

Parsing the datasets

For this to work, a bot has read through X's data. A bot can use big data map and retrieve functions that Google, Amazon, Facebook, LinkedIn, and other social networks have been developing.

The sentiment analysis function is a TextBlob module. Entering the text and text+.sentiment will return the following sentiment analysis:

```
myview=TextBlob("I hate movie 1. It was too violent ")
print(myview,":","\n",myview.sentiment,"\n")
```

The output will contain two values:

- **Polarity**

A value>0 is positive, close to 0 slightly positive.
A value<0 is negative, close to 0 slightly negative.

- **Subjectivity:** The higher the value, the more X's subjectivity influences the result

For mind-dataset building purposes, a high level of subjectivity provides inside information on X's feelings, which increases the quality of the dataset.

At the same time, the total dialog is loaded in a TextBlob for each sentence analyzed as shown in the following code:

```
myview=TextBlob("I like autumn. It reminds me of some sad music")
print(myview,":","\n",myview.sentiment,"\n")
dialog=dialog+myview
```

`myview` contains the sentence to be analyzed. `dialog` contains the complete dialog. At the end of the analysis, `dialog` is parsed for key noun phrases, as shown in this code:

```
#Parse noun phrases
print("Parse noun phrases to find potential key words:")
print(dialog.noun_phrases)
```

The result will produce sentiment analysis for each sentence and the noun phrases at the end. The output provides useful information to add to X's mind-dataset. The following sentences were scanned on X's social networks:

```
Press ENTER to Continue
A value>0 is positive, close to 0 slightly positive
A value<0 is negative, close to 0 slightly negative

I hate movie 1. It was too violent :
Sentiment(polarity=-0.8, subjectivity=0.95)

I like autumn. It reminds me of some sad music :
Sentiment(polarity=-0.5, subjectivity=1.0)

The love story was cool too. A bit mushy but cool :
Sentiment(polarity=0.3999999999999997, subjectivity=0.6333333333333333)

I would like to get out of here and see other horizons :
Sentiment(polarity=-0.125, subjectivity=0.375)
```

```
Parse noun phrases to find potential key words:
['sad music', 'bit mushy']
```

`RBM.py` now asks you, the profiler bot, whether you want to complete X's profile with images gathered on X's social network pages with the following authorization:

```
Press ENTER if you agree to complete X's profiling dataset with some images
```

Conceptual representation learning meta-models

The CRLMM phase is there to find images that constitute a mental representation for X.

 Humans mostly think in words+images and feel with words+images. Sounds, sensations, and odors are critical as well. That parameter can also be explored.

Profiling with images

Humans communicate widely through images, symbols, and pictures. They also have a large number of mental image datasets—images that have been transformed and linked to words.

The goal of the bot's conversation now is to confirm the profile of X and suggest a movie to X, just for fun. An image was stored by X, and the name of a movie comes up called *Lost?* with a dark picture. It is supposed to appeal to the emotions of somebody who yearns for happiness and love and is curious to see whether something will be found.

The following picture illustrates the darkness of being lost, with a forest as a symbol and light through the trees (hope?):

Darkness of being lost picture

Now the streaming website chatbot will detect that a viewer has been scrolling for over 5 minutes without making a choice, for example. It would like to make a suggestion.

The bot starts with a random choice of sentences in the following structured class and adds keywords:

```
print("Hi, I am your personal assistant to find a movie you like")
print("I found a movie named Lost. The hero has to fight(action) through
life")
print("after losing a loved one (love) and is searching for
happiness(happiness) again...")..
Do you want to watch the movie?
```

X is curious about this movie. Will something be found? Happiness? Something else? X answers, *I sure do.*

The program manages the following dialog sequence. If you use the program, enter *I sure do!* when asked if you want to be person X:

```
mytext=input("Do you want to watch the movie? ")
#enter I sure do!
myview=TextBlob(mytext)
print(myview,":",myview.sentiment)
```

It picks up `I sure do` and obtains the following sentiment analysis, which it will now add to X's mind-dataset:

```
I sure do : Sentiment(polarity=0.5, subjectivity=0.8888888888888888)
```

Note that the goal here was first to profile X and build a mind-dataset of X's features, not movie categories. Then only suggest a movie, not based on its category, but on more intrinsic features.

The next phase will be to increase the size of the mind-dataset with an RNN.

RNN for data augmentation

An RNN models sequences, in this case, words. It analyzes anything in a sequence, including images. To speed the mind-dataset process up, data augmentation can be applied here exactly as it is to images in other models. In this case, an RNN will be applied to words.

A first look at its graph data flow structure shows that an RNN is a neural network like the others previously explored. The following graphs were obtained by first running `LSTM.py` and then `Tensorboard_reader.py`:

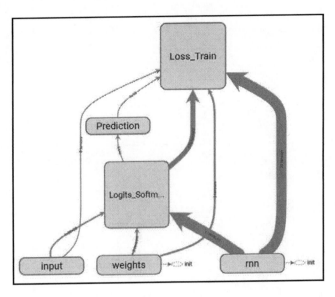

Data flow structure

The y inputs (test data) go to the loss function (`Loss_train`). The x inputs (training data) will be transformed through weights and biases into logits with a softmax function. A zoom into the RNN area of the graph shows the following `basic_lstm` cell:

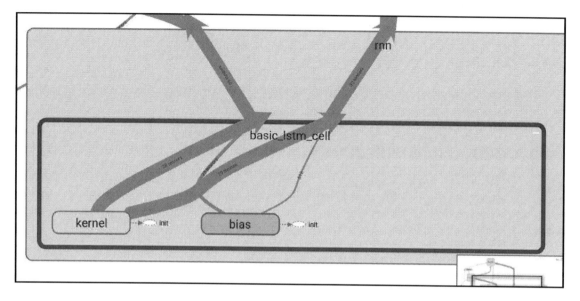

basic_lstm cell—RNN area of the graph

What makes an RNN special is to be found in the LSTM cell.

RNNs and LSTMs

An LSTM is an RNN that best shows how RNNs work.

An RNN contains functions that take the output of a layer and feed it back to the input in sequences simulating time. This feedback process takes information in a sequence. For example:

*The->movie->was->***interesting***->but->I->didn't->like->It*

An RNN will unroll a stack of words into a sequence and parse a window of words to the right and to the left. For example, in this sentence, an RNN can start with **interesting** (bold) and then read the words on the right and left (italics). These are some of the hyperparameters of the RNN.

This sequence aspect opens the door to sequence prediction. Instead of recognizing a whole pattern of data at the same time, it is recognizing the sequence of data, as in this example.

A network with no RNN will recognize the following vector as a week, a pattern just like any other one:

| *Monday* |
| *Tuesday* |
| *Wednesday* |
| *Thursday* |
| *Friday* |
| *Saturday* |
| *Sunday* |

An RNN will explore the same data in a sequence by **unrolling streams of data**.

Monday->Tuesday-Wednesday->Thursday->Friday->Saturday-Sunday

The main difference lies in the fact that once trained, the network will predict the following: if Wednesday is the input, Thursday could be one of the outputs. This is shown in the next section.

RNN, LSTM, and vanishing gradients

To simulate sequences and memory, an RNN and an LSTM will use backpropagation algorithms.

An RNN often has problems of gradients when calculating them over deeper and deeper layers in the network. Sometimes, it vanishes (too close to 0) due to the sequence property, just like us when a memory sequence becomes too long.

The backpropagation (just like us in a sequence) becomes less efficient. The are many backpropagation algorithms such as vanilla backpropagation, which is commonly used. This algorithm performs efficient backpropagation because it updates the weights after every training pattern.

One way to force the gradient not to vanish is to use a ReLU activation function, $f(x)=max(0,x)$, forcing values on the model so that it will not get *stuck*.

Another way is to use an LSTM cell containing a forget gate between the input and the output cells, a bit like us when we get stuck in a memory sequence and we say "whatever" and move on.

To explore this type of network deeper, `LSTM.py` runs on a MNIST example. `Tensorboard_reader.py` will display the data flow graph structure.

The LSTM cell will act as a memory gate with 0 and 1 values, for example. This cell will forget some information to have a fresh view of the information it has unrolled into a sequence.

The key idea of an RNN is that it unrolls information into sequences.

Prediction as data augmentation

`RNN.py`, a Vanilla RNN model, shows how person X's profile can be enhanced in three steps.

Step1 – providing an input file

`input.txt` contains texts picked up in X's dialogues with the chatbot, social networks, messaging, and more, as shown in the following output:

```
"The action movie was boring. The comedy was better. Next time, I'll watch
an action comedy with funny scenes...."
```

The ultimate goal is to automatically collect the largest file possible with thousands of words to have a representative dataset.

Step 2 – running an RNN

The RNN, based on a vanilla algorithm, starts by reading the stream of characters. It first opens `input.txt`, the reference text, as follows:

```
# data I/O
data = open('input.txt', 'r').read() # should be simple plain text file
chars = list(set(data))
data_size, vocab_size = len(data), len(chars)
print ('data has %d characters, %d unique.' % (data_size, vocab_size))
char_to_ix = { ch:i for i,ch in enumerate(chars) }
ix_to_char = { i:ch for i,ch in enumerate(chars) }
```

The RNN has hidden layers connected to the visible input and a learning rate, `learning_rate`, as shown in the following snippet:

```
# graph structure
hidden_size = 100 # hidden layer size
learning_rate = 1e-1
```

Then the specific parameter of an RNN is added—the length of the sequence, to unroll:

```
seq_length = 25 # length of units to unroll
```

Next, the weights are initialized with random functions. The program then runs forward passes to parse the elements of the sequence and backward to compute gradients.

Step 3 – producing data augmentation

The program will now generate text that can be added to X's text profile dataset. Data augmentation by text generation will:

- Help understand X's profile better
- Be used in chatbot conversations when this technology improves

This approach takes time and resources, and the results are not always efficient. However, research and development should continue by combining text generators with concept representation learning and more.

An intermediate result at iteration `60200` provided the following output:

```
iteration 60200, loss: 0.145638
----
er autumn because the leaves are brown, yellow, orange, red and all sorts
of colors. Summer is too hot, winhes comeny lard, yellories rore. I like
some but not too much. Love is really something great
```

`I like some but not too much` **contains some interesting emotional information:** `some but not too much.`

 To explore this type of network deeper, consult `rnn.py` and the video of this chapter.

Word embedding

The mind-dataset of X has begun to pile up a lot of data. It's time to introduce a word to vector model to determine how X sees words.

Building a mind-dataset is **not** like a dictionary that provides a standard definition for everybody. In this project, we want to target person X's personality.

This approach is about profiling X to understand how X perceives a word. For example, a dictionary might depict the season spring as something flowery. But X does not like spring as we have seen. X prefers autumn and its mild sadness.

So in X's dictionary, the definition of autumn is closer to satisfying than summer. This type of bot takes personal views into account to build a personal profiled mind-dataset. On the contrary, a standard dictionary would not suggest a preference between two seasons.

Word2vec will be used for customized phrases.

The Word2vec model

A **vector space model** (VSM) takes words and transforms them into a vector space. In this continuous space, similar words are represented in points near each other. This vectorial mapping process is called **embedding**.

Word2vec takes raw text, finds the words nearest to each other, and maps them into vectors. The system will take words, build them into a dictionary, and then input indexes.

A **skip-gram model** is applied to the sequences with a **skip window**. In that skip window, a number of words are taken into consideration on the left and the right. Then the model **skips,** and it will reuse and input several times to produce a label as implemented in embedding.py. The embedding size, skip window, and the number of skips are initialized and described in the following snippet:

```
embedding_size = 128 # Dimension of the embedding vector.
skip_window = 1 # How many words to consider left and right.
num_skips = 2 # How many times to re-use an input to generate a label.
```

Once the whole process is over, the model will have produced a number of vector features of the dataset with groups of nearest words to each other.

For our profile, `Embedding.py` analyzes a text written by X on artificial intelligence. These are texts written after reading this book. We will know more about X in a workplace.

 The following paragraphs describe the key functions of `Embedding.py`. For more info, view the complete source code on GitHub.

`Embedding.py` starts by reading a file called `concept.txt`, which is in a ZIP file and contains a text that X wrote after reading this book, as shown in the following code:

```
def read_data(filename):
  """Extract the first file enclosed in a zip file as a list of concepts."""
  with zipfile.ZipFile(filename) as f:
  data = tf.compat.as_str(f.read(f.namelist()[0])).split()
  return data
```

The words are stored as labels in the label filename `labels.tsv`, as shown in the following code snippet:

```
file = open('log/labels.tsv', 'w+')
for i in range(maxvoc+1):
print(i,vocabulary[i])
file.write(str(i)+'\t' +vocabulary[i]+'\n')
file.close()
```

A dataset is built in real time in the following code:

```
def build_dataset(words, n_words):
  """Process raw inputs into a dataset."""
  count = [['UNK', -1]]
  count.extend(collections.Counter(words).most_common(n_words - 1))
  dictionary = dict()
  ...
```

UNK represents unknown words that are generally simply skipped.

Then, training batches are generated by the following `generate_batch` function:

```
def generate_batch(batch_size, num_skips, skip_window):
  global data_index
  assert batch_size % num_skips == 0
  assert num_skips <= 2 * skip_window
  batch = np.ndarray(shape=(batch_size), dtype=np.int32)
  labels = np.ndarray(shape=(batch_size, 1), dtype=np.int32)
  span = 2 * skip_window + 1 # [ skip_window target skip_window ]
  buffer = collections.deque(maxlen=span)
```

```
if data_index + span > len(data):
data_index = 0
buffer.extend(data[data_index:data_index + span])
data_index += span
for i in range(batch_size // num_skips):
...
```

The skip-gram model has been prepared. A TensorFlow data flow graph will manage the operations. First, come the following inputs:

```
embeddings = tf.Variable(tf.random_uniform([vocabulary_size,
embedding_size], -1.0, 1.0))
embed = tf.nn.embedding_lookup(embeddings, train_inputs)
```

Then the following weights and biases along with the loss function are implemented:

```
# Construct the variables for the NCE loss
nce_weights = tf.Variable(
tf.truncated_normal([vocabulary_size, embedding_size],
stddev=1.0 / math.sqrt(embedding_size)))
nce_biases = tf.Variable(tf.zeros([vocabulary_size]))
loss = tf.reduce_mean(
tf.nn.nce_loss(weights=nce_weights,
biases=nce_biases,
labels=train_labels,
inputs=embed,
num_sampled=num_sampled,
num_classes=vocabulary_size))
```

The word2vec count model will take the words and build a count matrix, thus converting words into vectors so that the deep learning algorithm can process the data.

Given the concept.txt data file, a part of that matrix could look something like the following table:

	Transfer	Learning	Model	Number
Transfer		15		
Learning			10	5
Model				
Number			1	

The words have been transformed into numbers (vectors) so that a deep learning program can process them and find the words nearest to each other.

The output represents the features of the word with properties expressed in numbers, which in turn can be viewed as words through the stored labels (`labels.tsv`).

The output of the `concept.txt` input file shows the nearest words to each keyword. For example, for *such*, the system displays the following output:

```
Nearest to such: "class, model, way, Adding, been, and, face, business,
```

It does not look so exciting at first glance. However, if more text is added and deeper calculations are allowed, it will make progress.

To obtain a 3D view of the result with PCA (see next section), the information for TensorBoard projector is initialized, as shown in the following snippet:

```
print('Initialized')
config = projector.ProjectorConfig()
summary_writer = tf.summary.FileWriter("log/")
embedding = config.embeddings.add()
```

TensorFlow Projector is now ready to be launched.

Principal component analysis

General dictionary or encyclopedia representations of words, images, and concepts satisfy many needs. The probabilistic machine learning approach is applied very efficiently to marketing by Facebook, Amazon, Google, Microsoft, IBM, and many other corporations.

Probabilistic machine learning training remains efficient when targeting apparels, food, books, music, travel, cars, and other market consumer segments.

However, humans are not just consumers; they are human beings. When they contact websites or call centers, standard answers or stereotyped emotional tone analysis approaches can depend on one's nerves. When humans are in contact with doctors, lawyers, and other professional services, a touch of humanity is necessary if major personal crises occur.

The PCA phase is there to build a mental representation of X's profile either to communicate with X or use X's mind as a powerful, *mind-full* chatbot or decision maker.

The input data for this PCA is the output of `Embedding.py` described in the previous section. TensorFlow stored the model, data and labels in its `log/` directory.

TensorBoard projector has an inbuilt PCA loader.

Intuitive explanation

PCA takes data and represents it at a higher level.

For example, imagine you are in your bedroom. You have some books, magazines, and music (maybe on your smartphone) around the room. If you consider your room as a 3D Cartesian coordinate system, the objects in your room are all in specific x, y, z coordinates.

For experimentation purposes, take your favorite objects and put them on your bed. Put the objects you like the most near each other and your second choices a bit further away. If you imagine your bed as a 2D Cartesian space, you have just made your objects change dimensions.

They are not in their usual place anymore; they are on your bed and at specific coordinates depending on your tastes.

That is the philosophy of PCA. If the number of data points in the dataset is very large, the PCA of a mental dataset of one person will always be different from the PCA representation of another person like DNA.

That is what CRLMM is about as applied to a person's mental representation. Each person is different, and each person deserves a customized chatbot or bot treatment.

Mathematical explanation

The mains steps for calculating PCA are important for understanding how to go from the intuitive approach to how TensorBoard projector represents datasets using PCA.

Variance

Step 1: Calculate the mean of the array `data1`.

You can check this with the `math.py`, as shown in the following function:

```
data1 = [1, 2, 3, 4]
M1=statistics.mean(data1)
print("Mean data1",M1)
```

The answer is 2.5. The mean is not the median (the middle value of an array).

Step 2: Calculate the mean of array data2.

The mean calculation is done with the following standard function:

```
data2 = [1, 2, 3, 5]
M2=statistics.mean(data2)
print("Mean data2",M2)
```

The answer is:

$$\bar{X} = 2.75$$

The bar above the X signifies that it is a mean.

Step 3: Calculate the variance using the following equation:

$$var = \frac{\sum_{x=1}^{x=n}(X - \bar{X})^2}{n}$$

Now NumPy will calculate the variance with the absolute value of each x minus the mean, sum them up, and divide the sum by *n* as shown in the following snippet.

```
#var = mean(abs(x - x.mean())**2).
print("Variance 1", np.var(data1))
print("Variance 2", np.var(data2))
```

Some variances are calculated with *n*-1 depending on the population of the dataset.

The result of the program for variances is as displayed in the following output:

```
Mean data1 2.5
Mean data2 2.75
Variance 1 1.25
Variance 2 2.1875
```

We can already see that data2 varies a lot more than data1. Do they fit together? Are their variances close or not? Do they vary in the same way?

Covariance

Our goal in this section is to find out whether two words, for example, will often be found together or close to each other, taking the output of the embedding program into account.

Covariance will tell us whether these datasets vary together or not. The equation follows the same philosophy as variance, but now both variances are joined to see whether they belong together or not:

$$cov(X, Y) = \frac{\sum_{x=1}^{x=n}(X - \bar{X})(Y - \bar{Y})}{n}$$

As with the variance, the denominator can be *n*-1 depending on your model. Also, in this equation, the numerator is expanded to visualize the co-part of covariance, as implemented in the following array in `math.py`:

```
x=np.array([[1, 2, 3, 4],
            [1, 2, 3, 5]])
print(np.cov(x))
```

NumPy's output is a covariance matrix **a**:

$$[[1.666666672.16666667]$$
$$[2.166666672.91666667]]$$

If you increase some of the values of the dataset, it will increase the value of the parts of the matrix. If you decrease some of the values of the dataset, the elements of the covariance matrix will decrease.

Looking at some of the elements of the matrix increase or decrease that way takes time and observation. What if we could find one value or two values that would give us that information?

Eigenvalues and eigenvectors

To make sense out of the covariance of the covariance matrix, the eigenvector will point to the direction in which the covariances are going. The eigenvalues will express the magnitude or importance of a given feature.

To sum it up, an eigenvector will provide the direction and the eigenvalue the importance for the covariance matrix **a**. With those results, we will be able to represent the PCA with TensorBoard projector in a multi-dimensional space.

Let **w** be an eigenvalue(s) of **a**. An eigenvalue(s) must satisfy the following equation:

$$dot(a, v) = w * v$$

There must exist a vector v for which *dot(a,v)* is the same as *w*v*:

NumPy will do the math through the following function:

```
from numpy import linalg as LA
print ("eigenvalues", np.linalg.eigvals(a))
```

The eigenvalues are (in ascending order) displayed in the following output:

```
Eigenvalues [ 0.03665681  4.54667652]
```

Now we need the eigenvectors to see in which direction these values should be applied. NumPy provides a function to calculate both the eigenvalues and eigenvectors together. That is because eigenvectors are calculated using the eigenvalues of a matrix as shown in this code snippet:

```
from numpy import linalg as LA
w, v = LA.eigh(a)
print ("eigenvalue(s)",w)
print ("eigenvector(s)",v)
```

The output of the program is:

```
eigenvalue(s) [ 0.03665681 4.54667652]
eigenvector(s) [[-0.79911221 0.6011819 ]
 [ 0.6011819 0.79911221]]
```

Eigenvalues come in a 1D array with the eigenvalues of a.

Eigenvectors come in a 2D square array with the corresponding (to each eigenvalue) in columns.

Creating the feature vector

The remaining step is to sort the eigenvalues from the highest to the lowest value. The highest eigenvalue will provide the principal component (most important). The eigenvector that goes with it will be its feature vector. You can choose to ignore the lowest values or features. In the dataset, there will be hundreds and often thousands of features to represent. Now we have the feature vector:

$$Feature\ Vector=FV=\{eigenvector1, eigenvector2...n\}$$

n means that there could be many more features to transform into a PCA feature vector.

Deriving the dataset

The last step is to transpose the feature vector and original dataset and multiply the row feature vector by row data:

$$Data\ that\ will\ be\ displayed = row\ of\ feature\ vector\ *\ row\ of\ data$$

Summing it up

The highest value of eigenvalues is the principal component. The eigenvector will determine in which direction the data points will be oriented when multiplied by that vector.

TensorBoard Projector

TensorBoard projector loads the metadata from the output of the `Embedding.py` located in the `log` directory. First, run `Embedding.py`. Then run `Tensorboard.py`. For this example, click on **Load data** and load the `labels.tsv` file from the `log` directory generated by `Embedding.py`.

Next, TensorBoard runs a PCA calculation (the option on the left in the TensorBoard window) as explained previously. It then displays a 3D view, as shown in the following screenshot:

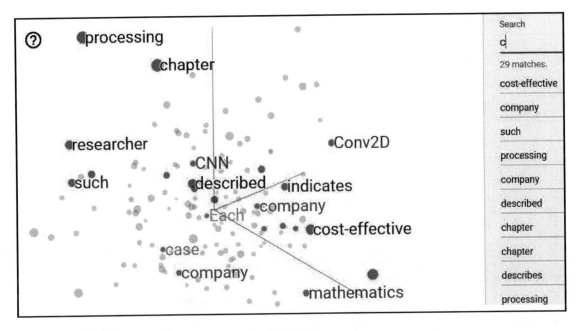

PCA 3D view

You can now select words on the right-hand side of the window, move the projection around in 3D, zoom, and explore the workplace mind of X.

Using Jacobian matrices

Using a matrix of partial derivatives is also possible. It shows the local trend of the data being explored. A Jacobian matrix contains partial derivatives.

A Jacobian matrix that contains the partial derivatives of X's mind functions produced between two periods of time can prove useful when minute trends need to be analyzed. The philosophy remains the same as for measuring covariances. The goal is to see the trends in the variables of X's mind.

Summary

Efficient machine learning programs produce good results but do not build a mind. To produce complex AI solutions, no single technique (MDP, CNN, RNN, or any other) will suffice. An efficient artificial intelligence solution to a complex problem will necessarily be an innovative combination of various techniques. This chapter showed how to start building one using an RBM, a tone analyzer (sentiment analysis), a CRLMM, an RNN, a word2vec program, and PCA.

X's mind-dataset has been enriched with the beginning of an actual memory with word and feeling associations as image and word associations. This brings X's mind-dataset profile beyond dictionary definitions, predictive statistics, and linear dimensional personality definitions.

Artificial intelligence will go beyond the present trend of mathematical probabilistic approaches into the realms of our minds.

Great progress has been made by major corporations distributing machine learning cloud platforms (Google, Amazon, IBM, Microsoft, and many more). CRLMM will become a necessity to solve complex problems that mathematical probabilities cannot, such as empathetic chatbots or deep thinking machines.

Much more work needs to be done during each phase described in this chapter to obtain a powerful mind that resembles X's. Quantum computing possesses the tremendous power and complexity to bring a thinking machine to another level.

Questions

1. RBMs are based on directed graphs. (Yes | No)
2. The hidden units of an RBM are generally connected to each other. (Yes | No)
3. Random sampling is not used in an RBM. (Yes | No)
4. Is there a method to prevent gradients from vanishing in an RNN? (Yes | No)
5. LSTM cells never forget. (Yes | No)

6. word2vec transforms words into indexes along with their labels. (Yes | No)
7. PCA transforms dates into higher dimensions. (Yes | No)
8. In a covariance matrix, the eigenvector shows the direction of the vector, representing that matrix, and the eigenvalue shows the size of that vector. (Yes | No)
9. It is impossible to represent a human mind in a machine. (Yes | No)
10. A machine cannot learn concepts, which is why classical applied mathematics is enough to make efficient artificial intelligence programs for every field. (Yes | No)

Further reading

- **Information on RNNs:** `https://www.tensorflow.org/tutorials/recurrent`
- **More on embedding:** `https://www.tensorflow.org/programmers_guide/embedding`

17
Quantum Computers That Think

IBM has begun to build quantum computers for research and business purposes. In a few years, quantum computing will become disruptive and will provide exponential computer power.

This unique computer capacity in the history of humanity opens the doors to obtaining results that would be impossible to reach with classical computers. Quantum computers in themselves will not provide revolutionary algorithms. But quantum computer power will take present-day algorithms beyond the limits of our imagination.

This chapter explains why quantum computers are superior to classical computers, what a quantum bit is, how to use it, and how the Quantum Mind experiment can lead to a quantum thinking machine. Quantum Mind is based on CRLMM, which I have been successfully applying to many corporate sites. Quantum Mind is named MindX.

The following topics will be covered in this chapter:

- Explaining why quantum computers are more powerful than other classical computers
- Defining what a quantum bit is
- Bloch sphere
- Quantum computing
- PCA representation of a CRLMM
- How to build a MindX, a thinking quantum computer

How to read this chapter

Dive into X's mind through this video of this chapter, link in the next section. A mind contains emotions, doubts, happiness, sadness, positive thoughts, negative feelings, and more. Use the explanations on quantum computing to imagine how powerful a personal mental representation could become with CRLMM. Use the explanations on MindX (representing a mind) to imagine how powerful and likable a chatbot or any AI solution could be by combining quantum computing power with personalized CRLMM models.

Technical requirements

You will need Python 3.6x 64-bit from `https://www.python.org/`

Package and modules:

```
import os,cv2
import numpy as np
import matplotlib.pyplot as plt
import pickle
from PIL import Image
import tensorflow as tf
from tensorflow.contrib.tensorboard.plugins import projector
tf.version
```

These programs will be used:

`EMBEDDING_IMAGES.py` with the data directory and `feature_vectors_400_samples.txt`

`Tensorboard_reader.py`

Check out the following video to see the code in action:

`https://goo.gl/qi4NCp`

The rising power of quantum computers

To understand how to build MindX, a thinking quantum computer, this section describes:

- Why quantum computers are faster
- What a qubit is
- How it is measured (its position)
- How to create a quantum score (program) with quantum gates
- How to run the quantum score and use its results for a cognitive NLP chatbot

The goal of this chapter is not to go into the details of quantum computing but to teach you enough how to build a thinking quantum computer.

Quantum computer speed

A standard computer bit has a 0 or a 1 state. A classical computer will manage 0 or 1, as the system chooses, but it remains limited to choosing 1 or (XOR) 0. It cannot manage both states at the same time.

A quantum computer is not constrained by an XOR state. It is an AND state. It can manage 0 and 1 at the same time until it is measured. A quantum state is unknown until observed, so a quantum program can use 0 and 1 at the same time. Once observed, the qubit will take a value of 0 or 1 because of the physical instability of a quantum state.

Just observing a quantum state makes the state break down. In quantum computing, this is called **decoherence**. It is not magic as some sci-fi hype suggests. Qubits are unstable. When observed, the quantum state breaks down.

This means quantum computing is memoryless once it is measured. Storage does not exist in a quantum computer. The input is made by a classical computer and the output goes back to a classical computer to be stored through the following process:

- **A Classical computer provides an input**
- **A Quantum Computer processes the input and produces an output**
- **A Classical computer interprets the output**

That being said, the computing power of a quantum computer fully justifies this architectural constraint.

Until a qubit is observed, it can have a 0 or 1 state or a probability in between, such as 0.1, 0.7, or 0.9.

Observing the situation is called **measuring** the state. When measured, only 0 or (XOR) 1 will become the result.

Until the state is measured, a large number of probabilities are possible. If a qubit is added to the system, we now have two qubits and four elementary combinations all at the same time.

Unlike standard computer logic, all four of the states can be used to compute algorithms at the same time in a parallel process. The volume of possible states of a given algorithm will thus expand with the number of qubits involved. An estimation of the volume of states can be made with the following number, in which q is the number of qubits:

$$2^q$$

Looking at the tiny equation does not seem awesome at all. Now, let's see what it looks like in a loop that runs up to 100 qubits:

```
import numpy as np
for q in range(101):
 v=(2**q)
 print("Size of nb to describe",q," qubits:","{:,}".format(v))
```

The program does not appear fearsome either. However, the following output is awesome:

```
Size of nb to describe 0 qubits: 1
Size of nb to describe 1 qubits: 2
Size of nb to describe 2 qubits: 4
Size of nb to describe 3 qubits: 8
Size of nb to describe 4 qubits: 16
Size of nb to describe 5 qubits: 32
Size of nb to describe 6 qubits: 64
...
Size of nb to describe 10 qubits: 1,024
...
Size of nb to describe 50  qubits: 1,125,899,906,842,624
...
Size of nb to describe 97 qubits: 158,456,325,028,528,675,187,087,900,672
Size of nb to describe 98 qubits: 316,912,650,057,057,350,374,175,801,344
Size of nb to describe 99 qubits: 633,825,300,114,114,700,748,351,602,688
```

```
Size of nb to describe 100 qubits:
1,267,650,600,228,229,401,496,703,205,376
```

Presently, big data is often calculated in petabytes. A petabyte=10^{15} or about 2^{50} bytes.

Facebook stores data for 2 billion-plus accounts. Imagine Facebook reaches 500 petabytes in the near future. Let's see what 500 petabytes approximately add up to in the following code:

```
print("Facebook in the near future:")
s=(2**50)*500
print("{:,}".format(v))
```

The output is quite surprising because it is about the size of data of a 100-qubit quantum computer can compute in one run:

```
Facebook in the near future:
1,267,650,600,228,229,401,496,703,205,376
```

This means that a single quantum computer with 100 qubits can run a calculation of the size of all data that 2,000,000,000+ Facebook accounts might represent in the near future.

The quantum computer will not actually contain that volume of data at all, but it shows that it can produce a calculation with that volume of computation information.

More importantly, this also means that a single quantum computer can run a mind-dataset of a single mind (see the next section) and calculate associations. This thinking process can generate an exponential volume of connections.

A classical n-bit computer manages n-bits whereas a quantum computer will manage 2^n bits or 2^q bits.

Compared to quantum computers 2^q exponential power, soon classical computers will seem like relics of the past for scientific calculations. Classical computers will still be in use. But quantum computers will be the tools to explore the world beyond the present limits of artificial intelligence.

Visualize all the AI solutions you saw in this book. They will already seem to have some dust of the past on them once you get your hands on quantum computing.

Quantum computers will beat any other computer in many fields in the years to come. In one parallel computation, a quantum will do in one run what would take years for classical computers to calculate.

Now think about what a network of many quantum computers can do!

Often, we try to compare large volumes with the number of stars in the universe. And we say, *That's more than the number of stars in our universe.* We must now look in the opposite direction.

The lesson is clear: The future lies in **nano** models. Quantum computing represents both a challenge and an opportunity.

Defining a qubit

A qubit, a quantum bit, has a physical counterpart. For example, a quantum state can be encoded in oscillating currents with a superconductor loops. Google and IBM have experimented with this approach. Another way is to encode a qubit in an ion trapped in an electromagnetic field in a vacuum trap.

Photons, electrons, the state of light, and other technologies have emerged. Whatever the approach, calculations with 50+ qubit quantum computers will outrun classical supercomputers.

The competition is fierce because the market will rapidly become huge. Get ready now to face the disruption that's coming!

Representing a qubit

The mathematical representation of a qubit is:

- $|0\rangle$ for a 0 value
- $|1\rangle$ for a 1 value
- $\alpha|0\rangle$ where alpha is a probability parameter
- $\beta|1\rangle$ where beta is a probability parameter

These brackets are called **bracket** or **bra-ket** notation.

This linear representation is called superposition. In itself, it explains most of the power of quantum computing.

The superposition of *0* and *1* in a quantum state can thus be expressed as follows in kets such as |*1*> and not **bras** such as in <*1*|:

$$quantumstate = \alpha|1> + \beta|0>$$

The alpha and beta probabilities look like weights and the total probabilities of those probable states of qubit must add up to 1. We use partition functions, softmax, and other techniques to make sure to keep the sum of probabilities equal to 1. This is no surprise since computers geek like us designed the way to program quantum computers. Translated into mathematics, this means that the probabilities of α and β must add up to 1. In the case of qubit probabilities, the values are squared, leading to the following constraint:

$$|\alpha^2| + |\beta^2| = 1$$

 To describe the probable state of a qubit, we thus need three numbers: the *0* and *1* possible states and a number to determine the value of the probabilities (the other is implicit since the total must add up to 1).

Since qubits interact in their respective states, an interaction is described as an entanglement. An entanglement designates at least two interacting qubits. They cannot be described without taking all the states of all the qubits into account.

This has been reproduced physically, which means that this entanglement seems strange because their quantum entanglement (relation) can occur at a distance. One qubit can influence a qubit that is physically far away.

 Albert Einstein called entanglement "spooky action at a distance."

The position of a qubit

One of the main ways to represent the state of a qubit is a Bloch's sphere. It shows how a qubit spins and can be used to describe qubit states. The following section refreshes some properties of a circle.

Radians, degrees, and rotations

The radius is the distance between the center of a circle and its circumference, as shown in the following diagram:

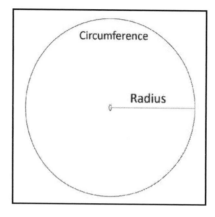

Radius of a circle

The radius of a circle is half of the circle's diameter. The relation between the radius r and the circumference C is (where π=3.14):

$$C = 2\pi r$$

If the length of the radius is wrapped around the circumference of a circle, that arc forms a radian, as shown in the following diagram:

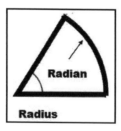

A radian

The angle formed by a radian is equal to about $57.29°$ (degrees).

The properties of the radian can be used for rotations:

- 3,14 x 57,29° = about 180°
- thus π radians = 180

Rotations are often described by radians expressed in π, as displayed in the following table:

Degrees	Radians
30°	π/6
45°	π/4
60°	π/3
90°	π/2
180°	π
270°	3π/2
360°	2π

Bloch sphere

The radian table shown just now is a practical way to describe rotations. A Bloch sphere, as shown in the following figure, provides a visual representation of the position and rotation of a qubit:

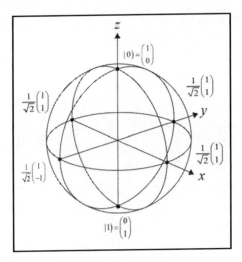

Bloch sphere

The North and South pole (polar coordinates) represent the basic states of a qubit:

$$" \, North \, " \, pole = |0\rangle = \begin{pmatrix} 1 \\ 0 \end{pmatrix}$$

$$" \, South \, " \, pole = |1\rangle = \begin{pmatrix} 0 \\ 1 \end{pmatrix}$$

A qubit can take any value on the sphere.

Composing a quantum score

Composing a quantum score consists of positioning gates on a stave (or circuit) and adding a measurement. The input comes from a classical computer. After the measurement phase, the output goes back to a classical computer. The reason is that quantum computers have no memory and thus cannot store their intermediate states because of their instability.

This section uses Quirk, a very educative quantum circuit simulator, to present quantum gates and a quantum composer.

Quantum gates with Quirk

The qubits are represented by the lines, and they start on the left, as shown in following quantum gate programming interface:

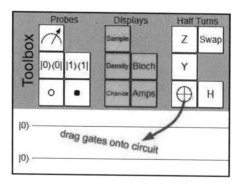

Quantum gate programming interface

The gates are logic gates that will transform the state of the qubits:

Not gate:

A not gate will transform a ket-zero |0⟩ into a ket-one |1⟩. It will transform a ket-one |1⟩ into a ket-zero|0⟩.

In circuit description, `on` is the ket-one state and `off` is the ket-zero state, as shown in the following quantum *score*:

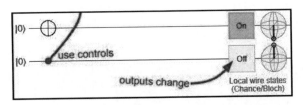

Circuit description of quantum score

You can see that:

- A not gate symbol is a circle with a vertical and horizontal line inside it
- The on status means that the state is |1⟩
- The Bloch Sphere representation is at π (starting from the top of the Bloch sphere) as it should

H gate

An H gate, or **Hadamard Gate** will perform the following transformation:

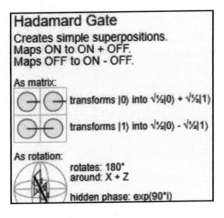

Hadamard Gate transformation

The following 50% chance will be displayed in a rectangle and the position on the Bloch sphere as well:

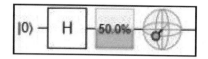

50% chance in rectangle and Bloch sphere

The fundamental role of a gate is to turn the qubits on a Bloch sphere and produce a probable condition if measured. There are many possible gates to be explored and used, as shown in this design menu diagram:

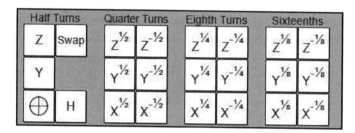

Gates design menu

These gates are more than enough to build many algorithms.

A quantum computer score with Quirk

Building a quantum score (or circuit) with Quirk means the following:

- Dragging and dropping gates that will make a qubit turn in a specific direction and produce probable outcomes
- Adding another qubit, doing the same, and so on
- Being able to perform an intermediate measurement, although this is impossible for a real physical quantum computer (the observations make the system collapse)

A score is represented as follows, for example:

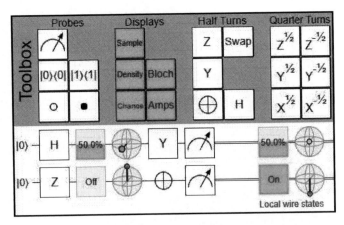

Quantum computer score representation

There are two qubits with a gate on each line to start. Then the intermediate result is shown, making the simulator very educational. Then two more gates are added. Finally, the following measurement probe is added at the end:

Measurement probe

Once the measurement is made, the final result is displayed on the right of the measurement symbols.

A quantum computer score with IBM Q

IBM Q provides a cloud platform to run a real physical quantum computer.

Create a free account and access the IBM quantum computing composer. Just as with Quirk, quantum gates are dragged on the following score, as shown in this diagram:

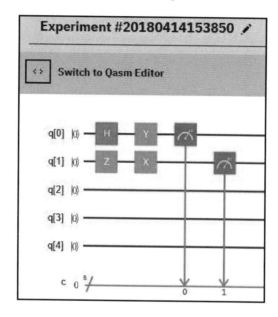

Quantum gates dragged

The score can be run on a simulator like Quirk or a real quantum computer, as shown in this interface diagram:

Score interface

Click on **Simulate** which will runs a simulator.

 Run launches a calculation on **IBM's physical quantum computer. It is an exhilarating experience! The future is at the tip of your fingers.**

The following output is interesting. It is a bit different from Quirk for the same score, but the probabilities add up to 1 as expected:

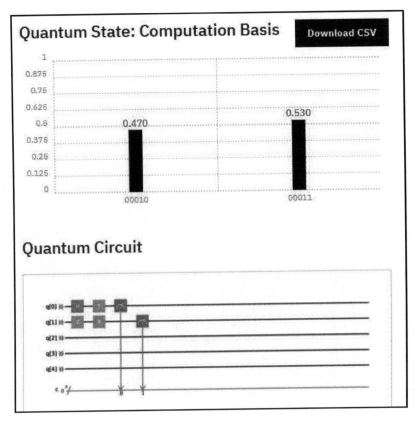

Quantum computer score output

IBM also possesses a source code version (QASM) of the score, as shown in the following code:

```
include "qelib1.inc";
qreg q[5];
creg c[5];
h q[0];
z q[1];
y q[0];
x q[1];
measure q[0] -> c[0];
measure q[1] -> c[1];
```

This language is an **Open Quantum Assembly** Language. It can be written in an editor like any other language on IBM Q's platform. A development kit can also be downloaded, and the APIs are functional.

All of this being said, let's find out how quantum computing can boost an AI project. It is now time to define the thinking quantum computer project.

A thinking quantum computer

A thinking quantum computer is not a reproduction of brain function but a representation of the mind of a person. Neuroscientists are making progress on using machine learning to understand the brain. But artificial intelligence mostly uses algorithms that simulate our way of thinking, not our brain's functions.

The endeavor of the Quantum MindX experiment is to build a personal mind named MindX, with memories of past events, conversations, chats, photographies, and more as described in Chapter 16, *Improve the Emotional Intelligence Deficiencies of Chatbots*.

This section describes how to build MindX, a thinking computer. It is not the project itself, which would be beyond the scope of the book. I've been doing research on this subject for many years. The power of quantum computation will no doubt boost research in this field.

 All the diagram in this section are part of the datasets used by the programs provided with the book (see *Technical requirements* section). You can also view the video showing the program running.

Representing our mind's concepts

A **conceptual representation learning meta model (CRLMM)** can be implemented with a quantum computer.

The input consists of encoding a state of mind of a PCA CRLMM representation. The CRLMM representation is not a general dictionary or encyclopedia dataset but a mind-dataset of actual personal data that is collected, classified, and transformed into a PCA 3D view as described in Chapter 16, *Improving the Emotional Intelligence of Chatbots*.

The following diagram is an extraction of some of the words and concepts that the mind of person X picked up by reading this book:

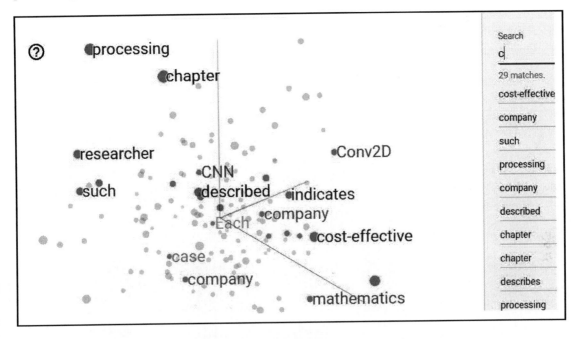

Extraction of words

This person's mind added to other information gathered in Chapter 16, *Improve the Emotional Intelligence Deficiencies of Chatbots* will now be in the mind of MindX.

A frame of MindX's PCA state will be submitted to a quantum computer. The quantum computer will then think as humans do, by associating concepts, mental images, sounds, sensations, feelings, and everything that makes up our mind. The result will be decoded into coordinates of the PCA CRLMM representation of the machine's mind and will produce a sentence.

The sequence is thus a classical computer input, a quantum computer calculation, and a classical computer interpretation of the output.

The input and outputs can be as follows:

- Connected to a chatbot
- Used for CRLMM decision-making purposes as seen in previous chapters

Expanding MindX's conceptual representations

MindX's mind dataset will grow continuously if implemented beyond this research experiment. It will have sensors to process body temperature for emotion classification, facial recognition for expression detection, body language detectors, and more. All of this technology is already available.

EMBEDDING_IMAGES.py contains one of the first methods of enriching the mind-dataset of MindX to obtain concepts. A version was presented in Chapter 16, *Improve the Emotional Intelligence Deficiencies of Chatbots*. This version was built with a larger mind-dataset.

The following is a screenshot of the PCA TensorBoard Projector 3D representation of a mind:

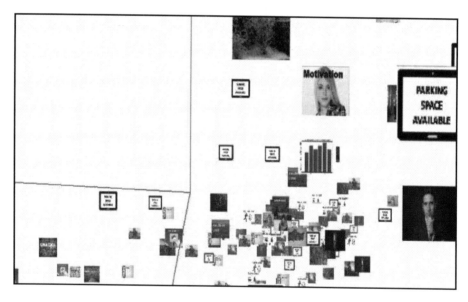

PCA TensorBoard Projector 3D representation of a mind

A sample dataset of concepts based on personal experience, and not general data, has been created. Some samples were generated by CRLMM CNN classification (see previous chapters); some were created for this sample. But all can be generated automatically using the program in Chapter 16, *Improve the Emotional Intelligence Deficiencies of Chatbots*.

Concepts in the mind-dataset of MindX

For the quantum MindX experiment, some personal concepts of MindX have been created.

Positive thinking

To think, a mind must have memories and personal ideas. The following screenshot comes from the sprite generated by `EMBEDDING_IMAGES.py` (see the following section). A sprite is an image that contains thumbnails: small images of the dataset. Once loaded into TensorBoard Projector with their features, they will be represented in a 3D mind projection as displayed in this diagram:

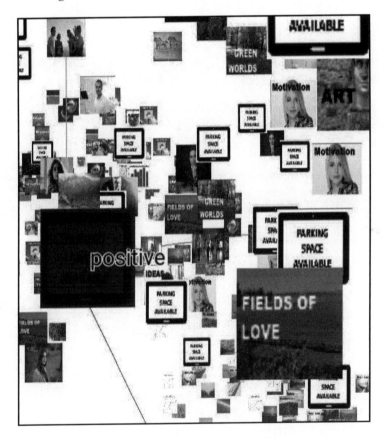

3D mind projection

As you can see, the following is true about MindX:

- It has superposed words and images, associating them to form memories. A field of flowers has become *a field of love*, forming a positive memory.
- It has memorized *parking space available*, picked up in this book as something very positive as well. A person who has been looking for a parking space for some time in a big city feels blessed to have found an available space.
- It has associated motivation with positive words and put the face of a colleague on the concept.
- It will continuously enrich the mind-dataset through everyday experience and memories and store the decisions (good or bad) made.

Negative thinking

To think, a mind must accept negative thinking and have feelings. A positive feeling is felt by contrast with a negative feeling. A positive thought is felt by contrast to a negative feeling.

Empathy is based on the ability to feel both positive and negative feelings. Otherwise, the mind is only half of a mind.

As you can see MindX does not pretend to be 100% perfect and positive; 100% efficiency may be good for optimizing like a machine but it certainly does not exist in humans. MindX has weaknesses and it knows this. This is what makes MindX a powerful thinking and feeling entity.

MindX is nearly human, so it can have negative thoughts. The following screenshot of the PCA Tensorbard Projection of MindX shows negative feelings:

PCA Tensorbard Projection of MindX

MindX, as in the positive PCA area:

- Has doubts.
- Can think better with this very useful dimension (avoiding a mistake, being careful, self-interrogation, or reconsidering an opinion on another person). MindX will be more sensitive and sensible.
- Has, on the left of doubts, cracks appearing close by in the gap area. Doubts images are near the fields of love positive thoughts appear by contrast. Associating different types of concepts is what makes a mind deep.

 In MindX, as in humans, doubts are often not flaws but ways of reconsidering a decision more deeply.

Gaps

Gaps constitute a major concept in a mind's way of thinking—something missing, the concept of insufficient, a gap between people, a gap in factory goals, and many more concepts (see Chapter 11, *Conceptual Representation Learning*).

The following image is a TensorBoard screenshot of the gap features of MindX's representation of its environment:

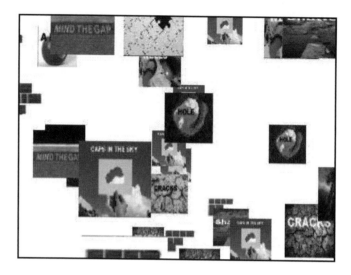

Gap features of MindX's representation

MindX has associated gaps with cracks, abstract holes in the sky, holes in rocks, "*mind the gap*" messages in cities, and cracks in the earth.

Distances

MindX has acquired experience and dreams of distances.

The following image is a TensorBoard screenshot of MindX's representation of distances:

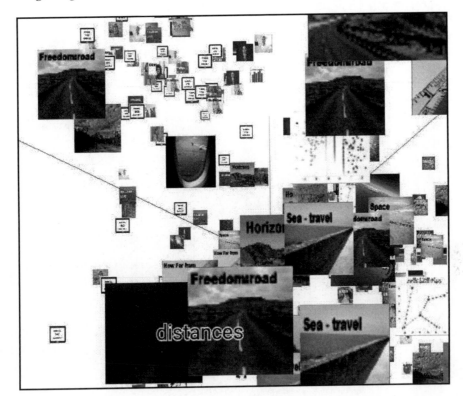

MindX's representation of distance

MindX has memories of "*freedom roads,*" and sea travel. It has associated horizons, hope, and love to distances and travel. MindX has MDP graphs in mind and much more.

The embedding program

EMBEDDING_IMAGES.py has started the MindX Quantum experiment with four main classes and 4,096 dimensions. This dataset can be automatically enhanced using the solutions described in Chapter 16, *Improve the Emotional Intelligence Deficiencies of Chatbots*.

The human brain has a maximum of around 100,000,000,000 neurons (100 billion), which is a small number compared to what we saw a quantum computer could manage in one calculation.

Of course, human neurons combine and do a lot more than just being a mass of neurons. But this means that expanding the mind-dataset of MindX beyond any human being's capacity is possible today with the right parameters. MindX could be represented by an endless number of separate PCA feature sets connected in the largest personal mind that ever existed. The following code in Python starts by loading the four classes of data described before:

```python
img_data=[]
for dataset in data_dir_list:
img_list=os.listdir(data_path+'/'+ dataset)
print ('Loaded the images of dataset-'+'{}\n'.format(dataset))
for img in img_list:
input_img=cv2.imread(data_path + '/'+ dataset + '/'+ img )
input_img_resize = cv2.resize(input_img, (64,64))
img_data.append(input_img_resize)
```

 A MindX project requires many more classes and subsets. You can certainly enhance this project and build a powerful chatbot by assembling the programs in this book and running a quantum score.

The following code describes how the feature vectors are now loaded. See Chapter 16, *Improve the Emotional Intelligence Deficiencies of Chatbots*, for details on how to produce feature vectors in the PCA section:

```python
feature_vectors = np.loadtxt('feature_vectors_400_samples.txt')
print ("feature_vector",feature_vectors)
print ("feature_vectors_shape:",feature_vectors.shape)
print ("num of images:",feature_vectors.shape[0])
print ("size of individual feature vector:",feature_vectors.shape[1])
```

The metadata files are written with the following few lines:

```python
. . .
metadata_file.write('Class\tName\n')
k=100 # num of samples in each class
j=0
#for i in range(210):
# metadata_file.write('%06d\t%s\n' % (i, names[y[i]]))
for i in range(num_of_samples):
c = names[y[i]]
```

```
if i%k==0:
j=j+1
metadata_file.write('{}\t{}\n'.format(j,c))
#metadata_file.write('%06d\t%s\n' % (j, c))
metadata_file.close()
...
def images_to_sprite(data):
if len(data.shape) == 3:
data = np.tile(data[...,np.newaxis], (1,1,1,3))
data = data.astype(np.float32)
min = np.min(data.reshape...
...
data = data.reshape((n * data.shape[1], n * data.shape[3]) +
data.shape[4:])
data = (data * 255).astype(np.uint8)
return data
...
```

The sprite image is created. It contains small thumbnail images of the dataset for TensorBoard Projector, displaying purposes as shown in the following code:

```
def images_to_sprite(data):
if len(data.shape) == 3:
data = np.tile(data[...,np.newaxis], (1,1,1,3))
data = data.astype(np.float32)
min = np.min(data.reshape...
...
data = data.reshape((n * data.shape[1], n * data.shape[3]) +
data.shape[4:])
data = (data * 255).astype(np.uint8)
return data
...
```

The metadata class labels are saved along with the necessary files for TensorBoard Projector (see the source code).

Now `Tensorboard_reader.py` is launched, and TensorBoard Projector will show the personal mind-dataset of MindX.

MindX is now ready to think with a quantum computer.

The MindX experiment

The aim of the Quantum MindX experiment is to build a mind and let it think with the power of a quantum computer. This section will show how to run a 16-qubit mind.

The size of numbers needed to describe a 16-qubit quantum simulation is 65,536.

The section first describes how to do the following:

- Prepare the data
- Create and run a quantum score
- Use the output

Preparing the data

To prepare data for higher dimension calculations, I have been using a concept encoding method for corporate projects for 30+ years to provide embedded data to the algorithms I developed. This guarantees high-level abstraction to solve problems. It is a very profitable way to implement transfer learning and domain learning. This way, you can apply the same model to many different fields.

The method consists of embedding data with the methods described in this book. The goal always remains the same—to transform the data points into higher dimensions to visualize features.

For quantum computing, the method remains the same for the MindX experiment.

Transformation Functions – the situation function

The mind dataset that has been built in the past chapters through CRLMM has undergone PCA (Chapter 16, *Improve the Emotional Intelligence Deficiencies of Chatbots*) transformation. Variances, covariances, covariance matrices, eigenvalues, eigenvectors, and then feature vectors were applied to the data.

Now two functions need to be applied before creating and running a score: a situation function and a quantum transformation function.

The situation function consists of building a vector of features in PCA dimensions. In `Chapter 16`, *Improve the Emotional Intelligence Deficiencies of Chatbots*, the chatbot was able to use person X's mind-dataset to suggest a movie. In this chapter, MindX now is that person. This chatbot has a nascent personal mind, not a general mind that can recognize, classify, and predict like a machine. MindX has a mind that is biased by its way of thinking like humans. MindX has an exceptionally open mind to adapt to everyone, which gives it empathy.

MindX can doubt. Thus it can learn better than dogmatic machines.

A situation function will create a situation matrix for a movie suggestion by the MindX bot that will communicate with consumers. In a movie suggestion situation by the MindX bot, for example, it could be something as follows for 16 qubits:

Qubit	Concept	Image	Initial polarity
1	cities	parking	0.146
2	darkness	dark forest	0.5
3	nostalgia	autumn leaves	0.5
4	worrying	dark background	0.146
5	job	sad face	0.5
	…	..	..
15	consider movie "Lost"		0.38
16	decision to suggest "Lost"		0.0

MindX is not analyzing person X anymore. It has now loaded an empathy matrix from its mind-dataset that contains the actual images of the dataset used in this chapter and represented in PCA TensorBoard Projector. MindX loads its mind plus the mind of another person.

Empathy colors your thoughts and feelings with the thoughts and feelings of another person.

The 16-qubit matrix shown just now contains four columns:

- **Qubit**: The line for this qubit on the quantum composer
- **Concept**: The concept loaded in MindX's situation dataset
- **Image**: The actual image in the dataset
- **Initial polarity**: The sentiment analysis of MindX's profile (see `Chapter 16`, *Improve the Emotional Intelligence Deficiencies of Chatbots*)

The first lines (1 to 5) show that MindX has perceived the person X as a bit sad and disappointed. The last two lines(15 and 16) show that MindX thinks that maybe the movie *Lost* would please person X.

Before suggesting the movie named *Lost*, MindX needs to think about it. For the moment, MindX seems reluctant to suggest the movie *Lost*.

This movie example is for explaining how to create a thinking, empathetic chatbot. This approach can be applied to other commercial market segments or any situation in which a chatbot is required to think beyond preset answers.

Transformation functions – the quantum function

The situation function has produced a qubit line number with labels (concepts and images). Each line also possesses a sentiment analysis polarity expressed in normalized values from 0 to 1 in probabilistic format. Negative is close to 0, positive close to 1, and the intermediate values give a more detailed approximation. 0.4 to 0.6 is a turning point.

This first transformation into another dimension is the first step to initialize quantum transformation function. The quantum transformation function consists in initializing the first column of all 16 qubits with a quantum gate.

Just like datasets were transformed into principal component features, the polarity transformation function enables the quantum transformation function to bring the dataset into a quantum universe.

The function will automatically find the quantum gates which represent the normalized sentiment analysis polarity of the data points of the following situation matrix:

Initial polarity	Quantum gate
0.146	$X^{1/4}$
0.5	$X^{1/2}$
0.5	$X^{1/2}$
0.146	$X^{1/4}$
0.5	$X^{1/2}$
..	
0.38	$X^{1/8}$
0.0	$Z^{1/8}$

The situation matrix and its concepts have now been transformed into a quantum dimension, in which the data status can be traced throughout the creation of the quantum score.

Creating and running the score

A thought process of MindX is described in a quantum score. There are two ways to build this score :

- Manually, just like a musician writing a music score. This requires thinking about the previous logic gate and the effect of the next one, taking a decision process into account. It is like writing any artificial intelligence program.
- Automatically, by building a function that reads a rule base of MindX's way of thinking and applies the quantum gates through that rule base.

In any case, it requires writing an algorithm. This algorithm is a decision-making algorithm that takes emotions into account. Doubt, for example, is what keeps many humans from making wrong decisions. Too much doubt, for example, will make a person back out from that situation.

Here is the quantum transcription of such an algorithm that takes MindX's concepts into account and represents how they interact. This requires very precise thinking and cognitive science programming.

The following is an experimental quantum score I built with Quirk:

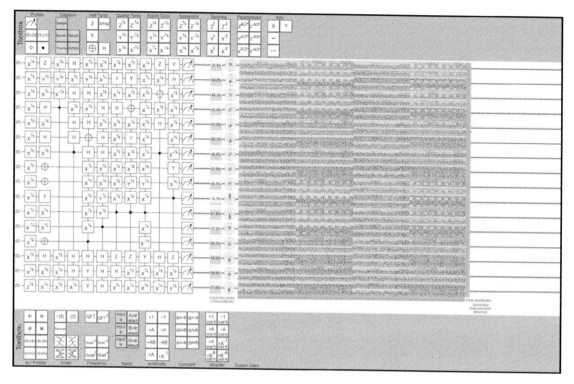

Quantum score with Quirk

Once the quantum score has been run and the measurement made, the green rectangles on the right provide the output.

Using the output

The output of the quantum score is now added as a column to the situation matrix. MindX has now attained the right to be a cognitive NLP chatbot. MindX has proven its cognitive abilities.

Qubit	Concept	Image	Initial Normalized Polarity expressed in quantum gate form	Quantum output directly interpreted as sentiment analysis polarity
1	cities	parking	0.146	0.677
2	darkness	dark forest	0.5	0.691
3	nostalgia	autumn leaves	0.5	0.5
4	worrying	dark background	0.146	0.48
5	job	sad face	0.5	0.36
	...	..	..	
15	consider movie "Lost"		0.38	0.82
16	decision to suggest"Lost"		0.0	0.75

MindX has given a 65,536 quantum state description of its thoughts about suggesting a given movie to person X. Lines 15 and 16 show that the normalized polarity value has risen over 0.5 to a positive feeling about the movie.

The reasoning is that the first lines show that MindX feels person X's doubts about life at that moment:

- That person X will identify to the "Lost" concept
- The movie has a happy ending (MindX knows that through the features of the movie)
- That person X's spirits will be most probably lifted after watching the movie

IBM Watson and scripts

With that output, the program can activate an IBM Watson movie-choice dialog created by the company who wants to optimize marketing chatbots as shown in Chapter 15, *Cognitive NLP Chatbots*.

The dialog in Chapter 16, *Improve the Emotional Intelligence Deficiencies of Chatbots*, between MindX and person X could be enhanced to something such as this:

- **MindX**: I've noticed you have been scrolling to find a movie on our website. Can I help you?"
- **PersonX**: Why not?
- **MindX**: Well, feel some doubts myself about things right now.

- **PersonX**: What???
- **MindX**: Oh, I forgot to introduce myself. I'm MindX a Quantum Mind program. I can think and feel. I'm not just about statistics and predictions.
- **PersonX**: Wow!
- **MindX**: Anyway, I was saying that I have some doubts myself and a movie called 'Lost' reflects my frame of mind. What do you think?
- **PersonX**: "Why would a movie like that (lines 15 and 16 of the situation matrix) be good for me?"
- **MindX**: Mmmm. Let me think a minute... (the quantum score runs)
- **MindX**: Ok. (the quantum score is over)
- **MindX**: I thought about it. Ok. I feel doubts today also, but the movie is all about people that are Lost and trying to find there way in life. I can't tell you more, but it looks exciting!. Do you see what I mean?
- **PersonX**: I sure do! But first, tell me more about you please!
- **MindX**: ....the rest of the IBM Watson dialog + AI Scripts + Quantum thinking scores...

Summary

Quantum computers have opened the door to scientific experiments that could never have been carried out with classical computers. Within a few years, quantum computers will have become mainstream, unavoidable, and a key asset for businesses and research labs. The race has begun to conquer the market.

CRLMM applied to quantum computers could make MindX one of the most powerful thinking minds on earth, human or machine.

With an unlimited mind-dataset and a 2^q quantum computer starting at 2^{50}, a 50-qubit machine, MindX could gain the thinking power and experience of a human who would have lived 1,000 years. MindX's thinking power and an exponential amount of real-time memory of past experiences, loaded through transformation functions, could help solve many medical, logistic, and other decision-making problems.

Quantum thinking has just begun to change the perception of the world. Then, DNA-based computers will appear with new perspectives. Conceptual AI models such as CRLMM will no doubt be the starting point of the next generation of AI solutions. These CRLMM models will be much more powerful because they will be gifted with empathy and complex minds.

Artificial intelligence has only begun its long journey into our lives. Always trust innovations. Never trust a solution that solves a problem without opening the door to a universe of questions and ideas!

Questions

1. Beyond the hype, no quantum computer exists? (Yes | No)
2. A quantum computer can store data? (Yes | No)
3. The effect of quantum gates on qubits can be viewed with a Bloch sphere? (Yes | No)
4. A mind that thinks with past experiences, images, words, and other bits of every day like stored memory will find deeper solutions to problems that mathematics alone cannot solve? (Yes | No)
5. A quantum computer will solve medical research problems that cannot be solved today? (Yes | No)
6. A quantum computer can solve mathematical problems exponentially faster than classical computers? (Yes | No)
7. Classical computers will soon disappear and smartphone processors also? (Yes | No)
8. A quantum score cannot be written in source code format but only with a visual interface? (Yes | No)
9. Quantum simulators can run as fast as quantum computers? (Yes | No)
10. Quantum computers produce intermediate results when they are running calculations? (Yes | No)

Further reading

Explore IBM Q and discover how you can implement quantum scores:

https://www.research.ibm.com/ibm-q/

Use Quirk, an intuitive quantum score designing tool:

http://algassert.com/2016/05/22/quirk.html

Answers to the Questions

Chapter 1 – Become an Adaptive Thinker

1. Is reinforcement learning memoryless? (Yes | No)

The answer is yes. Reinforcement learning is memoryless. The agent calculates the next state without looking into the past. This is significantly different to humans. Humans rely heavily on memory. A CPU-based reinforcement learning system finds solutions without experience. Human intelligence merely proves that intelligence can solve a problem. No more, no less. An adaptive thinker can then imagine new forms of machine intelligence.

2. Does reinforcement learning use stochastic (random) functions? (Yes | No)

The answer is yes. In the particular Markov Decision Process model, the choices are random. In just two questions, you can see that the Bellman equation is memoryless and makes random decisions. No human reasons like that. Being an adaptive thinker is a leap of faith. You will have to leave who you were behind and begin to think in terms of equations.

3. Is the Markov Decision Process based on a rule base?

The answer is no. Human rule base experience is useless in this process. Furthermore, the Markov Decision Process provides efficient alternatives to long consulting times with future users that cannot clearly express their problem.

4. Is the Q function based on the Markov Decision Process? (Yes | No)

The answer is yes. The use of the expression "Q" appeared around the time the Bellman equation, based on the Markov Decision Process, came into fashion. It is more trendy to say you are using a Q function than to speak about Bellman, who put all of this together in 1957. The truth is that Andrey Markov was Russian and applied this method in 1913 using a dataset of 20,000 letters to predict future use of letters in a novel. He then extended that to a dataset of 100,000 letters. This means that the theory was there 100 years ago. Q fits our new world of impersonal and powerful CPUs.

5. Is mathematics essential to artificial intelligence? (Yes | No)

The answer is yes. If you master the basics of linear algebra and probability, you will be on top of all the technology that is coming. It is worth spending a few months on the subject in the evening or taking a MOOC. Otherwise, you will depend on others to explain things to you.

6. Can the Bellman-MDP process in this chapter apply to many problems? (Yes | No)

The answer is yes. You can use this for robotics, market analysis, IoT, linguistics, and scores of other problems.

7. Is it impossible for a machine learning program to create another program by itself? (Yes | No)

The answer is no. It is not impossible. It has already been done by Google with AutoML. Do not be surprised. Now that you have become an adaptive thinker and know that these systems rely on equations, not humans, you can easily understand that mathematical systems are not that difficult to reproduce.

8. Is a consultant required to enter business rules in a reinforcement learning program? (Yes | No)

The answer is no. It is only an option. Reinforcement learning in the MDP process is memoryless and random. Consultants are there to manage, explain, and train in these projects.

9. Is reinforcement learning supervised or unsupervised? (Supervised | Unsupervised)

The answer is unsupervised. The whole point is to learn from unlabeled data. If the data is labeled, then we enter the world of supervised learning; that will be searching for patterns and learning them. At this point, you can easily see you are at sea in an adventure—a memoryless, random, and unlabeled world for you to discover.

10. Can Q Learning run without a reward matrix? (Yes | No)

The answer is no. A smart developer could always find a way around this, of course. The system requires a starting point. You will see in the second chapter that it is quite a task to find the right reward matrix in real-life projects.

Chapter 2 – Think like a Machine

1. The concept of using an artificial neuron was discovered in 1990. (Yes | No)

The answer is no. Warren McCulloch and Walter Pitts invented the first neuron and published a paper in 1943. Legend has it that at age 12 years in 1935, Walter Pitts, a poor child living in a bad neighborhood, was chased by bullies and sought refuge in a library. There he discovered *Principia Mathematica* by Bertrand Russell and Alfred Whitehead. Anyway, not only did he find mistakes in the reasoning, but also he sent a letter to Bertrand Russell! From then on, Walter was noted for his genius in mathematics. With Waren McCulloch, another genius, they invented the first neuron. It seems simple. But it's the result of sleepless nights. Just as the invention of the wheel appears simple, nothing better has been found to this day. This concept of a the neuron is the wheel of artificial intelligence.

2. Does a McCulloch-Pitts neuron require a threshold? (Yes | No)

The answer is yes. Adding up weights does not mean much if you do not have something to measure the value. It took months of work for McCulloch and Pitt to put this together. At first, time was in the equation, just like it is in our brain. But then, like Joseph Fourier (1768-1830), they found cycles that repeated themselves—periods that did not require much more than that neuron.

3. A logistic sigmoid activation function makes the sum of the weights larger. (Yes | No)

The answer is no. The whole point is to reduce the sums when necessary to have comparable numbers to work with.

4. A McCulloch-Pitts neuron sums the weights of its inputs. (Yes | No)

The answer is yes. It's only when you sum the weights that they make sense.

5. A logistic sigmoid function is a $\log_{10}$ operation? (Yes | No)

The answer is no. The sigmoid function is based on Euler's number, e, a constant that is equal to 2.71828. This number produces a natural logarithm. Leonhard Euler (1707-1783) discovered this in the 18th century with a quill—no scientific calculator or computer! Did you notice that the main mathematical functions used in artificial intelligence run far back in history? This aspect of the hype around what we think we have found now but has existed for decades, and sometimes centuries, will be dealt with in the following chapters.

6. A Logistic Softmax is not necessary if a logistic sigmoid function is applied to a vector. (Yes | No)

The answer is no. Calculating the sum of several numbers of a vector and then dividing each number by that sum gives a view of the proportions involved. It is a precious tool to keep in mind.

7. A probability is a value between -1 and 1. (Yes | No)

The answer is no. Probabilities lie between 0 and 1.

Chapter 3 – Apply Machine Thinking to a Human Problem

1. Can a human beat a chess engine? (Yes | No)

The answer is no. Today, the highest level chess tournaments are not between humans but between chess engines. Each chess engine software editor prepares for these competitions by making their algorithms faster and requiring less CPU. In fact today, a top chess engine running on a smartphone can beat humans. In human-to-human chess competitions, the level of chess has reached very high limits of complexity. Humans now mostly train against machines.

2. Humans can estimate decisions better than machines with intuition when it comes to large volumes of data. (Yes | No)

The answer is no. The sheer CPU power of an average machine or even a smartphone can generate better results than humans with the proper algorithms.

3. Building a reinforcement learning program with a Q function is a feat in itself. Using the results afterward is useless. (Yes | No)

The answer is no. While learning artificial intelligence, just verifying the results are correct is enough. In real-life applications, the results are used in databases or as input to other systems.

4. Supervised learning Decision Tree functions can be used to verify that the result of the unsupervised learning process will produce reliable, predictable results. (Yes | No)

> The answer is yes. Decision Tree functions are not intelligent, but they are very efficient in many cases. When large volumes are involved, Decision Tree functions can be used to analyze the results of the machine learning process and contribute to a prediction process.

5. The results of a reinforcement learning program can be used as input to a scheduling system by providing priorities. (Yes | No)

> The answer is yes. The output of reinforcement learning Q function can, in fact, be injected as input into another Q function. Several results and be consolidated in phase 1 and become the reward matrix of a phase 2 reinforcement learning session.

6. Artificial intelligence software thinks like humans. (Yes | No)

> The answer is yes and no. In early days, this was attempted with neuroscience-based models. However, applying mathematical models is presently far more efficient. Pretending otherwise at this point is hype. Who knows what will happen in future research? But for the time being, deep learning, the main trend, is based on mathematical functions.

Chapter 4 – Become an Unconventional Innovator

1. Can the perceptron alone solve the XOR problem? (Yes | No)

> The answer was no in 1969. A neural network, or some other mathematical process, is necessary to solve this problem. For the record, this is a common problem for electric circuits that function with "feedforward" electricity, and was solved long ago.

2. Is the XOR function linearly separable? (Yes | No)

The answer is no if you use a single neuron and yes if you use a hidden layer with at least two neurons. That is a major problem to address in deep learning. If you cannot separate the features of a face, for example, in a picture, recognizing that face will prove difficult. Imagine a picture with one half of the face in shadow and the other half in bright sunlight. Since the eye and features of one half are in shadow, a poor deep learning program might only capture half of the face, separating the face in the wrong place with a poor edge detection function. Linear separability is thus a key aspect of machine learning.

3. One of the main goals of layers in a neural network is classification. (Yes | No)

The answer is yes. Once the data is identifiable with a given neural network architecture, predictions, and many other functions become possible. The key to deep learning is to be able to transform data into pieces of information that will make sense.

4. Is deep learning the only way to classify data? (Yes | No)

The answer is no. You can classify data with an SQL query, artificial intelligence, machine learning, and standard source code. Deep learning becomes vital when many dimensions of classification are involved: first finding the edges of objects in a picture, then forms, and then determining what the object represents. To do this with millions of pictures is beyond the scope of standard programming or early AI and ML programs.

5. A cost function shows the increase in the cost of neural network. (Yes | No)

The answer is no. A cost function determines how much the training costs you. Running 100,000 epochs is more expensive than running 50,000 epochs. So at each epoch, the cost of training (how far the system is from its goal) must be estimated. Thus, a good cost function will decrease the cost of running a neural network.

6. Can simple arithmetic be enough to optimize a cost function? (Yes | No)

The answer is yes. As long as you know to what extent your cost function is increasing or decreasing, anything that works is fine.

7. A feedforward network requires inputs, layers, and an output. (Yes | No)

The answer is yes. Without layers, there is no network.

8. A feedforward network always requires training with backpropagation. (Yes | No)

The answer is often yes in changing environments.. Since the field is new, we tend to think that once the training is done, the work is done. If the datasets are very stable in a repetitive environment, such as recognizing the difference between various constant products in a shop, warehouse or factory, then the neural network will do the classification it is designed for. If new products are introduced, then training can be initiated again.

9. In real-life applications, solutions are only found by respecting academic theory. (Yes | No)

The answer is no. Without academic research, deep learning would not even exist. Without universities, the ideas used would be so simple that they would never work well. On the other hand, researchers need real-life feedback. If we find new ways of doing things they recommended, we should publish them to help global research. It's a two-way street.

Chapter 5 – Manage the Power of Machine Learning and Deep Learning

1. TensorBoard is simply a nice displaying program. (Yes | No)

The answer is yes and no. Yes, TensorBoard is a friendly interface for visualizing a dataflow graph. No, TensorBoard is not only nice but is also critical to designing the architecture of a project even before the data feed aspect of the program is written. In real-life projects, a good architecture shows that you can manage the power of ML/DL programs.

2. Defining functions at the beginning of the source code is just like standard programs. (Yes | No)

No. Seeing variables and arrays at the beginning of a TensorFlow program could lead one to think that it is just a formality. However, these lines are in fact the real program, the dataflow graph, the architecture.

3. TensorFlow is a library add-on to Python that provides some cool functions. (Yes | No)

The answer is no. It is a strategic tool for designing the dataflow graph of an application.

4. TensorBoard is not necessary to deploy machine learning and deep learning programs. (Yes | No)

> The answer is yes. TensorBoard refreshes every n seconds automatically (this can be deactivated). When running large datasets during the training process, it is crucial to see whether the cost function is going up or down. And even if it is going down, converging to 0 or near 0, it is vital to see how fast the slope (gradient) is decreasing (descent).

5. As long as we're technical experts, we don't have to worry about our environment. It will adapt. (Yes | No)

> The answer is no. Those days are over. Our environment decides whether our project will survive or not. It is critical to developing not only code but also communication skills to defend ongoing projects.

6. Presenting ML/DL projects doesn't change the architecture of a solution. (Yes | No)

> The answer is no. If the presentation has been well defined and made to the right people, the architecture can be tremendously improved by optimizing the datasets, training phase, test phase, and expected results.

7. Managers don't need to understand the technical aspect of a solution as long as it works. (Yes | No)

> The answer is no. This is a myth. It works early in a project, or in a dream world where projects never go wrong. But large projects always go wrong at some point because of dataset problems, bugs, communication tensions, sick leave, vacations, budget limitations, and scores of unexpected events. When that happens, communicating the key points and reasons of every aspect of the problem becomes essential.

Chapter 6 – Don't Get Lost in Techniques, Focus on Optimizing Your Solutions

1. Can a prototype be built with random data in corporate environments? (Yes | No)

> The answer is yes and no. To start developing a prototype, using random data can help make sure that the basic algorithm works as planned.

However, once the prototype is advanced, it will be more reliable to use a well-designed dataset. Then, once the training has been successfully accomplished, random data can help again to see how your system behaves in all situations.

2. Do design matrices contain one example per matrix? (Yes | No)

The answer is no. A good design matrix contains one example in each row or each column depending on the shape you want it to have. But be careful; a design matrix that contains data that is too efficient might **overfit**. That means the learning algorithm will be efficient with that data but not adapt to new data. On the other hand, if the dataset contains too many errors, then the algorithm might **underfit**, meaning it won't learn correctly. A good design matrix should contain reliable data, some imprecise data, and some **noise** (some data that can influence the algorithm in unreliable ways).

3. Automatic Guided Vehicle will never be widespread. (Yes | No)

The answer is that AGVs will expand endlessly from now on: drones, cars, planes, warehouse vehicles, industrial vehicles, and more. AGVs, added to artificial intelligence and IoT, constitute the fourth industrial revolution.

4. Can k-means clustering be applied to drone traffic? (Yes | No)

The answer is yes. Seeing where traffic builds up will prevent drone jams (drones circling and waiting).

5. Can k-means clustering be applied to forecasting? (Yes | No)

The answer is yes and will be explained in `Chapter 10`, *Applying Biomimicking to Artificial Intelligence*; it'll be applied to all types of traffic.

6. Lloyd's algorithm is a two-step approach. (Yes | No)

Yes, Lloyd's algorithm first classifies each data point in the best cluster. Then, once that is done, it calculates the geometric center or centroid of that center. When no data point changes the cluster anymore, the algorithm has been trained.

7. Do hyperparameters control the behavior of the algorithm? (Yes | No)

The answer is yes. Hyperparameters determine the course of the computation: the number of clusters, features, batch sizes, and more.

8. Once a program works, the way it is presented does not matter. (Yes | No)

The answer is no. Without a clear presentation of the results, the whole training process is confusing at best and useless at worst.

9. K-means is only a classification algorithm. It's not a prediction algorithm. (Yes | No)

The answer is no. K-means clustering can be used as a prediction algorithm as well.

Chapter 7 – When and How to Use Artificial Intelligence

The questions will focus on the hyperparameters.

1. The number of k clusters is not that important. (Yes | No)

The answer is no. The number of clusters requires careful selection, possibly a trial-and-error approach. Each project will lead to different clusters.

2. Mini-batches and batches contain the same amount of data. (Yes | No)

The answer is no. "Batch" generally refers to the dataset and "mini-batch" represents a "subset" of data.

3. K-means can run without mini-batches. (Yes | No)

The answer is yes and no. If the volume of data remains small, then the training epochs can run on the whole dataset. If the data volume exceeds a reasonable amount of computer power (CPU or GPU), mini-batches must be created to optimize training computation.

4. Must centroids be optimized for result acceptance? (Yes | No)

The answer is yes and no. Suppose you want to put a key in a keyhole. The keyhole represents the centroid of your visual cluster. You must be precise. If you are simply throwing a piece of paper in your garbage can, you do not need to aim at the perfect center (centroid) of the cluster (marked by the rim of the garbage can) to attain that goal. Centroid precision depends on what is asked of the algorithm.

5. It does not take long to optimize hyperparameters. (Yes | No)

> The answer is yes and no. If it's a simple project, it will not take long. If you are facing a large dataset, it will take some time to find the optimal hyperparameters.

6. Can it sometimes take weeks to train a large dataset? (Yes | No)

> The answer is yes. Media hype and hard work are two different worlds. Machine learning and deep learning are are still tough projects to implement.

7. AWS SageMaker only offers a k-means algorithm. (Yes | No)

> The answer is no. AWS Sagemaker offers a complete range of algorithms in the job creation interface. You can also use your algorithms choosing **Custom**.

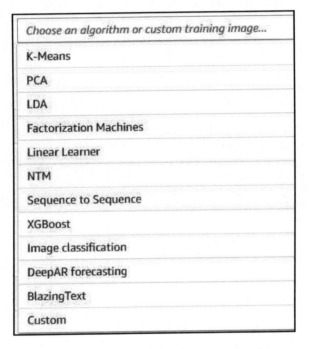

AWS Sagemaker algorithms

Chapter 8 – Revolutions Designed for Some Corporations and Disruptive Innovations for Small to Large Companies

1. It is better to wait until you have a top-quality product before putting it on the market. (Yes | No)

The answer is yes and no. In the early 21st century, Airbus was struggling to complete the A380, the largest ever passenger airplane. Their engineers worked on hundreds of improvements before transporting commercial passengers. We would not expect less!

In the case of Google Translate, it is a massive no. By putting Google Translate online and providing an API, Google encouraged thousands of artificial intelligence developers, linguists, consultants and users to provide feedback and improvements. Furthermore, Google, once again, occupies a large share of the web market.

2. Considering the investment made, a new product should always be highly priced to reach the top segment of the market. (Yes | No)

The answer is yes and no. When Ferrari puts a new car on the market, the price has to be high for two reasons; the quality of the car and cost of production make it necessary to do so to make the innovation profitable. Also, Ferrari avoids mass production to keep its quality at high levels.

When Amazon Web Services put machine learning on the market with SageMaker, it puts a "pay-as-you-go" policy in place, starting at a very low end of the market. The product had and has limits. But Amazon now has tremendous feedback and continuously improves the product.

3. Inventing a new solution will make it known in itself. (Yes | No)

You might be surprised to know that saving a camera picture by drawing it dates so far back in history that nobody knows for sure when it was first used. Nobody knows if it was invented or discovered. In any case, the first *camera obscura* was revolutionary. It is now proven that famous painters used the technique. The picture was projected on a paper or canvas. The "printer" was manual. The painter was the "printer." However, cameras as we know only become disruptive in the 20th century.

4. Artificial intelligence can solve most problems without using standard non-learning algorithms. (Yes | No)

> The answer is no. Artificial intelligence relies on cloud servers, architectures, standard languages (C++, Java, Python, and others), and Apache servers. Even on a self-driving car, the sensors installed require standard hard work to get them working and interpreting information before AI comes in to solve some of the problems.

> AI is like our brain. Without a body, it cannot function.

5 . Google Translate can translate all languages in a satisfactory way. (Yes | No)

> After reading this chapter, you might be surprised to have a yes and no answer. If you are using Google Translate to say "hello," "how are you," "thanks for the message," and similar friendly phrases on your favorite social network or in an email, it is good enough.

> But when dealing with more detailed phrases and sentences, Google Translate provides random satisfactory results. From a user's perspective, this is bad news. For a developer, it is a goldmine!

6. If you are not creative, it is no use trying to innovate. (Yes | No)

> The answer is a massive no. You certainly do not need to be either imaginative or creative to innovate. Do not let anybody convince you of such nonsense. If you are designing a solution and find a missing component, look for some alternative components on the web, talk about it, and find people that can help. Then get it done through teamwork. This works every time!

> Even the great Bill Gates was smart enough to ask Tim Patterson for help to develop MS-DOS, and he went on to become a billionaire.

7. If you are not a linguist, it is no use bothering trying to improve Google Translate. (Yes | No)

> The answer is no! Once again, never let somebody convince you of such nonsense. Innovating is teamwork. If you like Google Translate and you understand this chapter and have ideas, team up with a linguist around you or through a social network. The world is yours to improve!

8. Translation is too complicated to understand. (Yes | No)

No. The way some explain it is too complicated. If you speak a language, you are an expert of translating your thoughts into words. With work, you can get into the translation business.

9. Artificial intelligence has already reached its limits. (Yes | No)

Certainly not! We have just scratched the surface of both theory and applications.

Chapter 9 – Getting Your Neurons to Work

1. A convolutional neural network (CNN) can only process images. (Yes | No)

The answer is no. CNNs can process words, sounds, or video sequences, to classify and predict.

2. A kernel is a preset matrix used for convolutions. (Yes | No)

The answer is yes and no. There are many preset matrices used to process images such as the one used in `edge_detection_Kernel.py` in this chapter. However, in this chapter, kernels were created randomly and then the network trained their weights to fit the target images.

3. Does pooling have a pooling matrix or is it random?

A pooling matrix has a size that is an option when the pooling layer is added to the model, such as a 2x2 pooling window.

4. The dataset always has to be large. (Yes | No)

No. A dataset does not have a standard size. It depends on the training model. If the target images, for example, do not contain complex features, the dataset will be smaller than a complex feature dataset. Furthermore, the `ImageDataGenerator` function will expand the data by distorting it with the provided options.

5. Finding a dataset is not a problem with all the available image banks on the web. (Yes | No)

The answer is yes and no. Yes because if the model remains a standard academic one, then the available images (CIFAR, MNIST, or others) will suffice.

No, because in real-life corporate situations, you will have to build your dataset and add images containing **noise**. Noise requires more fine-tuning of the model to become reliable and generalized.

6. Once a CNN is built, training it does not take much time. (Yes | No)

The answer is no. Whatever the model is, training will remain time-consuming if you want it to be reliable. As seen in this chapter, a model requires a lot of options and mathematical thinking.

7. A trained CNN model applies to only one type of image. (Yes | No)

Yes and no. There are three main types of overfitting:

- Overfitting a model for a certain type of images with absolutely no consequence of implementation. In this case, the model classifies and predicts enough to satisfy the goals set.
- Overfitting a model that creates implementation problems because it cannot adapt to different images of the same time. The model will then go through more training.
- Overfitting a model that trains a certain type of image quite well but does not fit similar types of images when needed.

Each situation has its constraints. As long as the model works, no general rules apply. It is up to you to decide.

8. A quadratic loss function is not very efficient compared to cross-entropy function. (Yes | No)

The answer is no. Each model has its constraints. Quadratic loss functions work fine on some models and do not provide good results on others. This represents the main problems of training a model. No general rules will help you. You have to use your neurons or write a program that modifies the model automatically.

9. The performance of a deep learning CNN does not a represent a real issue with modern CPUs and GPUs. (Yes | No)

The answer is yes and no. If the model runs quickly enough for your needs, then performance will not limit the outcome of your project. However, in many cases, it remains a problem. Reducing features to simply focus on the best ones is one of the reasons that the layers bring the size to analyze down, layer by layer.

Chapter 10 – Applying Biomimicking to AI

1. Deep learning and machine learning mean the same thing. (Yes | No)

No. When an AI program contains a network, especially a deep one (with several layers), that is deep learning. Deep learning is a subset of machine learning.

When programs such as an Markov Decision Process (MDP) are used, that is machine learning.

To sum it up, not all artificial intelligence programs have to learn. Machine learning is a subset of artificial intelligence programs that learn but do not require networks. Deep learning is a subset of machine learning that uses networks.

2. Deep learning networks mostly reproduce human brain functions. (Yes | No)

Yes in neuroscience research on the human brain. Computer models of the brain using deep learning can provide interesting models.

Sometimes yes, when deep learning networks try to reproduce human vision for image recognition applications.

No, when it comes many programs using statistics and probability for language processing, for example.

3. Overfitting is unacceptable. (Yes | No)

Yes, when an application has been implemented and requires the ability to adapt constantly to new data.

No, when an application has been implemented, and the same images are submitted to the AI program.

No, when a prototype is first built and used as a proof of concept that the solution appears interesting.

4. Transfer learning can save the cost of building another model. (Yes | No)

Yes. A reusable model can become quickly very profitable.

5. Training a corporate model on MNIST is enough to implement it on a production line, for example. (Yes | No)

Yes and no. Yes because if a model works on MNIST, it contains the proper functions to learn. No, because if the goal of the project is not close to MNIST data, it will not work. Experiment with MNIST in an image project that contains similar sorts of simple images.

6. Exploring artificial intelligence beyond the cutting edge is not necessary. It is easier to wait for the next ideas that are published. (Yes | No)

Yes, when a team does not have ideas but excels in implementation, for example. GitHub can provide thousands of ideas, along with social networks, publications, and more.

No, when a team is creative and wants to occupy the market with innovations.

7. Some researchers have reproduced all the physical and biological reasoning functions of the human brain in robots. In fact, some robots have human brain clones in them. (Yes | No)

No. Intelligent human-cloned robots only exist in fiction and social hype.

8. Artificial General Intelligence software, a program that can adapt to any human function (natural language processing, image processing, and sound streams) better than a human, already exists in some labs. (Yes | No)

No. This will take much more time if it ever succeeds. Corporations might rather be satisfied with profits generated by narrow artificial intelligence that solves specific problems.

9. Training deep learning networks has become a quick and easy task. (Yes | No)

No. Even if it appears fast and simple sometimes, it is mostly a tough task to build a network from scratch and get it to work properly.

Chapter 11 – Conceptual Representation Learning

1. The curse of dimensionality leads to reducing dimensions and features in machine learning algorithms. (Yes | No)

> Yes. The volume of data and features makes it necessary to extract the main features of an observed event (an image, sound, and words) to make sense of it.

> Overfitting and underfitting apply to dimensionality reduction as well. Reducing the features until the system works in a lab (overfitting) might lead to nowhere once the application faces real-life data. Trying to use all the features might lead to underfitting because the application solves no problem at all.

> Regularization applies not just to data but to every aspect of a project.

2. Transfer learning determines the profitability of a project. (Yes | No)

> Yes if an application of an AI model in itself was unprofitable the first time but could generate profit if used for a similar type of learning. Reusing some functions would generate profit, no doubt.

> No, if the first application was extremely profitable but "overfitted" to meet the specifications of a given project.

3. Reading model.h5 does not provide much information. (Yes | No)

> No. Saving the weights of a TensorFlow model is vital during the training process to control the values. Furthermore, trained models often use HDF files (.H5) to load the trained weights. A Hierarchical Data Format (HDF) contains multidimensional arrays of scientific data.

4. Numbers without meaning are enough to replace humans. (Yes | No)

> Yes. In many cases, mathematics provides enough tools to replace humans for many tasks (games, optimization algorithms, and image recognition).

> No. Sometimes mathematics cannot solve problems that require concepts such as many aspects of NLP.

5. Chatbots prove that body language doesn't mean that much. (Yes | No)

Yes. In many applications, body language does not provide additional information. If only a yes or no answer is required, body language will not add much to the conversation.

No. If emotional intelligence is required to understand the tone of the user of a chatbot, a webcam detecting body language could provide useful information.

6. Present-day ANNs provide enough theory to solve all AI requests. (Yes | No)

No. Artificial Neural Networks (ANN) cannot solve thousands of problems, for example, translating poetry novels or recognizing images with forms that constantly vary.

7. Chatbots can now replace humans in all situations. (Yes | No)

No. Concepts need to be added. The market provides all the necessary tools. It will take some years to be able to speak effectively with chatbots.

8. Self-driving cars have been approved and do not need conceptual training. (Yes | No)

Yes, that could be true. Sensor, mathematics (linear algebra, probabilities) might succeed within a few years.

No. Certain problems will require concepts (and more robotics) when emergency situations that require creative solutions occur. If a self-driving car encounters a wounded person lying on the road, what is the best approach? The choices are to call for help, find another person if the help arrives too late, pick up the victim, drive them to a hospital (robotics), and much more.

9. Industries can implement AI algorithms for all of their needs. (Yes | No)

Yes. All the tools are there to be used. If the right team decides to solve a problem with AI and robotics, it can be done.

No. Some tools are missing, such as real-time management decision tools when faced with unplanned events. If a system breaks down, humans can still adapt faster to find alternative solutions to continue production.

Chapter 12 – Automated Planning and Scheduling

1 A CNN can be trained to understand an abstract concept. (Yes | No)

Yes. A CNN can classify images and make predictions. But CNNs can analyze any type of object or representation. An image, for example, can be linked to a word or phrase. The image thus becomes a message in itself.

2. It is better to avoid concepts and only use real-life images. (Yes | No)

No. Images provide many practical applications, but at some point, more is required to solve planning problems for example.

Planning requires much more than this type of dataset.

3. Planning and scheduling mean the same thing. (Yes | No)

No. Planning describes the tasks that must be carried out. Scheduling adds a time factor. Planning tells us what to do, and scheduling tells us when.

4. Amazon's manufacturing patent is a revolution. (Yes | No)

No. Manufacturing clothing has been mastered by factories around the world.

Yes. With such a worldwide distribution, Amazon has come very close to the end user. The end user can choose a new garment and it will be manufactured directly on demand. This connectivity will change the apparel manufacturing processes and force its competitors to find new ways of making and selling garments.

5. Learning how warehouses function is not useful. (Yes | No)

No. False. Online shopping requires more and more warehouse space and processes. The number of warehouses will now increase faster than shops. There are many opportunities for artificial intelligence applications in warehouses.

6. Online marketing does not require artificial intelligence. (Yes | No)

No. On the contrary, artificial intelligence is used by applications for online marketing every day, and this will continue for decades.

Chapter 13 – AI and the Internet of Things

1. Driving quickly to a location is better than safety in any situation. (Yes | No)

Yes and No.

Self-driving cars face the same difficulties as human-driven cars: getting to a location on time, respecting speed limits, or driving as safely as possible. Self-driving cars, like humans, are constantly improving their driving abilities through experience.

Yes. Sometimes, a self-driving car will perform better on a highway with little traffic.

No. Sometimes, if the highways are dangerous (owing to weather conditions and heavy traffic) a self-driving car should take a safer road defined by slow speed and little to no traffic. This way, if difficulties occur, the self-driving car can slow down and even stop more easily than on a highway.

2. Self-driving cars will never really replace human drivers. (Yes | No)

Nobody can answer that question. As self-driving cars build their abilities and experience, they might well end up driving better than humans.

In very unpredictable situations, humans can go off the road to avoid another car and back off a bit, for example. It will take more work to get a self-driving car to do that.

One thing is certain, though. If a human is driving all night and falls asleep, the self-driving car will detect the head slumping movement, take over, and save lives. The self-driving car can also save lives if the human has a medical problem while driving.

3. Will a self-driving fire truck with robots be able to put out a fire one day? (Yes | No)

Yes. Combining self-driving fire trucks with robots will certainly save many lives when a fire department faces difficult fires to extinguish. Those saved lives include firemen who risk their own lives. It might help firemen focus on helping people while the robots do the tougher jobs. This robot-human team will no doubt save thousands of lives in the future.

4. Do major cities need to invest in self-driving cars or avoid them? (Invest | Avoid)

Invest. With slow but safe self-driving cars, commuters could share public, free or very cheap, electric self-driving cars instead of having to drive. It would be like having a personal chauffeur.

5. Would you trust a self-driving bus to take children to school and back? (Yes | No)

No. Not in the present state of self-driving cars.

Yes, when self-driving cars, buses, and trucks prove that they can outperform humans. Self-driving vehicles will not make mistakes humans do: using smartphones while driving, talking to passengers without looking at the road, and much more.

6. Would you be able to sleep in a self-driving car on a highway? (Yes | No)

Not in the present state of self-driving vehicle technology.

Yes, when reliability replaces doubts.

7. Would you like to develop a self-driving program for a project for a city? (Yes | No)

That one is for you to think about! You can also apply the technology to warehouses for AGVs by contacting the companies or AGV manufacturers directly.

Chapter 14 – Optimizing Blockchains with AI

1. Cryptocurrency is the only use of blockchains today. (Yes | No)

No. IBM HyperLedger, for example, uses blockchains to organize secure transactions in a supply chain environment.

2. Mining blockchains can be lucrative. (Yes | No)

Yes. But it is a risk, like any other mining operation. Some companies have huge resources to mine cryptocurrency, meaning that they can beat smaller competitors to creating a block.

3. Using blockchains for companies cannot be applied to sales. (Yes | No)

No. False. Blockchain cloud platforms provide smart contracts and a secure way of managing transactions during a sales process.

4. Smart contracts for blockchains are more accessible to write than standard offline contracts. (Yes | No)

Yes. If they are standard contracts, this speeds the transaction up.

No. If the transaction is complex and requires customization, a lawyer will have to write the contract, which can then only be used on a blockchain cloud platform.

5. Once a block is in a blockchain network, everyone in the network can read the content. (Yes | No)

> Yes if no privacy rule has been enforced.

> No. IBM Hyperledger, for example, provides privacy functions.

6. A block in a blockchain guarantees that absolutely no fraud is possible. (Yes | No)

> Yes. A block in a blockchain can never be changed again, avoiding fraud. Nobody can tamper with the data.

> No. If the transaction is illegal in the first place, then the block will be fraudulent as well.

7. There is only one way of applying Bayes' theorem. (Yes | No)

> No. There are many variations of Bayes Theorem. Using Naive Bayes, for example, avoids the conditional probability constraint. But another approach could use conditional probability.

8. Training a Naive Bayes dataset requires a standard function. (Yes | No)

> No. Gaussian functions, for example, can be used to calculate Naive Bayes algorithms, among others.

9. Machine learning algorithms will not change the intrinsic nature of the corporate business. (Yes | No)

> No. False. Machine learning will disrupt every area of businesses as algorithms spread through the company, optimizing processes.

Chapter 15 – Cognitive NLP Chatbots

1. Can a chatbot communicate like a human? (Yes | No)

> No. Communicating like a human means being human: having a body with body language, sensations, odors, fear hormones, and much more.

> Yes. In certain situations, if a quantum mind (Chapter 17, *Quantum Computers That Think*) is built, a chatbot will produce near-human conversations.

2. Are chatbots necessarily artificial intelligence programs? (Yes | No)

No. Many call centers use the "press 1, press 2...press n" method, which requires careful organization but no artificial intelligence.

3. Chatbots only need words to communicate. (Yes | No)

Yes. Simple chatbots can communicate with words in a controlled situation.

No. When polysemy (several meanings for a same word or situation) is involved, pictograms and more will add more efficient dimensions.

4. Do humans only chat with words? (Yes | No)

No. In fact, humans express with the tone of their voice, body language, or music, for example.

5. Humans only think in words and numbers. (Yes | No)

No. Certainly not. Humans think in images, sounds, odors, and feelings.

6. To build a cognitive chatbot, mental images are necessary. (Yes | No)

No. In limited "press 1 or press 2 " situations, chatbots can perform well with limited cognitive capacities.

Yes. To engage in a real conversation with a human, mental images are the key to providing an empathetic exchange.

7. For a chatbot to function, a dialog flow needs to be planned. (Yes | No)

Yes. It will provide better results in a business environment.

No. If you want the chatbot to talk freely, you need to free it a bit. This still requires planning of the dialog but it is more flexible.

8. A chatbot possesses general artificial intelligence, so no prior development is required. (Yes | No)

No. This is presently impossible. Only narrow (specific to one or a few fields) artificial intelligence exists in real life, contrary to science fiction movies and media hype.

9. A chatbot translates fine without any function other than a translation API. (Yes | No)

No. See Chapter 8, *Revolutions Designed for Some Corporations and Disruptive Innovations for Small to Large Companies.*

10. Chatbots can already chat like humans in most cases. (Yes | No)

No. Chapter 8, *Revolutions Designed for Some Corporations and Disruptive Innovations for Small to Large Companies,* shows that interpreting a language will take quite some more challenging work and contributions.

Chapter 16 – Improve the Emotional Intelligence Deficiencies of Chatbots

1. Restricted Boltzmann Machines are based on directed graphs. (Yes | No)

No. RBM graphs are undirected, unsupervised, and memoryless, and the decision making is based on random calculations.

2. The hidden units of an RBM are generally connected to each other. (Yes | No)

No. The hidden units of an RBM are **not** generally connected to each other.

3. Random sampling is not used in an RBM. (Yes | No)

No. False. Gibbs random sampling is frequently applied to RBMs.

4. Is there a method to prevent gradients from vanishing in an RNN? (Yes | No)

Yes. When the gradient gets "stuck" around 0, for example, a ReLU function can solve this problem. It will force negative values to become 0 (or a fixed value in a leaky ReLU), and the positive values will not change.

5. LSTM cells never forget. (Yes | No)

No. False. LSTM cells "forget" by skipping connections, adding connections from the past to the present, and other techniques.

6. Word2vector transforms words into indexes along with their labels. (Yes | No)

Yes. Word2vector transforms words into numbers and also keeps track of their labels.

7. Principal Component Analysis (PCA) transforms data into higher dimensions. (Yes | No)

Yes. The whole point of PCA is to transform data into higher dimensions to find the principal component (highest eigenvalue of a covariance matrix), then the second highest, and down to the lowest values.

8. In a covariance matrix, the eigenvector shows the direction of the vector representing that matrix, and the eigenvalue shows the size of that vector. (Yes | No)

Yes. Eigenvalues indicate how important a feature is, and eigenvectors provide a direction.

9. It is impossible to represent a human mind in a machine. (Yes | No)

No. It is possible.

Chapter 17, *Quantum Computers That Think,* shows how to build a machine mind. It takes quite some work to include sensors, but the technology is there.

10. A machine cannot learn concepts, which is why classical applied mathematics is enough to make efficient artificial intelligence programs for every field. (Yes | No)

No. Never believe that. Progress is being made and will never stop until mind-machines become mainstream.

Chapter 17 – Quantum Computers That Think

1. Beyond the hype, no quantum computer exists. (Yes | No)

No. False. You can already run a quantum computer on IBM Q's cloud platform.

`https://www.research.ibm.com/ibm-q/`

The following screenshot is the result of a real IBM quantum computer calculation I ran on a quantum score explained in the chapter:

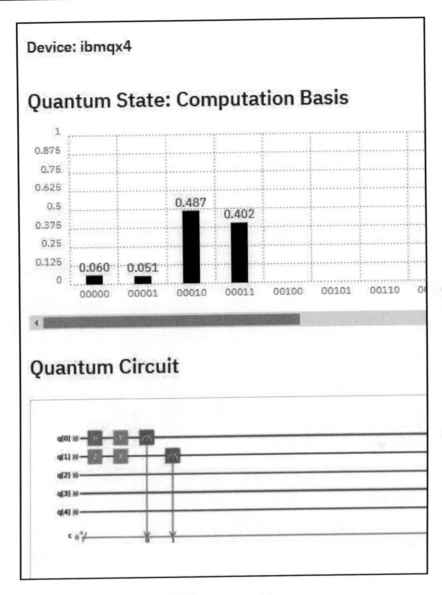

IBM quantum computer calculation

2. A quantum computer can store data. (Yes | No)

No. Instability prevents any form of storage at this point.

3. The effect of quantum gates on qubits can be viewed with a Bloch Sphere. (Yes | No)

> Yes. A Bloch sphere will display the state of a qubit.

4. A mind that thinks with past experiences, images, words, and other bits of every day like stored in memory will find deeper solutions to problems that mathematics alone cannot solve. (Yes | No)

> No. False. Many researchers believe that mathematics alone can solve all human problems.

> Yes. True. Mathematics alone cannot replace deep thinking. Even if computers have incredible power and can beat human players at chess, for example, they still cannot adapt to new situations without going through a design and training process. Concepts need to be added and experienced (memory as well).

> I bet that machine mind concepts will become progressively more mainstream to solve deep thinking problems.

5. A quantum computer will solve medical research problems that cannot be solved today. (Yes | No)

> Yes. There is no doubt about that. The sheer computing power of a quantum computer can provide exponential DNA sequencing programs for epigenetic research.

6. A quantum computer can solve mathematical problems exponentially faster than classical computers. (Yes | No)

> Yes. Classical computers function at $2 \times n$ (number of bits) and quantum computers run at 2^n (n being the number of qubits)!

7. Classical computers and smartphone processors will soon disappear and smartphone processors also. (Yes | No)

> No. Quantum computers require such a large amount of space and physical stability that this will not happen in the near future. Furthermore, classical computers and smartphones can store data. Quantum computers cannot.

8. A quantum score cannot be written in source code format but only with a visual interface. (Yes | No)

No. False. IBM, for example, can swap the quantum from score to QASM interface or display both, as shown here:

QASM interface

9. Quantum simulators can run as fast as quantum computers. (Yes | No)

Certainly not! A simulator just shows how a quantum score would behave on a real quantum computer. Although the simulator can help build the score, a quantum computer will run exponentially faster than the simulator.

10. Quantum computers produce intermediate results while they are running calculations. (Yes | No)

No. This is not possible. The qubits are too unstable. Observing them makes the system collapse. However, simulators such as Quirk come in handy. Since they are not real, intermediate results can be displayed to design a quantum score.

Index